The Internet

Illustrated Introductory
Third Edition

Gary P. Schneider ♦ Jessica Evans

THOMSON
COURSE TECHNOLOGY

Australia • Canada • Mexico • Singapore • Spain • United Kingdom • United States

The Internet, Third Edition - Illustrated Introductory

Gary P. Schneider and Jessica Evans

Adapting Author:
Sasha Vodnik

Managing Editor:
Nicole Jones Pinard

Production Editor:
Elena Montillo

QA Manuscript Reviewers:
Max Prior, Vitaly Davidovich, Shawn Day

Senior Product Manager:
Emily Heberlein

Developmental Editor:
Holly Lancaster

Text Designer:
Joseph Lee, Black Fish Design

Associate Product Manager:
Christina Kling Garrett

Editorial Assistant:
Elizabeth M. Harris

Composition House:
GEX Publishing Services

Printed in the United States of America

2 3 4 5 6 7 8 9 BM 05 04 03 02

For more information, contact Course Technology, 25 Thomson Place, Boston, Massachusetts, 02210.

Or find us on the World Wide Web at: www.course.com

ISBN 0-619-10958-0

The Illustrated Series Vision

Teaching and writing about the Internet and its applications can be extremely rewarding and challenging. How do we engage students and keep their interest? How do we teach them skills that they can easily apply on the job? As we set out to write this book, our goals were to develop a textbook that:

- works for a beginning student
- provides varied, flexible and meaningful exercises and projects to reinforce the skills
- serves as a reference tool
- makes your job as an educator easier, by providing resources above and beyond the textbook to help you teach your course

Our popular, streamlined format is based on advice from instructional designers and customers. This flexible design presents each lesson on a two-page spread, with step-by-step instructions on the left, and screen illustrations on the right. This signature style, coupled with high-caliber content, provides a comprehensive yet manageable introduction to the Internet—it is a teaching package for the instructor and a learning experience for the student.

ACKNOWLEDGMENTS

Thanks to the New Perspectives Series for providing a great starting point for the Third Edition. Thanks to Holly Lancaster, my developmental editor; her friendliness, skill at communicating clearly, and strong sense of how to pull a good idea out of less than stellar writing and make it clear and understandable have been instrumental in creating a book of which I'm immensely proud. Thanks to Emily Heberlein, this book's product manager, for the behind-the-scenes coordination that made this project such a pleasure to work on. Thanks to Tom Ace for technical consultations. Thanks to my parents, Diana and Jim Vodnik, for unfailing lifelong love and support. Thanks to Jan Nathan Long for the many shared dinners and for keeping me company on work nights. Finally, thanks to Gracie for constantly pointing out the exciting minutiae of life that a computer can't replicate.

Sasha Vodnik, Adapting Author

We want to thank the outstanding team of professionals at Course Technology for making this book possible. The editing, development, and production staff members have done their usual outstanding job. We are grateful for the continuous support and encouragement of our spouses, Cathy Cosby and Richard Evans. We also thank our children for tolerating our absences while we were busy writing.

Gary Schneider and Jessica Evans, New Perspectives Series Authors

Preface

Welcome to *The Internet, Third Edition –Illustrated Introductory*. This highly visual book offers students a comprehensive hands-on introduction to the Internet. Each lesson in the book contains elements in the sample two-page spread pictured to the right.

► How is the book organized?

This book is organized into 10 units. Students first learn basic Internet concepts, then learn how to use Internet e-mail with Netscape Mail and Microsoft Outlook Express, how to navigate, browse, and search the Web using Internet Explorer and Netscape, and how to download programs and files. Mailing Lists and newsgroups are also covered. This edition includes two new units that cover using Web-based tools and increasing browser capabilities and security.

► What kinds of assignments are included in the book? At what level of difficulty?

Each unit includes a different case study, developed specifically to suit the concepts and skills covered in that unit. The assignments on the blue pages at the end of each unit increase in difficulty. Project Files and case studies, including international examples, provide a great variety of interesting and relevant business applications for skills. Assignments include:

- **Concepts Reviews** include multiple choice, matching, and screen identification questions.
- **Skills Reviews** provide additional hands-on, step-by-step reinforcement.
- **Independent Challenges** are case projects requiring critical thinking and application of the skills learned in the unit. The Independent Challenges increase in difficulty, with the first Independent Challenge in each unit being the easiest (most step-by-step with the most detailed instructions). Independent Challenges become increasingly open-ended, requiring more independent thinking and problem solving.
- **Visual Workshops** show a completed file or Web page and require that the file be created or Web page located without any step-by-step guidance, involving problem solving and an independent application of the unit skills.

Each 2-page spread focuses on a single skill.

Concise text introduces the basic principles in the lesson and integrates the brief case study (indicated by the paintbrush icon).

Unit F Internet

Evaluating Web Resources

Like a library, the Web makes a huge variety of information readily available without a failsafe standard for differentiating reliable data from less reliable data. As a result, it's important to evaluate and verify the information you view. Table F-1 summarizes how you can evaluate the three major components of any Web page: authorship, content, and appearance. A client of Cosby Promotions is a nonprofit group that is concerned about global warming. While doing research for this organization, you have found a Web site that appears to contain relevant information. Before you pass along your findings, you need to evaluate the quality of the Web site.

Steps

QuickTip: If the Web site has changed, follow the alternate instructions on the Student Online Companion.

1. Go to www.course.com/illustrated/internet3, click the Unit F link, then click the PSR Environment and Health link under Lesson 10
   A Web page opens, similar to Figure F-22.
2. Evaluate the three components of a Web page: authorship, content, and appearance
   The Web page shown in Figure F-22 has a simple, clear design. The .org domain in the URL verifies that the publisher is a not-for-profit organization. The grammar and spelling are correct, and the content is clearly presented. In addition, the text cites such authorities as the U.S. Department of Energy. The reputable references and the consistent style of the Web page suggest that this Web site is a quality resource. However, the author or publisher of the Web page is identified only as "PSR."
3. Scroll to the bottom of the Web page
   As you can see, "PSR" is an acronym for Physicians for Social Responsibility. The organization's address, telephone number, and e-mail address are listed along with contact information for key individuals in PSR's Environment and Health Program.
4. Click in the Address text box or Location text box, click to the right of the URL, then press [Backspace] as many times as necessary to delete all of the text to the right of the .org/ domain name portion of the URL
   The URL should appear similar to *http://www.psr.org/*.
5. Press [Enter]
   The PSR home page appears. This Web page includes links to information about the organization, including its goals, activities, directors, and membership.
6. To view an additional resource, go to www.course.com/illustrated/internet3, click the Unit F link, then click the LibrarySpot link under Lesson 10
   The LibrarySpot includes many of the same things you would expect to find in a public or school library. This library is, however, open 24 hours a day and seven days a week. The LibrarySpot Web site lets you access reference materials, electronic texts, and other library Web sites from one central Web page.

Clues to Use

Citing Web research resources

For academic research, the two most widely followed standards for citing Web resources are those of the American Psychological Association (APA) and the Modern Language Association (MLA). You can use a search engine to find Web pages that describe how to cite Web resources using both standards.

INTERNET 164 GETTING INFORMATION FROM THE WEB

Hints and troubleshooting advice appear right where you need them – next to the step itself.

Clues to Use boxes provide concise information that either expands on the major lesson skill or describes an independent task that in some way relates to the major lesson skill.

Every lesson features large, full-color representations of what the screen should look like as students complete the numbered steps.

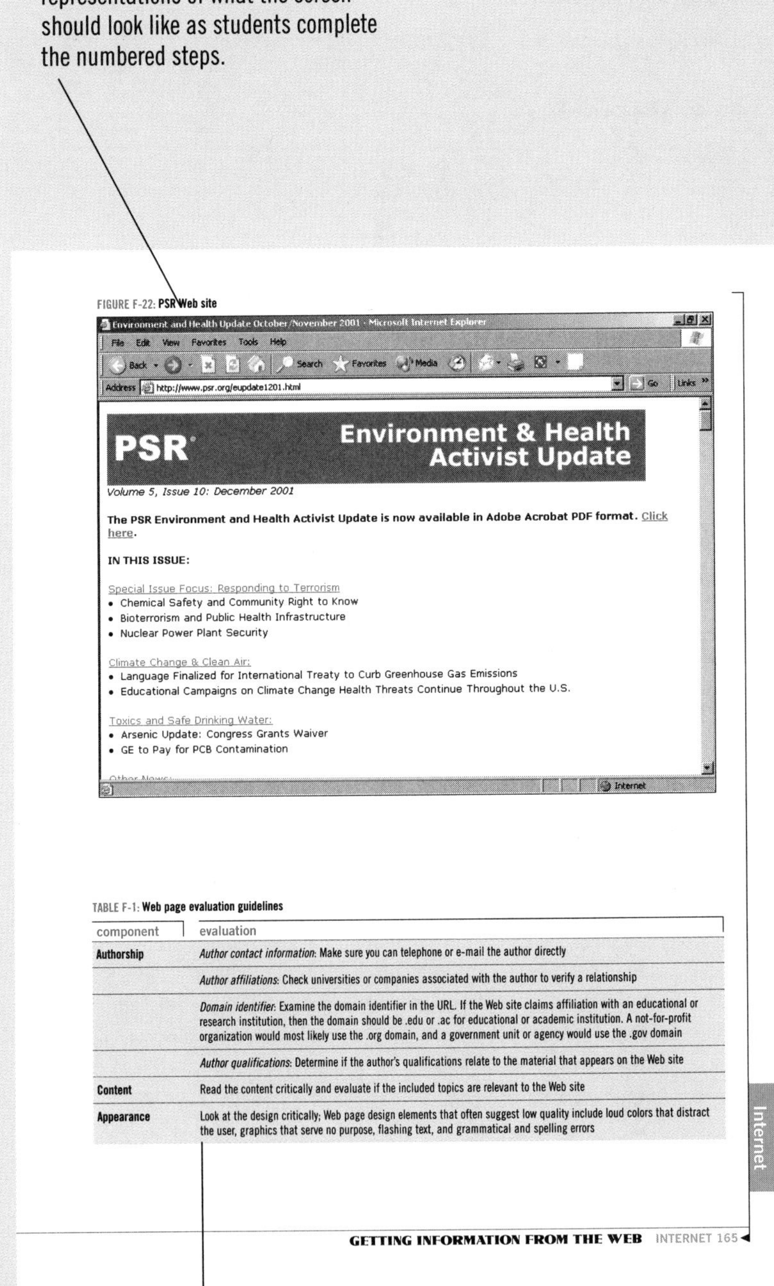

FIGURE F-22: **PSR Web site**

TABLE F-1: **Web page evaluation guidelines**

component	evaluation
Authorship	*Author contact information:* Make sure you can telephone or e-mail the author directly
	Author affiliations: Check universities or companies associated with the author to verify a relationship
	Domain identifier: Examine the domain identifier in the URL. If the Web site claims affiliation with an educational or research institution, then the domain should be .edu or .ac for educational or academic institution. A not-for-profit organization would most likely use the .org domain, and a government unit or agency would use the .gov domain
	Author qualifications: Determine if the author's qualifications relate to the material that appears on the Web site
Content	Read the content critically and evaluate if the included topics are relevant to the Web site
Appearance	Look at the design critically; Web page design elements that often suggest low quality include loud colors that distract the user, graphics that serve no purpose, flashing text, and grammatical and spelling errors

Tables provide quickly accessible summaries of key terms, toolbar buttons, or keyboard alternatives connected with the lesson material. Students can refer easily to this information when working on their own projects at a later time.

▶ What Web resources supplement the book?

This edition features a Student Online Companion (SOC) Web site. Use the SOC to access all the links referenced in the book, and to access other resources for further information. Since the Internet changes frequently, the SOC will also contain any updates or clarifications to the text after its publication.

▶ What distance learning options are available to accompany this book?

Options for this title include a testbank in MyCourse 2.0, WebCT, and BlackBoard ready formats to make assessment using one of these platforms easy to manage. Visit www.course.com for more information on our online learning materials.

Instructor Resources

The Instructor's Resource Kit (IRK) CD is Course Technology's way of putting the resources and information needed to teach and learn effectively into your hands. All the components are available on the IRK (pictured below), and many of the resources can be downloaded from www.course.com.

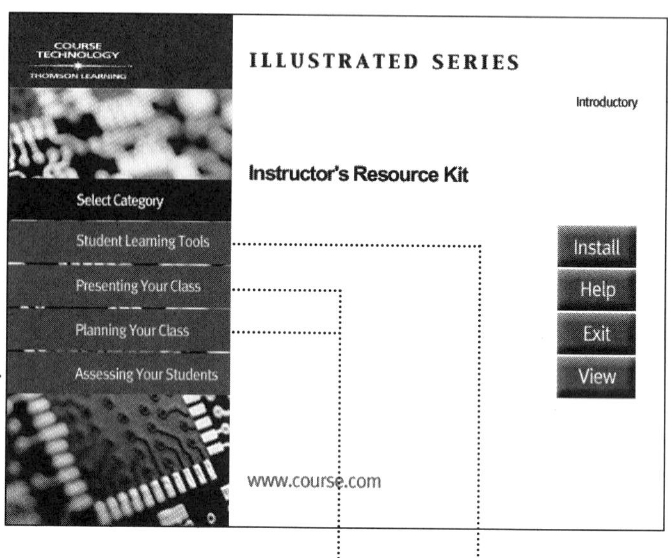

ASSESSING YOUR STUDENTS

Solution Files

Solution Files are Project Files completed with comprehensive sample answers. Use these files to evaluate your students' work. Or, distribute electronically or in hard copy so students can verify their own work.

ExamView

ExamView is a powerful testing software package that allows you to create and administer printed, computer (LAN-based), and Internet exams. ExamView includes hundreds of questions that correspond to the topics covered in this text, enabling students to generate detailed study guides that include page references for further review. The computer-based and Internet testing components allow students to take exams at their computers, and also save you time by grading each exam automatically.

PRESENTING YOUR CLASS

Figure Files

Figure Files contain all the figures from the book in .bmp format. Use the Figure Files to create transparency masters or a PowerPoint presentation.

STUDENT LEARNING TOOLS

Project Files and Project Files List

To complete some of the units in this book, your students will need **Project Files**. Put them on a file server for students to copy. The Project Files are available on the Instructor's Resource Kit CD-ROM, the Review Pack, and can also be downloaded from www.course.com.

PLANNING YOUR CLASS

Instructor's Manual

Available as an electronic file, the Instructor's Manual is quality-assurance tested and includes unit overviews, detailed lecture topics for each unit with teaching tips, comprehensive sample solutions to all lessons and end-of-unit material, and extra Independent Challenges. The Instructor's Manual is available on the Instructor's Resource Kit CD-ROM, or you can download it from www.course.com.

Sample Syllabus

Prepare and customize your course easily using this sample course outline (available on the Insturctor's Resource Kit CD-ROM).

Brief Contents

Contents

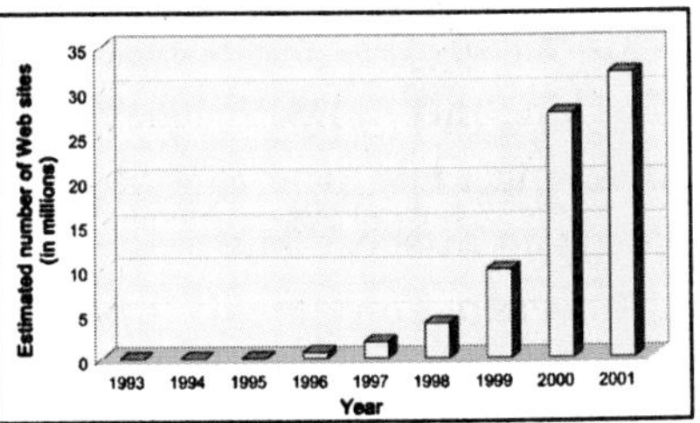

Estimated number of Web sites (in millions)
35
30
25
20
15
10
5
0
1993
1994
1995
1996
1997
1998
1999
2000
2001
Year

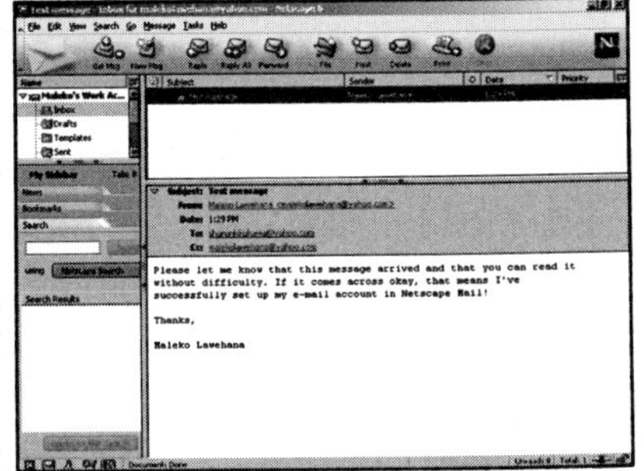

Contents

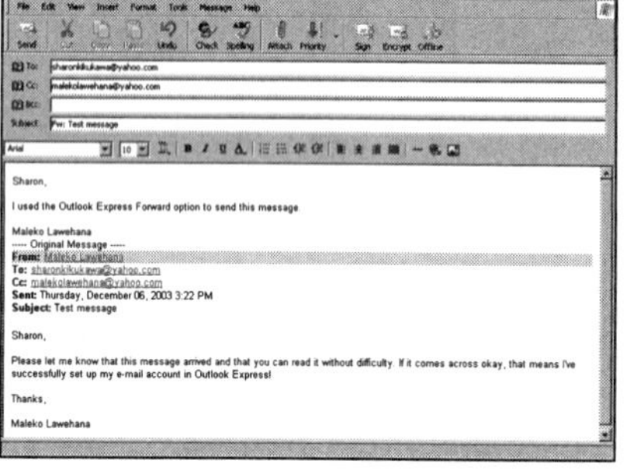

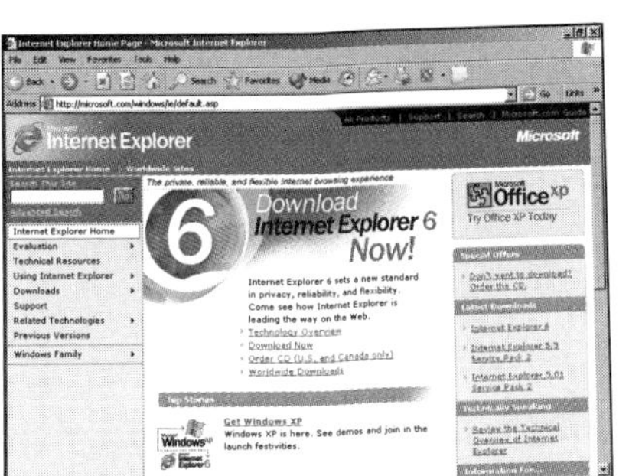

Unit E: Searching the Web 121

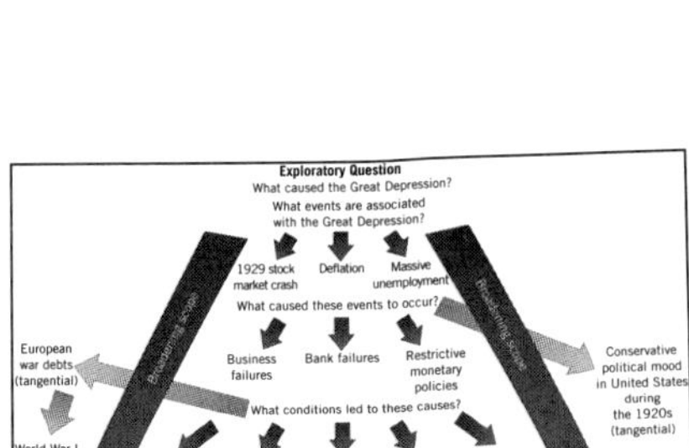
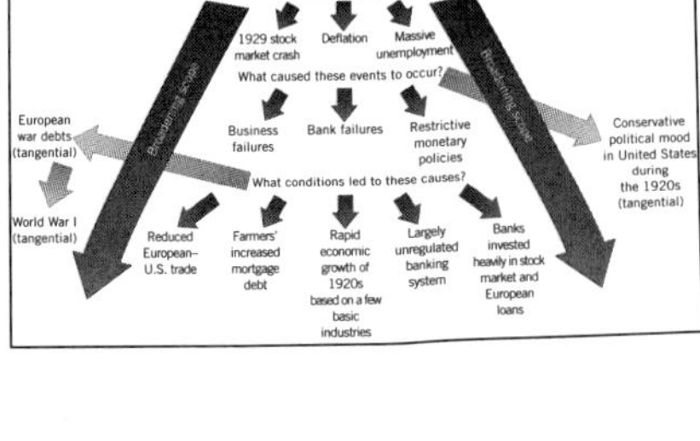

Exploratory Question
What caused the Great Depression?
What events are associated with the Great Depression?
1929 stock market crash
Deflation
Massive unemployment
What caused these events to occur?
Business failures
Bank failures
Restrictive monetary policies
What conditions led to these causes?
Reduced European–U.S. trade
Farmers' increased mortgage debt
Rapid economic growth of 1920s based on a few basic industries
Largely unregulated banking system
Banks invested heavily in stock market and European loans
European war debts (tangential)
World War I (tangential)
Conservative political mood in United States during the 1920s (tangential)

Unit F: Getting Information from the Web 145

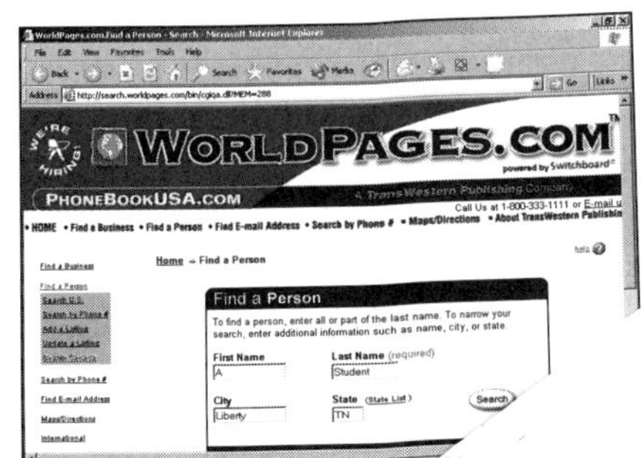

Contents

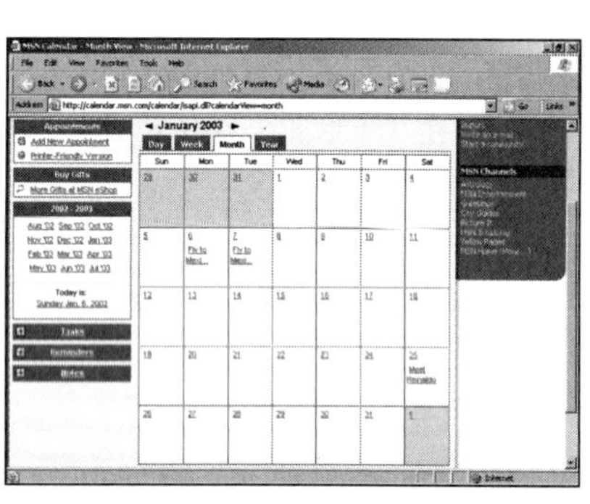
January 2003

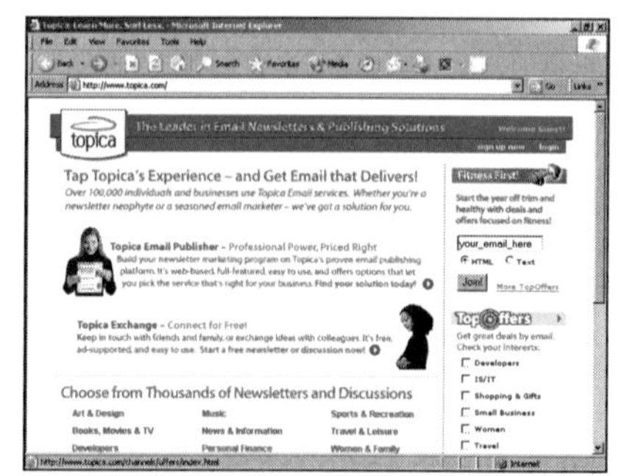
topica
Tap Topica's Experience – and Get Email that Delivers!
Choose from Thousands of Newsletters and Discussions

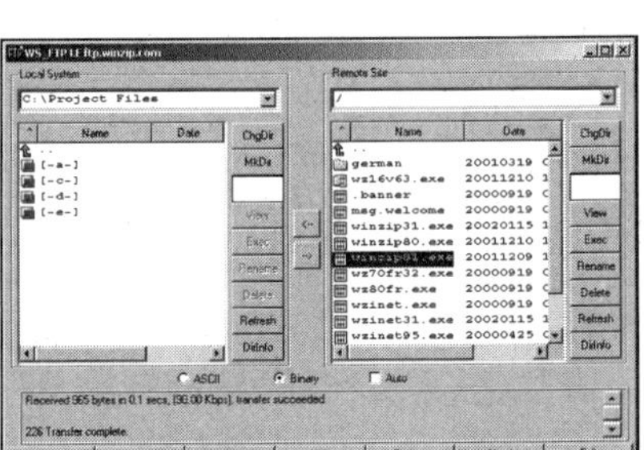

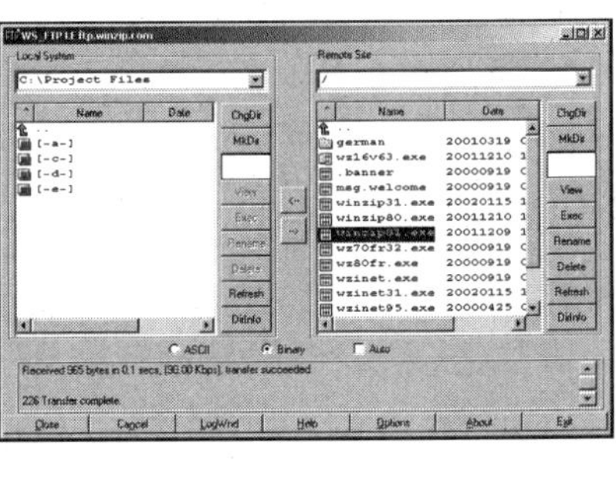

symantec.
security response
latest virus threats
security advisories
virus definitions
updates

Read This Before You Begin

Software Information and Required Installation

Browser and operating system information

This book was written using Microsoft Internet Explorer 6.0 and Windows XP with the Windows Classic theme. All of the steps and exercises have been tested using Internet Explorer 6.0 with the typical installation of both Microsoft Windows XP and Microsoft Windows 2000.

This book was written and tested using the two most commonly used Web browsers: Microsoft Internet Explorer (version 6) and Netscape (version 6.2). In most cases, the steps can be performed with either browser. For steps that are specific to Microsoft Internet Explorer, Outlook Express, or Netscape, separate steps, lessons, or units have been included so you can work through the entire book using either browser or e-mail program.

E-mail requirements

For Units B and C, you must use a POP e-mail account. HTTP or IMAP accounts, including Hotmail accounts, will not work with the steps as written. In Unit G, the steps for the lessons on Hotmail were based on the US version of Hotmail. Other versions of Hotmail might require different steps.

Student installation of software for Units I and J

In Unit I, students will be unable to follow the instructions in the lesson "Using FTP to Download a Program" if WinZip is already installed on their computer. In this case, students should read through the steps without actually doing them.

In Unit I, if students do not have installation privileges, they should read the steps without completing them starting with the lesson "Installing an FTP Client Program." Additionally, in Unit J students without installation privileges should read through the lessons "Installing Browser Extensions with Netscape" and "Installing Browser Extensions with Internet Explorer" without completing the steps.

In Unit I, if students do have installation privileges, they also need 10 MB of disk space on their computer or on a network drive, in order to download and unzip files for installation. See the Project Files List for more information.

Why your screens may differ from those in the book

To maximize the display area for Web pages that students open, the sidebar is hidden in figures showing the Netscape browser. To hide the sidebar, move the mouse pointer over the border separating the sidebar from the Web page content so that the pointer changes to a double-headed arrow, then drag the border to the left edge of the browser window.

The figures in this book show filenames including extensions. To display extensions, double-click My Computer on the desktop, click Tools on the menu bar, click Folder Options, click the View tab, click the "Hide extensions for known file types" check box to remove the checkmark, then click OK.

What is the Student Online Companion?

Units D through J of this book are integrated with the Student Online Companion (SOC), a Web-based resource that contains the links necessary to work through the units. The SOC also contains any updates to steps or other content since the book was published; therefore, it's important to check the SOC before beginning each unit. To open the Student Online Companion, go to www.course.com/downloads/illustrated/internet3.

If you are using your own computer, or if your computer lab allows you to make such changes, you can set the SOC home page as your browser home page by following these steps:

Internet Explorer:

1. Open the Student Online Companion
2. Click **Tools** on the menu bar, then click **Internet Options**
3. Click **Use Current**, then click **OK**

Netscape:

1. Open the Student Online Companion
2. Click **Edit** on the menu bar, then click **Preferences**
3. Click **Use Current Page**, then click **OK**

If setting the SOC as your browser home page is not an option, you can instead make the SOC easily accessible by adding its URL to your list of Bookmarks or Favorites (again, if you are using your own computer or if your computer lab allows it).

To create an Internet Explorer Favorite:

1. Open the Student Online Companion.
2. Click **Favorites** on the menu bar, then click **Add to Favorites**
3. Click **OK**

To create a Netscape Bookmark:

1. Open the Student Online Companion.
2. Click the **Bookmarks button** under the Location text box, then click **Add Bookmark**

For more information on creating and using Internet Explorer Favorites and Netscape Bookmarks, see Unit D.

If you choose not to change your home page or add a Favorite or Bookmark, you can still easily complete all the steps. Each unit and practice section includes the URL for the Student Online Companion.

Understanding

Internet Basics

- ► Define Internet tools and resources
- ► Understand networks
- ► Understand network connectors
- ► Learn the origins of the Internet
- ► Understand the development of the Internet
- ► Explore uses for the Internet
- ► Understand how the World Wide Web works
- ► Connect to the Internet
- ► Define Internet service options
- ► Understand e-mail

The Internet offers many communication tools and information resources. To use the Internet effectively, you need to know what it is, what tools and information are available on it, and how you can connect to it. As the sales manager for the Tropical Exotic Produce Company (TEPCo), you are responsible for finding new and innovative ways to market the company's line of organically grown, exotic fruits and vegetables from South America, Africa, and Asia in the United States. You know that many businesses are using the Internet as a marketing tool. The president of TEPCo has asked you to research the Internet to determine its potential for TEPCo.

Defining Internet Tools and Resources

The **Internet** is a large collection of computers all over the world that are connected to one another in various ways. Of all the technological developments in the last century, the Internet is perhaps the most amazing. You can use the Internet to communicate with other people throughout the world; read online versions of newspapers, magazines, academic journals, and books; join discussion groups on almost any conceivable topic; participate in games and simulations; and obtain free computer software. Figure A-1 shows some of the tools and resources available on the Internet today. The president of TEPCo has asked you to prepare a report on the use of the Internet for commercial purposes. As you begin your study of the Internet, you find that you need to familiarize yourself with new terms. You start by learning just a few of the most common terms associated with the Internet.

E-Mail

You can use **e-mail** (short for **electronic mail**) to communicate electronically with people all over the world. Although similar to other forms of correspondence, such as letters and memos, e-mail has the added advantage of being fast and inexpensive. Instead of traveling through a complicated, expensive, and frequently slow mail delivery service such as a postal system, e-mail travels quickly, efficiently, and inexpensively to its destination across the city or around the world. You can send a message any time you want, without worrying about when the mail is picked up or delivered and without adding postage.

Newsgroups

Just about any topic you can imagine is probably already being discussed somewhere on the Internet in a **newsgroup**, which is an electronic discussion group. Suppose you enjoy traveling to exotic places and want to talk with other adventurous travelers. You can find an adventure travel newsgroup on the Internet that other like-minded travelers have joined to share tips and ask or answer questions. Through newsgroups, you can meet people with interests similar to your own and correspond with them quickly and inexpensively.

Commercial Services

All kinds of businesses provide information about their products and services on the Internet. Many of these businesses use the Internet to market and sell their products and services. Figure A-2 shows an example of a commercial business marketing its goods on the Internet.

World Wide Web

The part of the Internet known as the **World Wide Web** (or the **Web**) is a subset of the computers on the Internet. The purpose of the Web is to organize resources on the Internet to make them easily accessible to all users. Often, you find information presented on the Web in a multimedia format that includes graphics, music, and video clips. This format makes the Web user-friendly.

FIGURE A-1: Communication tools and information resources on the Internet

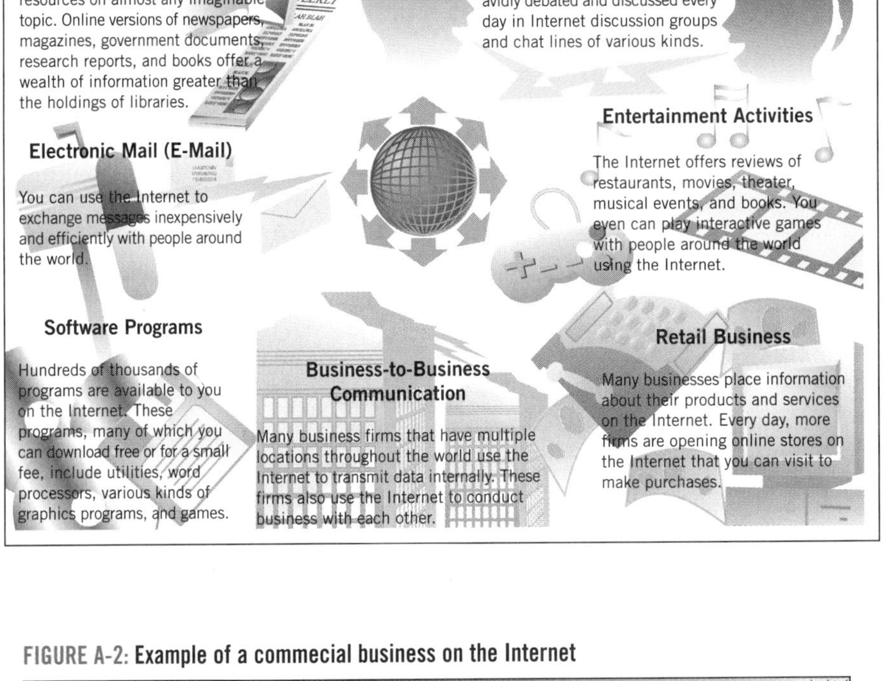

Information Resources
The Internet contains information resources on almost any imaginable topic. Online versions of newspapers, magazines, government documents, research reports, and books offer a wealth of information greater than the holdings of libraries.
Discussions
Thousands of different topics are avidly debated and discussed every day in Internet discussion groups and chat lines of various kinds.
Electronic Mail (E-Mail)
You can use the Internet to exchange messages inexpensively and efficiently with people around the world.
Entertainment Activities
The Internet offers reviews of restaurants, movies, theater, musical events, and books. You even can play interactive games with people around the world using the Internet.
Software Programs
Hundreds of thousands of programs are available to you on the Internet. These programs, many of which you can download free or for a small fee, include utilities, word processors, various kinds of graphics programs, and games.
Business-to-Business Communication
Many business firms that have multiple locations throughout the world use the Internet to transmit data internally. These firms also use the Internet to conduct business with each other.
Retail Business
Many businesses place information about their products and services on the Internet. Every day, more firms are opening online stores on the Internet that you can visit to make purchases.

FIGURE A-2: Example of a commecial business on the Internet

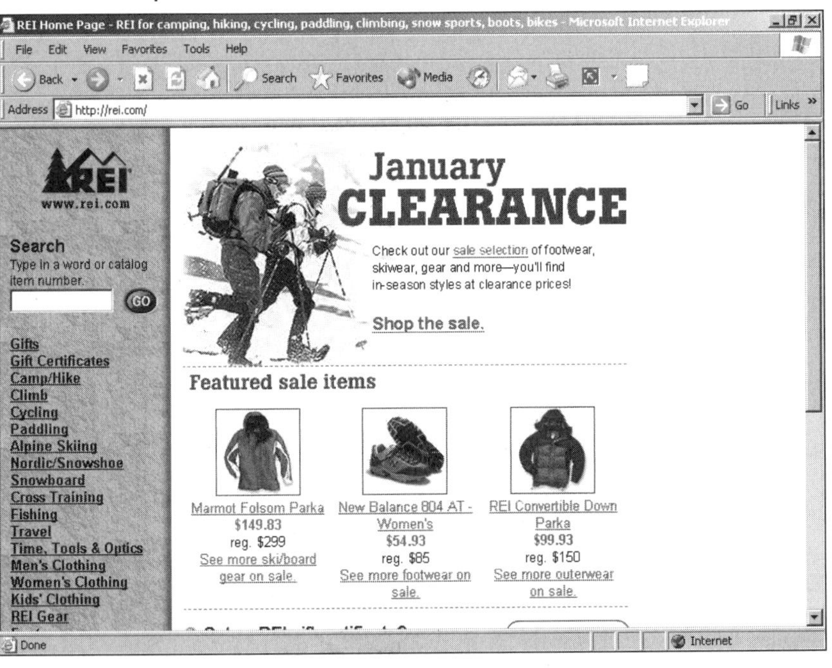

CLUES TO USE

What is the difference between the Internet and the World Wide Web?

The terms "Internet" and "World Wide Web" are often used interchangeably to refer to the many electronic resources you can access from a computer connected to the global network of computers. However, the Internet is the entire system of networked computers, and the World Wide Web is a method used to access information contained on a subset of those networked computers. Think of the difference this way: You connect to the Internet, and then use the World Wide Web to access information.

Internet

Understanding Networks

You will often hear the Internet referred to as a collection of networks. A **network** is created when two or more computers are connected to each other. A computer can become part of a network by connecting to a nearby computer or to the Internet. A network allows computers to share resources, such as printers or programs. As you continue your research, you encounter the concept of computer networks. You know that TEPCo does not have its computers networked, that is, connected to each other or to the Internet. You decide to learn more about what computer networks are and how to connect computers to form a network.

Network Interface Card

A **network interface card (NIC)**, or **network card**, is a removable circuit board that connects a computer to a network. After inserting a NIC into a computer, you can connect it to a network by running a cable from the NIC to the network's main computer or to another computer in the network.

Server

A **server** is any computer that accepts requests from other computers that are connected to it and shares some or all of its resources, such as printers, files, or programs, with those connected computers. A server can be a powerful personal computer (PC) or a larger computer, such as a minicomputer or a mainframe computer.

Client

Each computer connected to a server is called a **client**. The server runs software that coordinates how information flows among its various clients.

Network Operating System

The software that runs on the server is called a **network operating system**.

Client/Server Network

A **client/server network** is a network consisting of one server that shares its resources with multiple clients. Client/server networks commonly are used to connect computers that are located close together (for example, in the same room or building) so that each computer can share resources, such as a printer or a scanner.

Local Area Network

A **local area network (LAN)** consists of a group of computers connected through NICs. This network is described as "local" because the direct connection from one computer to another through NICs works only over relatively short distances (no more than a few thousand feet). Figure A-3 shows how a typical client/server LAN could be set up in an office environment.

Wide Area Network

Several LANs connected together form a **wide area network (WAN)**. For example, a typical college has several computer labs scattered throughout its many buildings. Each computer lab is a client/server LAN. The LANs in the college are interconnected to form the WAN.

FIGURE A-3: A client/server LAN

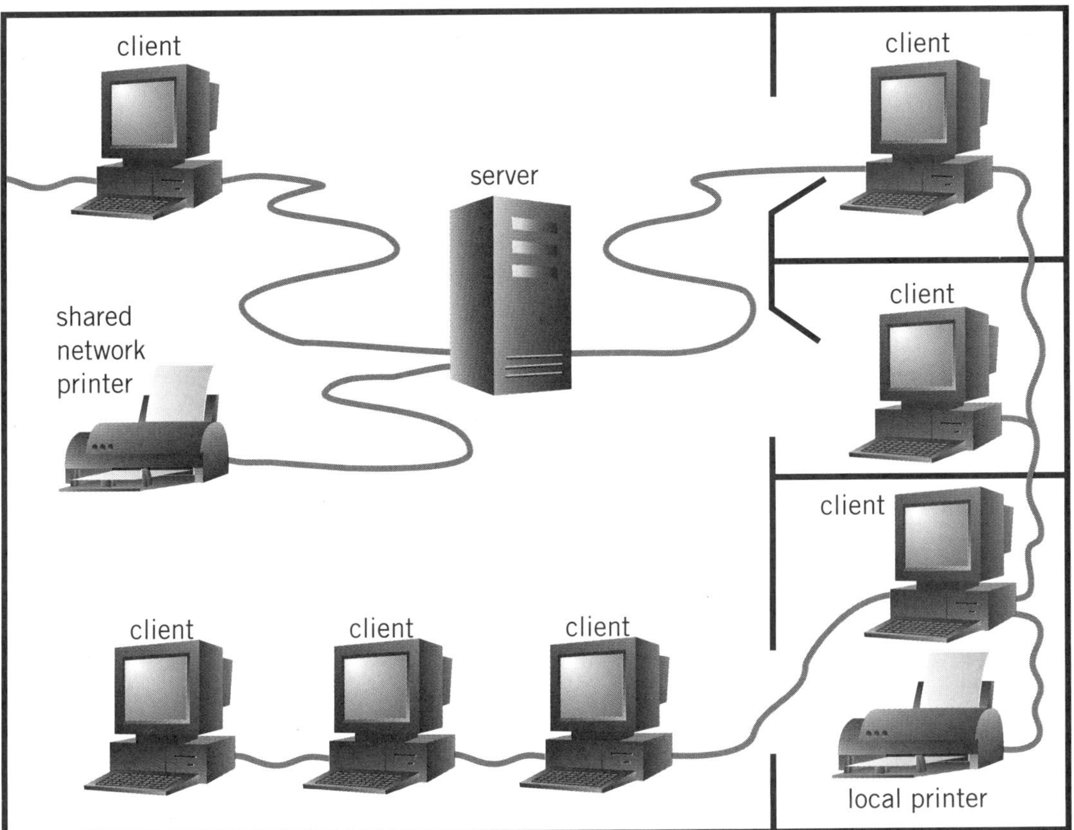

CLUES TO USE

What is the difference between an internet and the Internet?

The word "internet" (lowercase "i") is short for interconnected network. Computer lab LANs are networks, whereas a college's WAN is a network of networks, or an internet. In fact, any network of networks is an internet. The college's WAN is also connected to an internet called the Internet (capital "I"). The Internet is a specific worldwide collection of interconnected networks whose owners have voluntarily agreed to share resources and network connections with one another.

Internet

Understanding Network Connectors

Networks are connected in a variety of ways, depending on the available technology. Network connections create **communications circuits** through which data can travel. You can connect computers using old-fashioned twisted-pair cables, more powerful coaxial cables, or ultra-modern fiber-optic cables. Figure A-4 shows these three types of cables. Alternatively, you could dispense with cables altogether and use a wireless network. After researching networks, you decide to include in your report the suggestion that TEPCo create a LAN, which will be connected to the Internet. To be better informed, you decide to further investigate the different types of network connectors.

► Twisted-Pair Cable

The oldest cable type is **twisted-pair cable**, which consists of two or more insulated copper wires twisted around each other and enclosed in a layer of plastic insulation. The wires are twisted to reduce interference from any current-carrying wires located nearby. Twisted-pair cable is much less expensive than other cable types. Telephone companies have used one type of twisted-pair cable, called **Category 1 cable**, for years to wire residences and businesses. Category 1 cable transmits information more slowly than other cable types. Newer types of twisted-pair cables, called **Category 5 cable** and **Category 5e cable**, are used in computer networks.

► Coaxial Cable

Coaxial cable is an insulated copper wire encased in a metal shield that is enclosed with plastic insulation. The signal-carrying wire is completely shielded, so it resists electrical interference better than twisted-pair cable. Coaxial cable carries signals about 20 times faster than Category 1 cable, but Category 5 and 5e cable transmit information 10 to 100 times faster than coaxial cable. Additionally, coaxial cable is considerably more expensive than Category 1, 5, or 5e cable. Most cable television connections use coaxial cable.

► Fiber-Optic Cable

Fiber-optic cable transmits information by pulsing beams of light through very thin strands of glass. It does not use an electrical signal. Fiber-optic cable transmits signals much faster than coaxial cable and, because it does not use electricity, it is completely immune to electrical interference. Fiber-optic cable is lighter and more durable than coaxial cable, but it's more difficult to work with and much more expensive. Because of these drawbacks, in general, only large computer networks that transmit huge volumes of data use fiber-optic cable.

► Wireless Networks

Wireless networks use technologies such as radio frequency (RF) and infrared (IR) systems to link computers. These types of networks are becoming more common as the cost of the wireless transmitters and receivers that plug into NICs continues to drop. Wireless LANs are well suited to organizations that occupy old buildings that were built before electricity and telephones were widely available, or offices in which cables are difficult to install.

FIGURE A-4: Twisted-pair, coaxial, and fiber-optic cables

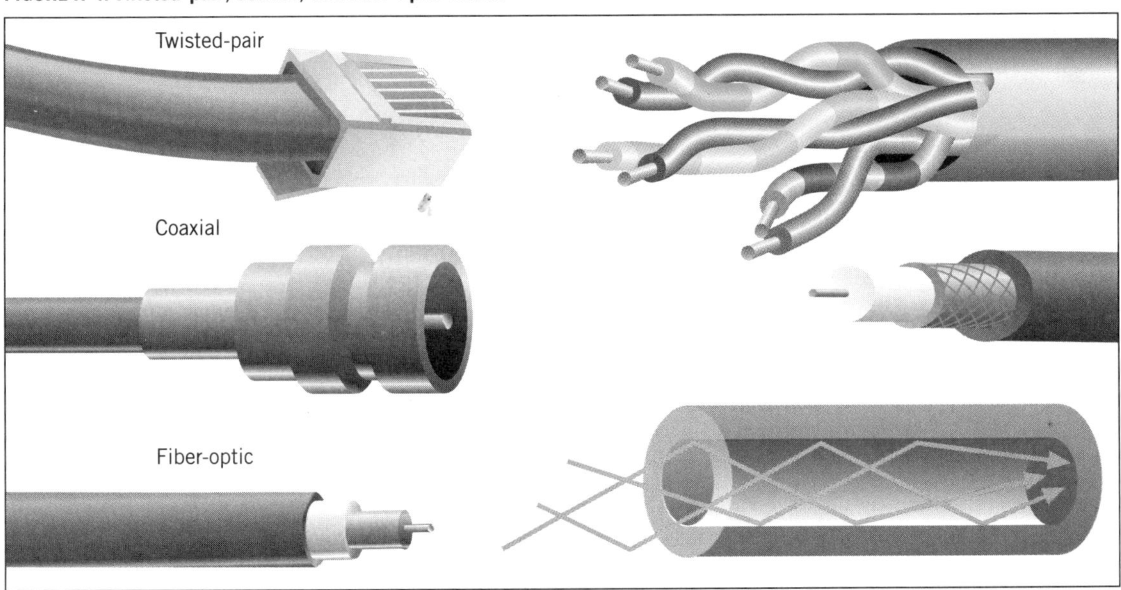

Transporting data

Bandwidth is a measure of the amount of data that can be transmitted simultaneously through a communications circuit. Bandwidth is commonly used to compare the maximum possible transmission speed through different connectors and to evaluate transmission speed through a given circuit. The circuit's bandwidth is limited to the narrowest bandwidth in the network, so the amount of data transmitted through any connector, known as **throughput**, is much lower than each connector's maximum value. Bandwidth is measured in multiples of **bits per second (bps)**. A bandwidth of 28,800 bps means that 28,800 bits of data are transferred each second. The following terms are often used when discussing Internet bandwidth: **kilobits per second (Kbps)**, which is 1,024 bps; **megabits per second (Mbps)**, which is 1,048,576 bps; and **gigabits per second (Gbps)**, which is 1,073,741,824 bps.

Internet

Learning the Origins of the Internet

In the early 1960s, the U.S. Department of Defense (DOD) became very concerned about the possible effects of nuclear attack on its computing facilities. As a result, it began to examine ways to connect its computers to one another and to weapons installations that were distributed all over the world. The DOD created the Defense Advanced Research Projects Agency (DARPA). DARPA's research led to the creation of a worldwide network. Intrigued by the military origins of the Internet, you decide to find out how the Internet developed from the activities of DARPA into the vast network of computers now available to anyone.

Details

ARPANET

The **Advanced Research Projects Agency Network (ARPANET)** was an experimental WAN that consisted of four computers networked together by DARPA researchers in 1969. These first four computers were located at the University of California at Los Angeles, SRI International, the University of California at Santa Barbara, and the University of Utah. By 1990, a network of networks, now known as the Internet, had grown from the four computers on the ARPANET to more than 300,000 computers on many interconnected networks.

Protocols

As ARPANET grew to include more computers, researchers realized that each connected computer needed to conform to the same set of rules. The **Network Control Protocol (NCP)** was developed as the first collection of rules for formatting, ordering, and error-checking data sent across a network. Vincent Cerf, who is often referred to as the Father of the Internet, along with his colleague Robert Kahn, developed the Transmission Control Protocol and the Internet Protocol (referred to by their combined acronym **TCP/IP**), which are still used today. The **Transmission Control Protocol (TCP)** includes rules that computers on a network use to establish and break connections. The **Internet Protocol (IP)** includes rules for routing individual **data packets** (small chunks of data). The term "Internet" was first used in 1974 in an article written by Cerf and Kahn about TCP.

Open Architecture Philosophy

The **open architecture philosophy** ensured that each network connected to the ARPANET could continue using its own protocols and data-transmission methods internally. Four key points characterize the open architecture philosophy:

- Independent networks should not require internal changes to have a connection to the Internet.
- Data packets that do not arrive at their destinations must be retransmitted from their source network.
- Computers that route data packets do not retain information about the data packets they handle, which makes the transmission network-independent.
- No global control exists over the network. This feature is perhaps one of the most amazing features of the Internet, because the Internet began as a way for the military to maintain control while under attack.

Interconnecting Networks

The Internet is a network of networks. These networks are connected via a **network backbone**, the long-distance lines and supporting technology that transport large amounts of data between major network connection points. As shown in Figure A-5, many of the networks that developed in the wake of ARPANET eventually joined together into the Internet we know today. Table A-1 describes some of the most well-known networks that eventually became the Internet.

FIGURE A-5: Networks that became the Internet

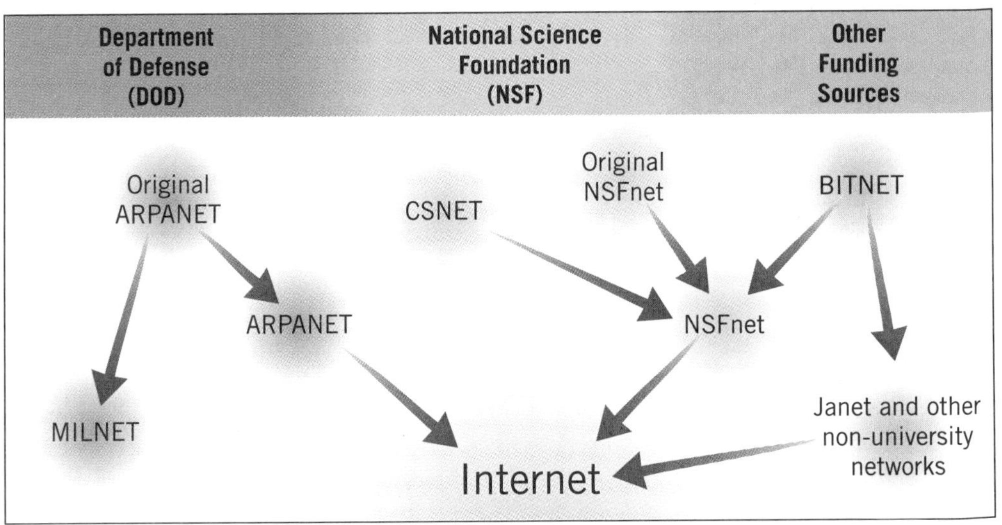

TABLE A-1: Interconnecting networks

network	descriptions
ARPANET (Advanced Research Projects Agency Network)	Specialized network used for advanced research studies that originated in 1984 when the DOD split the original ARPANET into ARPANET and MILNET
BITNET (Because It's Time Network)	Developed by City University of New York to link IBM mainframes at universities
CSNET (Computer Science Network)	Funded by the National Science Foundation (NSF) for educational and research institutions that did not have access to the ARPANET
Janet (Joint Academic Network)	Developed in the United Kingdom to link universities
MILNET (Military Network)	Specialized network reserved for high-security military uses that originated in 1984 when the DOD split the original ARPANET into ARPANET and MILNET
NSFnet (National Science Foundation Network)	Developed as an addition to CSNET

CLUES TO USE

Understanding packet switching and routers

In the conventional **circuit switching** method for data transmission (once commonly used by telephone companies), all data transmitted from a sender to a receiver traveled along a single path. This method could not be easily secured. DARPA researchers needed to find a more secure method for sending information. As a result, DARPA developed an alternative: the **packet switching** method, which breaks down files and messages into data packets. Each data packet is labeled electronically with codes that describe its origin and destination, and it travels from computer to computer along the network until reaching its destination. The destination computer collects the data packets and reassembles the original data. Each computer that an individual data packet encounters while traveling through the network determines the best way to move the data packet forward to its destination. The computers that perform this function on networks are often called **routers**, and the programs they use to determine the best path for data packets are called **routing algorithms**.

Internet

Understanding the Development of the Internet

As PCs became more powerful, affordable, and available during the 1980s, firms increasingly used them to construct intranets. **Intranets** are LANs or WANs that use the TCP/IP protocol but do not connect to sites outside the firm. Prior to 1989, most universities and businesses could not communicate with people outside their intranet. Because the National Science Foundation (NSF) prohibited commercial network traffic on the networks it funded, businesses that wanted to communicate outside their intranets turned to commercial e-mail services. Larger firms built their own TCP/IP-based WANs that used leased telephone lines to connect field offices to corporate headquarters. As you continue your research about the Internet, you learn more about how the Internet evolved from a resource used primarily by the academic community to one that became accessible to commercial services.

Details

► Commercial E-Mail Services

In 1989, the NSF permitted two commercial e-mail services, MCI Mail and CompuServe, to establish limited connections to the Internet. These commercial providers allowed their subscribers to exchange e-mail messages with members of the academic and research communities who were connected to the Internet. These connections allowed commercial enterprises to send e-mail directly to Internet addresses and allowed members of the research and education communities on the Internet to send e-mail directly to MCI Mail and CompuServe addresses. The NSF justified this limited commercial use of the Internet by describing it as a service that would primarily benefit the Internet's noncommercial users.

► Internet Engineering Task Force

People from all walks of life, not just scientists or academic researchers, started thinking of these networks as a global resource that we now know as the Internet. Information systems professionals began to form volunteer groups, such as the **Internet Engineering Task Force (IETF)**, which first met in 1986. The IETF is a self-organized group that makes technical contributions to the engineering of the Internet and its technologies; it is also the main body that develops new Internet standards.

► Federal Networking Council

The National Science and Technology Council's Committee on Computing, Information and Communications (CCIC) set up the **Federal Networking Council (FNC)** to meet the CCIC's research and education goals. The FNC also coordinates the use of its agencies' technologies by the commercial sector. In 1995, the FNC adopted the formal definition of Internet shown in Figure A-6. Many people find it interesting that a formal definition of the term did not appear until 1995. The Internet was a phenomenon that surprised the world.

► Commercialization of the Internet

In 1991, the NSF eased its restrictions on Internet commercial activity and began implementing plans to eventually privatize much of the Internet. Businesses and individuals began to connect to the Internet in ever-increasing numbers. Figure A-7 shows the dramatic growth of Internet host computers during these first years, 1991 through 2001.

FIGURE A-6: The Federal Networking Council's October 1995 resolution to define the term "Internet"

RESOLUTION: The Federal Networking Council (FNC) agrees that the following language reflects our definition of the term "Internet." "Internet" refers to the global information system that—

(i) is logically linked together by a globally unique address space based on the Internet Protocol (IP) or its subsequent extensions/follow-ons;

(ii) is able to support communications using the Transmission Control Protocol/Internet Protocol (TCP/IP) suite or its subsequent extensions/follow-ons, and/or other IP-compatible protocols; and

(iii) provides, uses or makes accessible, either publicly or privately, high level services layered on the communications and related infrastructure described herein.

Source: http://www.itrd.gov/fnc/Internet_res.html

FIGURE A-7: Growth of the number of Internet hosts

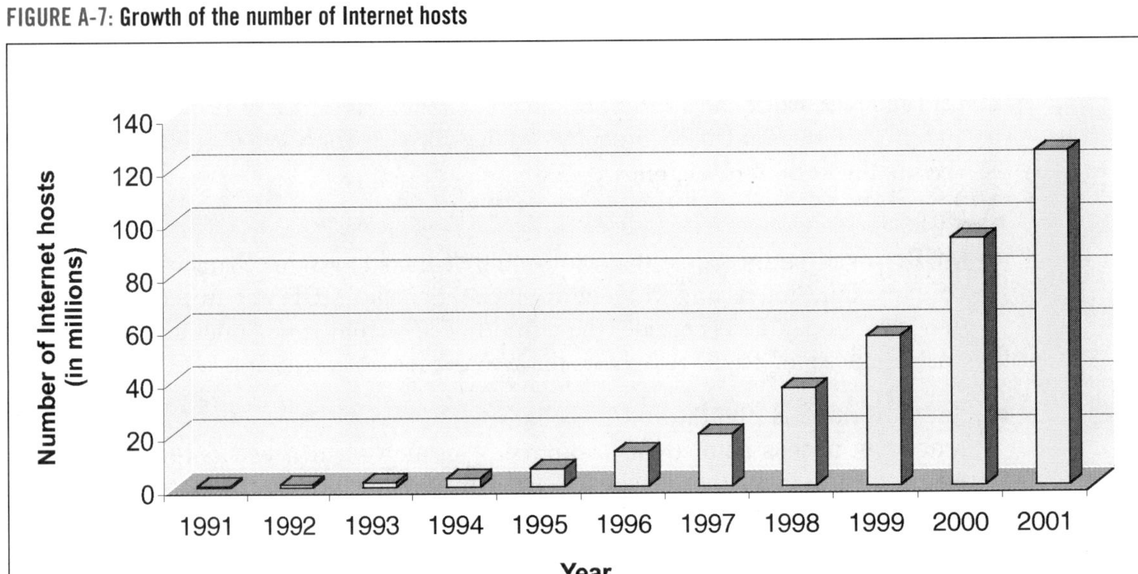

Internet

Exploring Uses for the Internet

Many people are surprised to learn that no one knows how many users are on the Internet. The Internet has no central management or coordination, and the routing computers do not maintain records of the data packets they handle. Therefore, no one has the capability of finding out how many individual e-mail messages or files travel on the Internet. Researchers estimate that at least 30 million host computers are connected to the Internet and that between 300 million and 400 million people worldwide use it. The Internet's phenomenal growth can be attributed, in part, to the development of a wide variety of uses for it. Your research about the Internet has introduced you to its popular uses, such as e-mail and newsgroups. As you continue your research, you encounter more new terms—many of which are written as acronyms. You decide to familiarize yourself with some of these terms and to learn how they helped shape the Internet.

TCP/IP Tools

The TCP/IP suite of protocols includes a tool to facilitate file transfer, and another to access **remote computers** (computers that aren't part of a user's immediate network) over the Internet:

- The **File Transfer Protocol (FTP)** enables users to transfer files between computers.
- **Telnet** enables users to log on to a remote server.

LISTSERV

LISTSERV software is used to create and manage e-mail mailing lists that users all over the world can join to discuss a variety of issues and topics. LISTSERV software was originally developed to run mailing lists on BITNET.

Usenet

Usenet, an acronym for User's News Network, allows anyone that connects to this network to read and post articles on a variety of subjects. Usenet was started in 1979 by a group of students and programmers at Duke University and the University of North Carolina. Today, Usenet survives in the form of newsgroups.

MUDs

MUDs are adventure games that allow multiple users to assume character roles and to play at the same time, interacting with one another. Originally, MUD was an acronym for "multiuser dungeon." Today, users consider the term to be an acronym for "multiuser domain" or "multiuser dimension." Figure A-8 shows the Web site for a MUD game.

Network Access Points

A **network access point (NAP)** is a physical location where networks connect to the Internet. Figure A-9 shows the four network access points on the Internet backbone. Each NAP is operated by a different company, which sells access to the Internet to organizations and businesses. Presumably, these companies will continue to invest in developing and refining network architecture to attract new Internet users and to ensure continued growth of the Internet. Already, computers are located in almost every country of the world, and millions of dollars change hands each day over the Internet to purchase all kinds of products and services.

FIGURE A-8: Sample MUD game on the Internet

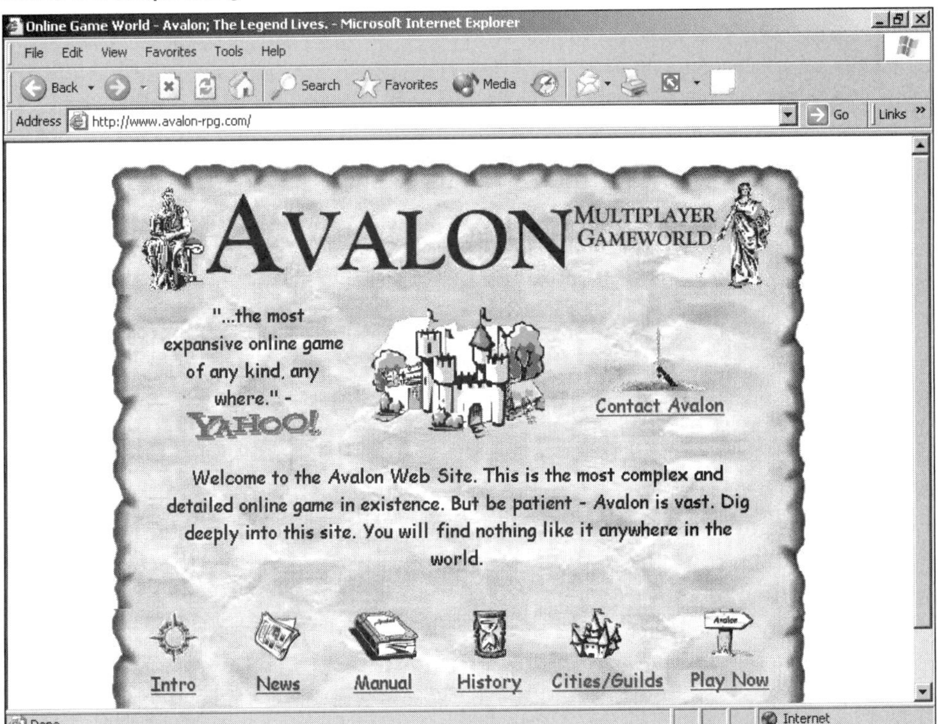

FIGURE A-9: Network access points on the Internet backbone

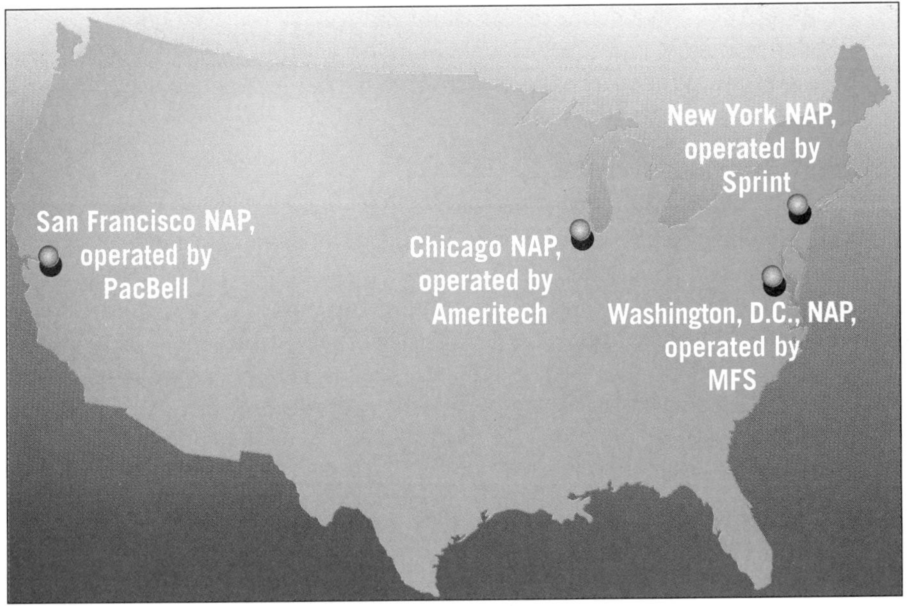

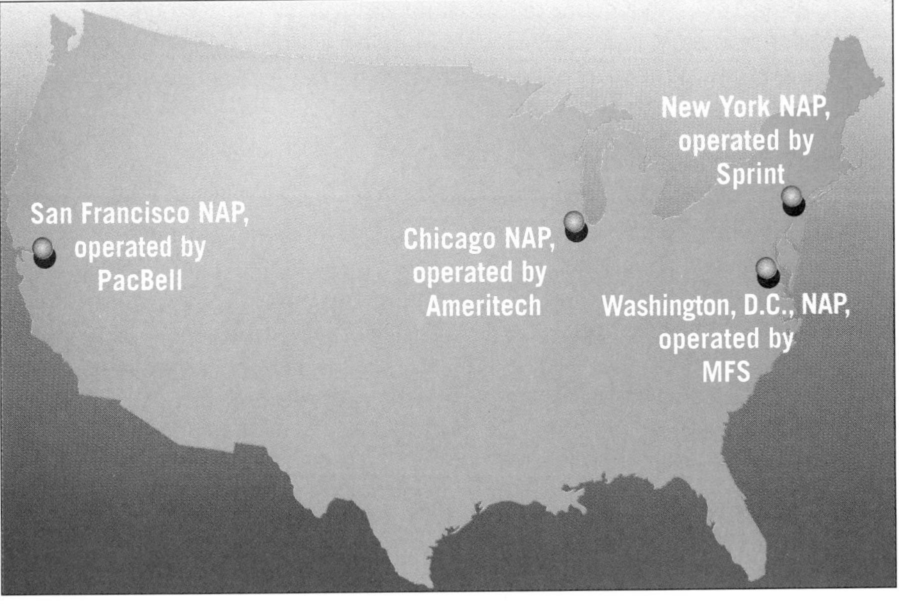

Future of the TCP/IP numbering system

The TCP/IP numbering system for identifying users will run out of addresses in a few years if the Internet continues to grow at its current rate. In 1997, the IETF approved a new addressing scheme, **IP version 6** **(IPv6)** that permits many more addresses. The new addressing scheme will allow existing users to continue accessing the Internet while the new system is implemented.

Internet

Understanding How the World Wide Web Works

In a short amount of time, the number of Web sites has rapidly increased. Figure A-10 shows the fast growth of the Web during its initial years. The Web's success is due to links that enable you to connect to any document on the Web, and user-friendly Web tools that enable users to view and search for Web pages with ease. As you continue your research about the Internet, you decide to learn more about how the Web works.

Details

► Links

Links (also called **hypertext links**, or **hyperlinks**) are text, graphics, or other Web page elements that connect to additional data on the Web. On a Web page, a text link is usually underlined, and the mouse pointer typically appears as a pointing hand when positioned over a link. When you click a link, a new **Web document**, such as a page of text and graphics, or an audio or video file, appears. This Web document could be part of the Web site you are currently exploring or part of a Web site halfway around the world. Links allow you to easily locate and open information or resources related to the Web page you're viewing. Figure A-11 shows a Web page from the Course Technology Web site.

► Hypertext Markup Language

Hypertext Markup Language (HTML) is a computer language that marks text with a set of **tags**, or codes, that define the structure and behavior of a Web document. For example, HTML includes a tag to create a header, a numbered list, or a link. Every Web page is created using HTML tags. When you view a Web page on the Internet, however, you don't see the HTML tags—you see just the resulting formatted Web page.

► Web Browser

A **Web browser** is software that reads HTML documents. Web browsers let you read (or browse) HTML documents and move from one HTML document to another. You can use a Web browser to view any HTML document that resides on a computer connected to the Internet. Two of the most popular Web browser software programs currently available are Netscape Navigator and Microsoft Internet Explorer. The Web page shown in Figure A-11 was accessed using Internet Explorer. Web browsers use text, pictures, icons, and other graphical elements to present information and allow users to perform a variety of tasks. For example, you could click the Print icon, which displays a picture of a printer, to print a copy of a Web page.

FIGURE A-10: Growth of the World Wide Web

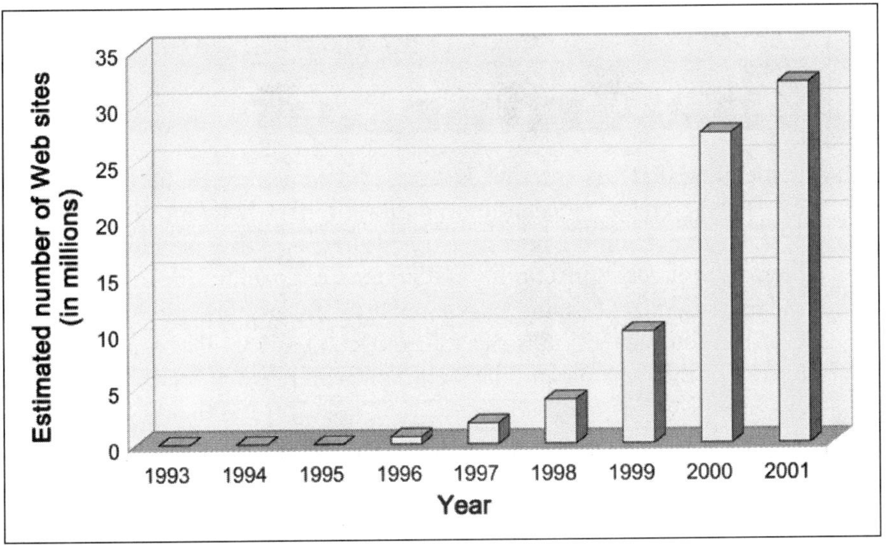

FIGURE A-11: Example of a Web page

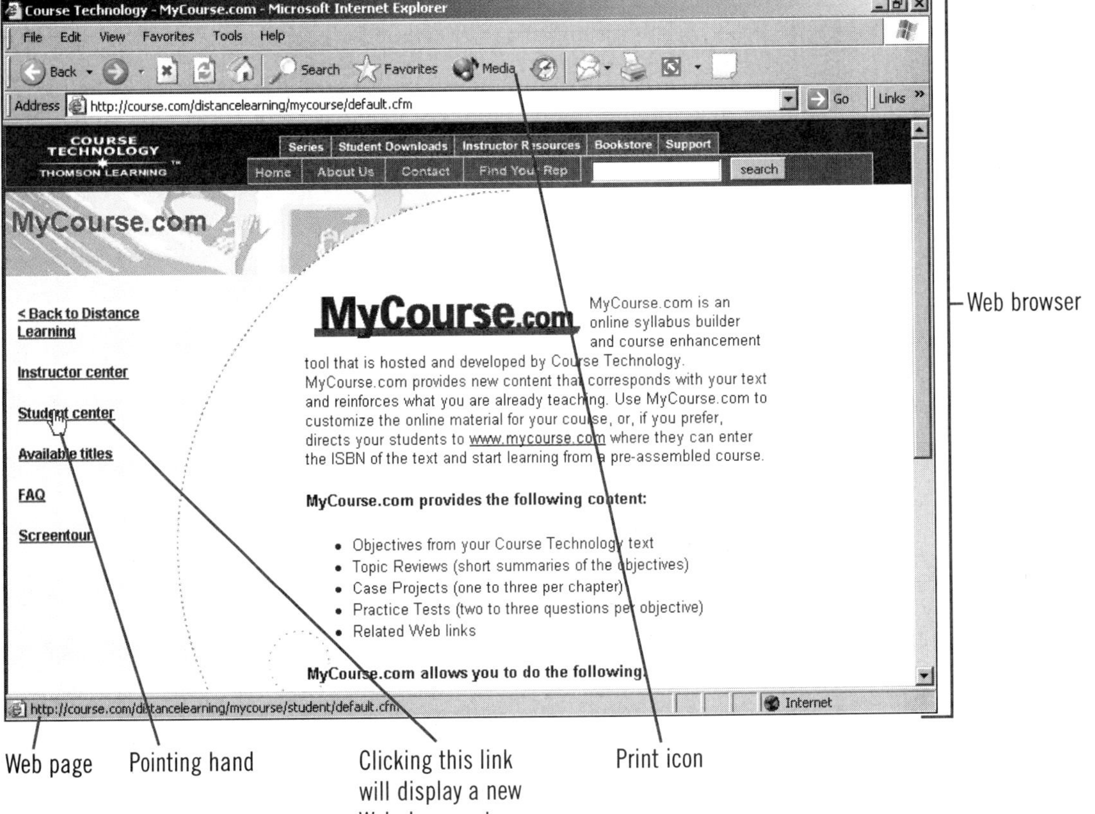

Internet

Internet

Connecting to the Internet

Remember that the Internet is a set of interconnected networks. To become a part of the Internet, you need to be part of a communications network. NAPs maintain the core operations of the Internet and the backbone used to transmit data over long distances. NAPs do not, however, offer direct connections to individuals or small businesses. Instead, they offer connections to large organizations and businesses that, in turn, provide Internet access to other organizations and individuals. Your research has provided you with a good background on the history of the Internet and the Web. Next, you research the nature of Internet connections. You can use this information to decide what TEPCo needs to access the Internet.

► Internet Service Provider

To connect to the Internet from your home or business, you need to set up an account with an **Internet service provider (ISP)**. Usually, the ISP provides you with the software you need to connect to the Internet, browse the Web, send and receive e-mail messages, and transfer files. ISPs also often provide advice and help in setting up networks, and some even help their customers design Web pages. Many larger ISPs not only sell Internet access to users, but also sell Internet access to other ISPs, which then sell access and service to their own customers. This hierarchy of Internet access is illustrated in Figure A-12.

► Line Connections

To connect to the Internet, data must be able to travel between your computer and the Internet. Common connections include the following: telephone service connection (sometimes referred to as **POTS**, or **plain old telephone service**); **T1** and **T3** line connections; **Digital Subscriber Line (DSL)**; and **cable**. Table A-2 summarizes the most popular types of connections currently used on the Internet.

► Modem

To connect to the Internet, you usually need a **modem**, which is a device that converts signals between a computer and the transmission line. The term modem is short for **modulator-demodulator**. When you connect your computer, which communicates using digital signals, to another computer through a twisted-pair or coaxial cable, which uses analog signals, the signal must be converted. Converting a digital signal to an analog signal is called **modulation**; converting that analog signal back into digital form is called **demodulation**. A modem performs both functions; that is, it acts as a modulator-demodulator. The general term modem usually refers to a device used with a telephone line; most computers sold today include this variety of modem. Other methods of connecting to the Internet require different types of modems. For example, a cable connection through a cable television company requires a **cable modem**. A **DSL connection**, a high-speed connection often provided by a telephone company, requires a **DSL modem**.

FIGURE A-12: The hierarchy of Internet service options

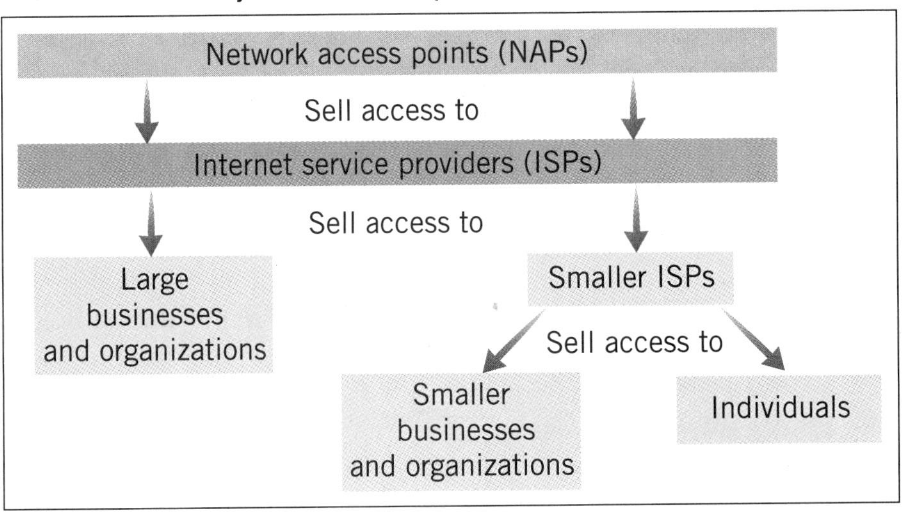

TABLE A-2: Types of Internet connections

type of service	description	speed
telephone service	Available through regular phone lines; used by individuals and small businesses to connect to an ISP	28.8 Kbps to 56 Kbps
T1 line	Offers a higher grade of service for connecting to the Internet than POTS does; used by large companies and organizations that must link hundreds or thousands of individual users to the Internet; more expensive than POTS connections	1.544 Mbps
T3 line	Same as T1 line	44.736 Mbps
Digital Subscriber Line (DSL)	Creates a high-speed connection using the customer's telephone wiring; used by individuals and businesses	up to 1.5 Mbps
cable	Uses the customer's television cable to connect to the Internet; used by individuals and businesses	Up to 170 times faster than regular phone service

Connecting with a mobile device

Mobile Internet connections are simply an extension of both the Internet and mobile communications. Wireless devices such as cell phones and personal digital assistants (PDAs) can upload and download e-mail, transfer files, and access the Web. Such connections use a wireless modem (which is built into most cell phones), and the organization providing the wireless connection service serves as the ISP.

Internet

Defining Internet Service Options

To connect to the Internet, individuals or small businesses must use an ISP. Users can choose one of four ways to link to an ISP. The first way, which is available only to individuals, is a connection through your school or employer. The second option is a connection over standard telephone lines. The third option is to connect through a cable television company. The fourth option is to use a satellite. As your research continues, you evaluate the various connection options to determine which option you will recommend for TEPCo.

School or Employer Connection

One of the easiest ways to connect to the Internet is through your school or employer, if it already has an Internet connection. Such a connection is generally free or very reasonably priced. Most schools and employers have an **acceptable use policy (AUP)** that specifies the conditions under which you can use their Internet connection. For example, many AUPs expressly prohibit you from engaging in commercial activities. In such cases, you could not use your Internet account to start a small business on the Web. An important concern when using your school's or employer's Internet connection is that the school or employer generally retains the right to examine any files or e-mail messages you transmit. You need to carefully consider whether the limitations placed on your use of the Internet are greater than the benefits of the low cost of this access option.

Standard Telephone Line Connection

Depending on where you live, you might find that a telephone line service (using either standard dial-in service or DSL) is the best way to connect to the Internet. In major metropolitan areas, many ISPs offering these services compete for customers and, therefore, connection fees are often very reasonable. Additionally, some companies offer free Internet access, in exchange for displaying advertising on your computer screen each time you connect. Smaller towns and rural areas have fewer ISPs offering these connection options, and therefore might be less competitive. Figure A-13 lists some of the information you need to learn about such an ISP before signing on. A telephone line service is the best option for many Internet users, in part because it usually provides a reliable connection at a reasonable price. Figure A-14 shows the main Web page (called the home page) of a dial-in ISP's Web site.

Cable Connection

One of the more recent developments in the Internet access business is the cable modem, which allows you to connect to the Internet through your cable television company. A cable connection can provide very fast downloads to your computer from the Internet (as much as 170 times faster than a telephone line connection). Although the cost of a cable connection is usually higher than the cost of a telephone line connection, you save the cost of a second telephone line. The greatest disadvantage for most people is that the cable connection might not be available yet in their area.

Satellite Connection

Many rural areas in the United States do not have cable television service and never will because their low population density makes it too expensive. A cable company simply cannot afford to run miles of cable to reach one or two isolated customers. People in these areas often buy satellite receivers to obtain television signals and Internet connections. The major advantage of a satellite connection is speed. Although the speeds are not as high as those offered by cable modems, they are approximately 5 to 10 times higher than those achieved with telephone connections. For users in remote areas, this technology often offers the best connection solution.

FIGURE A-13: Questions to ask when selecting an Internet service provider

What is the monthly base fee and how many hours of Internet service are included?

What is the hourly rate for time used over the monthly base amount?

Is the telephone access number local or long distance?

Which specific Internet services are included?

What software is included?

What user-support services are available?

FIGURE A-14: Web site of an Internet service provider

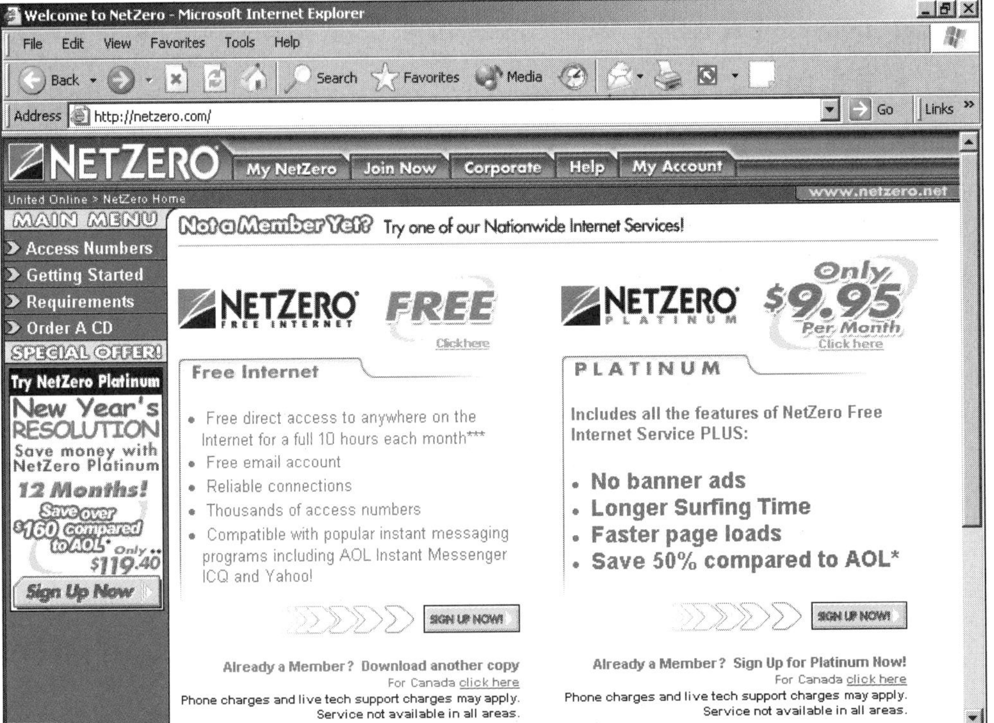

CLUES TO USE

Public-access Internet service

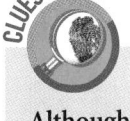

Although many options exist for setting up Internet service in your home, some people find that they can meet their Internet access needs for free using public facilities. For example, many public libraries offer free Internet access to library card holders, or to the general public. You might find it unnecessary to maintain Internet service at home if you have minimal Internet access requirements, and such public access is available in a convenient location.

Internet

Unit A

Internet

Understanding E-Mail

E-mail is one of the most prevalent forms of business communication and the most popular way individuals use the Internet. In fact, many people view the Internet as simply an electronic highway that transports e-mail messages, without realizing that the Internet provides a wide variety of other services. Whether for business or recreational use, people rely on e-mail as an indispensable way of sending messages and data to one another. Now that you have researched how to connect TEPCo to the Internet, you decide that you need to learn some of the principal characteristics of e-mail.

Mail Server

Like other Internet data, e-mail travels across the Internet in small data packets, which are reassembled at the destination and delivered to the addressee. When you send an e-mail message to a particular addressee, the message is sent to a **mail server**, which is a server that runs special software for handling e-mail tasks. Based on the recipient's e-mail address, the mail server determines which of several electronic routes it will use to send your message. When you send an e-mail message, the message is routed from one computer to another and passes through several mail servers until it reaches the recipient. Each mail server determines the next route for your message until it finally arrives at the recipient's electronic mailbox.

Mail Software

You can send and receive e-mail messages in two ways:

- **Mail client software** is a program that lets you send and receive e-mail, and store e-mail on your PC. An advantage of being able to store e-mail on your PC is that you can read e-mail that you've received even after disconnecting from the Internet. Two popular e-mail client programs are Netscape Mail and Microsoft Outlook Express. See Unit B for instructions on setting up and using Netscape Mail, and Unit C for the same information on Microsoft Outlook Express.
- A **Web-based e-mail service** allows you to send and receive e-mail using a Web browser. This service lets you read your stored e-mail messages from different computers (for example, at home, work, or school). However, you can only access e-mail when you're connected to the Internet. Popular Web-based e-mail services include Hotmail and Yahoo! mail. See Unit G for instructions on setting up and using Web-based e-mail.

E-Mail Addresses

E-mail addresses uniquely identify an individual or organization that is connected to the Internet. An e-mail address comprises a **user name** (the recipient's account name), an at sign (@), and a **host name** (the computer that stores the e-mail). For example, the e-mail address of a TEPCo employee called Sally Jones might be sjones@tepco.com, where "sjones" is the user name and "tepco.com" is the host name.

Anatomy of an E-Mail Message

An e-mail message consists of two major parts: the message header and the message body. The **message header** contains all the information about the message—the recipient's e-mail address (To), the sender's e-mail address (From), and a subject line (Subject), which indicates the topic of the message. In addition, the message header can list other people who have received copies of the message and, sometimes, the filename of an **attachment** (a separate file sent with an e-mail message). The **message body** contains the actual message. Figure A-15 shows a sample e-mail message.

FIGURE A-15: Structure of a typical e-mail message

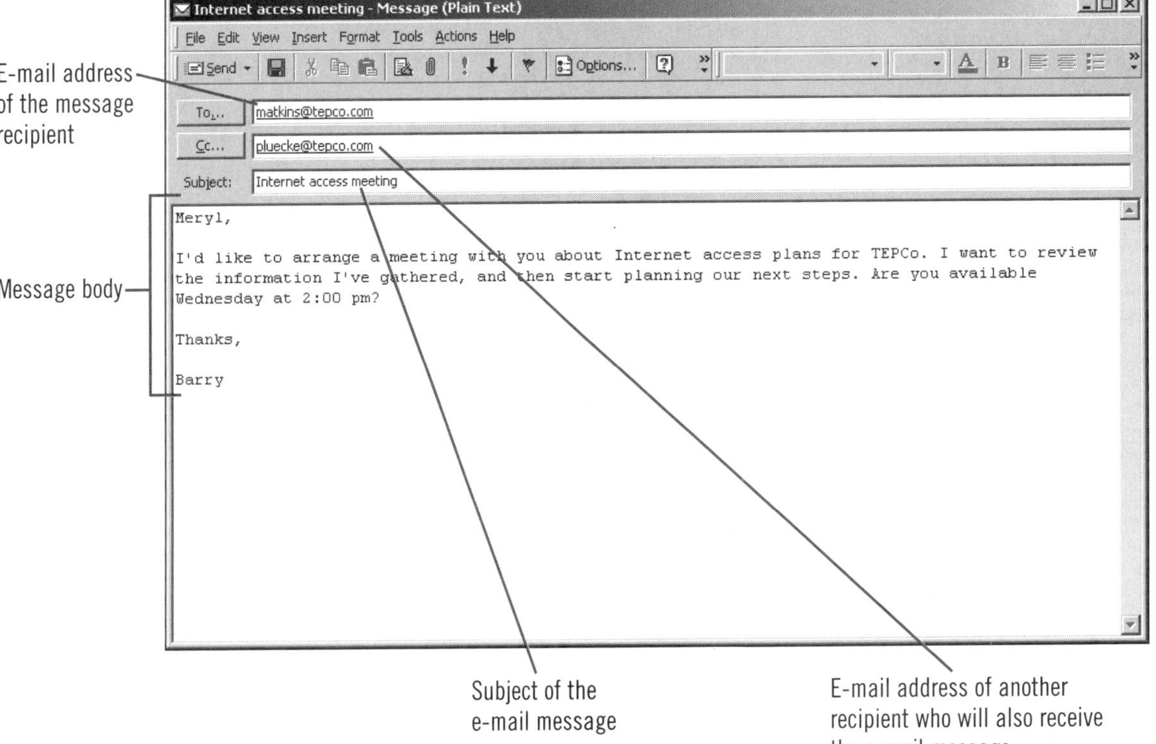

CLUES TO USE

Examining host names with multiple parts

A host name can consist of more than two parts. For example, in Figure A-16 the host name "condor.cs.missouri.edu" contains four parts. An e-mail message to someone named John Brown in the University of Missouri's Computer Science Department could be addressed to jbrown@condor.cs.missouri.edu.

FIGURE A-16: Host name elements

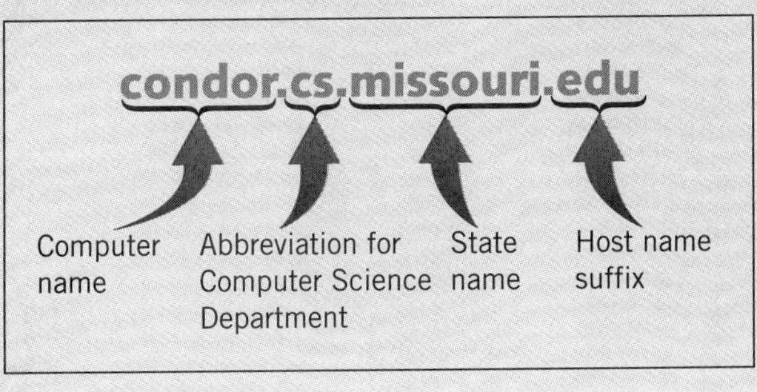

Internet

Practice

Concepts Review

Match each term with the statement that it describes.

1. **Internet**
2. **server**
3. **LAN**
4. **ISP**
5. **ARPANET**
6. **IETF**
7. **TCP/IP**
8. **FTP**
9. **links**
10. **HTML**

- **a.** An organization responsible for developing new Internet standards
- **b.** A computer that accepts requests from computers connected to it and shares resources with those computers
- **c.** A method used to transfer files over the Internet
- **d.** A business that offers an Internet connection to your home or office
- **e.** Clickable text, graphics, or other Web page elements that connect to other Web documents
- **f.** An experimental WAN
- **g.** A network of computers located close together
- **h.** A worldwide collection of interconnected networks
- **i.** The language used to create a Web page
- **j.** Protocols used by all computers connected to the Internet

Select the best answer from the list of choices.

11. The type of cable used in telephone connections is called a:
- **a.** Twisted-pair cable.
- **b.** TCP/IP cable.
- **c.** Coaxial cable.
- **d.** Fiber-optic cable.

12. Which of the following methods is the switching method used by the Internet?
- **a.** Cable switching
- **b.** Circuit switching
- **c.** Packet switching
- **d.** Transmission switching

13. Which of the following terms is the technical term for the collection of rules that computers follow when formatting, ordering, and error-checking data sent across a network?
- **a.** Router
- **b.** ARPANET
- **c.** Open architecture
- **d.** Protocol

14. The network developed by City University of New York is called:
- **a.** NSFnet.
- **b.** BITNET.
- **c.** Janet.
- **d.** CSNET.

Practice

15. Which of the following terms is used to describe computer networks that use the TCP/IP protocol but do not connect to sites outside the firm?
- **a.** Internet
- **b.** ARPANET
- **c.** World Wide Web
- **d.** intranet

16. Which of the following is a requirement for all home and business Internet connections?
- **a.** A T1 line
- **b.** Cable television service
- **c.** DSL service
- **d.** An ISP

17. Which network connector is capable of the highest possible bandwidth?
- **a.** Category 1
- **b.** Category 5/5e
- **c.** Coaxial
- **d.** Fiber-optic

18. A program that lets you read e-mail messages stored on your computer when you are not connected to the Internet is called:
- **a.** a Mail server.
- **b.** a Web-based service.
- **c.** Mail client software.
- **d.** Hotmail.

▶ Independent Challenge 1

Your school probably has a number of computer networks. At most schools, you can find information about computing facilities from the Department of Academic Computing, the school library, or the network administrator.

- **a.** What LANs and WANs do you have on your campus?
- **b.** Which of these LANs and WANs are interconnected?
- **c.** Determine if the file server is a PC or a larger computer.
- **d.** Which network operating system is used?

▶ Independent Challenge 2

You've decided to get connected to the Internet! Your first step is to determine which Internet service provider you should choose.

- **a.** Find the names of three ISPs in your area. If possible, include one ISP that provides Internet access via cable connection. Your local cable television company is a good place to start.
- **b.** Find out the following information about each of the three ISPs you have chosen:
  1. What is the monthly base fee?
  2. How many hours of Internet service are included in the base fee?
  3. What is the hourly rate for time used over the monthly base amount?
  4. Is the telephone access number local or long distance?
  5. Which specific Internet services are included?
  6. What software is included?
  7. What user-support services are available?

8. What is the best feature of the services provided by the ISP?
9. What is the worst feature of the services provided by the ISP?

c. Describe which ISP you would choose based on your answers to the preceding questions.

Independent Challenge 3

Most companies and public institutions that offer Internet access require users to sign, or at least be aware of, an acceptable use policy (AUP).

a. Obtain a copy of your school's or employer's AUP.
b. Outline the main restrictions that the AUP places on student (or employee) activities.
c. Compare those restrictions with the limits that it places on faculty (or employer) activities.
d. Analyze and evaluate any differences in treatment; if there are no differences, discuss whether the policy should be rewritten to include differences.
e. If your school or employer has no policy, outline the key elements that you believe should be included in such a policy.

Independent Challenge 4

As you learned in this unit, the Internet includes many resources. If you are new to the Internet, you might be wondering how you can use the Internet in your life. You will find learning about the Internet much more enjoyable if you approach it with some uses in mind.

a. List several topics that you are interested in exploring on the Internet. Think of your own hobbies and interests. Would you like to find travel information about Alaska? Gather information for a research paper on Mars? Learn new yoga techniques? Explore nuclear physics databases? Identify at least five topics that interest you.
b. Describe three specific activities you want to engage in on the Internet. For example, you might want to send your resume to an employer across the country, write messages to a distant pen pal, view a clip of your favorite movie, or listen to music performed by your favorite band.

Internet

Using the Netscape Mail E-Mail Program

- ► Explore Netscape Mail
- ► Set up Netscape Mail
- ► Send an e-mail message
- ► Check incoming e-mail
- ► Attach a file to an e-mail message
- ► Save an e-mail attachment
- ► Reply to an e-mail message
- ► Forward an e-mail message
- ► File an e-mail message
- ► Delete an e-mail message
- ► Maintain an address book
- ► Create a mailing list

Several programs for managing e-mail are currently available. You can use any of these programs to send e-mail to people who use the same or different e-mail programs. The recipient can read your e-mail just as you can read the e-mail you receive from other people, regardless of the e-mail programs they use. One of the most popular e-mail programs is Netscape Mail, an integral part of the Netscape suite. 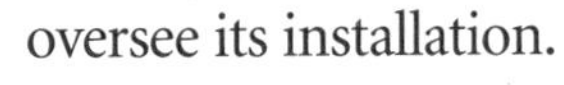 Kikukawa Air is an air charter service based in Maui, Hawaii, which offers service to all of the Hawaiian Islands. Sharon Kikukawa, one of the owners, wants to use e-mail as the company's primary means of communication to save on long distance phone bills. She hired you to evaluate Netscape Mail and to oversee its installation.

Internet

Exploring Netscape Mail

Netscape Mail includes three windows that let you manage e-mail: the Mail, Message, and Compose windows. After installing Netscape, you explore the various components of Netscape Mail. You decide to explore each of the three Netscape Mail windows.

Trouble?

Because you can customize the Mail window by resizing, hiding, and displaying different panes and their individual elements, your screen might look different from Figure B-1.

Mail Window

When you start Netscape Mail, the **Mail window** opens, as shown in Figure B-1. The Mail window contains up to four panes: the folders list, the message list, the Message pane, and My Sidebar. The **folders list** displays six default folders that you can use to receive, save, and store e-mail messages. The **message list** displays the contents of the folder selected in the folders list. Each message is listed as a **message header summary**, which includes the subject of the message, the sender, and the date or time the message was sent. When you select a message header summary in the message list, the **Message pane** shows the contents of the e-mail message. **My Sidebar** displays customizable Web shortcuts that allow you to access the Web without switching to a Web browser window.

Message Window

The **Message window** shown in Figure B-2 shows an individual e-mail message. To open an e-mail message in the Message window, you double-click its message header summary in the message list. The Message window displays the same information as the Message pane, and offers the same tools for managing a message. Because the Message window is a separate window, you can enlarge or maximize it to use more of the available screen area.

Compose Window

You use the **Compose window** shown in Figure B-3 to create new e-mail messages. To open the Compose window, you click the New Msg button on the Mail Toolbar in the Mail window or the Message window. The Mail Toolbar in the Compose window contains buttons to send the current message, find someone's e-mail address, attach files, check spelling, and save the current e-mail message as a draft.

CLUES TO USE

Downloading Netscape

You can download the Netscape browser suite (which includes Netscape Mail) for free from the Internet. If Netscape is not installed on your computer, see your network administrator. If your request is approved, you can then download Netscape from the Internet. Go to the Netscape home page at *www.netscape.com*, follow links to the Web page that tells you how to download the Netscape browser suite, then install it on your computer.

FIGURE B-1: Mail window

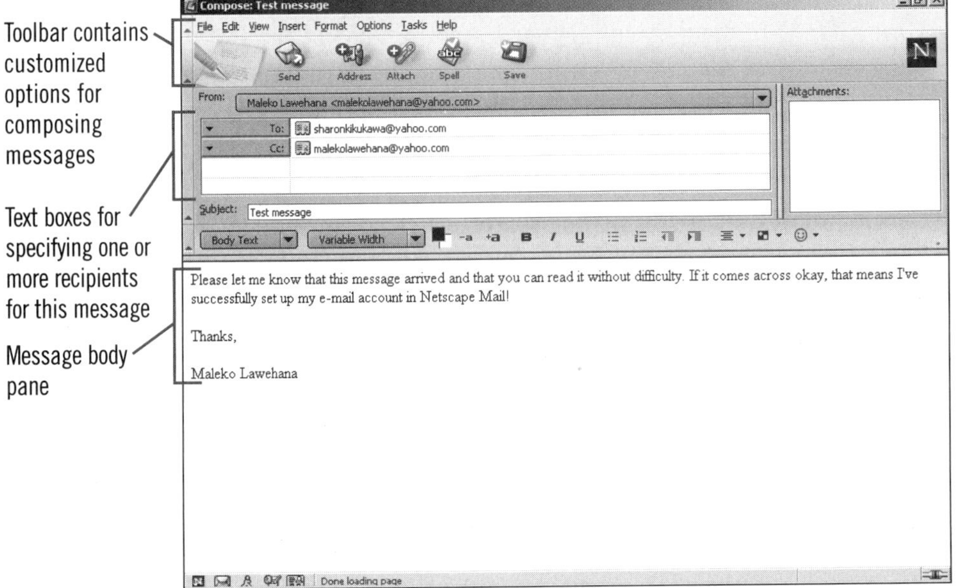

FIGURE B-2: Message window

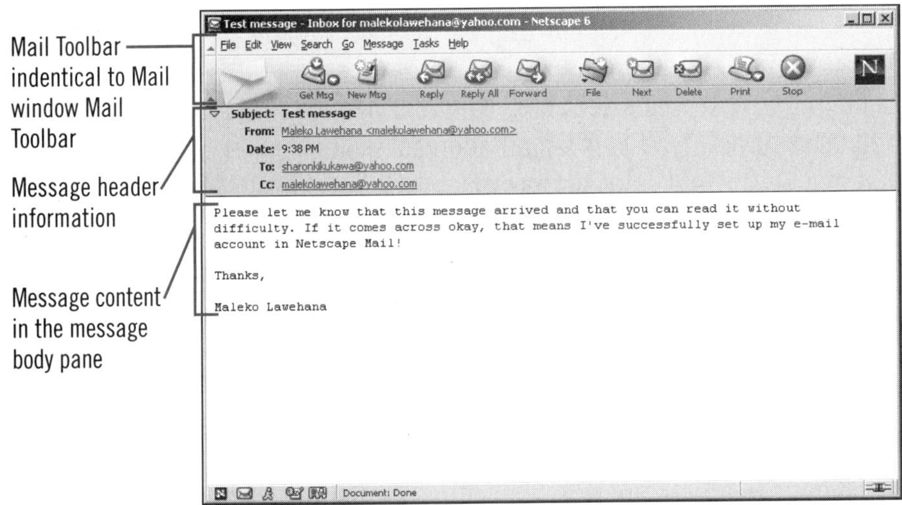

FIGURE B-3: Compose window

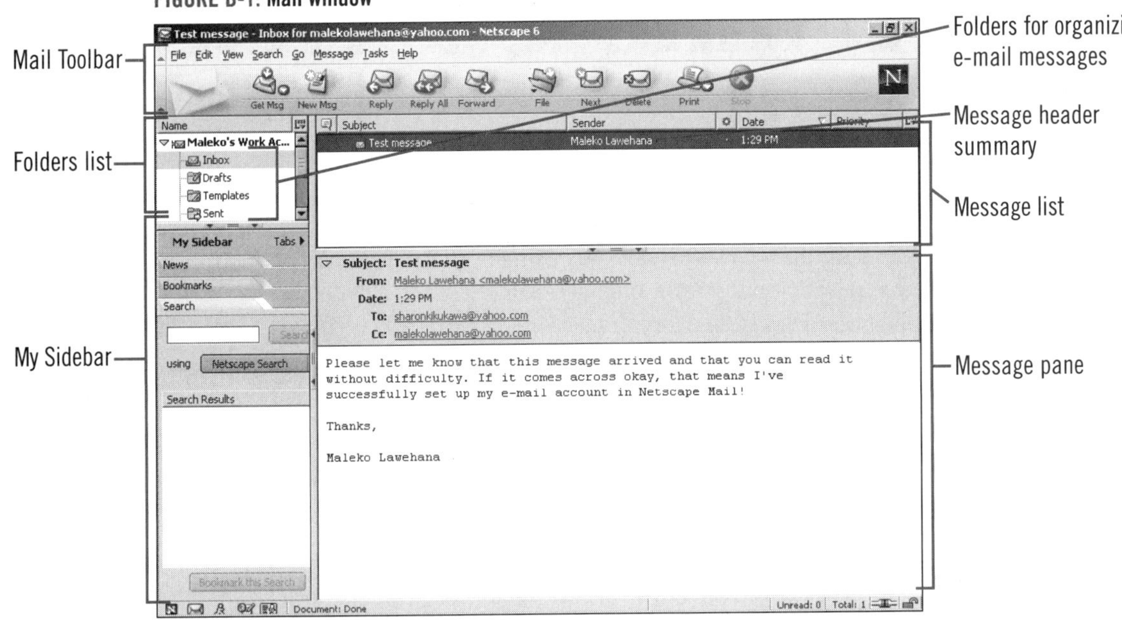

Internet

Internet

Setting Up Netscape Mail

After Netscape is installed on your computer, you need to **configure**, or set up, Netscape Mail to send and receive e-mail. As you learn about Netscape Mail, you discover that you must set it up before you can start using e-mail. You configure Netscape Mail by providing basic information about your e-mail account.

Steps

QuickTip

If necessary, click the Maximize button on the Mail window.

1. Click the **Start button** on the taskbar, point to either **Programs** or **All Programs**, point to **Netscape 6.2**, then click **Mail**
   The Mail window opens. If the Select a profile dialog box opens, then Netscape Mail is configured for more than one user. Click your user name, if available, or ask your instructor which user ID you should use to start Netscape.
2. Click **File** on the menu bar, point to **New**, then click **Account**
   The Account Wizard dialog box opens.

Trouble?

If you are unsure of which option to choose, ask your instructor or system administrator for help.

3. Click the **option button** for the type of service that describes your e-mail account, then click **Next**
   The Account Wizard dialog box displays the Identity page, containing fields for entering your name and e-mail address.
4. Click in the **Your Name text box**, type your name, press **[Tab]** to move to the Email Address text box, type your e-mail address, then click **Next**
   You should type your name the way you want it to appear in the message header summary for recipients of your messages. The values you enter in the Identity page have no effect on your ability to send or receive e-mail. When you send an e-mail message, these values simply tell the recipient who sent the message. If you selected "ISP or email provider" in Step 3, the Account Wizard dialog box displays the Server Information page shown in Figure B-4; skip to Step 5. If you selected "Netscape WebMail" or "AOL account" in Step 3, the Account Wizard dialog box displays the Congratulations! page, shown in Figure B-5, which summarizes the account settings that you entered; skip to Step 9.
5. In the Incoming Server section, click the **option button** corresponding to the type of incoming server you are using, click in the **Server Name text box**, then type the name of your incoming mail server
   The Incoming Server information tells Netscape how you receive e-mail through your ISP.

Trouble?

If you (or someone else) already set up an account on your computer, you don't need to provide Outgoing Server information; skip to Step 7.

6. Press **[Tab]** to move to the Server Name text box in the Outgoing Server section (if this text box is available), then type the name of your outgoing mail server
   Figure B-4 shows the completed Server Information page. The Outgoing Server information tells Netscape how you send e-mail through your ISP.
7. Click **Next**
   The Account Wizard dialog box displays the User Name page.
8. Type the user name assigned to you by your ISP in the User Name text box, then click **Next**
   The Account Wizard dialog box displays the Account Name page.

Trouble?

If any of the information listed is incorrect, click Back to open the appropriate page, edit the information, click Next to return to the Congratulations! page, then click Finish to finalize your settings.

9. Type a unique name for your account in the Account Name page, then click **Next**
   If Netscape is configured to send and receive e-mail for multiple e-mail accounts, the Account Name assists you in differentiating between accounts. The Account Wizard dialog box displays the Congratulations! page, shown in Figure B-5, which summarizes the account settings that you entered.
10. Click **Finish**
    The Account Wizard dialog box closes, and your copy of Netscape Mail is set up to send and receive messages using your e-mail account.

FIGURE B-4: Account Wizard Server Information page

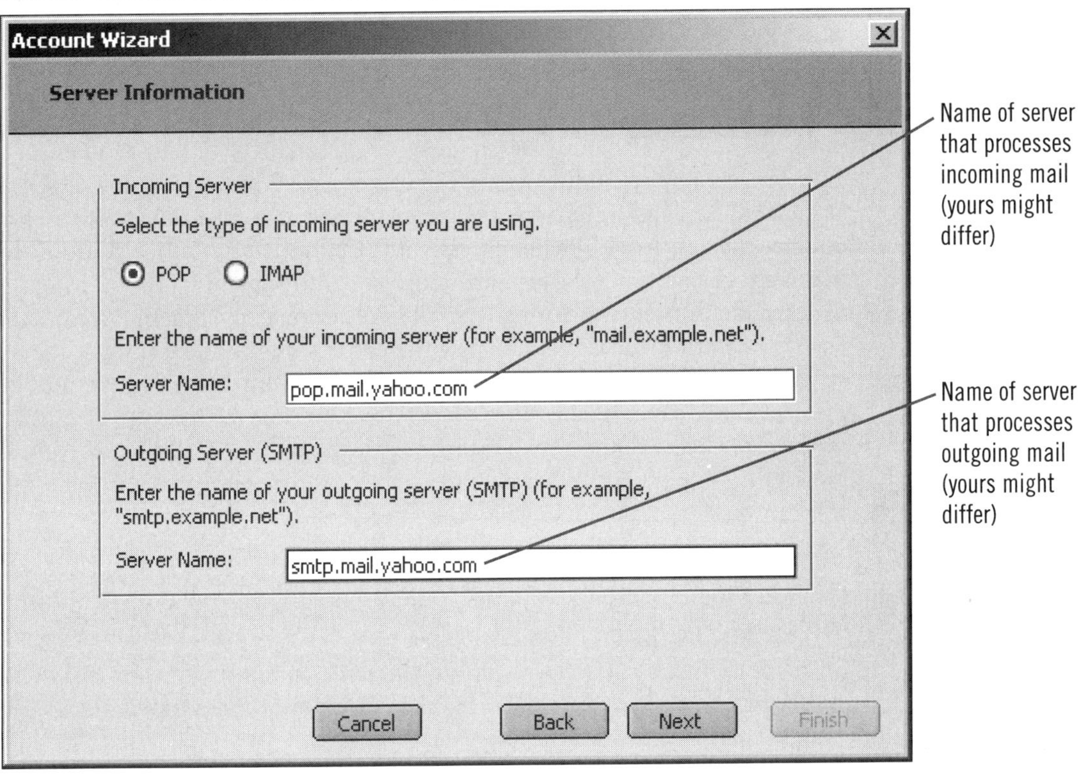

FIGURE B-5: Summary of e-mail account settings

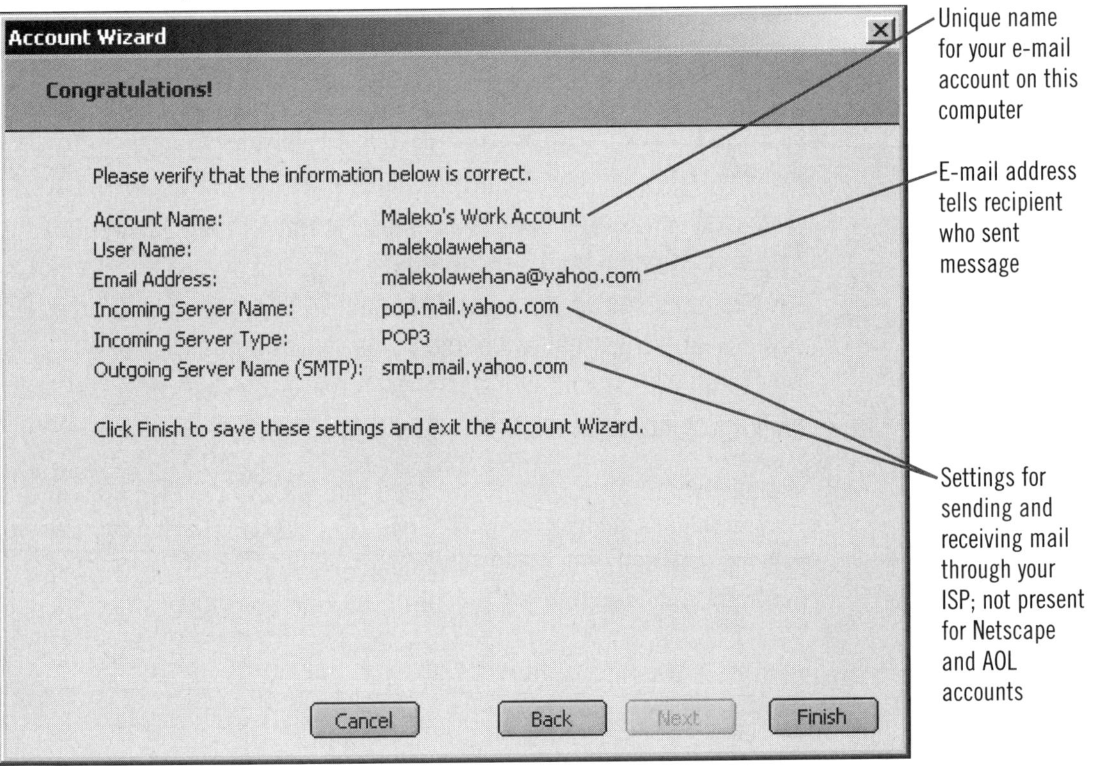

Internet

Internet

Sending an E-Mail Message

After your e-mail account is set up, you can use the Compose window to send e-mail messages. The Compose window includes fields for entering an e-mail address for each recipient. You can designate a recipient's e-mail address with "Cc," which stands for "Carbon copy." **Cc** indicates that the recipient is not the primary addressee; the recipient is just receiving a copy. You can also use the **Bcc** option (which stands for "Blind carbon copy") to send a copy without the knowledge of the other addressee(s). Below the address information, you use the Subject text box to summarize the main topic of an e-mail message. You then enter the message content in the message body pane. When you click the Send button, the message is transferred to your mail server for delivery to the e-mail recipient(s). You decide to use Netscape Mail to send a message to Sharon. You will also send a copy of the message to your own e-mail address so that you can verify that the message is sent correctly.

1. In the folders list, click the account name of your e-mail account, then click the **New Msg button** on the Mail Toolbar
   If multiple accounts are set up on the same computer, the message will be sent from the account selected in the folders list. The Compose window opens.
2. Type **sharonkikukawa@yahoo.com** in the To text box
3. Click in the empty text box below the e-mail address you just entered, then type your e-mail address
4. Click the **To button** to the left of your e-mail address, then click **Cc** on the menu that opens
   The text on the To button changes to "Cc." Your Compose window should resemble Figure B-6.
5. Click in the **Subject text box**, then type **Test message**
   The information in the Subject text box appears in the message header summary in the recipient's Inbox. It also becomes part of the title of the Compose window in the window's title bar.
6. Click in the **message body pane**, type **Please let me know that this message arrived and that you can read it without difficulty. If it comes across okay, that means I've successfully set up my e-mail account in Netscape Mail!**, press **[Enter]** twice, type **Thanks**, press **[Enter]** twice, then type your full name
   Your screen should look similar to Figure B-7.
7. Click the **Send button** on the Mail Toolbar
8. If a password dialog box opens, type your password, then click **OK**
   The message is sent to the mail server for delivery to Sharon and to you. The Compose window closes and the Mail window appears.

QuickTip

The address you're sending this message to is a working e-mail address; however, the messages are deleted without being opened or read, so do not send important messages to this address.

Trouble?

If you see a message that says "Unable to connect to the SMTP server," then the information about your mail server and/or your user name might have been entered incorrectly. Repeat the second lesson or contact your instructor or system administrator for help.

FIGURE B-6: Compose window containing address information

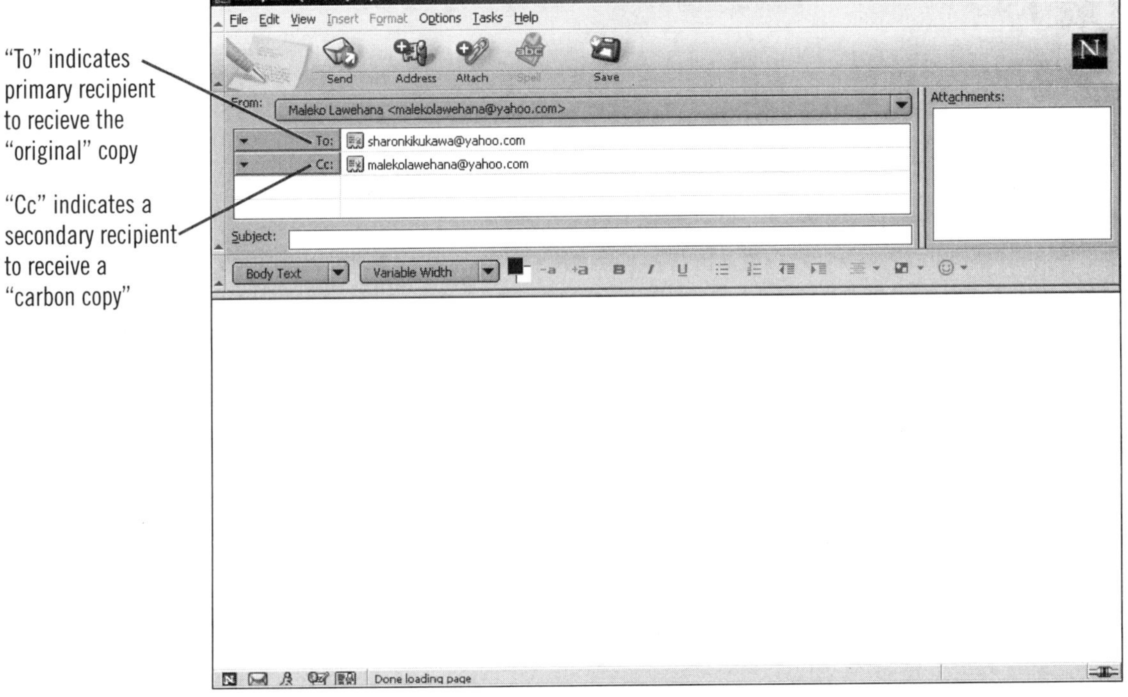

FIGURE B-7: Completed e-mail message

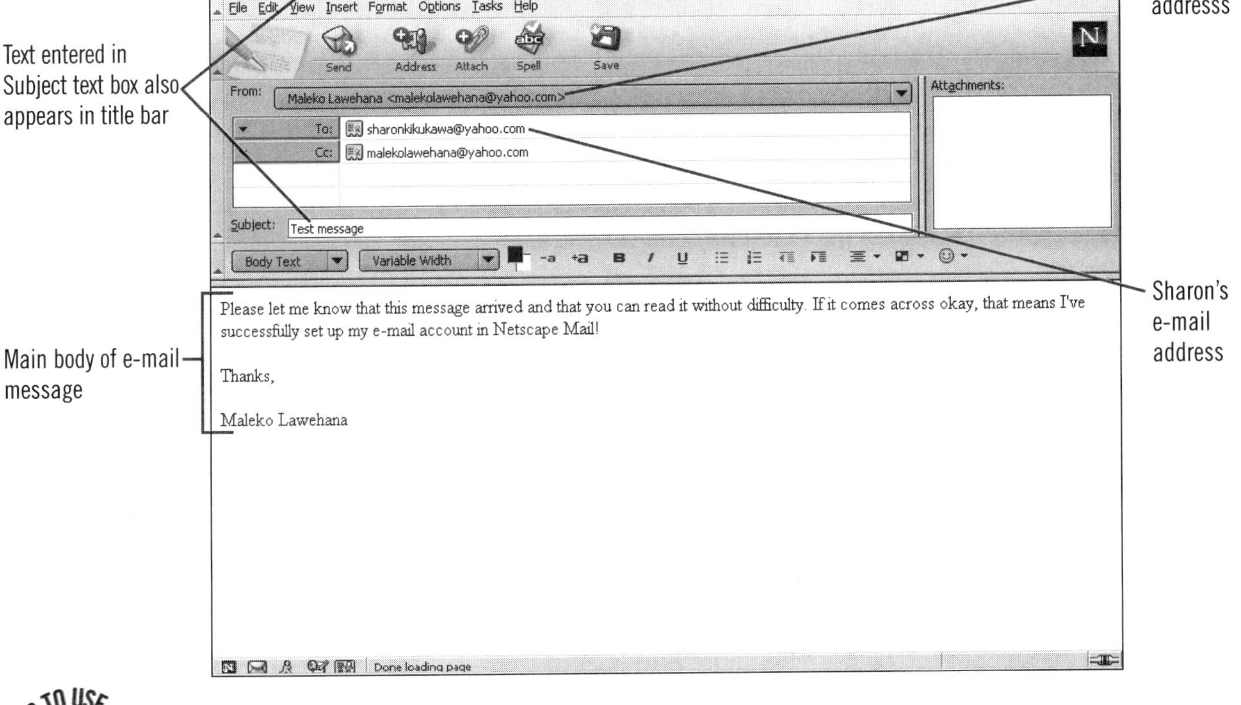

CLUES TO USE

Correcting your e-mail message content

If you notice a typing error before sending an e-mail message, you can select the error with your mouse pointer and then make the required correction. You can move the insertion point between the text boxes in the Compose window by pressing [Tab] to move forward or [Shift][Tab] to move backward, or by clicking in the desired text boxes. To check the spelling of your e-mail message, click the Spell button on the Mail Toolbar, then accept or reject the spelling suggestions just as you would in a word-processing program.

Internet

Checking Incoming E-Mail

You receive incoming e-mail messages in your Inbox folder (also called the Inbox). When the Inbox contains unread messages, the word "Inbox" and the number of unread messages appear in bold in the folders list. When you select Inbox in the folders list, message header summaries appear in the message list. An envelope icon with a green arrow appears next to the message header summary for an unread message, and the message header summary appears in bold. A plain envelope appears next to the message header summary for each message you have viewed, and the message header summary is not bold. When you sent the message to Sharon, you copied the message to yourself by typing your e-mail address in the Cc text box. You check your e-mail to see if you received the Cc of the message you sent to Sharon.

1. **Click the triangle at the bottom right of the Get Msg button on the Mail Toolbar, then click the name of your e-mail account**

Trouble?

Get the password from your instructor or system administrator, if necessary.

2. **If a password dialog box opens, type your password, then click OK**
   Depending on your system configuration, you might need to connect to your ISP to get your new e-mail. Within a few moments, your mail server transfers all new e-mail to your Inbox.

3. **If necessary, double-click your account name in the folders list so that the folders for your account are visible under your account name**

4. **Click Inbox under your account name in the folders list to select it**
   Your Mail window should look similar to Figure B-8. The message that you copied to yourself when you e-mailed the test message to Sharon appears in the message list. If you do not see any incoming messages in your Inbox, then either you did not receive any new e-mail or you are looking in the wrong folder. Be sure "Inbox" is selected in the folders list. If you still don't have any e-mail messages, wait a few minutes, then repeat Step 1 until you receive a message. Sometimes e-mail delivery slows down at peak times during the day.

Trouble?

If the message does not appear in the Message pane, click View on the menu bar, then click Message.

5. **Click Test message in the message list**
   The address information and the full message appear in the Message pane of the Mail window, as shown in Figure B-9.

FIGURE B-8: Mail window containing new message

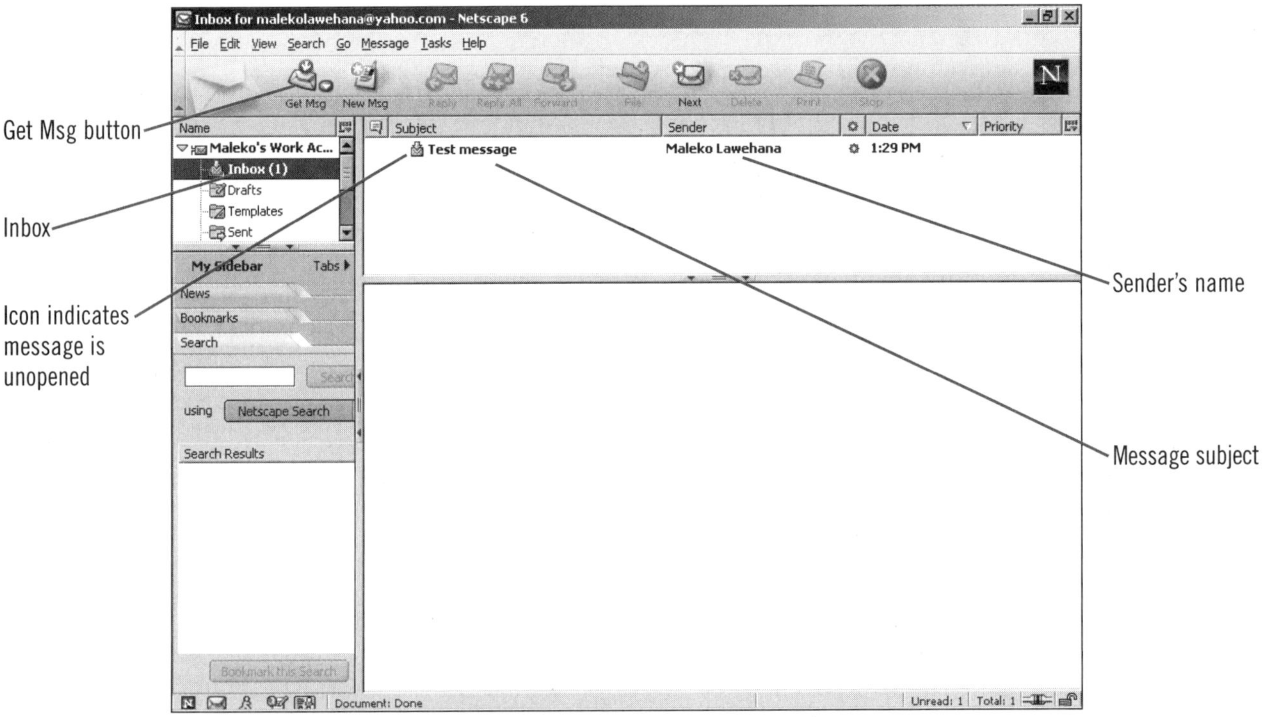

Get Msg button

Inbox

Icon indicates message is unopened

Sender's name

Message subject

FIGURE B-9: Reading new message

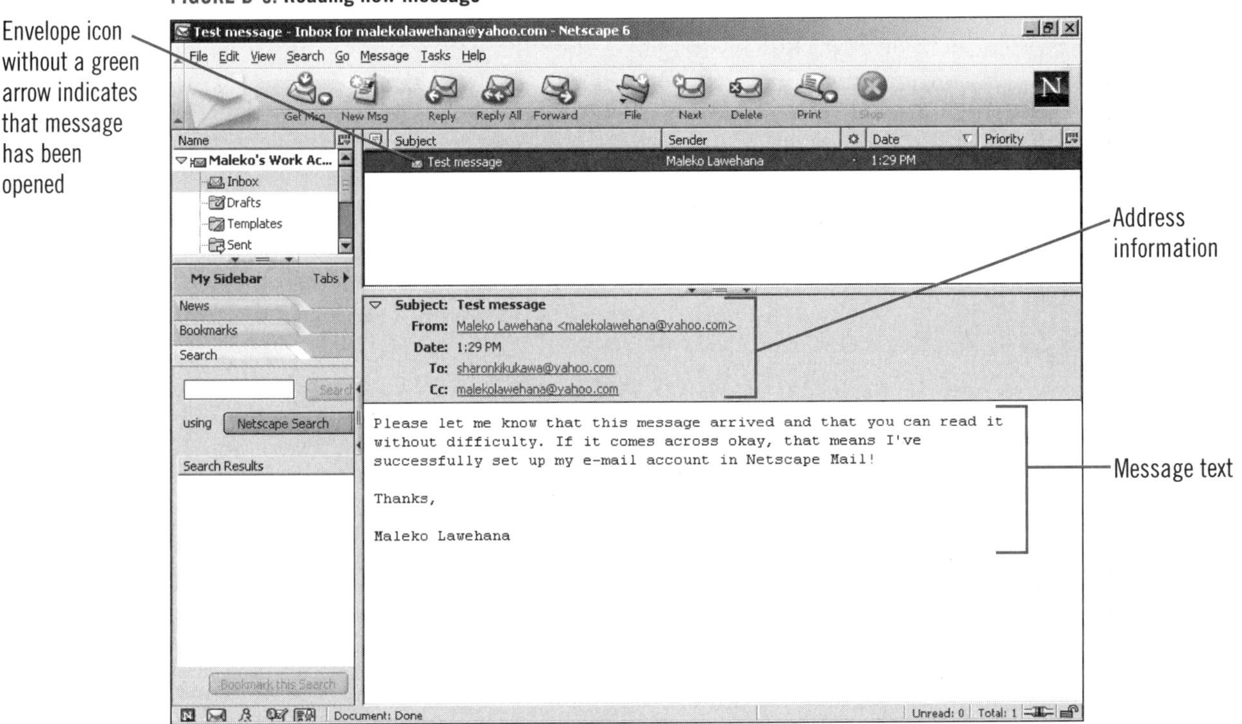

Internet

Internet

Attaching a File to an E-Mail Message

You might want to send an e-mail message that includes a file, such as a document created in a word-processing program or a spreadsheet program, or a picture. You can send any type of file over the Internet by attaching it to an e-mail message. A file linked to an e-mail message is called an **attachment**. Because e-mailing attachments between employees of Kikukawa Air would be useful for sharing information, such as maintenance schedules, you decide to explore how the attachment feature works. You use Netscape Mail to send a message with an attachment.

1. Click the **New Msg button** on the Mail Toolbar
2. Type your e-mail address in the To text box
3. Type **Test message with attachment** in the Subject text box
4. Type **A file is attached to this message as a test.** in the message body pane
5. Press **[Enter]** twice, then type your full name
6. Click the **Attach button** on the Mail Toolbar
   The Enter file to attach dialog box opens, as shown in Figure B-10.
7. Click the **Look in list arrow**, navigate to the drive and folder where your Project Files are stored, then double-click the file **Physicals.wri**
   The file Physicals.wri is attached to your e-mail message. Notice that the filename appears in the Attachments pane as shown in Figure B-11.
8. Click the **Send button** on the Mail Toolbar
   The message is sent to the mail server for delivery to you. The Compose window closes and the Mail window appears.

QuickTip

The extension "wri" might not appear on your screen.

FIGURE B-10: Enter file to attach dialog box

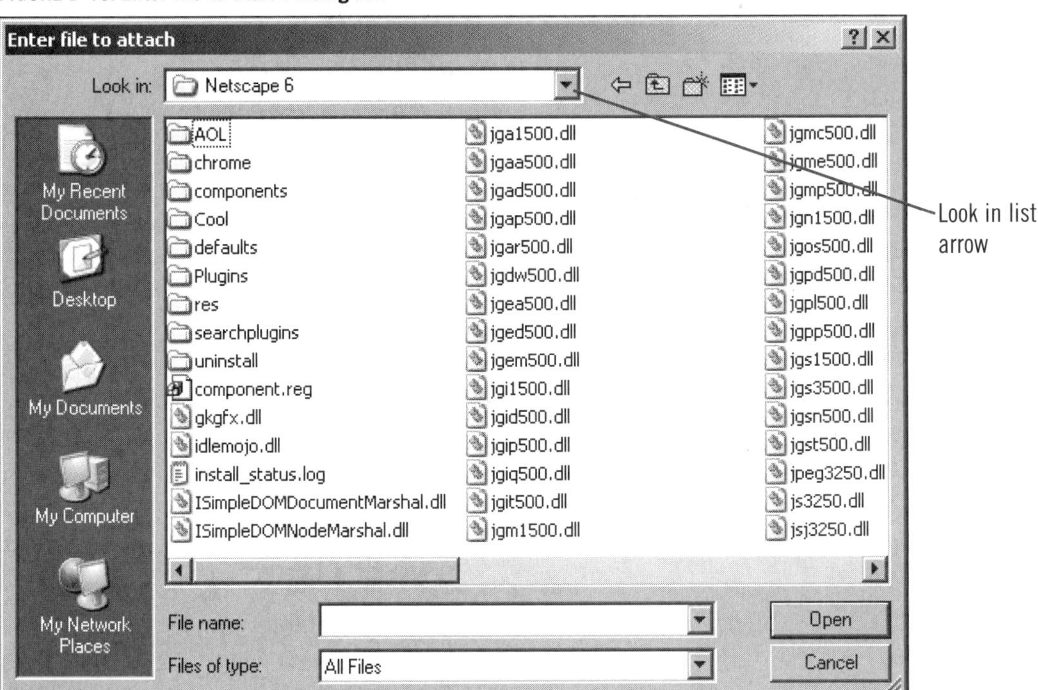

FIGURE B-11: Completed e-mail message with attachment

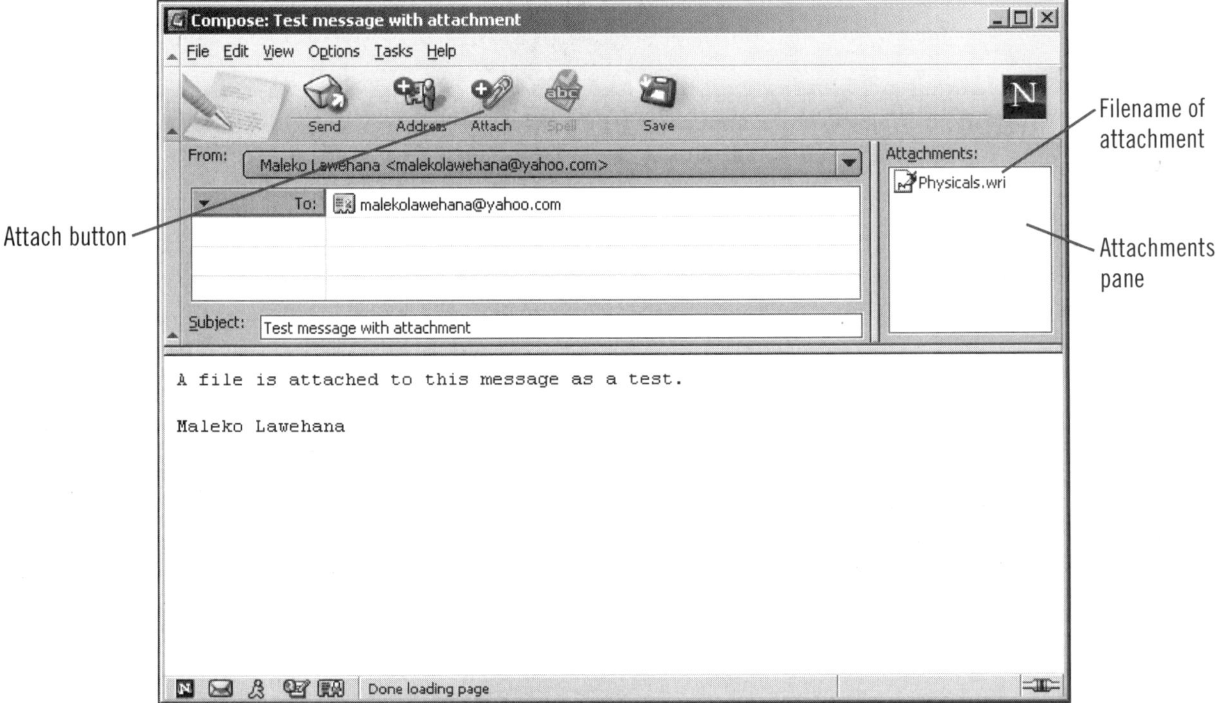

Internet

Internet

Saving an E-Mail Attachment

When you receive an e-mail message with a file attached, you can open the attachment in a Preview pane or you can save it to view later. You decide to experiment with the options for working with an attached file. You save the attachment on your computer.

1. Click the **Get Msg button** on the Mail Toolbar
2. Click **Test message with attachment** in the message list
   The message appears in the Message pane, as shown in Figure B-12. The envelope icon in the Subject column of the message header summary includes a paper clip, indicating that the message contains an attachment. The attachment filename appears in the Attachments pane to the right of the address information and might also appear in the Message pane below the message text.
3. Right-click the filename **Physicals.wri** in the Attachments pane
   A shortcut menu appears. The Open option allows you to specify the program Mail should use to open the file, and lets you specify how you want Mail to deal with this type of file in the future. The Save As option allows you to save the file on your computer.
4. Click **Save As** on the shortcut menu
   The Save Attachment dialog box opens, as shown in Figure B-13.
5. Click the **Save in list arrow**, then navigate to the drive and folder where your Project Files are stored
6. Select the text in the File name text box, then type **Unit B Physicals.wri**
7. Click **Save**
   The attached file is now saved where your Project Files are stored. You can open the saved attachment at any time just as you would open any other file.

QuickTip

If a gray background doesn't appear behind the filename before you right-click it, you might not successfully select the file.

Understanding e-mail viruses, worms, and Trojan horses

E-mail can carry malicious programs, such as viruses, worms, and Trojan horses. A computer **virus** is a piece of software that runs without your permission and performs undesired tasks, such as deleting the contents of your hard disk. Viruses **self-replicate**, meaning that they create, and in some cases distribute, copies of themselves to infect more computers. **Worms** and **Trojan horses** are variations on this idea, written with the intent of creating computer trouble and are of special concern to e-mail users, because they reproduce by using the functions of e-mail programs like Netscape Mail to send out copies of themselves as attachments. However, you can take a couple easy steps to protect yourself and those with whom you exchange e-mail. The most important precaution you can take is not opening a file attachment from a sender you don't know, because the attachment might contain a worm or Trojan horse. You could also install **anti-virus software**, which is a software package that protects your computer from malicious programs. Many schools and colleges distribute anti-virus software for free to students, staff, and faculty; check with your instructor, system administrator, or computing services center to see if this is available to you.

FIGURE B-12: "Test message with attachment" message in the message list

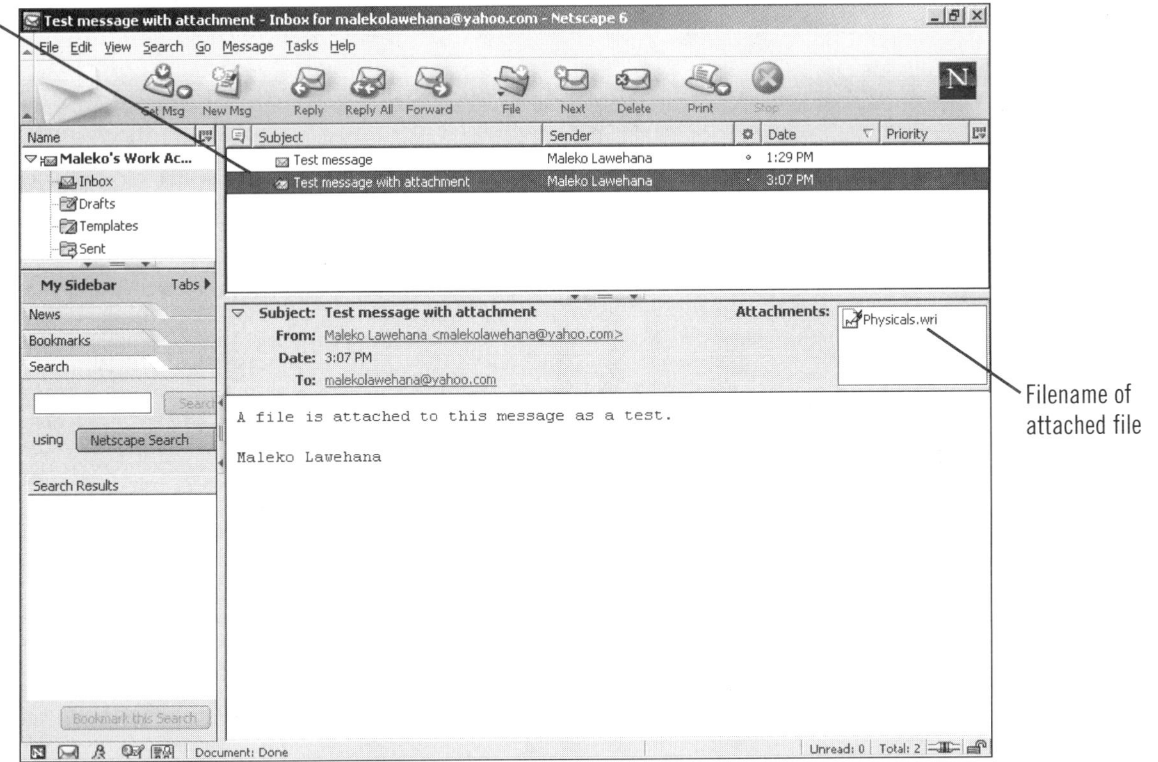

FIGURE B-13: Saving an attachment

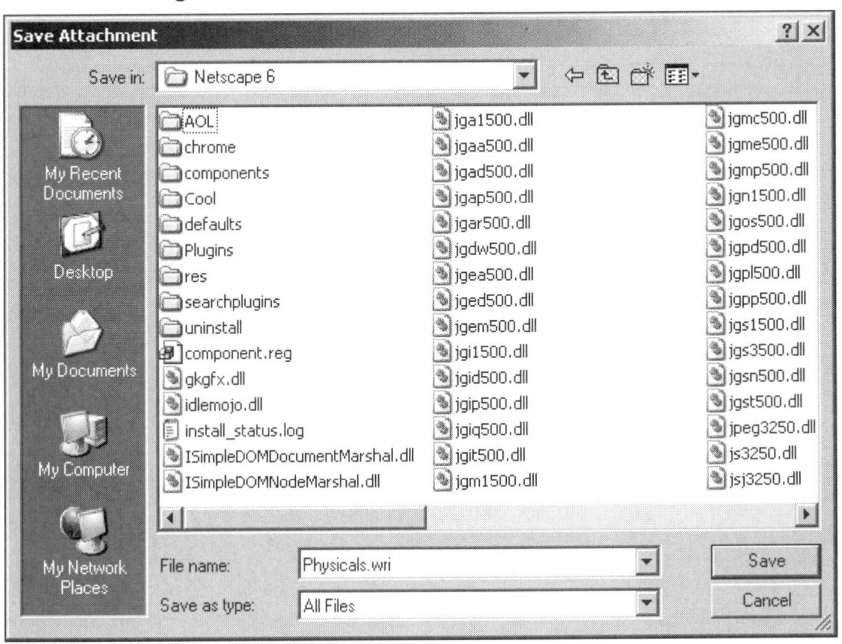

Internet

Internet

Replying to an E-Mail Message

You can use Netscape Mail's Reply option to respond to the sender of a message quickly and efficiently. When you reply to an e-mail message, the sender's name is automatically placed in the To text box, and the text of the original message appears in the body of the new message for reference. You practice using the Reply option by replying to the copy of the e-mail message you sent to Sharon.

Steps

1. Click **Test message** in the message list
2. Click the **Reply button** on the Mail Toolbar
   The Compose window opens and the original sender's address appears in the To text box. "Re:" appears at the beginning of the original subject text, indicating that this message is a response to the original message. If you want, you can replace this subject line with new text. The original message appears in the message body pane. The vertical line on the left edge of the message body pane indicates which part is the original message.
3. Type **I created this message using the Reply button in Netscape Mail.** in the message body pane, press **[Enter]** twice, then type your full name
   Your Compose window should look similar to Figure B-14.
4. Click the **Send button** on the Mail Toolbar
5. Click the **Get Msg button** on the Mail Toolbar
   The message appears in your Inbox.
6. Click **Re: Test message** in the message list
   Your screen should appear similar to Figure B-15.

QuickTip

You can reply to only the sender by clicking the Reply button or to the sender and all recipients of the original message by clicking the Reply All button. In either case, the e-mail address for each recipient appears in the address area.

FIGURE B-14: Replying to a message

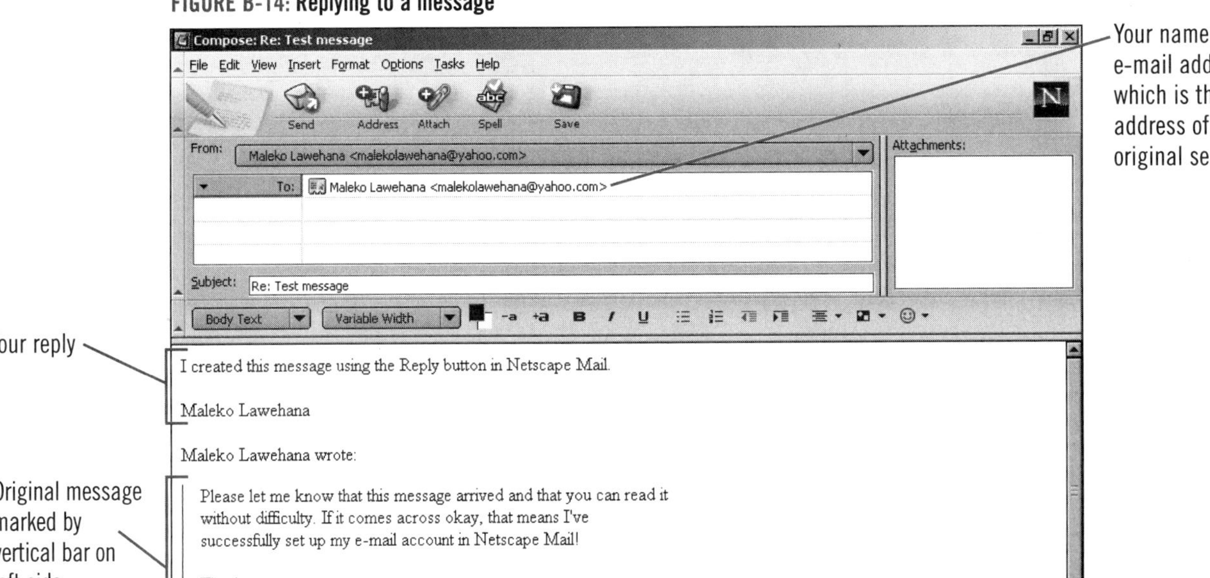

FIGURE B-15: Message reply received

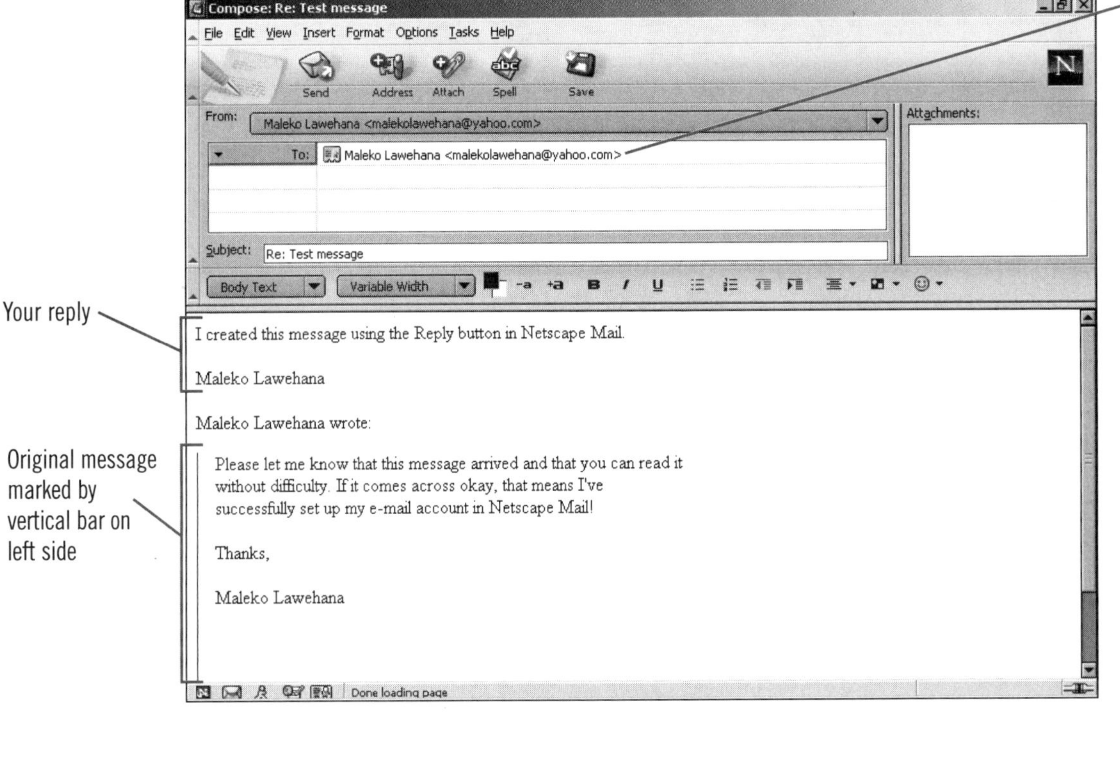

Internet

Forwarding an E-Mail Message

You can send any message you receive to someone else, which is called **forwarding**. When you use the Forward option, the original message appears in the Compose window. Forwarding is similar to replying, except that a forwarded message is not automatically addressed to the original sender; you must address the message to the desired recipients. To practice forwarding messages and to see how they look to recipients, you forward the "Test message" message to yourself and to Sharon.

1. Click **Test message** in the message list
2. Click the **Forward button** on the Mail Toolbar
   The Compose window opens and displays the text of the message to forward. Notice that the Subject text box includes Fwd: and the original subject text. The Fwd: indicates that the message is being forwarded. Just like when you reply to a message, you can edit the subject line if you want to clarify the subject of the message. Notice that instead of the vertical bar that accompanies the original message in a reply, the text of the forwarded message simply appears below the text "Original Message." You can enter your own comments above the original message.
3. Type **sharonkikukawa@yahoo.com** in the To text box, then type your e-mail address in the text box below Sharon's e-mail address
4. Click in the message body pane, type **Sharon,** press **[Enter]** twice, type **I used Netscape Mail's Forward option to send this message.**, press **[Enter]** twice, then type your full name
   Your screen should appear similar to Figure B-16.
5. Click the **Send button** on the Mail Toolbar
6. Click the **Get Msg button** on the Mail Toolbar, then click **[Fwd: Test message]**
   The forwarded message appears in your Inbox, and the message appears in the Message pane.

QuickTip

You can also forward an original message as a text file by clicking Message on the menu bar, pointing to Forward As, then clicking Attachment. The e-mail becomes an attachment, so it is not visible in the text of the message received by the recipient.

FIGURE B-16: Forwarding a message

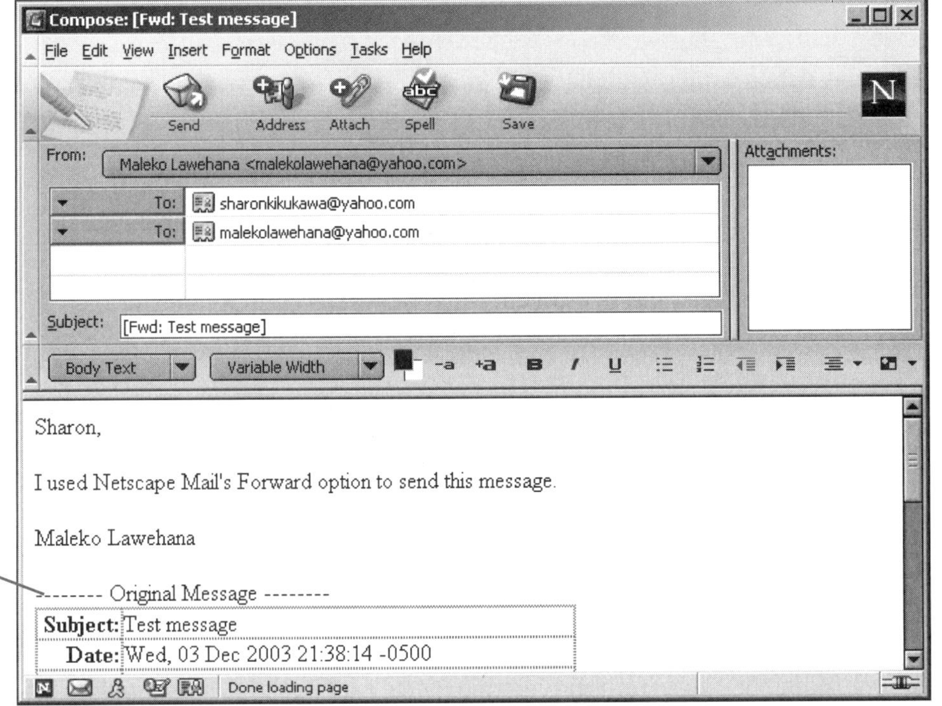

CLUES TO USE

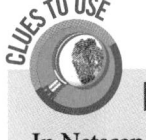

Formatting an e-mail message

In Netscape Mail, you can use the various features on the Formatting Toolbar to enhance text. The Formatting Toolbar allows you to change text and paragraph options including text size, text and background color, and paragraph alignment. Figure B-17 shows an e-mail message formatted using the Formatting Toolbar. Formatting a message can make it look more interesting or even increase its readability. However, not all e-mail programs can display formatted messages. When you send a formatted message, you are prompted to specify how you want to send the message. By selecting "Send in Plain Text and HTML" (the default option), you ensure that all e-mail programs can display your message.

FIGURE B-17: Formatted e-mail message

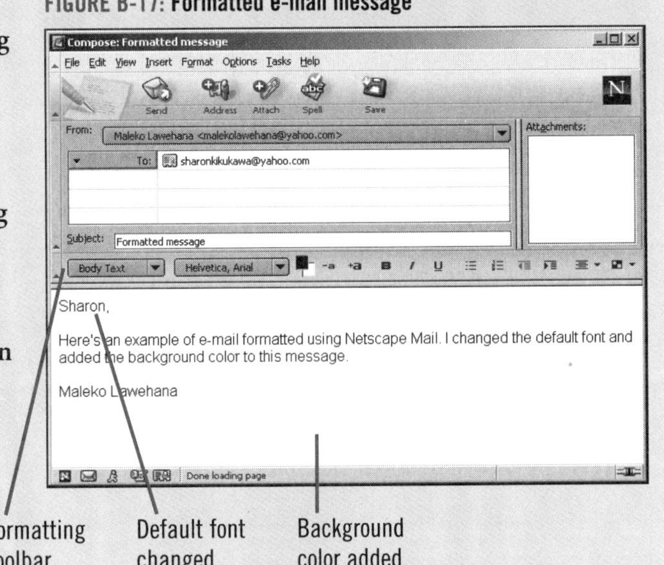

Internet

Internet

Filing an E-Mail Message

You can organize your e-mail messages by using Netscape Mail folders to file your messages by category. For example, you might file messages from friends in one folder, and file messages concerning a certain project in a different folder. When you file a message, you move it from the Inbox to another folder. You can also make copies of a message to store it in multiple folders. Sharon wants you to show employees of Kikukawa Air how they can organize their e-mail, so you practice creating a folder and copying a message into it.

1. In the Mail window, click **File** on the menu bar, point to **New**, then click **Folder**
   The New Folder dialog box opens.
2. Type **Personnel** in the Name text box, click the **list arrow** under the Create as a sub-folder of section, then point to the name of your e-mail account
   Figure B-18 shows the open menus.
3. Click **choose this for the parent**
4. Click **OK**, then if it's not already displayed, scroll down the folders list to view the new Personnel folder
5. Click **Inbox** in the folders list, then click **Test Message** in the message list
6. Click **Message** on the menu bar, point to **Copy Message**, point to the name of your e-mail account, then click **Personnel**
   Notice that the "Test message" message still appears in the Inbox. The Copy Message option places a copy of the current message in the folder you select, while leaving the original message in its current location. To move a message so that it no longer appears in its original location, click Move Message instead of Copy Message on the Message menu.
7. Click **Personnel** in the folders list
   The message list displays the contents of the Personnel folder. The "Test message" message has been copied to the Personnel folder.
8. Click **Test message** in the message list
   The message text appears in the Message pane, as shown in Figure B-19.
9. Click **Inbox** in the folder list
   The message list displays the message header summaries for the messages in your Inbox.

QuickTip

If you make a mistake and move or copy messages to the wrong folder, you can immediately click Edit on the menu bar, then click Undo to cancel the action.

FIGURE B-18: Menus in New Folder dialog box

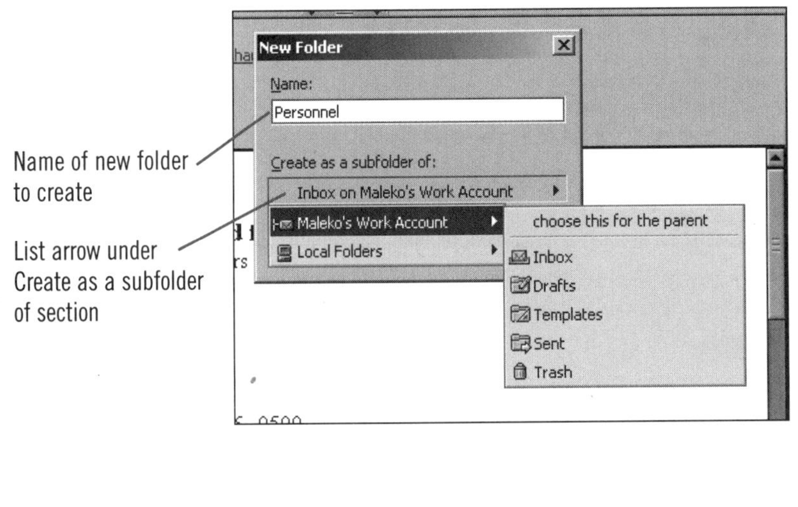

FIGURE B-19: Contents of new Personnel folder

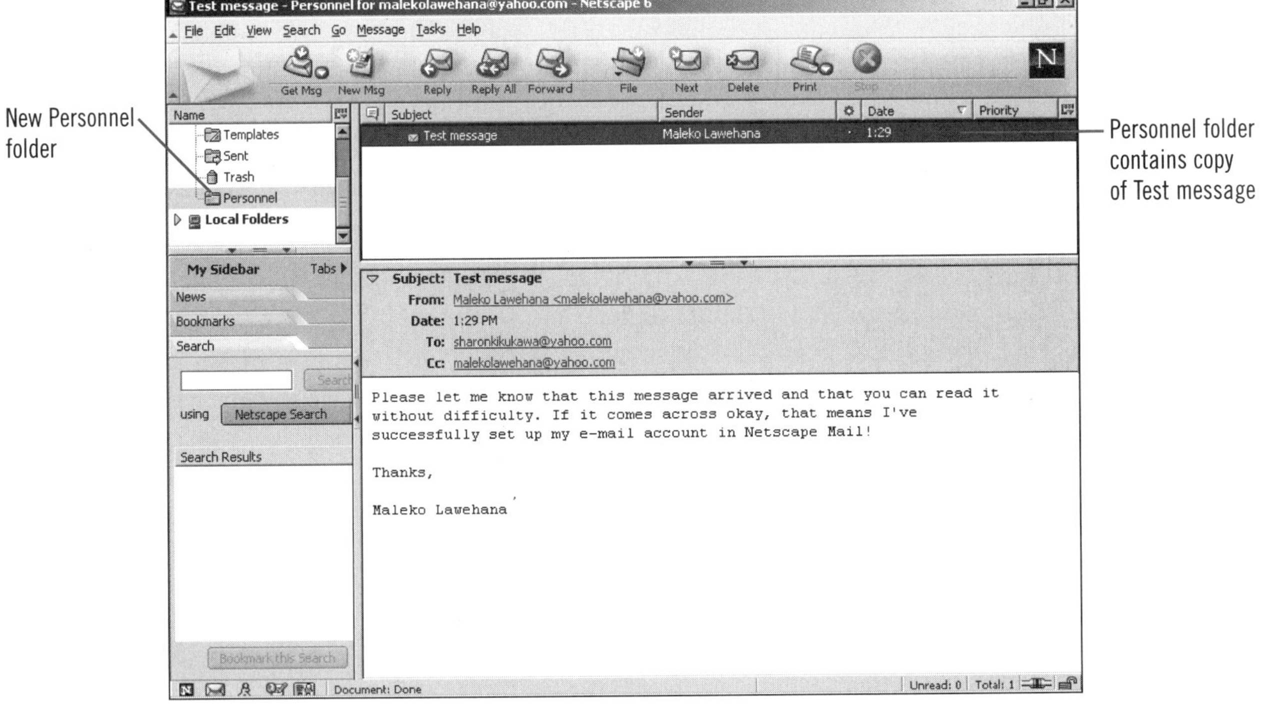

CLUES TO USE

Moving or copying multiple e-mail messages

You can move or copy several messages at once. Press and hold [Ctrl] and then click each message header summary that you want to move or copy. After you have selected all the messages, click Message on the menu bar, point to either Move Message or Copy Message, then click the folder to which you want to move or copy the selected files.

Internet

Deleting an E-Mail Message

Just as you can delete unnecessary files from your computer, you can also delete e-mail messages that you no longer need. When you delete a message, the message moves to the Trash folder. If you are using a public PC in a university computer laboratory, you should always delete your messages and then empty the Trash folder before you leave the computer. Otherwise, the next person who uses Netscape Mail will be able to access and read the messages you moved to the Trash folder. You practice deleting e-mail by removing some of the messages in your Inbox and a message in the Personnel folder, which you created in the previous lesson.

QuickTip

If you accidentally delete a message that you want to keep, you can recover it immediately after you delete it by clicking Edit on the menu bar, then clicking Undo. If the Undo option is no longer available, open the Trash folder, right-click the message, point to Move To, and select your Inbox or another folder.

QuickTip

You can also delete messages and folders by clicking a message or folder and clicking the Delete button on the Mail Toolbar.

1. Right-click **Re: Test message** in the message list
   A shortcut menu appears, as shown in Figure B-20.
2. Click **Delete** on the shortcut menu
   Netscape Mail moves the message from the Inbox to the Trash folder. Notice that the "Re: Test message" e-mail no longer appears in the Inbox.
3. Click **Trash** in the folder list
   The "Re: Test message" e-mail you deleted appears in the Trash folder. Although you do not need to view the Trash folder before you delete its contents, opening this folder before emptying it allows you to verify that you're not about to permanently delete a message you still want.
4. Click **File** on the menu bar, then click **Empty Trash**
   The e-mail message no longer appears in the Trash folder. When you empty the Trash folder, the message is permanently deleted.
5. If necessary, scroll down the folder list so that the Personnel folder is visible, then right-click the **Personnel folder**
   Figure B-21 shows the shortcut menu for deleting a folder.
6. Click **Delete Folder**
   The Confirm dialog box opens, asking if you're sure you want to move the selected folder into the Trash folder.
7. Click **OK**
   The Personnel folder moves into the Trash folder.
8. Click **Inbox** in the folder list
9. Click **File** on the menu bar, then click **Empty Trash**
   The Personnel folder and its contents are permanently deleted.

FIGURE B-20: Deleting a message

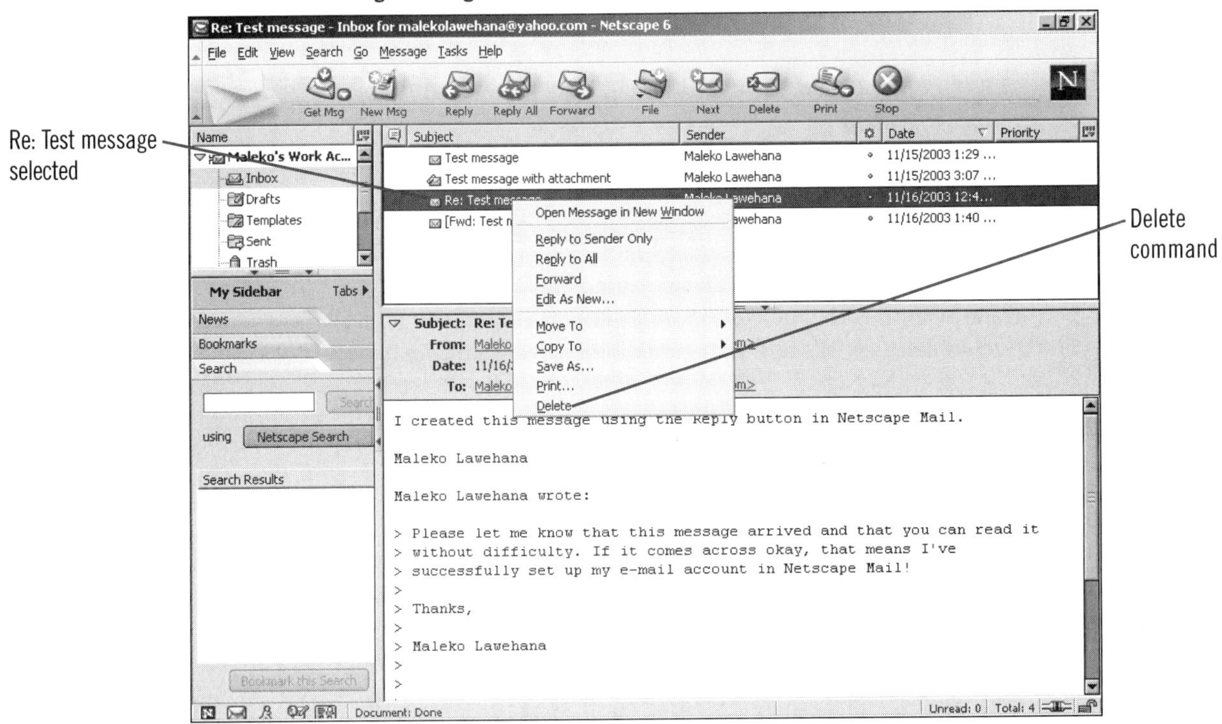

FIGURE B-21: Deleting a folder

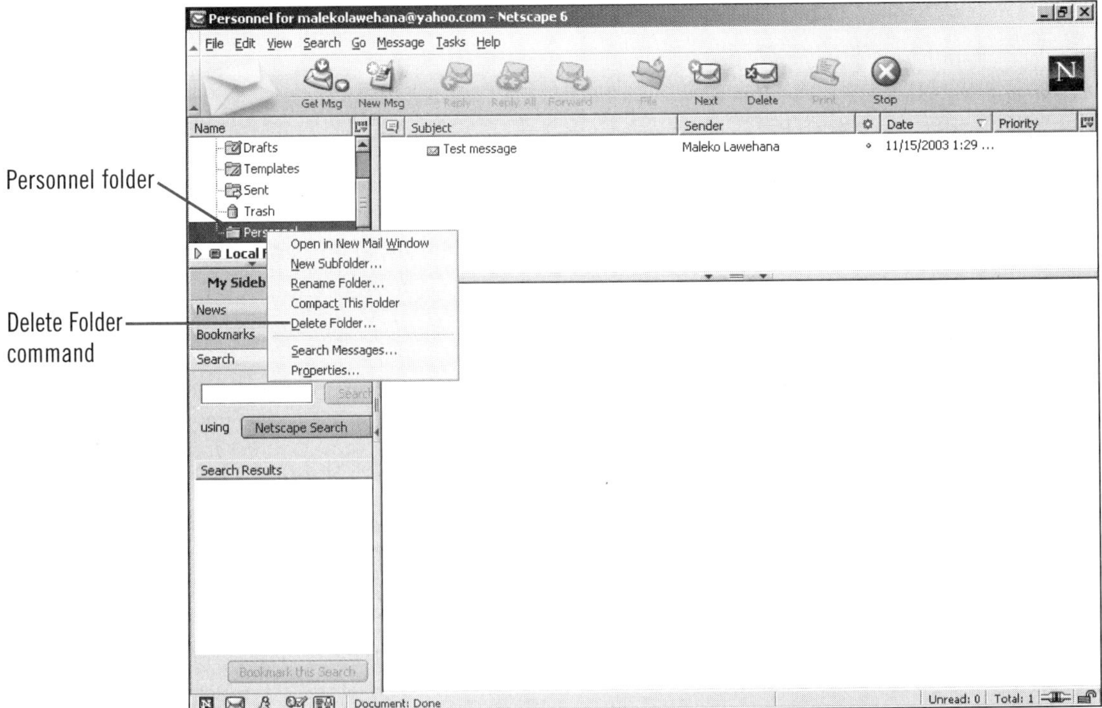

Internet

Maintaining an Address Book

You can save e-mail addresses and contact information, such as phone numbers and postal addresses, in the Address Book. The **Address Book** allows you to select e-mail addresses from a list, rather than typing them in the To text box, which saves time and avoids typing errors. You can also create **nicknames**, which are shortened names for the e-mail addresses of people you send e-mail to frequently. You can type a nickname in the To text box to send a message. You begin to create an address book for employees of Kikukawa Air using Netscape Mail.

Trouble?

If the Instant Messenger Setup dialog box opens, click Cancel to close it.

1. In the Mail window, click **Tasks** on the menu bar, then click **Address Book**
   The Address Book window opens, as shown in Figure B-22.
2. Click the **New Card button** on the Address Book Toolbar
   The New Card dialog box opens. You use this dialog box to add e-mail addresses to the Address Book. The Name tab stores a person's name, e-mail address, and telephone numbers. You can use the Address tab to store postal addresses, the Inst Msg tab to record user names for instant messaging systems, and the Other tab to record custom information.
3. Type **Sharon** in the First text box, press **[Tab]**, type **Kikukawa**, then press **[Tab]** twice
4. Type **Sharon** in the Nickname text box, press **[Tab]**, then type **sharonkikukawa@yahoo.com** in the Email text box
   Figure B-23 shows the completed New card dialog box.
5. Click **OK**
6. Use Steps 2 through 5 as a guide to create Address Book cards for the following Kikukawa Air employees:

First Name	Last Name	Nickname	E-Mail Address
Chris	**Breed**	**Chris**	**chrisbreed@kikukawa.com**
Jenny	**Mahala**	**Jen**	**jennymahala@kikukawa.com**
Richard	**Forrester**	**Rich**	**richardforrester@kikukawa.com**

QuickTip

To delete an address from the Address Book, select the name in the Address Book window, then click the Delete button on the Address Book Toolbar.

7. Click the **Close button** on the Address Book window, click the **New Msg button** on the Mail Toolbar in the Mail window, then click the **Address button** on the Mail Toolbar in the Compose window
8. Click **Sharon Kikukawa** in the Select Addresses window, click **To**, then click **OK**
   Sharon Kikukawa's e-mail address appears in the To text box.

QuickTip

You can also type Sharon's nickname in the To text box to address a message.

9. Type **Address Book test** in the Subject text box, click in the message body pane, type **I'm testing the Address Book feature in Netscape Mail.**, press **[Enter]** twice, then type your full name
   Figure B-24 shows the completed e-mail message.
10. Click the **Send button** on the Mail Toolbar

FIGURE B-22: Address Book window

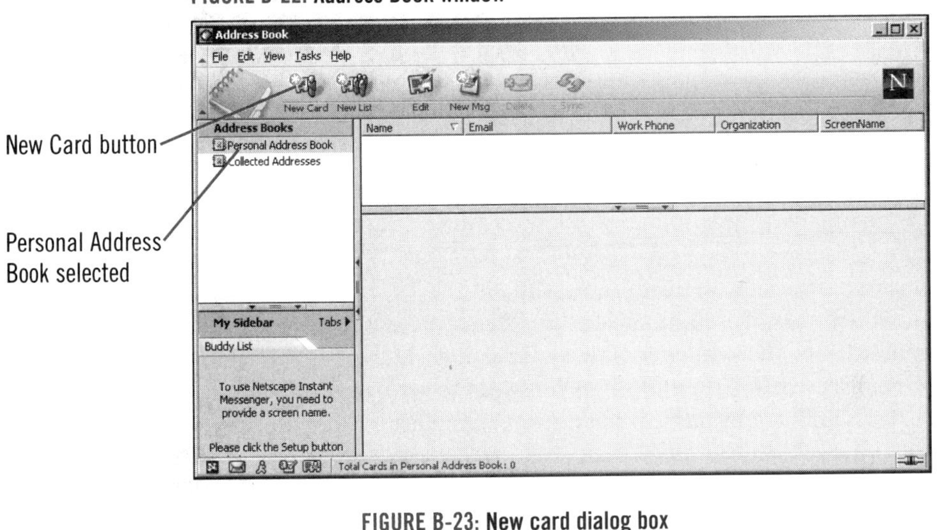

FIGURE B-23: New card dialog box

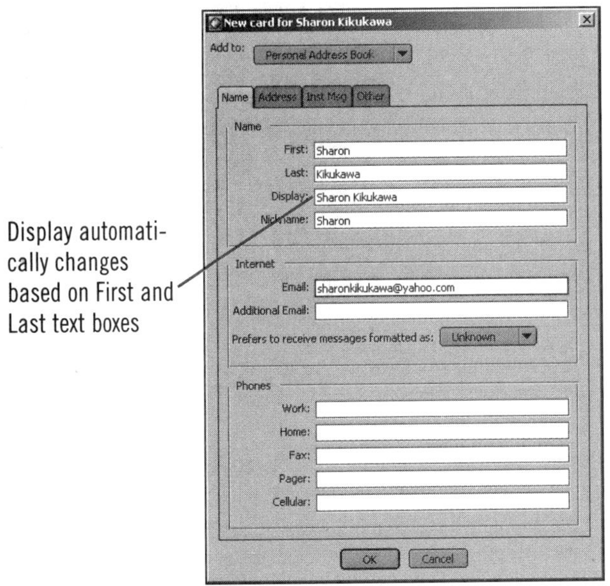

FIGURE B-24: Message addressed from the Address Book

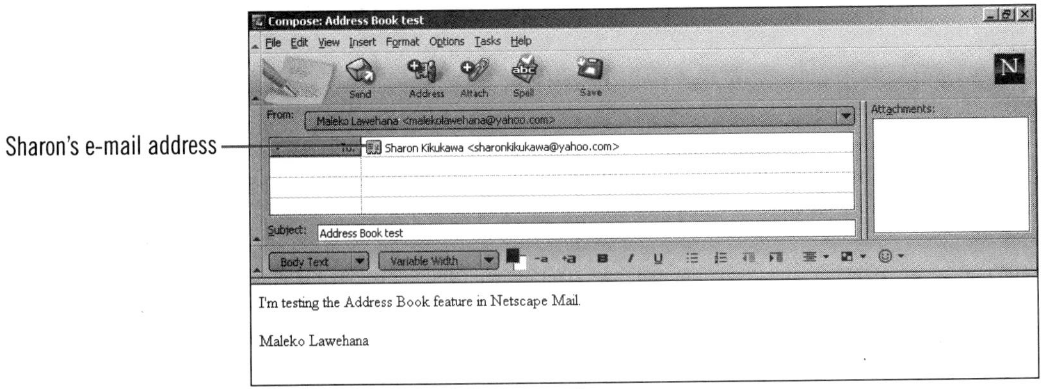

Sharon's e-mail address

CLUES TO USE

Updating the Address Book

You can quickly add a sender's e-mail address to the Address Book. When you receive a message from someone who is not listed in the Address Book, click the message header summary, right-click the sender's e-mail address in the Message pane, then click Add to Address Book on the shortcut menu.

Internet

Creating a Mailing List

You can quickly send an e-mail message to a group of people by creating a **mailing list**. You create a mailing list in the Address Book by creating a name for the mailing list, and then assigning e-mail addresses in the Address Book to the name. When you want to send an e-mail message to a group, simply type the group's name in the To text box to send a single message to all the mailing list members simultaneously. Because Kikukawa Air, like many companies, is organized into departments such as Personnel, Marketing, and Operations, you realize that mailing lists would be useful when you want to send messages to all the employees in a particular department. You start by creating a mailing list for the Personnel Department.

1. In the Mail window, click **Tasks** on the menu bar, then click **Address Book**
   The Address Book window opens.
2. Click the **New List button** on the Address Book Toolbar
   The Mailing List dialog box opens.
3. In the List Name text box, type **Personnel List**, press **[Tab]**, then type **Personnel** in the List Nickname text box
4. Press **[Tab]** three times, type **Chris** in the address list area, then press **[Enter]** twice
   Chris's address is already in the Address Book. As soon as you type the first few letters of Chris's name, Netscape Mail recognizes it and shows her name and e-mail address.
5. Use Step 4 as a guide to add Jenny Mahala and Richard Forrester to the mailing list
   Figure B-25 shows the Personnel List after three names have been entered.
6. Click **OK**, then in the Address Book window, scroll down the list of names, and click **Personnel List**
   As shown in Figure B-26, the Personnel List is listed among the Address Book entries just like the names of other contacts. You can address an e-mail message to the Personnel List just as you would to individuals by selecting it from the Select Addresses window and clicking the To button.
7. Click the **Close button** on the Address Book window
8. Click the **Close button** on the Mail window
   Netscape Mail closes.

FIGURE B-25: Mailing List dialog box

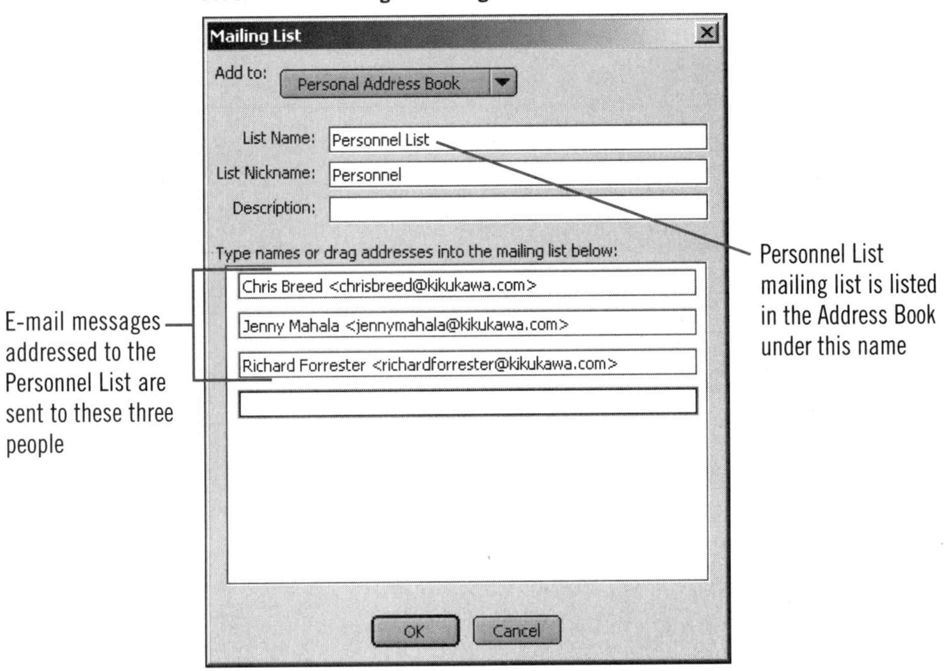

FIGURE B-26: Personnel List mailing list

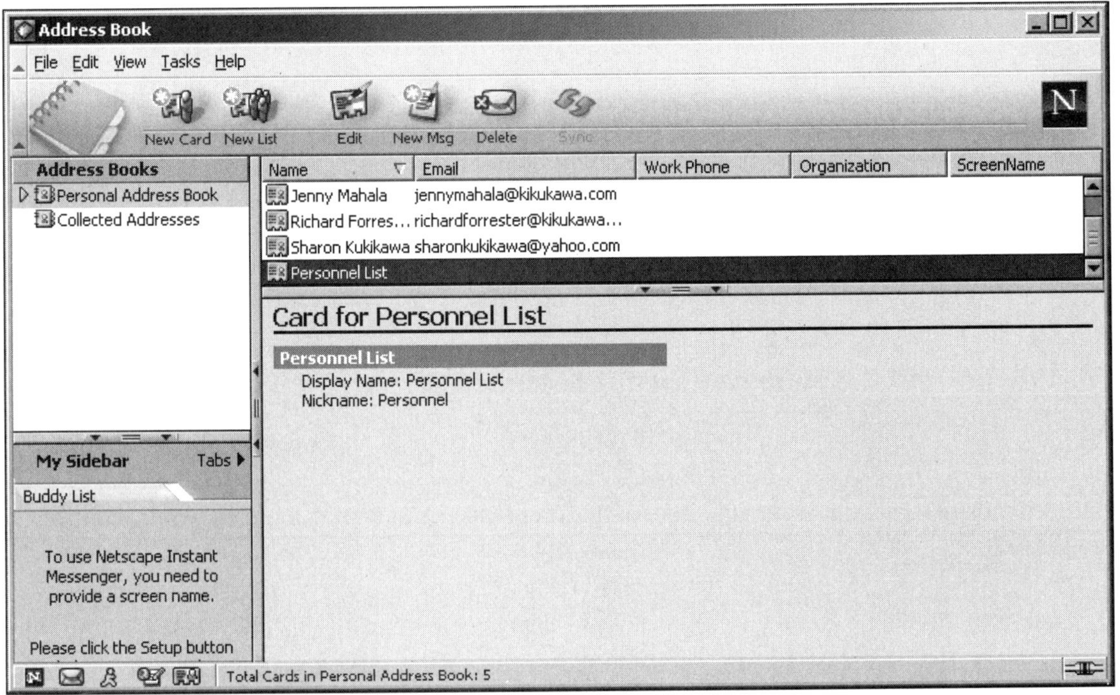

Practice

▶ Concepts Review

Identify the function of each element of the Compose window shown in Figure B-27.

FIGURE B-27

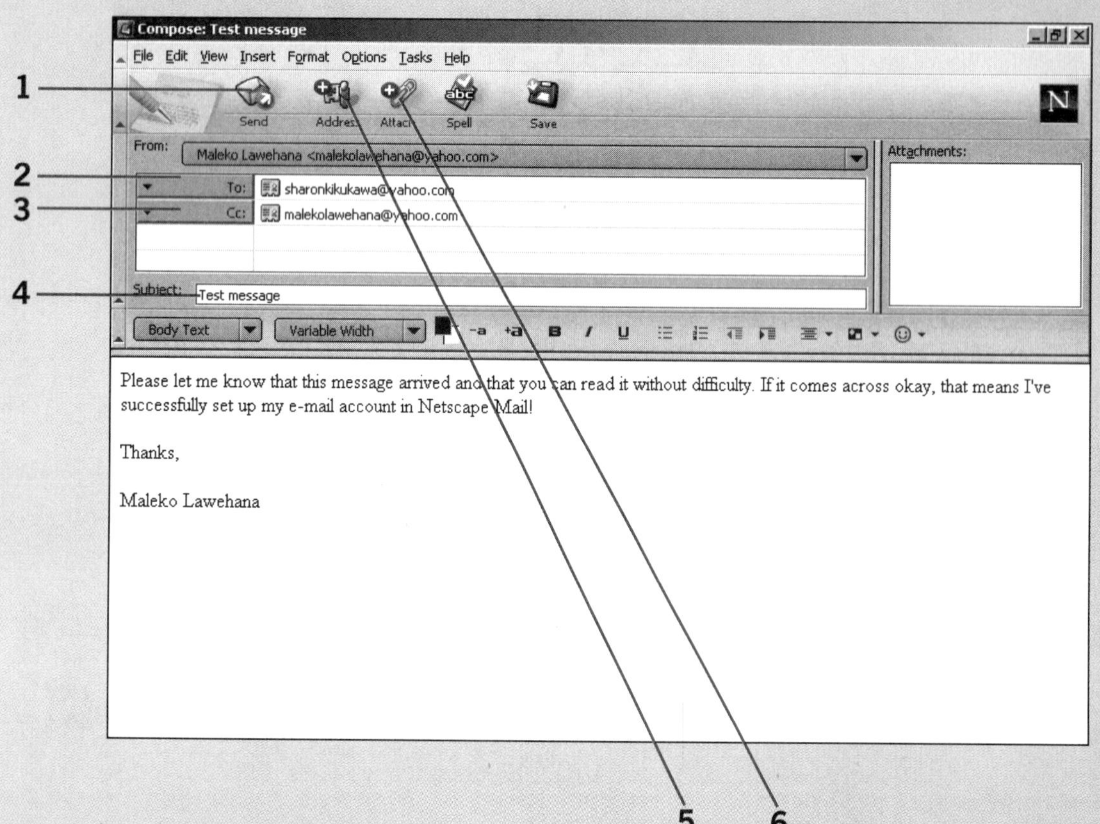

Match each term with the statement that it describes.

7. Inbox	**a.** A folder that contains all incoming messages
8. Address Book	**b.** A file that accompanies an e-mail message
9. Compose window	**c.** A feature that stores names and e-mail addresses for people with whom you correspond regularly
10. Message header summary	**d.** A window used to create messages
11. Attachment	**e.** A location where you type the main topic of an e-mail message
12. Subject text box	**f.** The summary information about a message, including sender, subject, and date

Practice

Select the best answer from the list of choices.

13. To view new messages, which button do you click on the Mail Toolbar in the Mail window?

- **a.** Messages
- **b.** Get
- **c.** Get Msg
- **d.** E-Mail

14. Sending an e-mail message you've received to a new recipient is called:

- **a.** Forwarding.
- **b.** Carbon copying.
- **c.** Messaging.
- **d.** Replying to sender.

15. You can organize your e-mail by placing messages into:

- **a.** Files.
- **b.** My Sidebar.
- **c.** Address books.
- **d.** Folders.

16. Shortened names that you give to the e-mail addresses of people you frequently send messages to are called:

- **a.** Quick names.
- **b.** New names.
- **c.** Nicknames.
- **d.** List names.

Skills Review

1. Send an e-mail message.

- **a.** Open Netscape Mail, then open the Compose window.
- **b.** Address the message to your instructor, a friend, or a colleague.
- **c.** Cc the message to yourself.
- **d.** Make **Dinner Meeting** the subject of your message.
- **e.** Compose the following message:
  Hi <<name of recipient>>**,**
  We are planning to meet for dinner at <<a local restaurant name>> **on November 30. Please bring the presentation on the Ford account.**
- **f.** Type your full name below the message.
- **g.** Send the message.

2. Check incoming e-mail.

- **a.** Retrieve your e-mail.
- **b.** Read the Dinner Meeting message.

3. Attach a file to an e-mail message.

- **a.** Open the Compose window.
- **b.** Address the message to your instructor, a friend, or a colleague.
- **c.** Cc the message to yourself.
- **d.** Make **Dinner Meeting Participants** the subject of your message.
- **e.** Compose the following message:
  Attached is a list of the people we have invited to attend the dinner meeting at <<restaurant name>> **on November 30. Please check the list and get back to me with any suggestions for additional participants.**
  (Be sure to add your name to the end of the message.)
- **f.** Attach the file named Dinner Meeting.wri located in the drive and folder where your Project Files are stored.
- **g.** Send the file with the attachment.

4. Save an e-mail attachment.

- **a.** Retrieve your e-mail.
- **b.** Open the Dinner Meeting Participants message in its own window.
- **c.** Save the attached file where your Project Files are stored as **Unit B Dinner Meeting.wri**.

5. Reply to an e-mail message.

- **a.** Reply to the sender of the Dinner Meeting Participants message.
- **b.** Change the subject to **Dinner Meeting R.S.V.P.**
- **c.** Compose the following message:
  I'll be delighted to attend the meeting on November 30.
- **d.** Add your full name to the message.
- **e.** Send the message.
- **f.** Retrieve and open your e-mail.

Practice

6. **Forward an e-mail message.**
   a. Forward the Dinner Meeting Participants message to your instructor, a friend, or a colleague.
   b. Cc the message to yourself.
   c. Compose the following message:
   I have reviewed the list of meeting participants. We should also include Juan Sanchez from the Marketing Department.
   d. Send the message.
   e. Retrieve and open your e-mail.

7. **File e-mail messages.**
   a. Create a new folder called **Meetings** in your e-mail account.
   b. Copy the following messages to the Meetings folder: Dinner Meeting, Dinner Meeting Participants, Dinner Meeting R.S.V.P., and [Fwd: Dinner Meeting Participants].
   c. View the contents of the Meetings folder to verify that all four messages appear.
   d. Display your Inbox.

8. **Delete e-mail messages.**
   a. Delete the following messages in the Meetings folder: Dinner Meeting, Dinner Meeting Participants, Dinner Meeting R.S.V.P., and [Fwd: Dinner Meeting Participants].
   b. Empty the contents of the Trash folder.
   c. Delete the Meetings folder, then empty the Trash folder.

9. **Maintain an address book.**
   a. Create a new Address Book card for Loree Erickson at lerickson@kikukawa.com. Loree's nickname is Lo.
   b. Create a new Address Book card for Lorenzo Seale at lseale@kikukawa.com. Lorenzo's nickname is Lor.
   c. Create a new Address Book card for Consuela Longue at clongue@kikukawa.com. Consuela's nickname is Con.

10. **Create a mailing list.**
    a. Create a mailing list called **Meetings**.
    b. Type **Meet** as the nickname.
    c. Add Loree Erickson and Consuela Longue to the list.
    d. Check the Address Book for the Meetings entry, then close the Address Book.
    e. Close Netscape Mail.

▶ Independent Challenge 1

Your instructor has asked you to submit your next assignment via e-mail. You are also asked to send a copy of the assignment to yourself.

a. Find a file from one of your own folders to include as an attachment with the e-mail message to your instructor. Make sure the file contains a very short document that will not take up a great deal of disk space. For example, you could select a short essay that you completed for another course or a short letter you wrote to a friend. Alternatively, you could use one of the Project Files. After you have determined which file you will attach to your e-mail, start Netscape Mail.
b. Add your instructor's name and full e-mail address to the Address Book. Use an appropriate nickname that is easy to remember.
c. Create a new message.
d. Use **E-Mail Assignment** for the subject.
e. In the To text box, type your instructor's nickname, then press **[Tab]**.
f. In the Cc text box, type your full e-mail address.
g. Type the following message in the message body pane:
Here's a copy of <<describe the file>> **as you requested. Please let me know as soon as you receive the file. Thanks.**
h. Leave a blank line after the end of your message, then type your name, class name, class section, and e-mail address on four separate lines.
i. Attach the file you have chosen to the message.
j. Carefully proofread your message for errors, then correct any problems.
k. Send the message.
l. Check for new e-mail to see if your message arrived in your Inbox.
m. Close Netscape Mail.

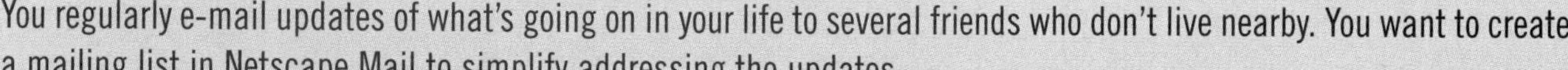

▶ Independent Challenge 2

You regularly e-mail updates of what's going on in your life to several friends who don't live nearby. You want to create a mailing list in Netscape Mail to simplify addressing the updates.

a. Start Netscape Mail.
b. Add the full names, appropriate nicknames, and e-mail addresses of three classmates to the Address Book.
c. Add your instructor's full name, nickname, and e-mail address to the Address Book, if necessary.
d. Create an Address Book card for yourself, if necessary.
e. Create a mailing list called **updates list** and nicknamed **updates**, which includes your three classmates, your instructor, and yourself.
f. Create a new e-mail message. Address the message using the updates mailing list.
g. Type a short message informing your classmates that your e-mail message is testing the use of your new mailing list.
h. Send the message.
i. Retrieve and open the message. You should receive the message because you are included in the mailing list.
j. Close Netscape Mail.

Independent Challenge 3

Bridgefield Engineering Company (BECO) is a small engineering firm in Somerville, New Jersey, that manufactures and distributes heavy industrial machinery for factories worldwide. Because BECO has trouble reaching its customers around the world in different time zones, the company has decided to implement an e-mail system to facilitate contact between BECO employees and their customers. BECO hired you to help employees set up and use this e-mail system. Your first task is to compile a list of typical industrial machines that BECO can manufacture and to send this list to several of BECO's marketing staff located throughout the country.

- **a.** Start Netscape Mail.
- **b.** If necessary, add your instructor and two classmates to the Address Book. Use an appropriate nickname for each person. Be sure you have a complete Address Book card for yourself. (*Hint:* If you already have an Address Book card, double-click your name in the Address Book list box and then fill in information for both the Name and Contact tabs.)
- **c.** Start a new message, and address the message to three people: your instructor and two of your classmates.
- **d.** Send a blind carbon copy (Bcc) of the message to yourself.
- **e.** Type an appropriate topic in the Subject text box.
- **f.** Compose the following message: **Bridgefield manufactures machines to your specifications. We can build borers, planers, horn presses, and a variety of other machines. E-mail us for further information.**
- **g.** Sign your name.
- **h.** Send the message.
- **i.** Retrieve the message.
- **j.** Close Netscape Mail.

Independent Challenge 4

You've recently set up office e-mail at Fiona's Hat Shop where you work. Now that clients and vendors have begun sending you e-mails, you need to set up a filing system to keep track of e-mail messages that you've received.

- **a.** Start Netscape Mail.
- **b.** Send brief messages to three or four classmates and copy the messages to yourself.
- **c.** Retrieve and view all e-mail messages in the message list.
- **d.** Create a folder named **Vendors** and a folder named **Clients**.
- **e.** Move one e-mail message into one folder, then copy one e-mail message into the second folder.
- **f.** View the contents of both folders.
- **g.** Close Netscape Mail.

▶ Visual Workshop

Use the skills you learned in this unit to create the message shown in Figure B-28. The file attachment is located where your Project Files are stored. When you have completed the message and attached the file, send the message to your instructor or a colleague.

FIGURE B-28

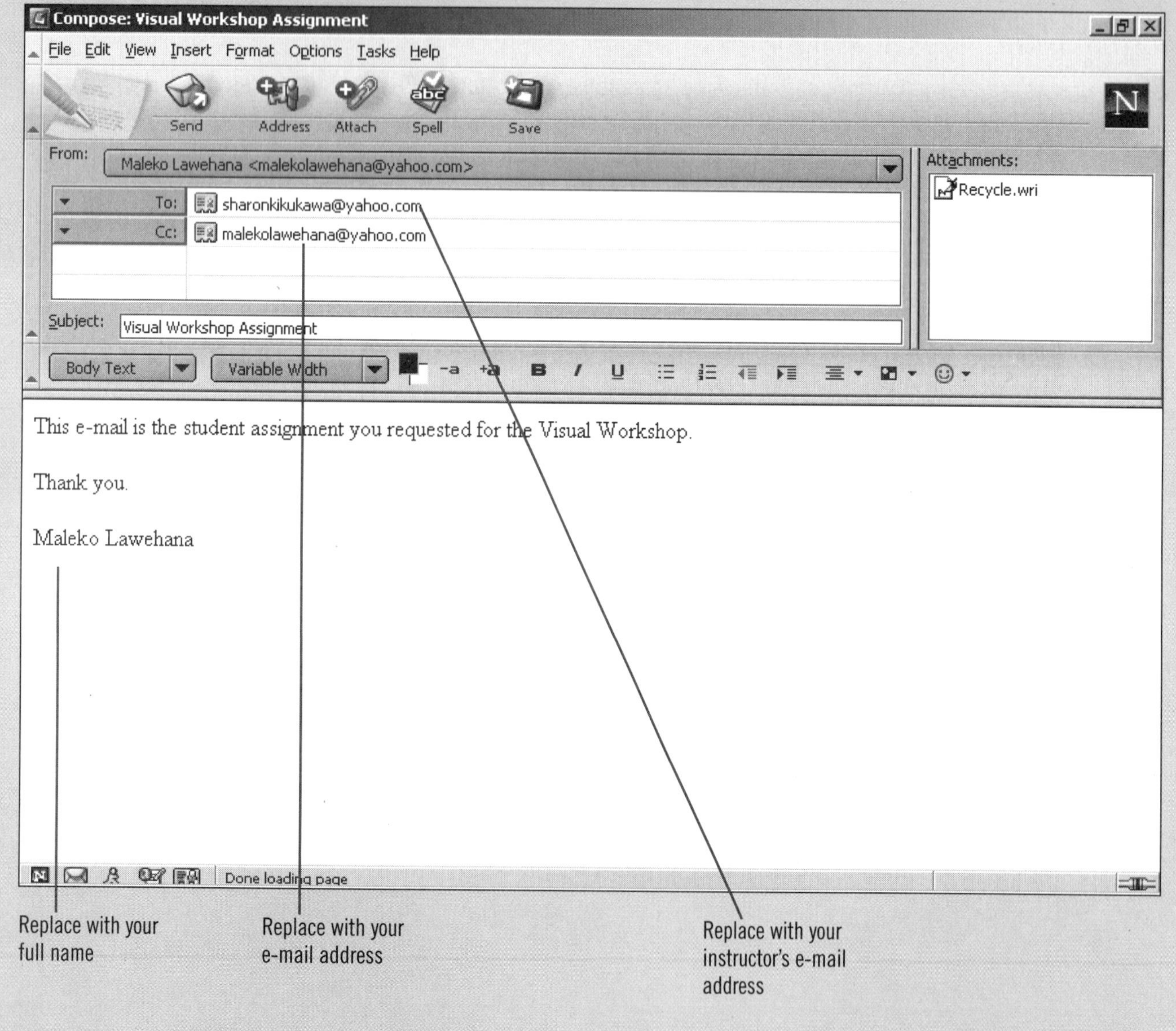

Internet

Unit C

Using the Microsoft Outlook Express E-Mail Program

- Explore Microsoft Outlook Express
- Set up Microsoft Outlook Express
- Send an e-mail message
- Check incoming e-mail
- Attach a file to an e-mail message
- Save an attached file
- Reply to an e-mail message
- Forward an e-mail message
- File an e-mail message
- Delete an e-mail message
- Maintain an address book
- Create a mailing list

Several programs for managing e-mail are currently available. You can use any of these programs to send e-mail to people who use the same or different e-mail programs. The recipient can read your e-mail just as you can read the e-mail you receive from other people, regardless of the e-mail programs they use. One of the most popular e-mail programs is Microsoft Outlook Express, which is installed as part of Microsoft Internet Explorer. Kikukawa Air is an air charter service based in Maui, Hawaii, which offers service to all of the Hawaiian Islands. Sharon Kikukawa, one of the owners, wants to use e-mail as the company's primary means of communication to save on long distance phone bills. She hired you to evaluate Microsoft Outlook Express and to oversee its installation.

Internet

Exploring Microsoft Outlook Express

Microsoft Outlook Express (usually referred to as Outlook Express) is an e-mail program that supports standard e-mail functions to manage, send, and receive e-mail. Figure C-1 shows the default Outlook Express window at startup; Figure C-2 shows the Outlook Express Inbox window. By default, the Outlook Express Inbox window displays five elements that allow you to manage e-mail: the Folder list, the Folder Bar, the Contacts list, the message list, and the Preview pane. You installed Outlook Express. Sharon has asked you to explore the various components of Outlook Express. You decide to explore each of the five default Outlook Express elements.

Details

► Folder List

The Folder list, shown in Figure C-2, displays a list of folders that you can use to receive, send, and delete e-mail messages. Because you can customize Outlook Express, your folders might be different from those that appear in Figure C-2.

- **Inbox folder**
  The Inbox folder stores messages that you have received.
- **Outbox folder**
  The Outbox folder stores messages waiting to be sent by Outlook Express.
- **Sent Items folder**
  The Sent Items folder contains copies of messages you sent.
- **Deleted Items folder**
  The Deleted Items folder contains messages you deleted from other folders.
- **Drafts folder**
  The Drafts folder contains saved messages that you are not yet ready to send.

► Folder Bar

The Folder Bar, just below the toolbar, displays the title of the folder that is currently open.

► Contacts List

The Contacts list displays the names of people and organizations for which you have saved contact information in Outlook Express. You can use the Contacts list to quickly address an e-mail message.

► Message List

The message list contains message header summaries. A **message header summary** includes the sender's name, message subject, message priority, an indication of any attached file, and the date and time on which the message was received.

► Preview Pane

The message header summary that is selected in the message list appears in the Preview pane. The Preview pane is normally located below the message list and displays the message's contents.

FIGURE C-1: Default Outlook Express window at startup

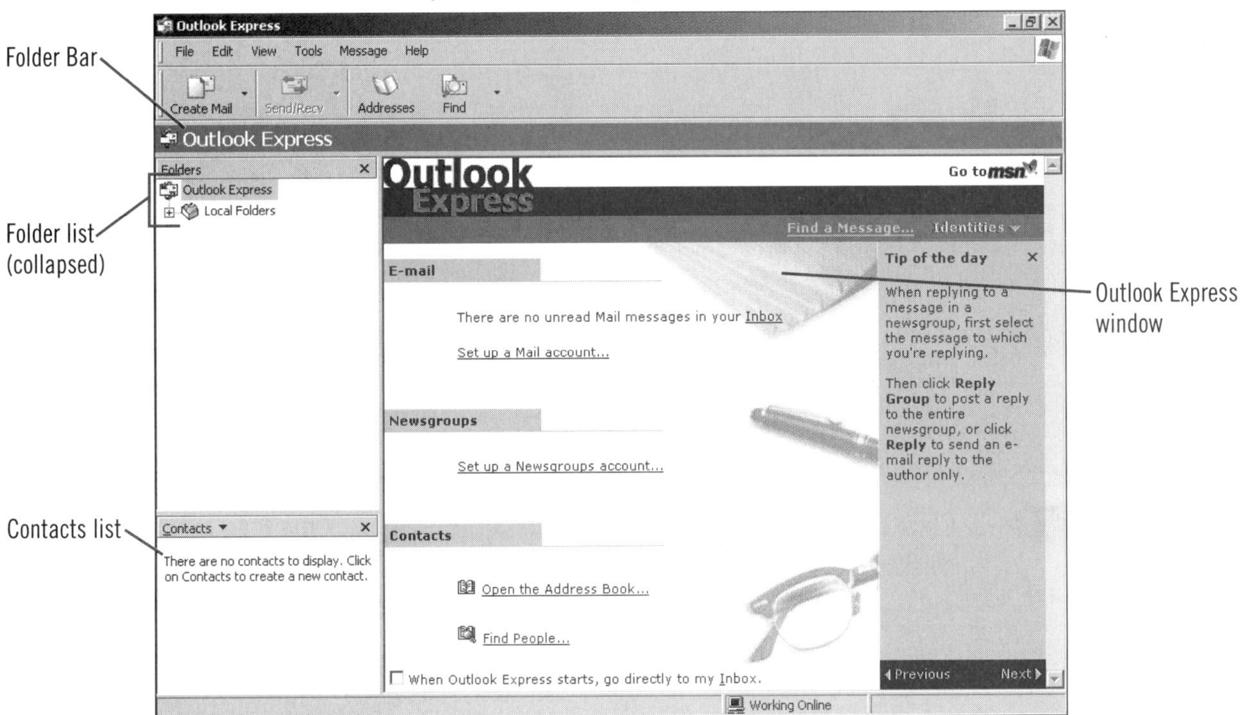

FIGURE C-2: Inbox window

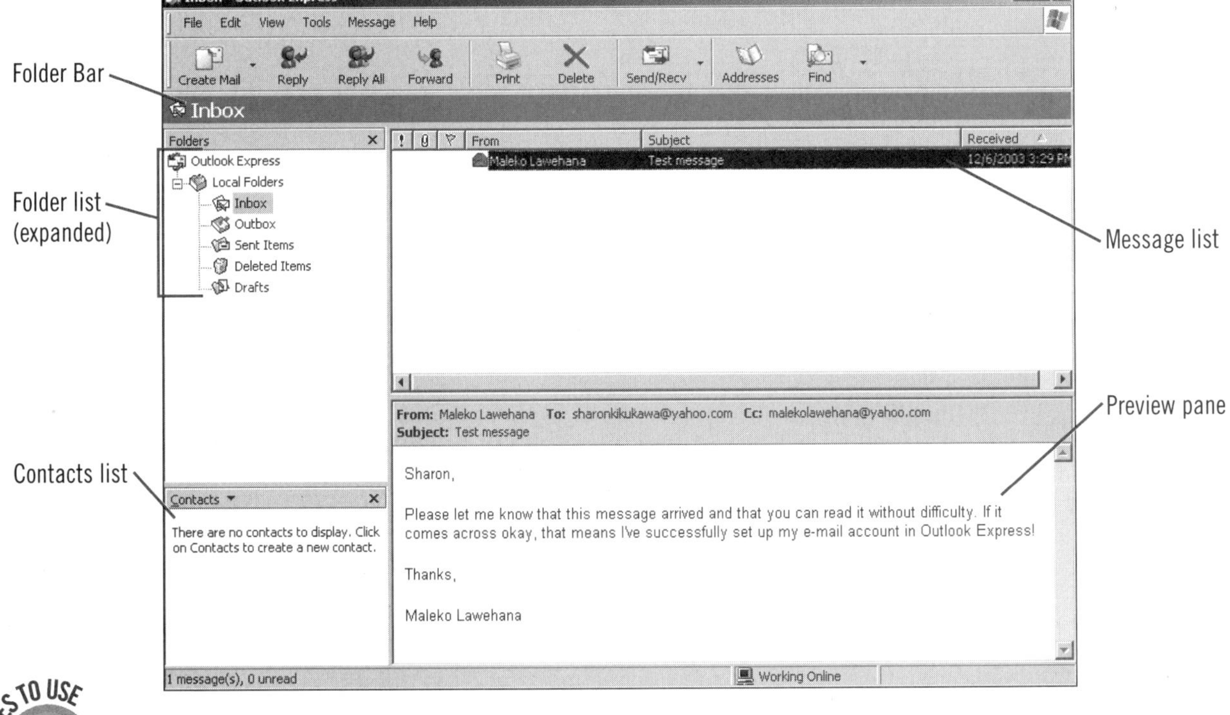

CLUES TO USE

Downloading Microsoft Internet Explorer

You can download Microsoft Internet Explorer (which includes Microsoft Outlook Express) for free from the Microsoft Web site. If Microsoft Internet Explorer is not installed on your computer, see your network administrator to obtain approval to download this program from the Web. Then go to the Microsoft home page at *www.microsoft.com*, follow the links to the Web page that tells you how to download Microsoft Internet Explorer, and install it on your computer.

Internet

Setting Up Microsoft Outlook Express

After Outlook Express is installed on your computer, you need to **configure**, or set up, Outlook Express to send and receive e-mail. You want to get a feel for Outlook Express. You start by customizing the program with basic information about your e-mail account.

Trouble?

If a dialog box appears asking if you want to set Outlook Express as your default e-mail client, click Cancel.

QuickTip

If you (or someone else) already set up your account, click Close to close the Accounts window and skip to the next lesson.

1. Click the **Start button** on the taskbar, point to either **Programs** or **All Programs**, then click **Outlook Express**
   Outlook Express opens. If an Outlook Express dialog box opens asking you to select the service to which you'd like to connect, click the list arrow, click the service you use to connect to the Internet, then click Connect. If the Internet Connection Wizard starts, skip to Step 4.
2. Click **Tools** on the menu bar, click **Accounts**, then click the **Mail tab** if it's not already selected
3. Click **Add**, then click **Mail**
   The Internet Connection Wizard starts, as shown in Figure C-3. You use this wizard to identify yourself and the settings for your mail server.
4. Type your full name in the Display name text box, click **Next**, type your e-mail address in the E-mail address text box, then click **Next**
5. Type the name of your incoming and outgoing mail servers in the appropriate text boxes
   Your instructor or system administrator will provide you with this information. Usually, your incoming mail server name is POP, POP3, or IMAP, followed by a domain name. Your outgoing mail server name is typically either SMTP or MAIL, followed by a domain name.
6. Click **Next**, then type your account name in the Account name text box, as supplied by your instructor or system administrator
7. Press **[Tab]**, then type a password in the Password text box
8. Deselect the **Remember password check box**, then click **Next**
9. Click **Finish**
   The mail account information is saved and the Internet Connection Wizard closes. The Internet Accounts dialog box reappears, and your account is listed on the Mail tab, as shown in Figure C-4.
10. Click **Close** in the Internet Accounts dialog box
    The Internet Accounts dialog box closes.

FIGURE C-3: Internet Connection Wizard dialog box

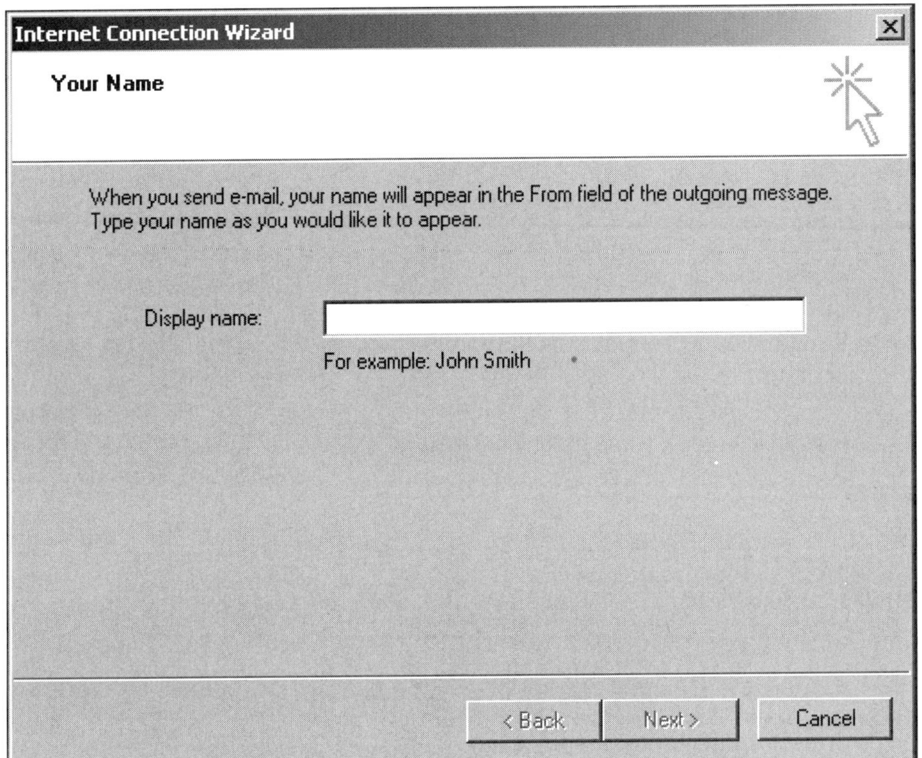

FIGURE C-4: Internet Accounts dialog box

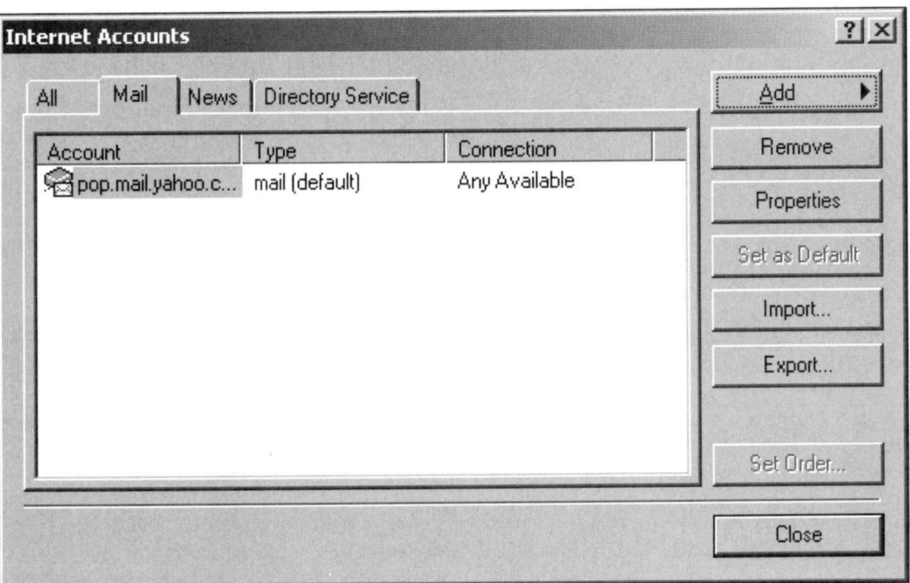

Internet

Internet

Sending an E-Mail Message

After your e-mail account is set up, you can use Outlook Express to send e-mail messages. Outlook Express includes fields for entering the e-mail address for each recipient. You can designate a recipient's e-mail address with "Cc," which stands for "Carbon copy." Cc indicates that the recipient is not the primary addressee; the recipient is just receiving a copy. You can also use the Bcc option (which stands for "Blind carbon copy") to send a copy without the knowledge of the other addressee(s). Below the address information, you can use the Subject text box to summarize the main topic of an e-mail message. You then enter the message content in the message body pane. When you click the Send button, the message is transferred to your mail server for delivery to the e-mail recipient(s). You decide to use Outlook Express to send a message to Sharon. You will also send a copy of the message to your own e-mail address so you can verify that the message is sent correctly.

Trouble?

If Inbox is not visible in the Folder list, click the plus sign next to Local Folders in the Folder list to display your local folders.

Trouble?

If the Bcc text box is not visible on your screen, click View on the menu bar, then click All Headers. If you have more than one e-mail account set up in Outlook Express, the new message window will contain an extra text box called the From text box, which shows your e-mail address.

1. Click **Inbox** in the Folder list, then click the **Create Mail button** on the toolbar
   Figure C-5 shows a new message window.
2. If necessary, click the **Maximize button** on the New Message window
3. Type **sharonkikukawa@yahoo.com** in the To text box
4. Press [Tab] to move to the Cc text box
5. Type your e-mail address
6. Press [Tab] twice to move to the Subject text box, then type **Test message**
7. Click in the message body pane, type **Sharon,** press [Enter] twice, type **Please let me know that this message arrived and that you can read it without difficulty. If it comes across okay, that means I've successfully set up my e-mail account in Outlook Express!**, press [Enter] twice, type **Thanks,** press [Enter] twice, then type your full name
   Your screen should look similar to Figure C-6.
8. Click the **Send button** on the toolbar
   The message is sent to the mail server for delivery to Sharon and to you. The Test message window closes and the Inbox window appears.

CLUES TO USE

Correcting your e-mail message content

If you notice a typing error before sending an e-mail message, you can select the error with your mouse pointer and then make the required correction. You can move the insertion point between the text boxes in the new message window by pressing [Tab] to move forward or [Shift][Tab] to move backward or by clicking in the desired text boxes. To check the spelling of your e-mail message, click the Spelling button on the toolbar, then accept or reject the spelling suggestions just as you would in a word-processing program.

FIGURE C-5: New Message window

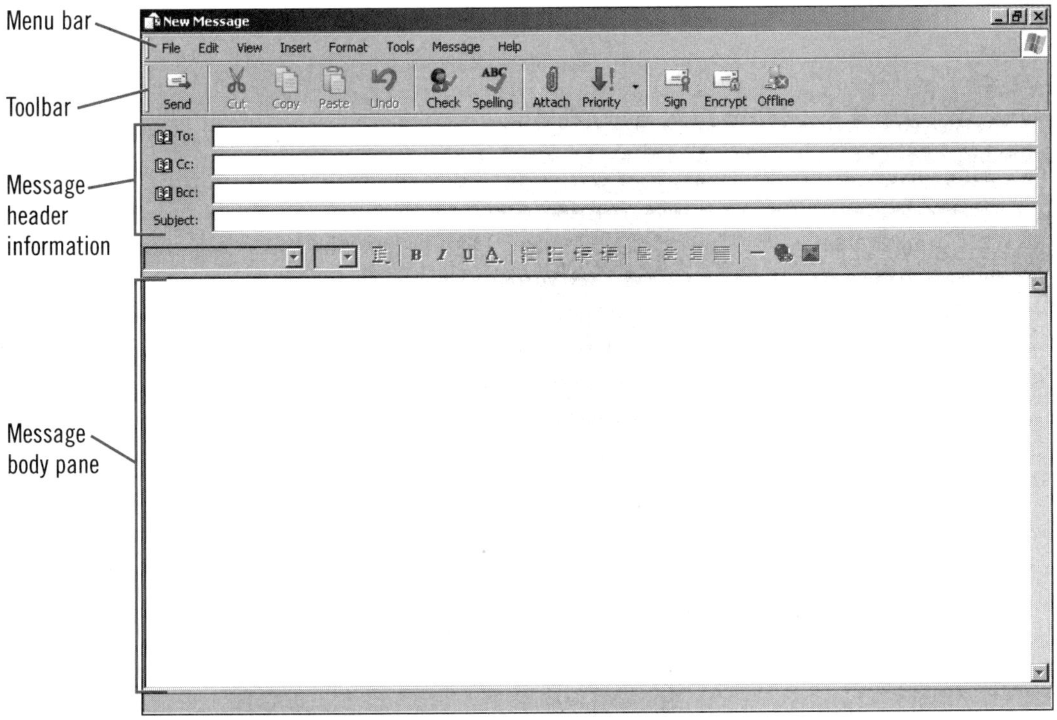

Menu bar

Toolbar

Message header information

Message body pane

New Message

File Edit View Insert Format Tools Message Help

Send Cut Copy Paste Undo Check Spelling Attach Priority Sign Encrypt Offline

To:

Cc:

Bcc:

Subject:

FIGURE C-6: Completed e-mail message

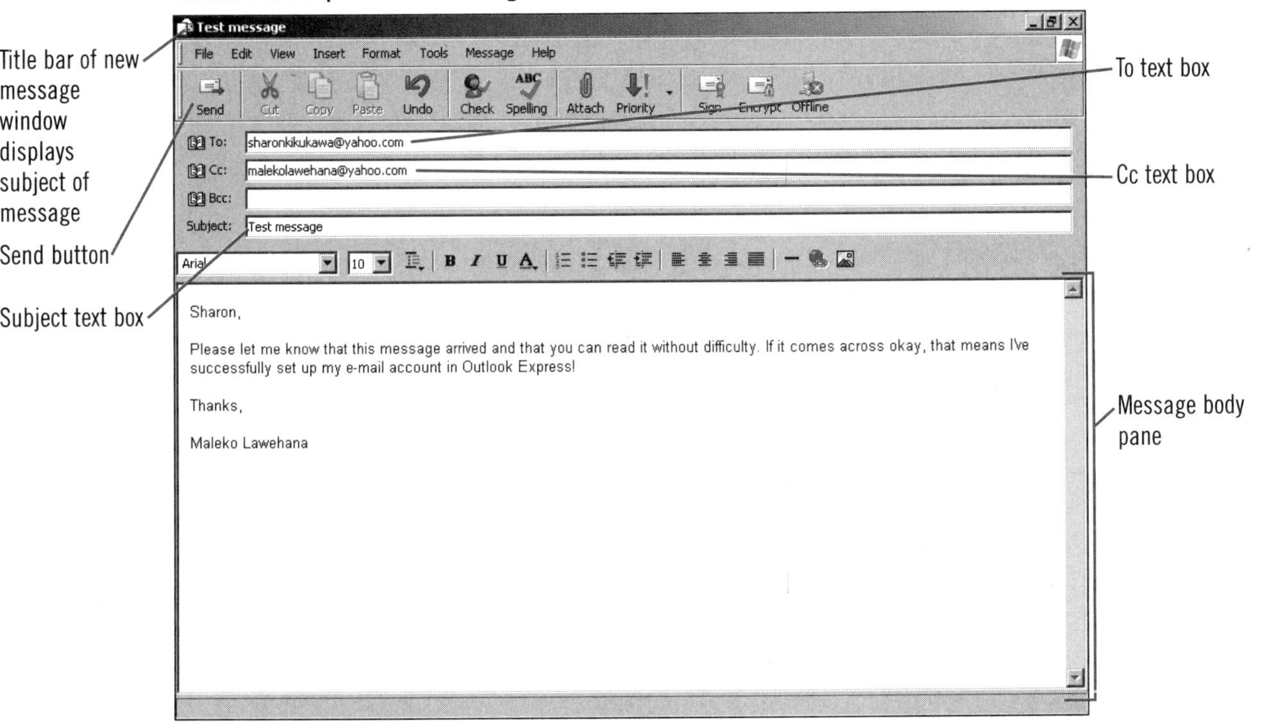

Internet

Internet

Checking Incoming E-Mail

You receive incoming e-mail messages in your Inbox folder (also called the Inbox). When the Inbox contains unread messages, the word "Inbox" (set in bold type) and the number of unread messages appear in the Folder list. When you select Inbox in the Folder list, message header summaries appear in the message list. A closed envelope icon appears next to the message header summary of an unread message, and the message header summary appears in bold. An open envelope icon appears next to the message header summary of each message you have viewed, and the message header summary does not appear in bold. When you sent the message to Sharon, you copied the message to yourself by putting your e-mail address in the Cc text box. You check your e-mail to see if you received the Cc of the message you sent to Sharon.

Steps

Trouble?

If an Outlook Express alert box opens telling you that it could not find your host, click the Hide button to close the alert box, click Tools on the menu bar, click Accounts, then click the Properties button. Verify that your incoming and outgoing server names are correct, then repeat Step 1. If you still have problems, ask your instructor or system administrator for help.

1. Click the **Send/Recv button** on the toolbar

   Depending on your system configuration, you might need to connect to your ISP or log on to your mail server to download your new e-mail. Within a few minutes, your mail server transfers all new e-mail to your Inbox. If you don't see any incoming messages in the Inbox after you click the Send/Recv button, wait a few moments, then click it again; sometimes e-mail delivery slows down at peak times during the day. Your Inbox window should look similar to Figure C-7. The message that you copied to yourself when you e-mailed the test message to Sharon appears in the message list. Notice that Inbox in the Folder list appears in bold, and a number appears next to the word "Inbox."

2. Click **Test message** in the message list

   The message appears in the Preview pane, as shown in Figure C-8.

FIGURE C-7: Message list containing new message

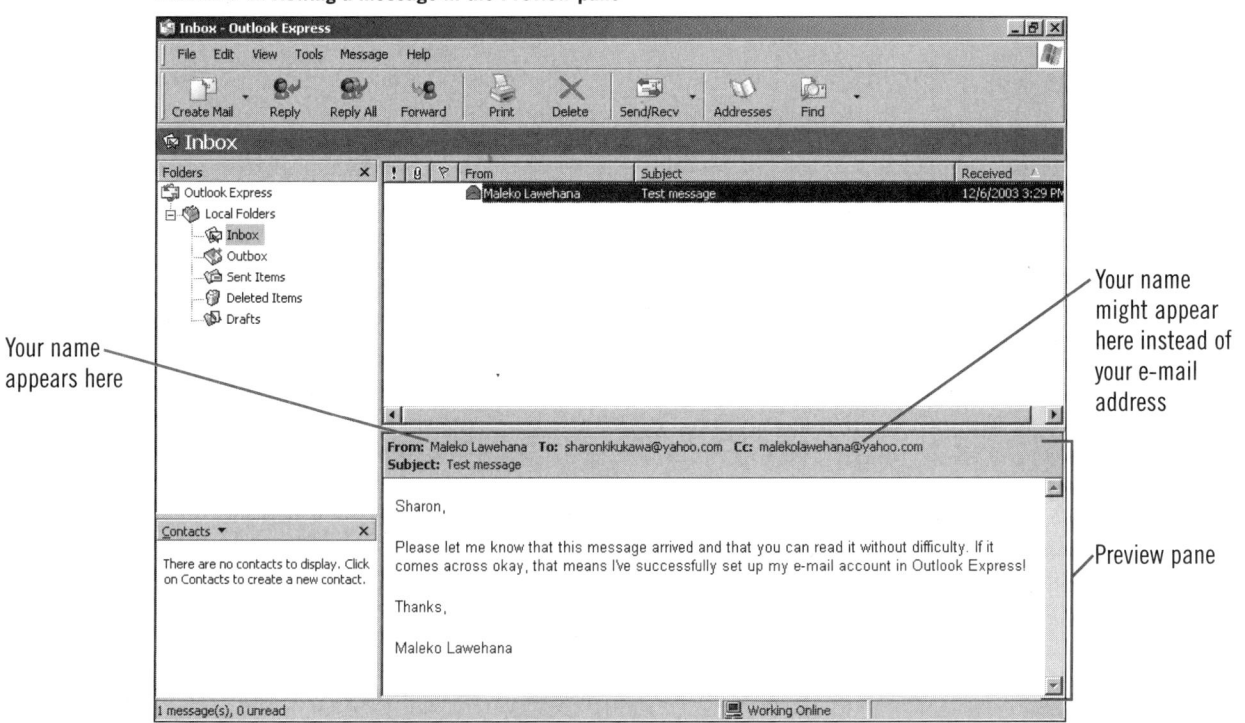

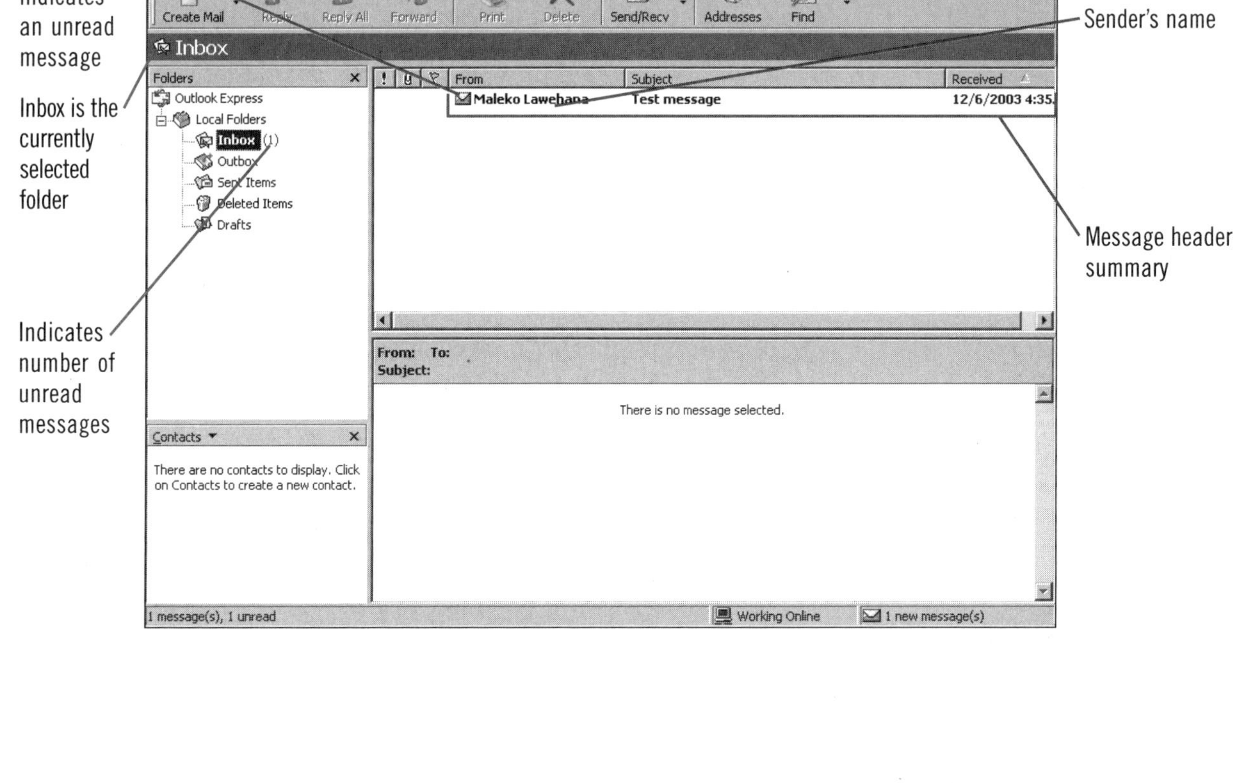

FIGURE C-8: Viewing a message in the Preview pane

Internet

Internet

Attaching a File to an E-Mail Message

You might want to send an e-mail message that includes a file, such as a document created in a word-processing program or a spreadsheet program, or a picture. You can send any type of file over the Internet by attaching it to an e-mail message. A file sent with an e-mail message is called an **attachment**. Because e-mailing attachments between employees of Kikukawa Air would be useful for sharing information, such as maintenance schedules, you decide to explore how the attachment feature works. You use Outlook Express to send a message with an attachment.

1. Click the **Create Mail button** on the toolbar, then maximize the New Message window
2. Type your e-mail address in the To text box
3. Type **Test message with attachment** in the Subject text box
4. Type **A file is attached to this message as a test.** in the message body pane
5. Press **[Enter]** twice, then type your full name
6. Click the **Attach button** on the toolbar
   The Insert Attachment dialog box opens, as shown in Figure C-9.
7. Click the **Look in list arrow**, and navigate to the drive and folder where your Project Files are stored, then double-click the file **Physicals.wri**
   The Insert Attachment dialog box closes, and the Attach text box appears below the Subject text box. The filename of the attached file appears in the Attach text box. Compare your screen to Figure C-10.
8. Click the **Send button** on the toolbar
   The Test message with attachment window closes and the Inbox window appears.

Trouble?

The filename might appear in the Insert Attachment dialog box on your computer as Physicals without the .wri at the end.

FIGURE C-9: Insert Attachment dialog box

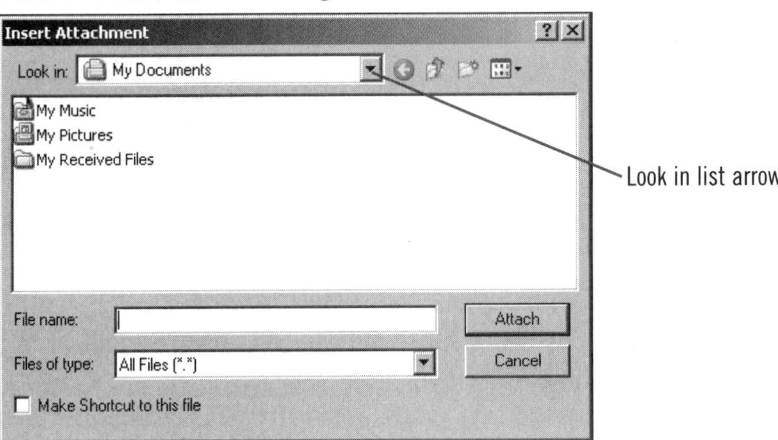

FIGURE C-10: Completed message with attachment

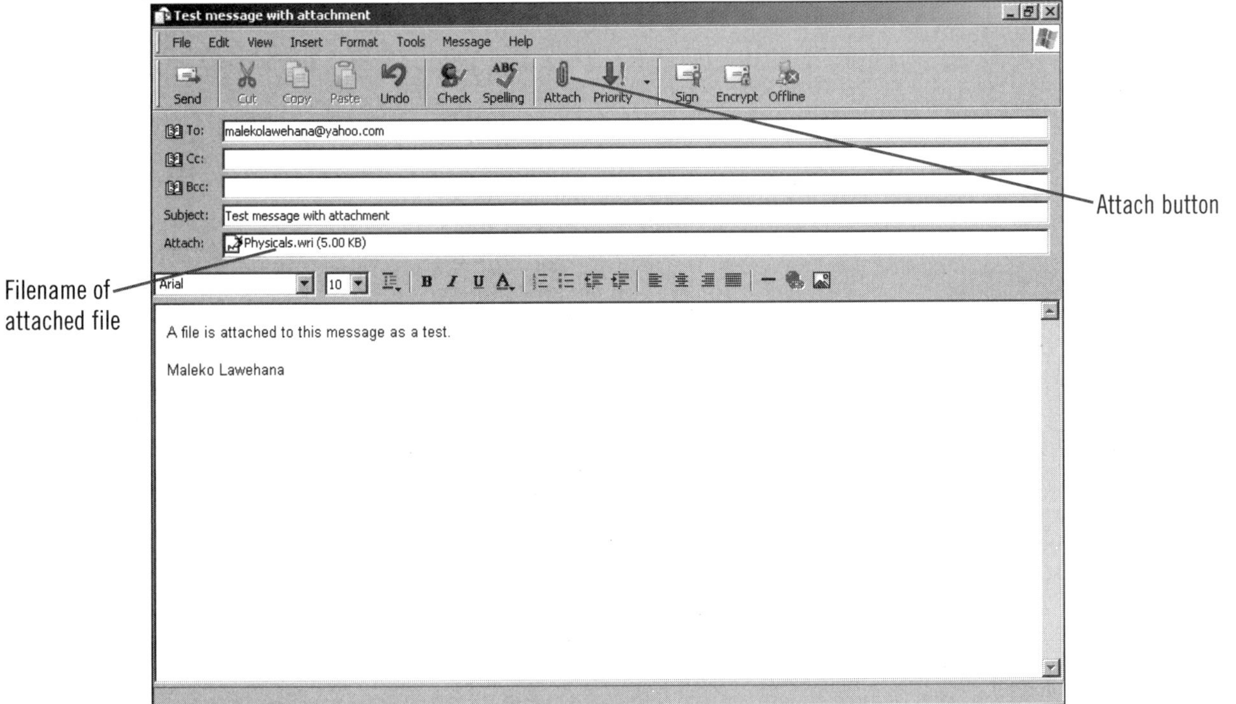

Internet

Saving an Attached File

When you receive an e-mail message with a file attached, you can open the attachment in the Preview pane or you can save it to view later. You decide to experiment with the options for working with an attached file by opening the file and then saving it.

1. Click the **Send/Recv button** on the toolbar, then click **Test message with attachment** in the message list
   The message text appears in the Preview pane. Your screen should look similar to Figure C-11.
2. Click the **paperclip icon** in the Preview pane, then click **Physicals.wri**
   The Open Attachment Warning dialog box opens, as shown in Figure C-12.
3. Click the **Open it option button**, then click **OK**
   The attachment opens in WordPad.
4. Click the **Close button** on the WordPad window
5. To save the attachment, click the **paperclip icon** in the Preview pane, click **Physicals.wri**, verify that the **Save it to disk option button** is selected, then click **OK**
   The Save Attachment As dialog box opens, similar to the one shown in Figure C-13.
6. Click the **Save in list arrow**, navigate to the drive and folder where your Project Files are stored, select the text in the File name text box, then type **Unit C Physicals**
7. Click **Save**
   The attached file is saved where your Project Files are stored. You can open the saved attachment at any time just as you would open any other file.

Understanding e-mail viruses, worms, and Trojan horses

E-mail can carry malicious programs, such as viruses, worms, and Trojan horses. A computer **virus** is a piece of software that runs without your permission and performs undesired tasks, such as deleting the contents of your hard disk. Viruses **self-replicate**, which means that they create, and in some cases distribute, copies of themselves to infect more computers. **Worms** and **Trojan horses** are variations on this idea, written with the intent of creating computer trouble, and are of special concern to e-mail users, because they reproduce by using the functions of e-mail clients like Outlook Express to send out copies of themselves as attachments. However, you can take a couple easy steps to protect yourself and those with whom you exchange e-mail. The most important precaution you can take is not opening a file attachment from a sender you don't know, because the attachment might contain a worm or Trojan horse. You could also install **anti-virus software**, which is a software package that protects your computer from malicious programs. Many schools and colleges distribute anti-virus software for free to students, staff, and faculty; check with your instructor, system administrator, or computing services center to see if this is available to you.

FIGURE C-11: Message with attachment in the messsage list

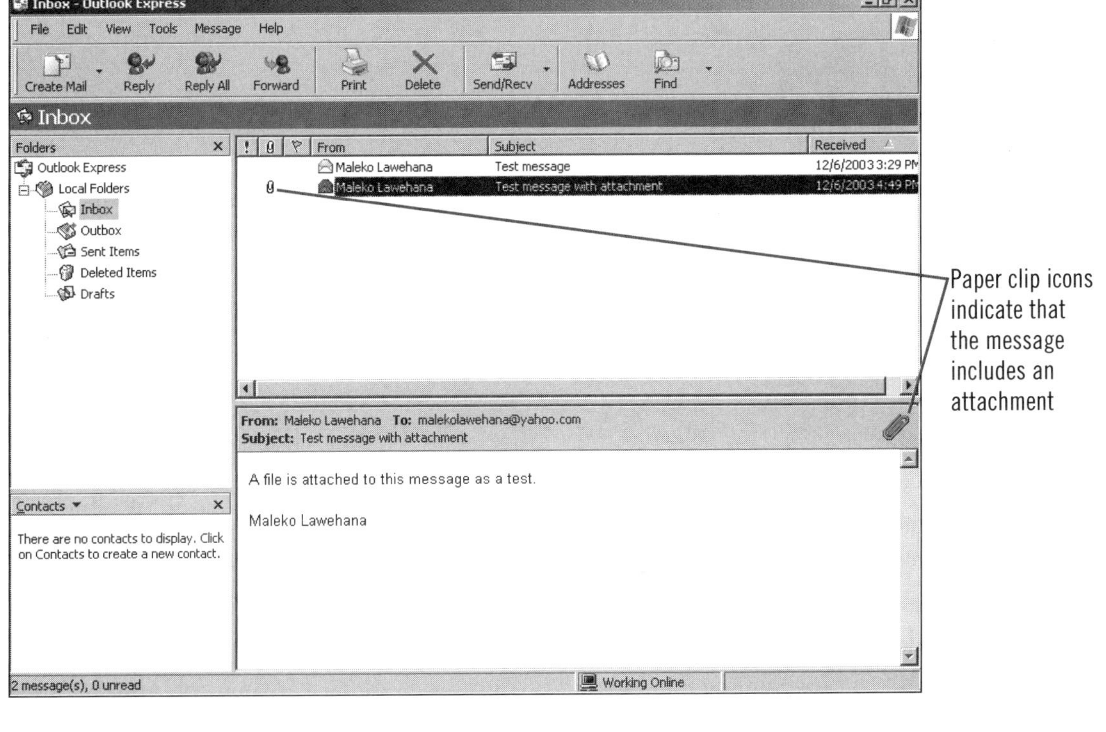

FIGURE C-12: Open Attachment Warning dialog box

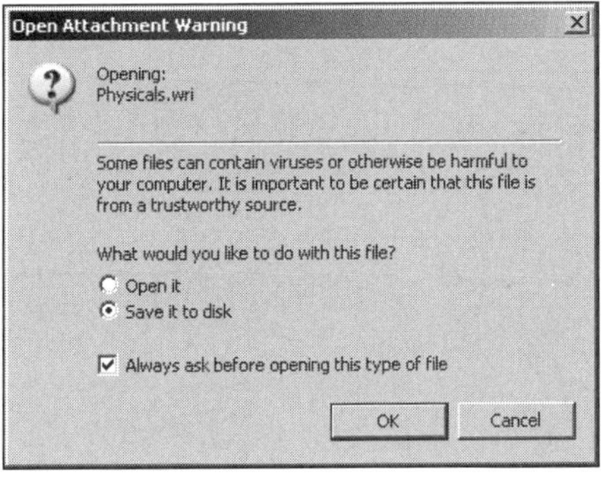

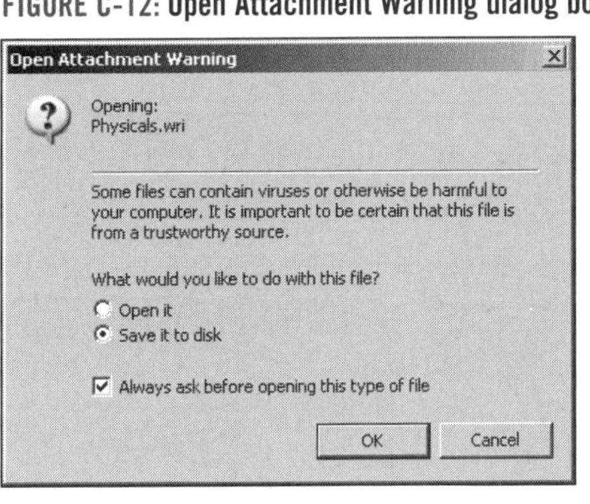

FIGURE C-13: Saving an attached file

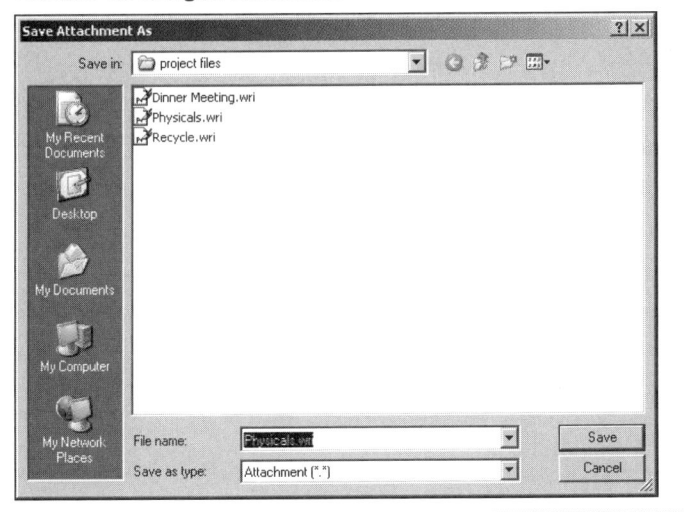

Internet

Internet

Replying to an E-Mail Message

You can use the Reply option to respond to the sender of a message quickly and efficiently. When you reply to an e-mail message, the sender's name is automatically placed in the To text box, and the text of the original message appears in the body of the new message for reference. You practice using the Reply option by replying to the copy of the e-mail message you sent to Sharon.

Steps

1. Click **Test message** in the message list
2. Click the **Reply button** on the toolbar, then maximize the Re: Test message window
   A new message window opens and the original sender's address appears in the To text box. "Re:" appears at the beginning of the original subject text, indicating that this message is a response to the original message. You can replace this subject line with new text if you desire. A copy of the original message appears in the message body pane. The vertical line on the left edge of the pane indicates which part is the original message.
3. Type **I created this message using the Reply button in Outlook Express.** in the message body pane, press **[Enter]** twice, then type your full name
   The Re: Test message window should appear similar to the one shown in Figure C-14.
4. Click the **Send button** on the toolbar
5. Click the **Send/Recv button** on the toolbar
   The message you sent appears in your Inbox.
6. Click **Re: Test message** in the message list
   Your screen should look similar to Figure C-15.

QuickTip

You can reply to only the sender by clicking the Reply button or to the sender and all recipients of the original message by clicking the Reply All button. In either case, the e-mail address for each recipient appears in the address area.

FIGURE C-14: Completed reply to a message

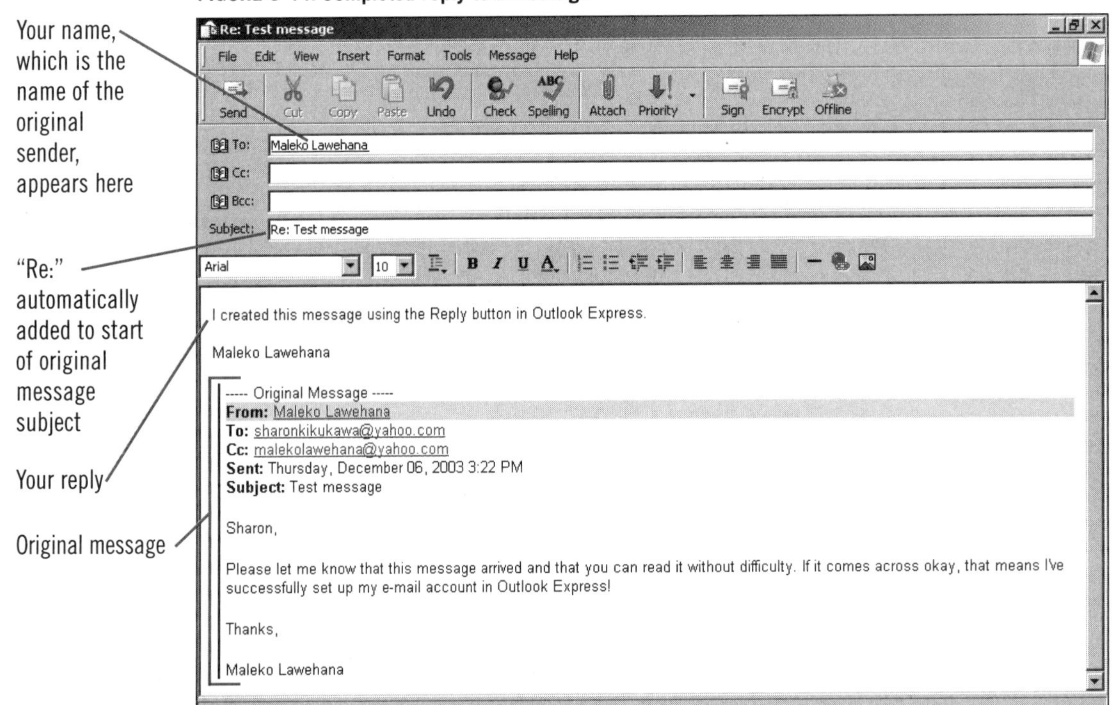

FIGURE C-15: Message reply received

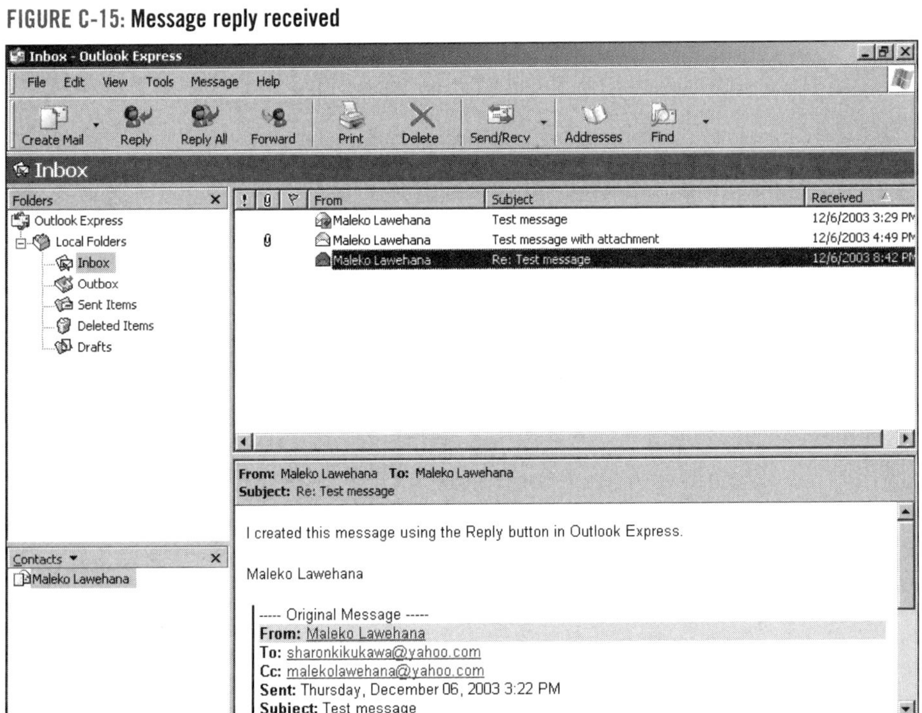

Internet

Internet

Forwarding an E-Mail Message

You can send any message you receive to someone else, which is called **forwarding**. When you use the Forward option, the original message appears in a new message window. Forwarding is similar to replying, except that a forwarded message is not automatically addressed to the original sender; you must address the message to the desired recipients. To practice forwarding messages and to see how they look to recipients, you forward the "Test message" message to yourself and to Sharon.

1. Click **Test message** in the message list
2. Click the **Forward button** on the toolbar, then maximize the Fw: Test message window
   A new message window opens and displays the text of the message to forward, along with a full message header summary. Notice that the Subject text box includes Fw: and the original subject text. The Fw: indicates that the message is being forwarded. Just like when you reply to a message, you can edit the subject line if you want to clarify the subject of the message. Also, notice that instead of the vertical bar that accompanies the original message in a reply, the text of the forwarded message simply appears below the text "Original Message." You can enter your own comments above the quoted message.
3. Type **sharonkikukawa@yahoo.com** in the To text box, then type your e-mail address in the Cc text box
4. In the message body pane, type **Sharon,** press **[Enter]** twice, type **I used the Outlook Express Forward option to send this message.**, press **[Enter]** twice, then type your full name
   Your window should look similar to Figure C-16.
5. Click the **Send button** on the toolbar
6. Click the **Send/Recv button** on the toolbar, then click **Fw: Test message** in the message list
   The forwarded message appears in your Inbox, and the message appears in the Preview pane.

QuickTip

You can also forward a message by clicking Message on the menu bar, then clicking Forward As Attachment; this selection attaches the original message as a text file, so it's not visible in the text of the message received by the recipient.

FIGURE C-16: Forwarding a message

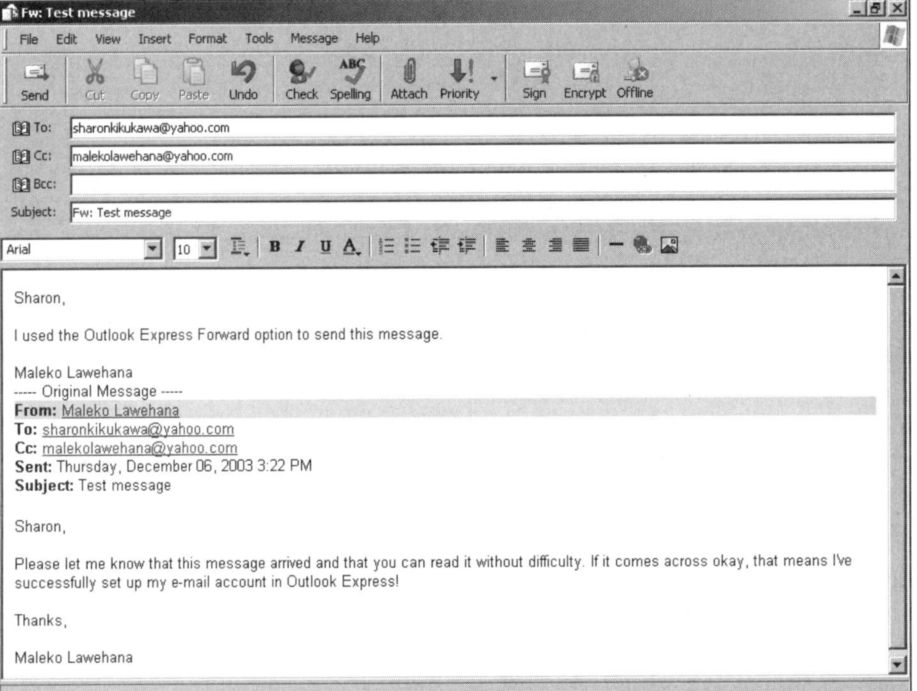

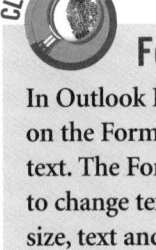

Formatting an e-mail message

In Outlook Express, you can use the various features on the Formatting Bar and Format menu to enhance text. The Formatting Bar and Format menu allow you to change text and paragraph options including text size, text and background color, and paragraph alignment. Figure C-17 shows a formatted e-mail message. Formatting a message can make it look more interesting or even increase its readability. However, not all e-mail programs can display formatted e-mail messages. You can send messages in plain text (no formatting) or HTML (with formatting) format. To specify the desired setting, in the Inbox window, click Tools on the menu bar, click Options, then click the Send tab. In the Mail Sending Format section, click the Plain Text option button to always send unformatted text, or the HTML option button to send formatting instructions when you specify formatting in a message.

FIGURE C-17: Message with formatting

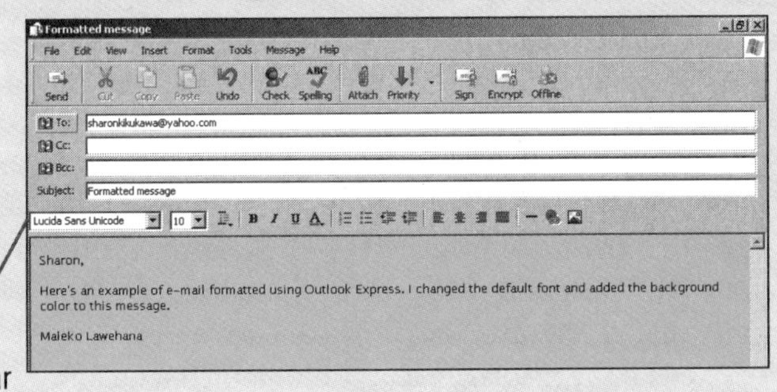

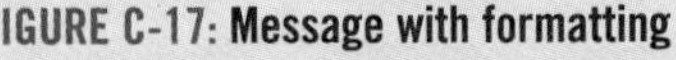

Internet

Filing an E-Mail Message

You can organize your e-mail messages by using Outlook Express folders to file messages by category. For example, you might file messages from friends in one folder and file messages concerning a certain project in a different folder. When you file a message, you move it from the Inbox to another folder. You can also make copies of a message to store it in multiple folders. Sharon wants you to teach employees of Kikukawa Air how to organize their e-mail. You practice creating a folder and copying a message into it.

Steps

QuickTip
You can also open the Create Folder dialog box by right-clicking Local Folders in the Folder list, then clicking New Folder.

1. In the Inbox window, click **File** on the menu bar, point to **Folder**, then click **New**
   The Create Folder dialog box opens, as shown in Figure C-18.
2. Click **Local Folders** in the list of folders
3. Click in the **Folder name text box**, type **Personnel**, then click **OK**
   The Create Folder dialog box closes. A new folder named Personnel appears in the Folder list.
4. Click **Test message** in the message list

QuickTip
You can also open the Copy to Folder dialog box by right-clicking the message you want to copy and clicking Copy to Folder on the shortcut menu.

5. Click **Edit** on the menu bar, click **Copy to Folder**, verify that Personnel is selected in the Copy dialog box that opens, then click **OK**
   Notice that the "Test message" e-mail message still appears in the Inbox. The Copy to Folder command places a copy of the selected message in the folder you select, while leaving the original message in its current location. To move a message so that it no longer appears in its original location, click Move to Folder instead of Copy to Folder on the Edit menu.
6. Click the **Personnel folder** in the Folder list
   The "Test message" e-mail message header summary appears in the Personnel folder's message list, as shown in Figure C-19.
7. Click **Inbox** in the Folder list
   The list of messages in your Inbox appears.

CLUES TO USE

Moving or copying multiple e-mail messages

You can move or copy several messages at once. Press and hold [Ctrl] and click each message header summary that you want to move or copy. After you have selected all the messages, click Edit on the menu bar, point to either Move to Folder or Copy to Folder, click the folder to which you want to move or copy the selected files, then click OK.

FIGURE C-18: Create Folder dialog box

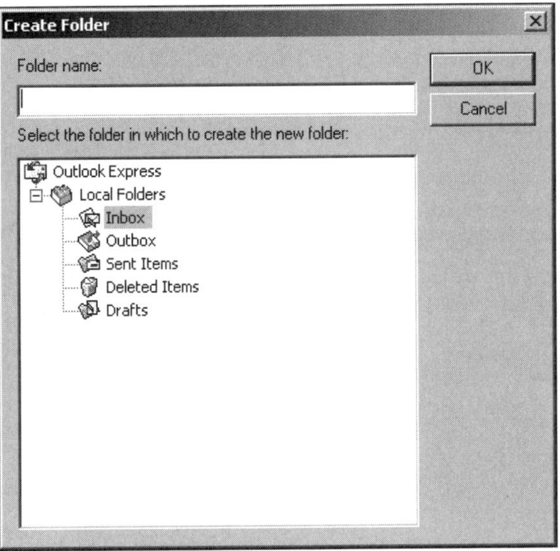

FIGURE C-19: Test message copied to the Personnel folder

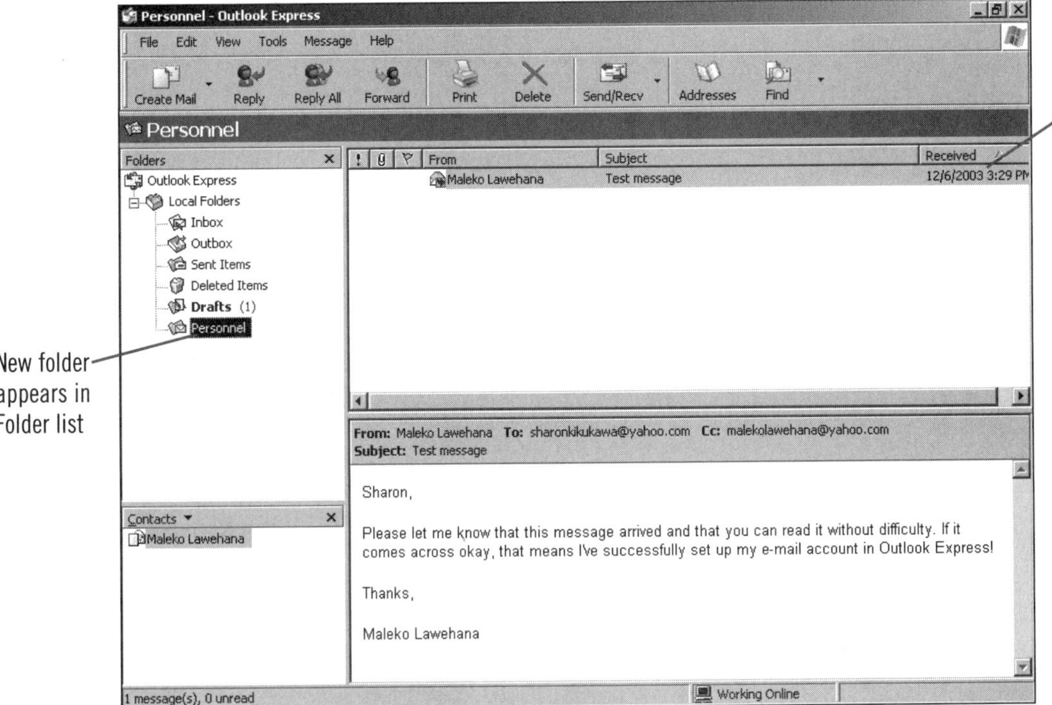

Internet

Internet

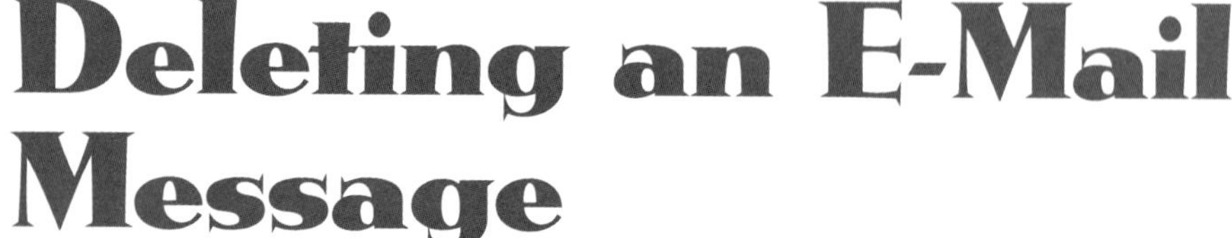

Deleting an E-Mail Message

Just as you can delete unnecessary files from your computer, you can also delete e-mail messages that you no longer need. When you delete a message, it moves to the Deleted Items folder. If you are using a public PC in a university computer laboratory, you should always delete your messages and then empty the Deleted Items folder before you leave the computer. Otherwise, the next person who uses Outlook Express will be able to read the messages you moved to the Deleted Items folder. You practice deleting e-mail by removing some of the messages in your Inbox and the Personnel folder that you created in the previous lesson.

1. Click **Re: Test message** in the message list
2. Click the **Delete button** ✕ on the toolbar
   The message moves from the Inbox to the Deleted Items folder. The "Re:Test message" e-mail message no longer appears in the Inbox.
3. Click **Deleted Items** in the Folder list to open it, then click **Re: Test message** in the message list
   The "Re: Test message" e-mail message you deleted appears in the Deleted Items folder. Although it is not necessary to view the Deleted Items folder before you delete its contents, opening this folder before emptying it allows you to verify that you're not permanently deleting a message you still want.
4. Right-click the **Deleted Items** folder, then click **Empty 'Deleted Items' Folder** on the shortcut menu
   An alert box appears, as shown in Figure C-20, warning you that the deletion will be permanent.
5. Click **Yes**
   All messages in the Deleted Items folder are permanently removed.
6. Right-click **Personnel** in the Folder list
   A shortcut menu appears, as shown in Figure C-21.
7. Click **Delete**, then click **Yes** in the alert box that appears
   The folder and its contents are moved to the Deleted Items folder.
8. Right-click **Deleted Items** in the Folder list
   A shortcut menu appears.
9. Click **Empty 'Deleted Items' Folder**, then click **Yes** in the alert box that appears
10. Click **Inbox** in the Folder list

QuickTip

You can also press [Delete] to move the selected message to the Deleted Items folder.

FIGURE C-20: Deletion warning

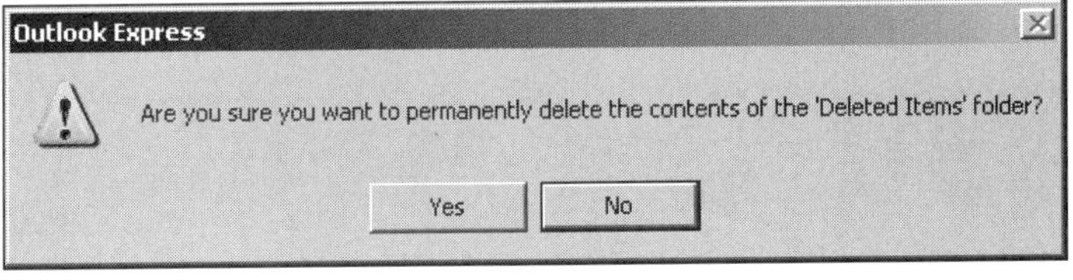

FIGURE C-21: Using the shortcut menu to delete a folder

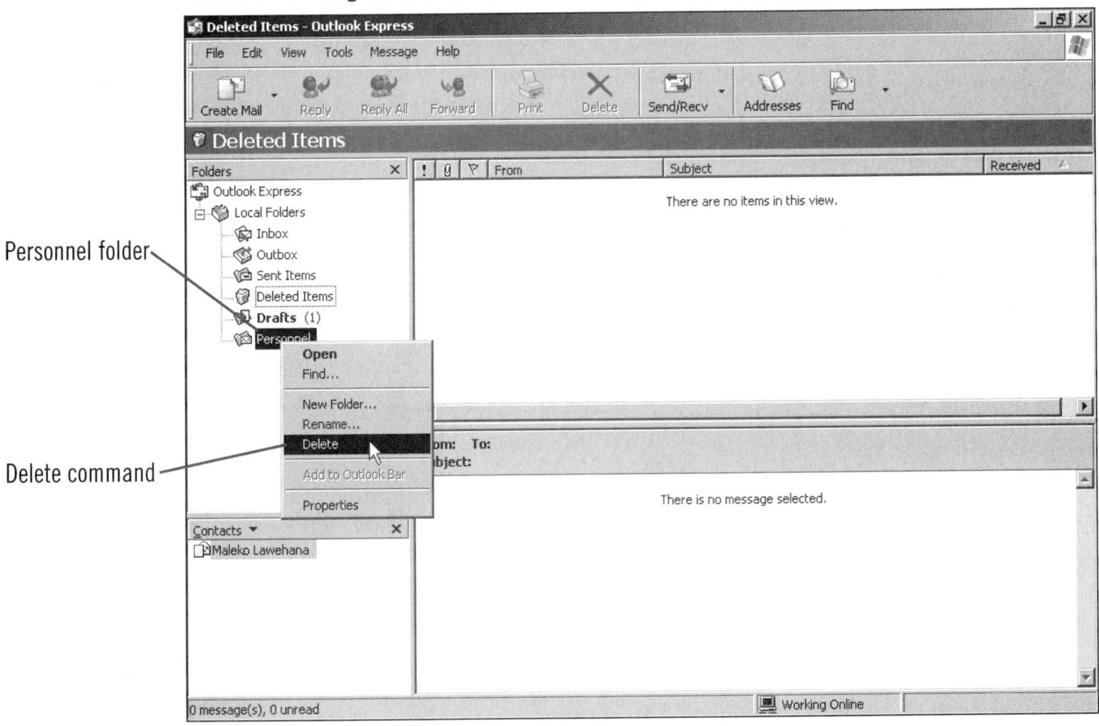

Internet

Maintaining an Address Book

You can save e-mail addresses and contact information, such as phone numbers and postal addresses, in the Address Book. The **Address Book** allows you to select e-mail addresses from a list, rather than typing them, which saves time and avoids typing errors. You can also create **nicknames**, which are shortened names for the e-mail addresses of people you send e-mail to frequently. You can type a nickname in the To text box to send a message. You begin to create an address book for employees of Kikukawa Air using Outlook Express.

1. Click the **Addresses button** on the toolbar
   The Address Book window opens. Notice that Outlook Express automatically created an entry for you, using the information you entered when setting up your e-mail account.
2. Maximize the Address Book window, click the **New button** on the toolbar, then click **New Contact**
   The Properties dialog box opens. You use this dialog box to add addresses to the Address Book. The Name tab stores information about a person's name and e-mail address. You can use the other tabs to store postal address information and other personal information.
3. Type **Sharon** in the First text box, press **[Tab]** twice to move to the Last text box, type **Kikukawa**, then press **[Tab]** three times to move to the Nickname text box
4. Type **Sharon** in the Nickname text box, press **[Tab]** to move to the E-Mail Addresses text box, then type **sharonkikukawa@yahoo.com**
   Figure C-22 shows the completed Properties dialog box.
5. Click **Add**, then click **OK**
   The Properties dialog box closes and the Address Book window appears.
6. Use Steps 2 through 5 as a guide to create address cards for the following Kikukawa Air employees:

First Name	Last Name	Nickname	E-Mail Address
Chris	**Breed**	**Chris**	**chrisbreed@kikukawa.com**
Jenny	**Mahala**	**Jen**	**jennymahala@kikukawa.com**
Richard	**Forrester**	**Rich**	**richardforrester@kikukawa.com**

QuickTip

To delete an address from the Address Book, click the name in the Address Book window, then click the Delete button on the toolbar.

7. Click the **Close button** on the Address Book window, click the **Create Mail button** on the toolbar, maximize the New Message window, then click the **To button**
   The Select Recipients dialog box opens.
8. Click **Sharon Kikukawa** in the list of names on the left side of the Select Recipients dialog box, then click **To**
   Sharon's name appears in the Message recipients list in the dialog box. Compare your screen to Figure C-23.
9. Click **OK**
   Sharon's name appears in the To text box. You can use Address Book entries to quickly address your e-mail messages.
10. Type **Address Book test** in the Subject text box, type **I'm testing the Address Book feature in Outlook Express.** in the message body pane, press **[Enter]** twice, type your full name, then click the **Send button**

QuickTip

You can also type Sharon's nickname in the To text box in the new message window.

FIGURE C-22: Completed Properties dialog box for Sharon Kikukawa

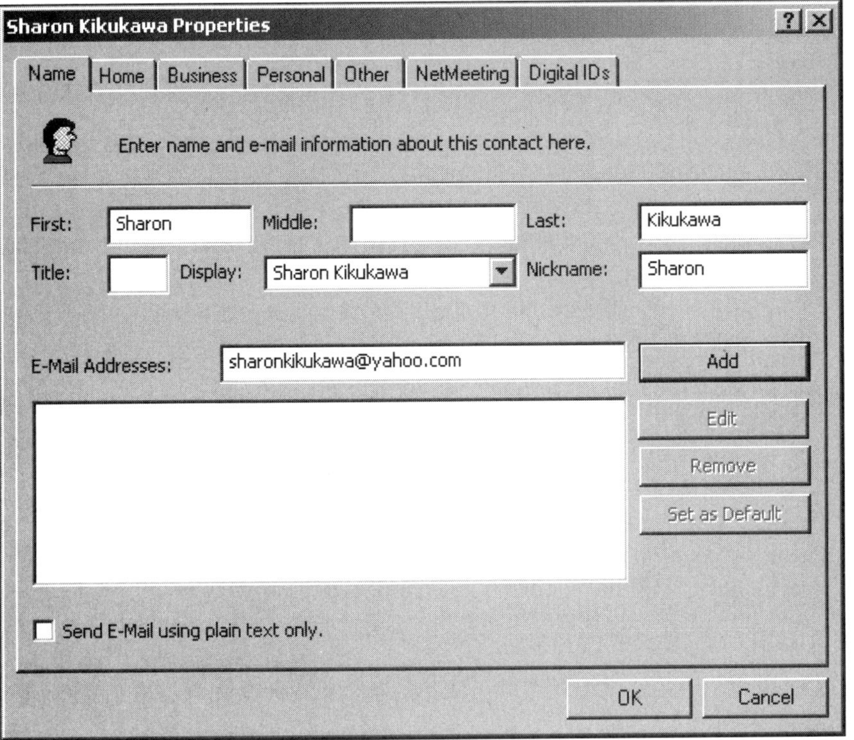

FIGURE C-23: Select Recipients dialog box

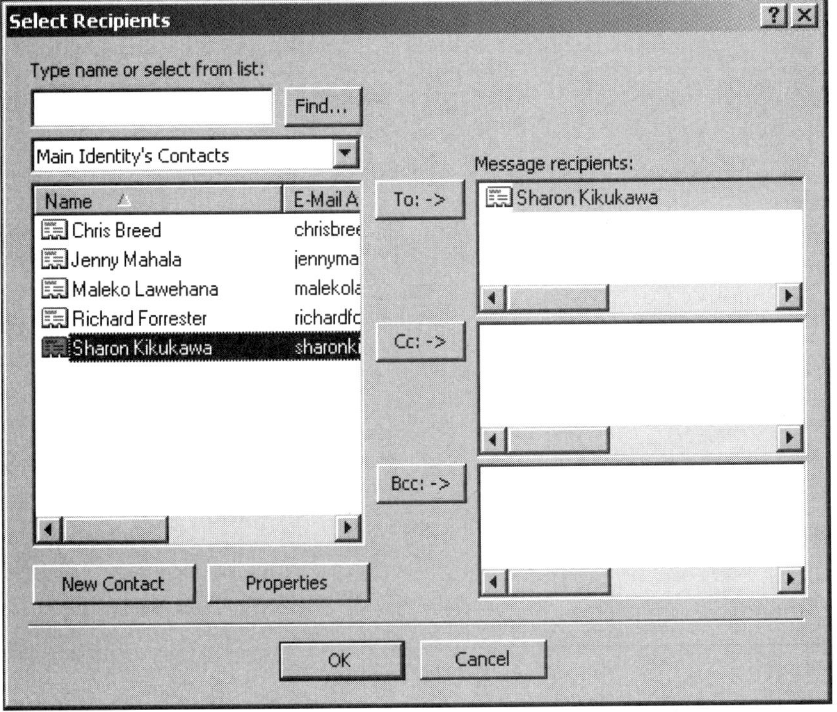

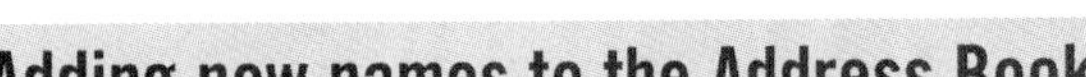

Adding new names to the Address Book

When you receive e-mail from someone who is not listed in the Address Book, you can right-click the message header summary, then click Add Sender to Address Book on the shortcut menu. The sender's name and e-mail address will be added to the Address Book.

Internet

Internet

Creating a Mailing List

You can quickly send an e-mail message to a group of people by creating a **mailing list**. You create a mailing list in the Address Book by creating a name for the mailing list, and then assigning e-mail addresses to the name. When you want to send an e-mail message to the group, you can simply type the name in the To text box to send a single message to all the mailing list members simultaneously. Because Kikukawa Air, like many companies, is organized into departments such as Personnel, Marketing, and Operations, you realize that mailing lists would be useful when you want to send messages to all the employees in a particular department. You start by creating a mailing list for the Personnel Department.

1. Click the **Addresses button** on the toolbar, click the **New button** on the toolbar in the Address Book window, then click **New Group**
2. Type **Personnel** in the Group Name text box
3. Click **Select Members** to add existing entries to the group
   The Select Group Members dialog box opens so that you can choose which names to add to the Personnel mailing list.
4. Select Chris Breed in the list, then click **Select** to add her name to the Members list
5. Use Step 4 as a guide to add Jenny and Richard to the group
   Figure C-24 shows the completed Select Group Members dialog box.
6. Click **OK**
   Compare your screen to Figure C-25.
7. Click **OK**
   Notice the entry named "Personnel" in the Address Book window. The icon shows people rather than an envelope, indicating that this entry is a mailing list.
8. Click the **Close button** on the Address Book window
9. Close all open Outlook Express windows

CLUES TO USE

Modifying a group

You can modify a group's members by opening the Address Book, double-clicking the group name, and then selecting the appropriate option from the group's Properties dialog box. To delete a member's name, click the name, then click Remove. To add a member, click Select Members.

FIGURE C-24: Select Group Members dialog box

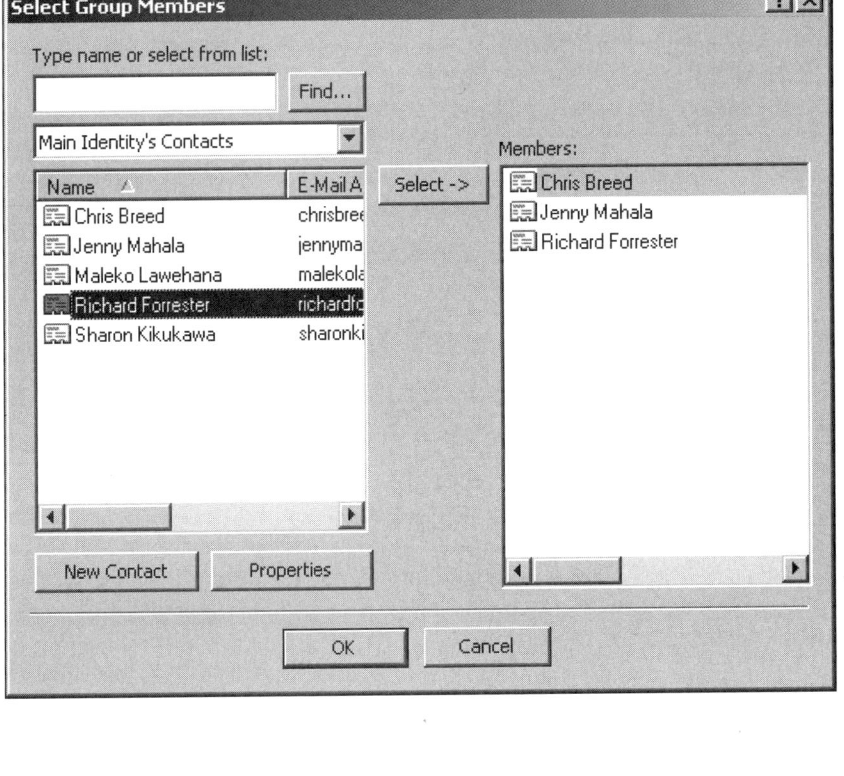

FIGURE C-25: Completed Personnel Properties dialog box

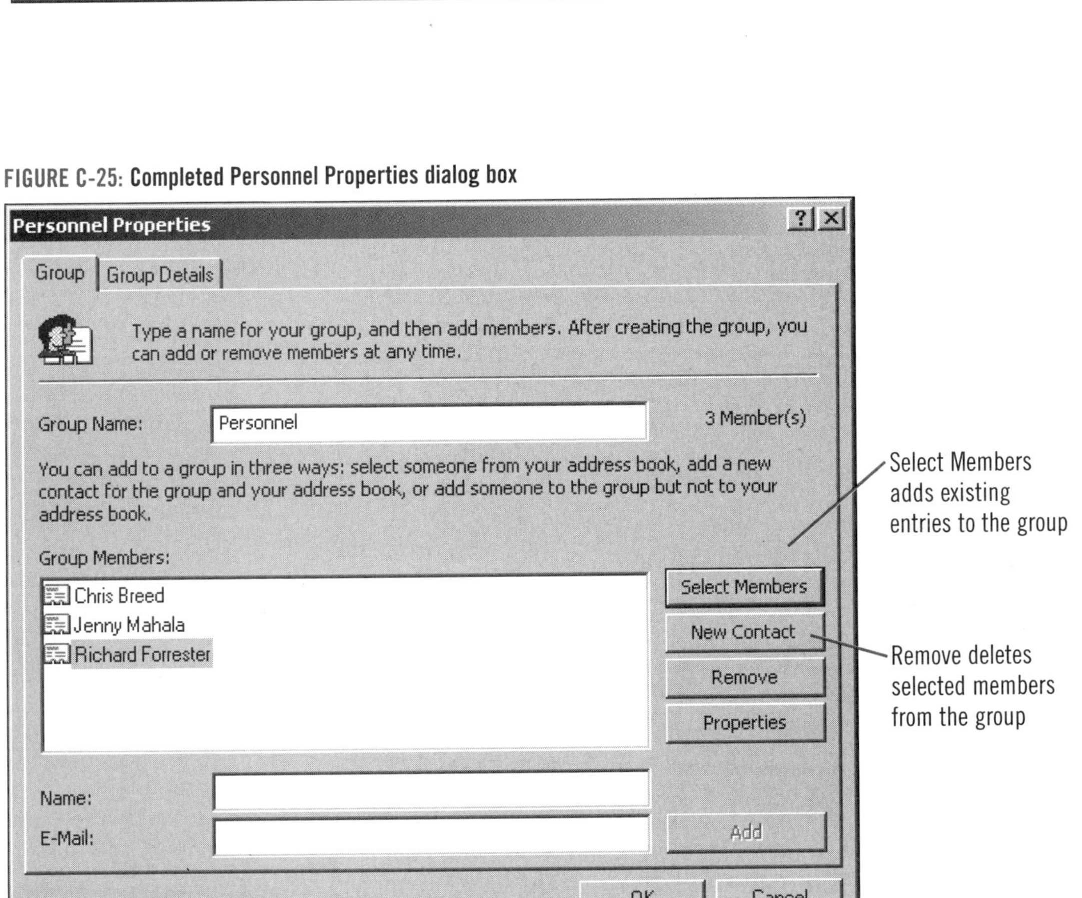

Internet

Practice

► Concepts Review

Explain the use of each element in the window shown in Figure C-26.

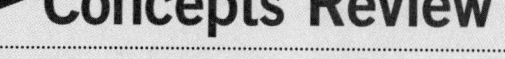

FIGURE C-26

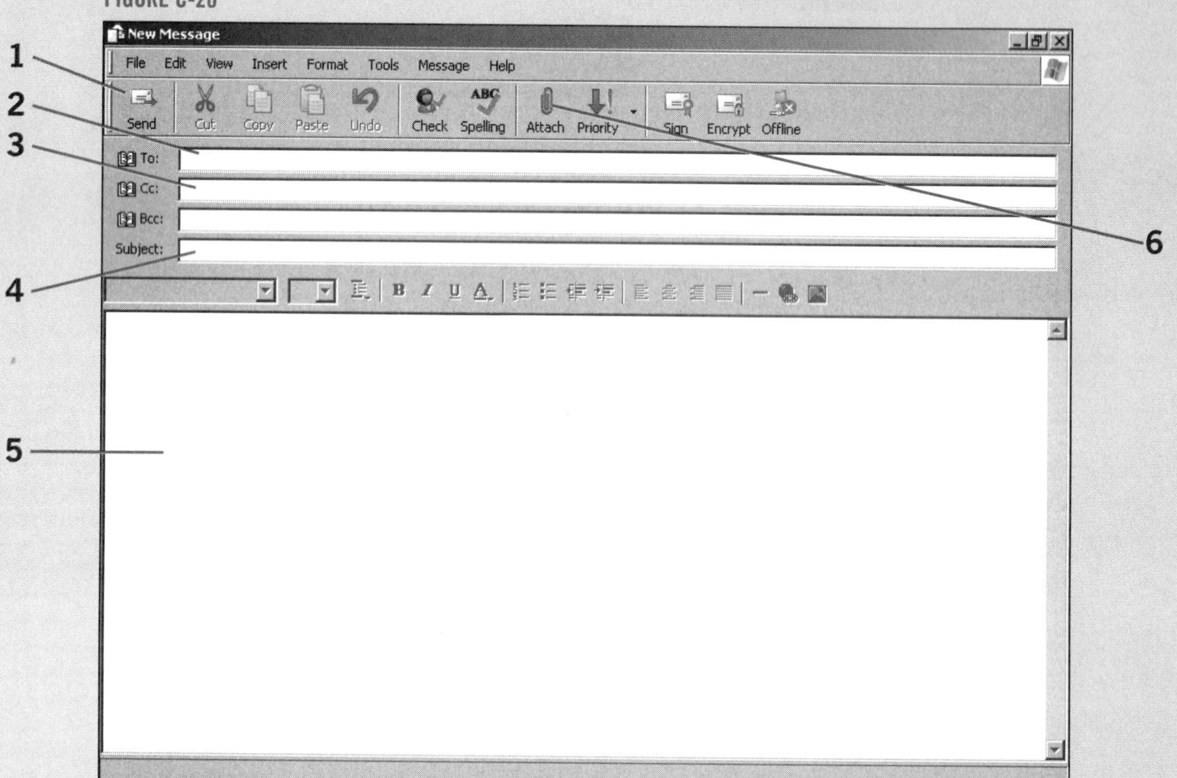

Match each term with the statement that describes it.

7. Inbox	**a.** A folder that contains all incoming messages
8. Address Book	**b.** A file that accompanies an e-mail message
9. New Message window	**c.** A feature that stores names and e-mail addresses for people with whom you correspond regularly
10. Message header summary	**d.** A window used to create messages
11. Attachment	**e.** A location where you type the main topic of an e-mail message
12. Subject text box	**f.** The summary information about a message, including sender, subject, and date

Practice

Select the best answer from the list of choices.

13. To retrieve new messages from the server, which button do you click on the toolbar in the Inbox window?

- **a.** E-Mail
- **b.** Messages
- **c.** Send/Recv
- **d.** Get Message

14. Sending an e-mail message you've received to a new recipient is called:

- **a.** Carbon copying.
- **b.** Replying.
- **c.** Forwarding.
- **d.** Messaging.

15. You can organize your e-mail by placing messages into:

- **a.** Files.
- **b.** Address books.
- **c.** Folders.
- **d.** Trash.

16. Shortened names you give to the e-mail addresses of people to whom you send messages frequently are called:

- **a.** Quick names.
- **b.** List names.
- **c.** Nicknames.
- **d.** New names.

Skills Review

1. **Send an e-mail message.**
   - **a.** Start Outlook Express, then open the New Message window.
   - **b.** Address the message to your instructor, a friend, or a colleague.
   - **c.** Cc the message to yourself.
   - **d.** Make **Dinner Meeting** the subject of the message.
   - **e.** Compose the following message:
     Hi <<name of recipient>>,
     We are planning to meet for dinner at <<a local restaurant name>> **on November 30. Please bring the presentation on the Ford account.**
   - **f.** Type your full name below the message.
   - **g.** Send the message.

2. **Check incoming e-mail.**
   - **a.** Retrieve your e-mail.
   - **b.** Read the copy of the Dinner Meeting message.

3. **Attach a file to an e-mail message.**
   - **a.** Open the New Message window.
   - **b.** Address the message to your instructor, a friend, or a colleague.
   - **c.** Cc the message to yourself.
   - **d.** Make **Dinner Meeting Participants** the subject of the message.
   - **e.** Compose the following message:
     Attached is a list of the people we have invited to attend the dinner meeting at <<restaurant name>> **on November 30. Please check the list and get back to me with any suggestions for additional participants.**
   - **f.** Add your full name to the bottom of the message.
   - **g.** Attach the file named Dinner Meeting.wri located where your Project Files are stored.
   - **h.** Send the file with the attachment.

4. **Save an e-mail attachment.**
   - **a.** Retrieve your e-mail.
   - **b.** Open the Dinner Meeting Participants message in its own window.
   - **c.** Save the attached file where your Project Files are stored as **Unit C Dinner Meeting.wri.**

5. **Reply to an e-mail message.**
   - **a.** Reply to the sender of the Dinner Meeting Participants message.
   - **b.** Change the subject to **Dinner Meeting R.S.V.P.**
   - **c.** Compose the following message:
     I'll be delighted to attend the meeting on November 30.
   - **d.** Add your full name to the bottom of the message.
   - **e.** Send the message.
   - **f.** Retrieve and open your e-mail.

Practice

6. Forward an e-mail message.

a. Forward the Dinner Meeting Participants message to your instructor, a friend, or a colleague.
b. Cc the message to yourself.
c. Compose the following message:
I have reviewed the list of meeting participants. We should also include Juan Sanchez from the Marketing Department.
d. Add your name to the bottom of the message, then send the message.
e. Retrieve and open the message.

7. File e-mail messages.

a. Create a new folder called **Meetings**.
b. Copy the following messages to the Meetings folder: Dinner Meeting, Dinner Meeting Participants, Dinner Meeting R.S.V.P., and Fw: Dinner Meeting Participants.
c. View the contents of the Meetings folder to verify that all four messages appear.
d. Display the Inbox again.

8. Delete e-mail messages.

a. Delete the following messages in the Inbox: Dinner Meeting, Dinner Meeting Participants, Dinner Meeting R.S.V.P., and Fw: Dinner Meeting Participants.
b. Empty the Deleted Items folder.
c. Delete the Meetings folder, then empty the Deleted Items folder.

9. Maintain an address book.

a. Create a new address card for Loree Erickson at lerickson@kikukawa.com. Loree's nickname is Lo.
b. Create a new address card for Lorenzo Seale at lseale@kikukawa.com. Lorenzo's nickname is Lor.
c. Create a new address card for Consuela Longue at clongue@kikukawa.com. Consuela's nickname is Con.

10. Create a mailing list.

a. Create a mailing list called **Meetings**.
b. Add Loree Erickson and Consuela Longue to the list.
c. Close the Address Book.
d. Check the Address Book for the Meetings entry, then close it.
e. Close Outlook Express.

Internet

▶ Independent Challenge 1

Your instructor has asked that you submit your next assignment via e-mail. You should also send a copy of the assignment to yourself.

a. Start Outlook Express.
b. Find a file from one of your own folders to include as an attachment with the e-mail message to your instructor. Make sure that this file contains a very short document that does not take up a lot of disk space. For example, you might select a short essay that you completed for another course or a short letter you've written to a friend. Alternatively, you could use one of the Project Files.
c. Add your instructor's name and full e-mail address to the Address Book. Use an appropriate nickname that is easy for you to remember.
d. Create a new message.
e. Type your instructor's nickname in the To text box.
f. Type your full e-mail address in the Cc text box.
g. Type **E-mail Assignment** in the Subject text box.
h. Type the following message in the message body pane:
Here's a copy of <<describe the file>> **as you requested. Please let me know as soon as you receive the file. Thanks.**
i. Leave a blank line after the end of your message, then type your name, class name, class section, and e-mail address on four separate lines.
j. Attach the file you have selected to the message.
k. Carefully proofread your message for errors, correcting any problems.
l. Send the message.
m. Check for new e-mail to see if your message arrived in your Inbox.
n. Close Outlook Express.

▶ Independent Challenge 2

You regularly e-mail updates of what's going on in your life to several friends who don't live nearby. You want to create a mailing list in Outlook Express to simplify addressing the updates.

a. Start Outlook Express.
b. Ask three classmates for their e-mail addresses.
c. Type the full names, proper nicknames, and e-mail addresses for these three classmates in the Address Book. Create an address card for yourself.
d. Type your instructor's full name, nickname, and e-mail address in the Address Book, if necessary.
e. Create a mailing list named Updates list that includes three classmates, your instructor, and yourself.
f. Create a new e-mail message and address the message to the Updates list mailing list.
g. Type a short message informing your classmates that you are testing the use of your new mailing list.
h. Send the message.
i. Retrieve and open the message. You should receive the message because you are included in the Updates list.
j. Close Outlook Express.

► Independent Challenge 3

Bridgefield Engineering Company (BECO) is a small engineering firm in Somerville, New Jersey, that manufactures and distributes heavy industrial machinery for factories worldwide. Because BECO has trouble reaching its customers who are located around the world in different time zones, the company decided to implement an e-mail system to facilitate contact between its employees and its customers. BECO hired you to help their employees set up and use this e-mail system. Your first task is to compile a list of typical industrial machines that BECO can manufacture and send this list to several of BECO's marketing staff located throughout the country.

a. Start Outlook Express.
b. If necessary, add your instructor and two classmates to the Address Book. Use an appropriate nickname for each person.
c. Start a new message. Address the message to three people: your instructor and two of your classmates.
d. Send a blind carbon copy (Bcc) of the message to yourself.
e. Type an appropriate topic in the Subject text box.
f. Compose the following message: **Bridgefield manufactures machines to your specifications. We can build borers, planers, horn presses, and a variety of other machines. E-mail us for further information.**, then add your full name to the end of the message.
g. Send the message.
h. Retrieve the message and view the Address Book card at the bottom of the message.
i. Close Outlook Express.

► Independent Challenge 4

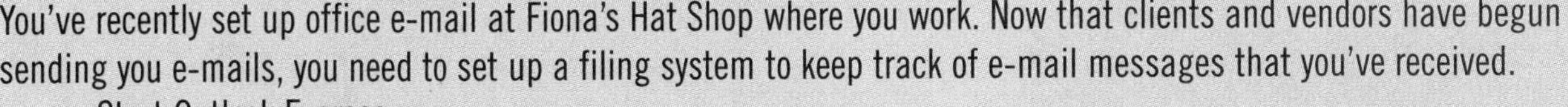

You've recently set up office e-mail at Fiona's Hat Shop where you work. Now that clients and vendors have begun sending you e-mails, you need to set up a filing system to keep track of e-mail messages that you've received.

a. Start Outlook Express.
b. Send a different brief message to four or more of your classmates, and copy each message to yourself.
c. Retrieve and view all of the e-mail messages in the Inbox.
d. Create a folder named **Vendors** and a folder named **Clients**.
e. Move one e-mail message into one folder, then copy and move one e-mail message into the second folder.
f. View the contents of both folders.
g. Close Outlook Express.

▶ Visual Workshop

Use the skills you learned in this unit to create the message shown in Figure C-27. The file attachment is located where your Project Files are stored. When you have completed the message and attached the file, send the message to your instructor or a colleague.

FIGURE C-27

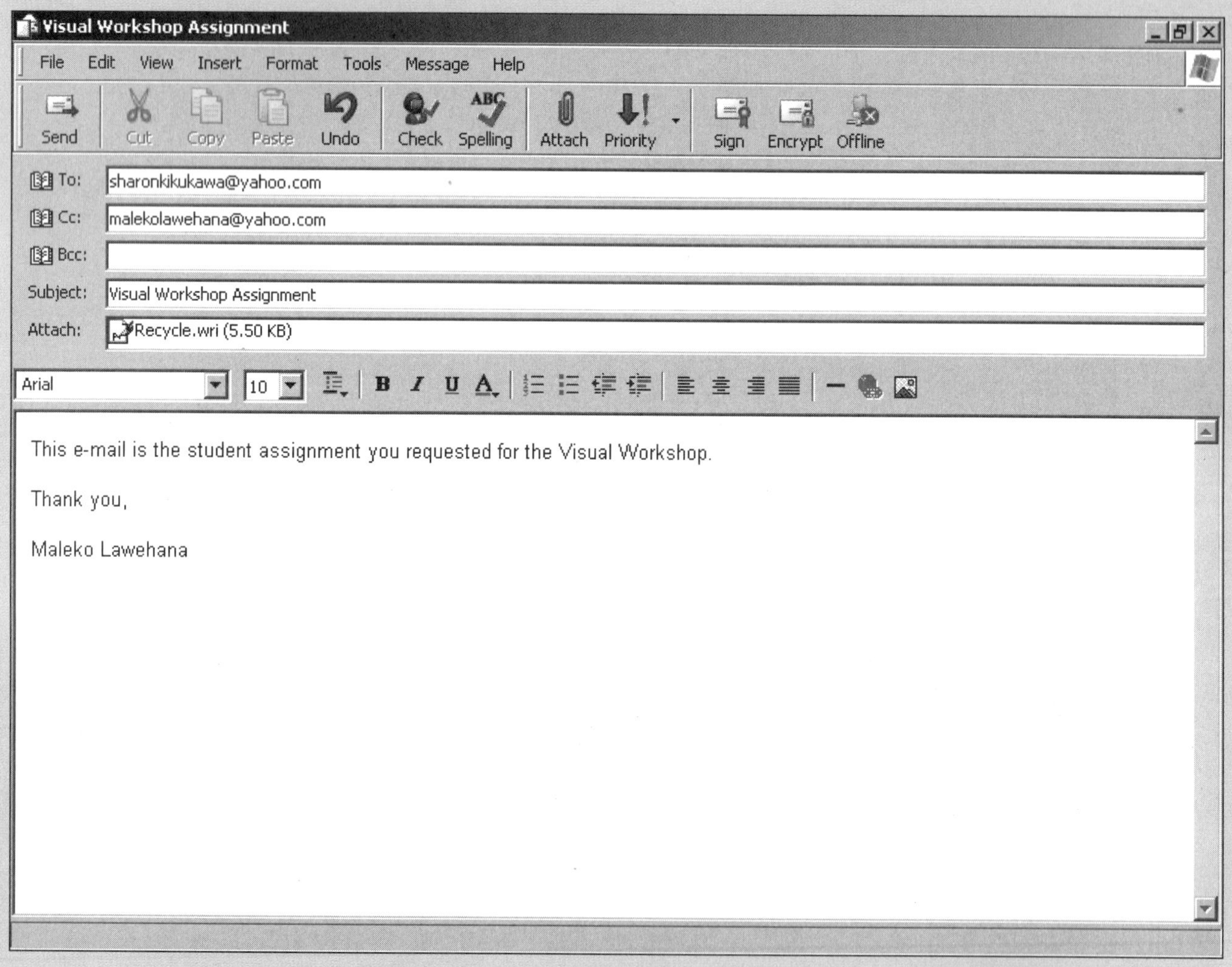

Understanding
Browser Basics

- Understand Web browser software
- Understand Hypertext Markup Language (HTML)
- Define a Web site
- Understand Web site addresses
- Start a Web browser
- Find a Web site
- Navigate through a Web site
- Use the History feature
- Create bookmarks or favorites
- Manage bookmarks in Netscape
- Manage favorites in Internet Explorer
- Check security features

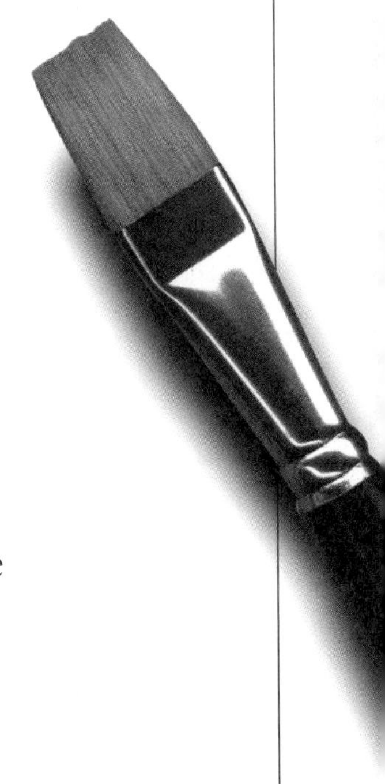

The Web consists of millions of Web sites, which are made up of millions of Web pages. To use the Web as an effective tool for both research and entertainment purposes, it's helpful to understand how the Web is structured and how to use a Web browser to find and view information. As the business manager for the Riverview Rowing Club in Victoria, British Columbia, you are responsible for organizing practices and competitions. You have decided to learn how to use the Web to find information about other rowing clubs, upcoming competitions, and sports and health issues of interest to club members.

Internet

Understanding Web Browser Software

The Web consists of a collection of files that reside on computers located all over the world. These computers are connected to one another through the Internet. If you have a computer, an Internet connection, and Web browser software, you can view these files. One of your goals as business manager for the Riverview Rowing Club is to learn to use the Web and its resources effectively. You decide to begin your exploration of the World Wide Web by learning some common terms related to the Web and Web browsing.

► Web Clients and Web Servers

When you use your Internet connection to become part of the Web, your computer becomes part of a worldwide client/server network. As a **Web client**, your computer makes requests of Web servers on the Internet. **Web servers** store the files that make up the Web, and Web clients make requests of Web servers to display and interact with those files. Figure D-1 shows how this client/server structure uses the Internet to provide multiple interconnections among the various kinds of client and server computers.

► Web Browser

A **Web browser** is the software that you run on your computer to make it work as a Web client. The Internet connects many different types of computers running different operating system software. Web browser software lets your computer communicate with all of these different types of computers. The two principal Web browsers are Netscape and Microsoft Internet Explorer. Figure D-2 shows these two popular Web browsers.

FIGURE D-1: Client/server structure of the Web

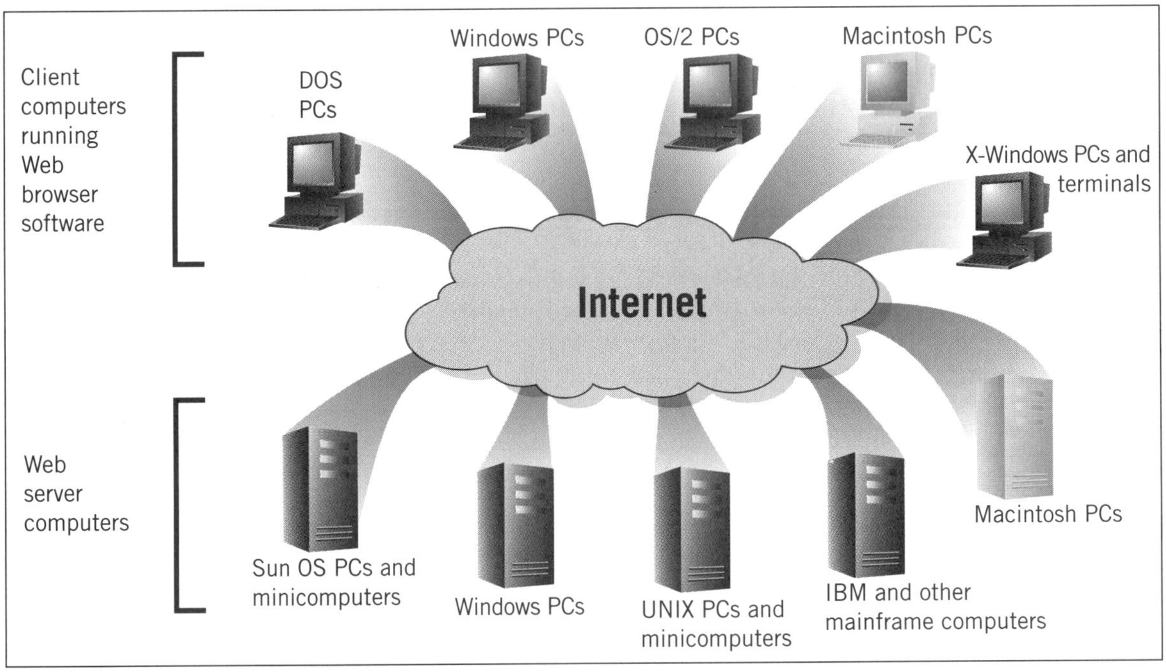

Client computers running Web browser software

DOS PCs

Windows PCs

OS/2 PCs

Macintosh PCs

X-Windows PCs and terminals

Internet

Web server computers

Sun OS PCs and minicomputers

Windows PCs

UNIX PCs and minicomputers

IBM and other mainframe computers

Macintosh PCs

FIGURE D-2: Popular Web browsers

Internet

Internet

Understanding Hypertext Markup Language (HTML)

The public files on Web servers are ordinary text files that contain text and codes. The text and codes must follow a generally accepted standard so that Web browser software can read these files. The standard used for formatting files viewed on the Web is **Hypertext Markup Language (HTML).** As you watch a Web-savvy friend use a Web browser to display various rowing Web sites, you are intrigued by how clicking the text on one Web page links to another Web page. You decide to research how text can be linkable.

Details

Hypertext Markup Language (HTML)

HTML uses codes known as **tags** to tell Web browser software how to display text and other elements contained in a document. Here is an example of a line of text that includes HTML code:

<B>Welcome to the <I>Riverview Rowing Club</I></B>

When the Web browser reads this line of HTML-coded text, it recognizes the <B> and </B> tags as instructions to display the enclosed text in bold and the <I> and </I> tags as instructions to display the enclosed text in italics. In a Web browser, the line of text would appear as follows:

Welcome to the *Riverview Rowing Club*

To view HTML codes in a Web page, you click View on the menu bar of your Web browser, then click Page Source or Source.

HTML Anchor Tag

An **HTML anchor tag** enables you to link multiple HTML documents together. Of all the HTML tags used to create a Web page, the HTML anchor tag is perhaps the most important because it enables you to easily open other Web pages that are relevant to the one you're viewing.

Links

When Web page authors use an anchor tag to reference another HTML document, they create a **link**, also known as a **hyperlink** or **hypertext link**. Links enable you to access other Web pages containing related information. As shown in Figure D-3, a Web page can link to other Web pages inside or outside a Web site. Links often appear as underlined text with a color different from the other text on the Web page so that they are easily distinguishable. An image, such as a picture or company logo, can also contain a link to another Web page. Figure D-4 shows a Web page that contains several links. When you move the mouse pointer over a link in a Web browser, the mouse pointer changes to 🖑 and the address of the linked Web page appears on the status bar.

Error Messages

Sometimes an error message appears when you click a link. Common messages are "Server busy," "DNS entry not found," and "File not found." These messages indicate that your Web browser cannot communicate with the Web server that stores the Web page you requested or cannot find the Web page because the server is busy, the Web page's location has changed permanently, or the Web page no longer exists on the Web.

FIGURE D-3: Linked Web pages

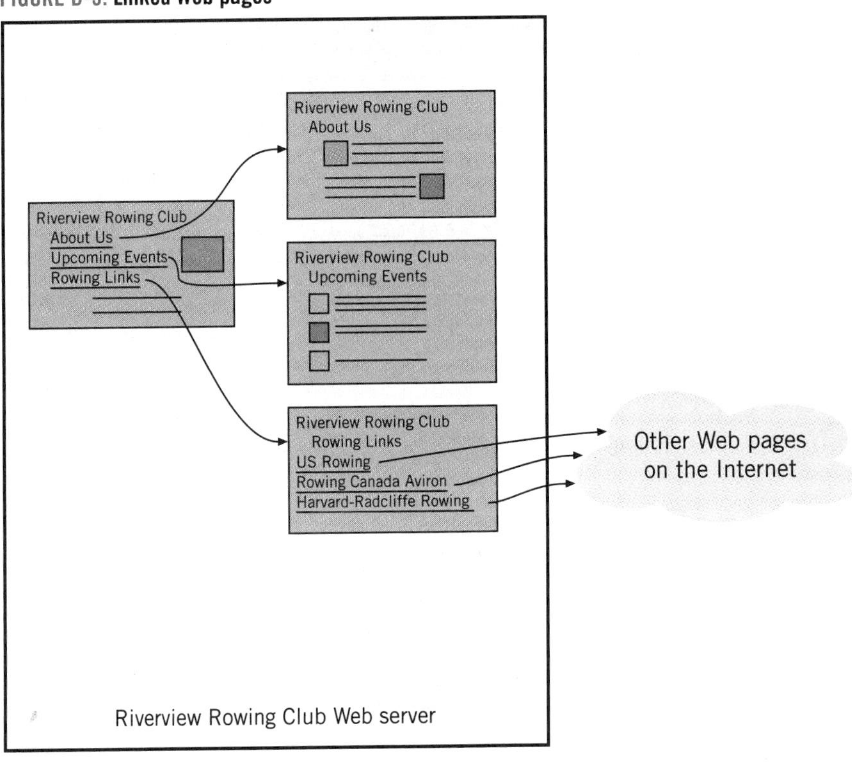

FIGURE D-4: Web page with links

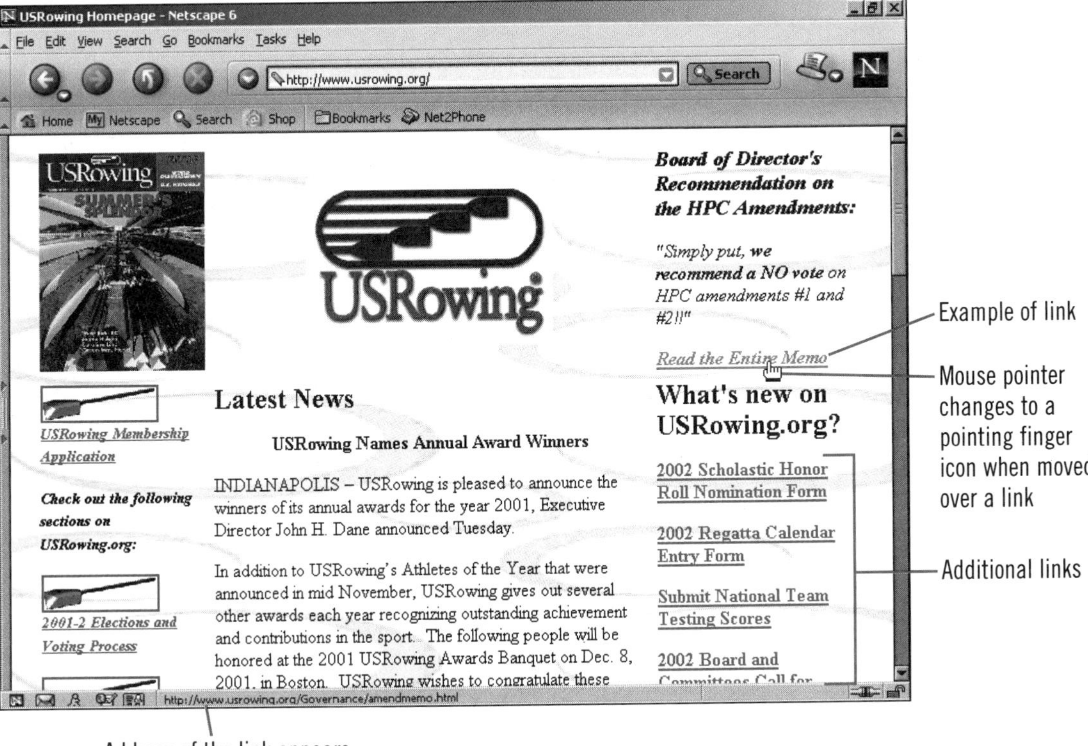

Internet

Internet

Defining a Web Site

A collection of linked Web pages that has a common theme or focus is called a **Web site**. For example, Netscape's Web site contains Web pages about Netscape products and services. Web sites are organized around a main Web page, known as a **home page**, through which you can enter the Web site and use links to open Web pages within the Web site. The first Web page that appears when you open your Web browser is also referred to as the home page. As you investigate how to use the Web for the Riverview Rowing Club, a few friends give you Web addresses for the home pages of rowing groups with which they're associated. You research to clarify what a home page is. You discover that the term is used in a few different ways.

Home Page

The term home page is commonly used when talking about the Web. It has three common meanings:

- A home page can be the main Web page that all the Web pages in a Web site are organized around and link back to; it is typically the first Web page that opens when you visit a Web site. Figure D-5 shows the Harvard-Radcliffe Rowing home page. Most of the links on this home page link to Web pages in the Harvard-Radcliffe Rowing Web site.
- A home page can be the first Web page that opens when you start your Web browser. This type of home page might be an HTML document on your own computer or the main Web page of a favorite Web site. If you are using a computer on your school's or employer's network, the Web browser might be configured to display the main Web page for the school or firm.
- A home page can be a Web page that a Web browser displays the first time you use it. This Web page is typically the main Web page of the firm or other organization that created the Web browser software.

Start Page

A home page (in the sense of the second or third definition previously listed) is sometimes called a **start page**. For example, Figure D-6 shows the home page for Capilano College in North Vancouver, British Columbia. This Web page appears when a student first opens a Web browser on a Capilano College computer. In this example, the Web page is the Web browser's start page as well as the college's home page.

FIGURE D-5: The Harvard-Radcliffe Rowing home page

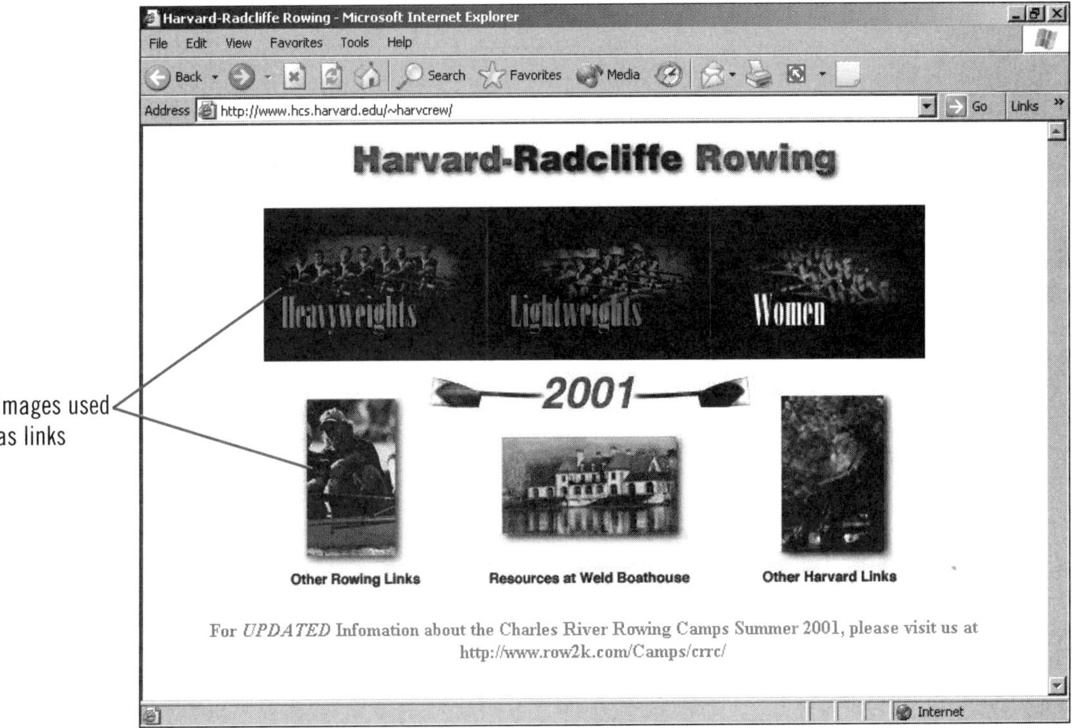

FIGURE D-6: Start page that appears on Web browsers at Capilano College

Internet

Understanding Web Site Addresses

The Internet contains many servers answering requests for Web documents from many clients. To facilitate these interactions, each computer, whether client or server, is identified by a unique number called an **Internet Protocol address (IP address).** Many servers and the individual Web sites on the servers can also be referenced by their **domain name**, a unique identifier composed of words and abbreviations. In addition, every document on the Web is identified by a unique address called a **Uniform Resource Locator.** You begin to research terms that will help you learn about the unique identification associated with each computer and each Web page.

IP Addressing
An IP address consists of a four-part number. Each part is a number ranging from 0 to 255. For example, one possible IP address is 106.29.242.17.

Domain Name Addressing
IP addresses can be difficult to remember, so most Web browsers use domain name addressing to identify a computer. Domain names are identifiers made up of words and abbreviations that are assigned to IP addresses. For example, the domain name gsb.uchicago.edu is an Internet server at the Graduate School of Business (gsb), which is an academic unit of the University of Chicago (uchicago), which is an educational institution (edu). No other computer on the Internet has the same domain name.

Top-Level Domain
The last part of a domain name is called its top-level domain. In the example gsb.uchicago.edu, the top-level domain is "edu." Figure D-7 shows the seven currently used top-level domain names.

Country Domain Names
In addition to the top-level domain names, Internet host computers outside the United States often use two-letter country domain names. Figure D-8 shows 10 frequently accessed country domain names.

Uniform Resource Locators
IP addresses and domain names identify particular computers on the Internet, but they do not identify where a Web page's HTML document resides on that computer. To find a specific Web page, you need to enter a URL, which tells the Web browser the following information:

- The transfer protocol to use when transporting the file (HTTP is the most common)
- The domain name of the computer on which the file resides
- The pathname of the folder or directory on the computer on which the file resides
- The name of the file

Figure D-9 shows an example of a URL. This URL for the parachuting club at the University of Glasgow uses the HTTP as the protocol and points to a computer at Glasgow University (gla), which is an academic institution (ac) in the United Kingdom (uk). Educational institutions in the United Kingdom use the ac domain instead of the edu domain. The Club's pathname refers to the folder in which the Parachute subfolder is stored, which contains the filename of the Web site's home page (index.html). The index.html filename is the default name for a Web site's home page.

Easy Domain Names
Many companies and organizations register unique and easy-to-remember domain names. For example, the domain name for the Disney Corporation is *www.disney.com*, and the domain name for Course Technology is *www.course.com*. Such domain names are easier to remember and enter in a Web browser than Web addresses that include pathnames and filenames.

FIGURE D-7: **Top-level Internet domain names**

Domain Name	Description
com	Businesses and other commercial enterprises
edu	Postsecondary educational institutions
gov	U.S. government agency, bureau, or department
int	International organizations
mil	U.S. military unit or agency
net	Network service provider or resource
org	Other organizations, usually charitable or not-for-profit

FIGURE D-8: **Examples of country domain names**

Domain Name	Country	Domain Name	Country
au	Australia	jp	Japan
ca	Canada	nl	Netherlands
de	Germany	na	Norway
fl	Finland	se	Sweden
fr	France	uk	United Kingdom

FIGURE D-9: **Structure of a URL and its Web page**

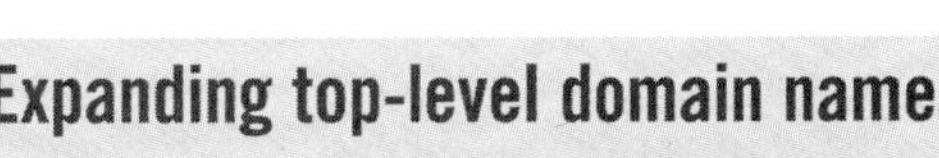

Expanding top-level domain names

ICANN, the nonprofit corporation responsible for making Internet domain names available, is adding seven new top-level domain names. Several of the top-level domains are designated to be used by a specific type of organization. The seven new top-level domain names include:

top-level domain	for use by
aero	Air-transport industry
biz	Businesses
coop	Cooperative organizations
info	Information service providers
museum	Museums
name	Individuals
pro	Accountants, lawyers, and physicians

Internet

Starting a Web Browser

You use a Web browser to access the millions of Web pages on the Web. The two most popular Web browsers are Netscape and Internet Explorer. You decide to practice starting a Web browser so that you can begin to use the Web as a source for rowing information.

In the steps that follow, you will start either Netscape or Internet Explorer, depending on which Web browser is installed on your computer.

Trouble?

The start page for your Web browser might be different from the Web pages shown in Figures D-10 and D-11.

1. To start your Web browser:
   - If you are using Netscape, click **Start** on the taskbar, point to **Programs** or **All Programs**, point to **Netscape 6.2**, then click **Netscape 6.2**
     Figure D-10 shows the Netscape Web browser window. If your Programs menu displays a different version number for Netscape, such as Netscape 6.1, click that instead. To match the figures in this unit, if necessary, press F9 to hide the My Sidebar pane in Netscape.
   - If you are using Internet Explorer, click **Start** on the taskbar, point to **Programs** or **All Programs,** then click **Internet Explorer**
     Figure D-11 shows the Internet Explorer Web browser window.
2. If the Web browser window is not maximized, click the **Maximize button**
3. Find the following components in your Web browser window, then read the description of each component:
   - **Title bar**: Shows the name of the open Web page and the Web browser's name and contains the Minimize, Restore Down/Maximize, and Close buttons.
   - **Menu bar**: Contains the File, Edit, View, and Help menus and other specialized menus that allow you to navigate the Web.
   - **Scroll bar**: Allows you to move a Web page up, down, right, and left if the Web page is longer or wider than the window.
   - **Status bar**: Indicates the name of the Web page that is loading, the load status (partial or complete), and important messages such as "Document: Done." When you point to a link, its URL also appears on the status bar.
4. Find the following buttons in your Web browser, then read the description of each button:
   - **Back button**: Allows you to go back to a previously viewed Web page. If you have just opened your Web browser, the Back button will be dimmed, or inactive.
   - **Reload button** or **Refresh button**: Allows you to load again a Web page that currently appears in your Web browser so that you can view the latest information (such as news headlines).
   - **Home button**: Allows you to return to the home page (or start page) for your Web browser.
   - **Stop button**: Allows you to stop loading the contents of a Web page. In Netscape, the Stop button will be dimmed if you just loaded the program.

FIGURE D-10: Netscape Web browser window

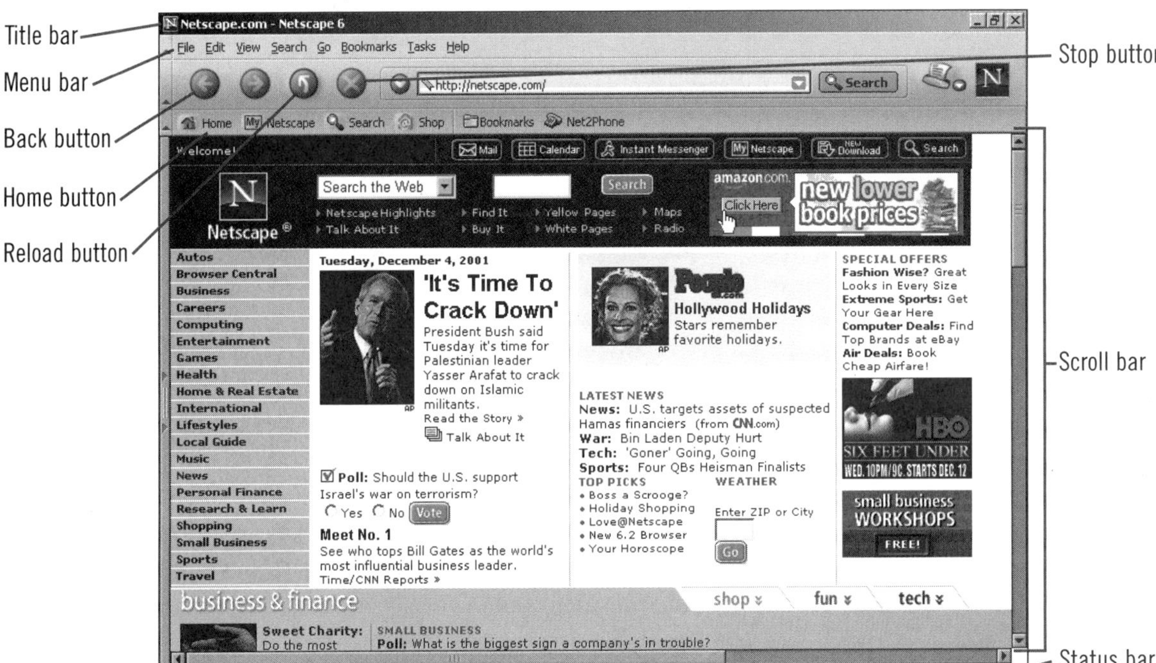

FIGURE D-11: Internet Explorer Web browser window

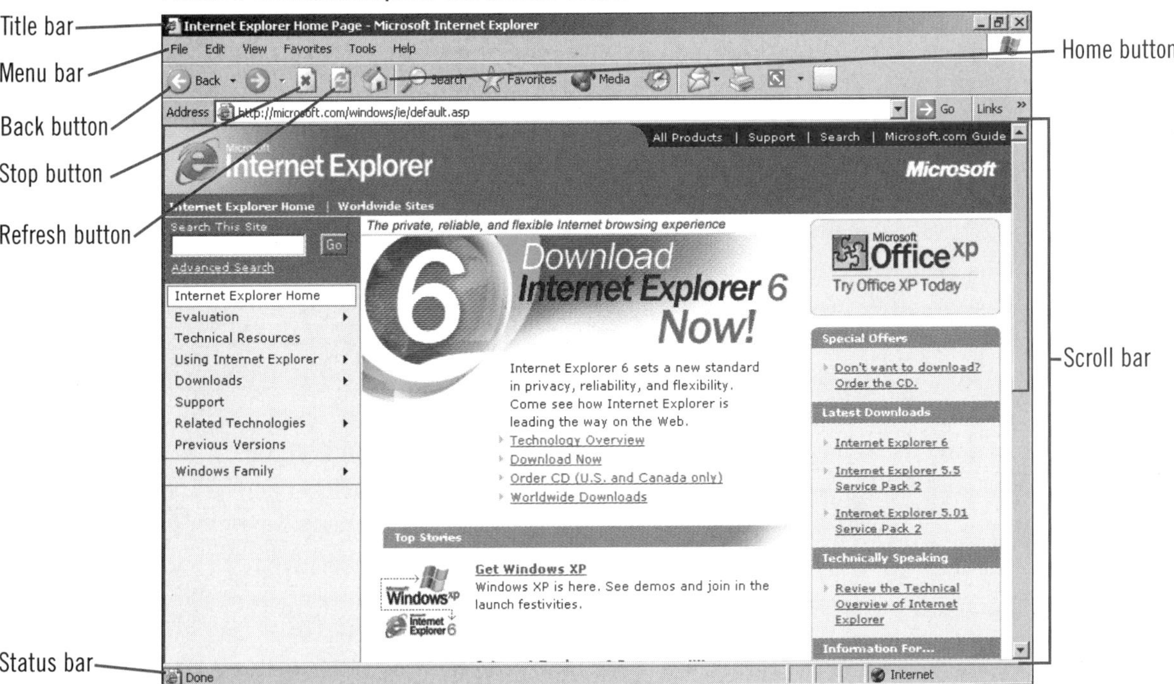

Internet

Unit D

Internet

Finding a Web Site

After you start your Web browser, you can begin learning how to use it to find information on the Web. The fastest way to go to a specific Web site on the Web is to enter its address in the Location text box in Netscape or in the Address text box in Internet Explorer. At a recent competition, you got the URLs for a couple rowing Web sites that friends recommended. You decide to check them out.

Steps

QuickTip

You can quickly select a URL by clicking to the right of the URL in the Address and Location text boxes.

Trouble?

If you cannot access the Web sites in this lesson, go to *www.course.com/illustrated/internet3*, click the Unit D link, then use the links under Lesson 6.

1. To enter a URL:
   - In Netscape, select the **URL** in the Location text box
     The URL in the Location text box is selected as shown in Figure D-12.
   - In Internet Explorer, select the **URL** in the Address text box
     The URL in the Address text box is selected as shown in Figure D-13.
2. Type **rowingcanada.org**
   As soon as you start to type the new URL, the old URL disappears. Even though a complete URL contains the protocol (such as http), followed by a colon and two slashes, both Netscape and Internet Explorer add this prefix automatically, making it unnecessary to type it.
3. Press **[Enter]**
   The Rowing Canada Web site appears in your Web browser window. Figure D-14 shows the Rowing Canada home page in Netscape. Because Web sites are constantly being updated, the Web site on your screen might appear differently from the one shown in Figure D-14.
4. Select the **URL** in the Location text box in Netscape or the **URL** in the Address text box in Internet Explorer
5. Type **row2k.com**, then press **[Enter]**
   The row2k home page appears in your Web browser window. Figure D-15 shows the row2k home page in Internet Explorer.

FIGURE D-12: Location text box in Netscape

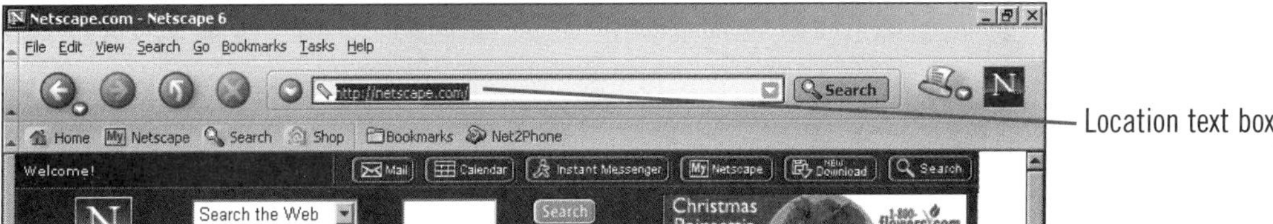

FIGURE D-13: Address text box in Internet Explorer

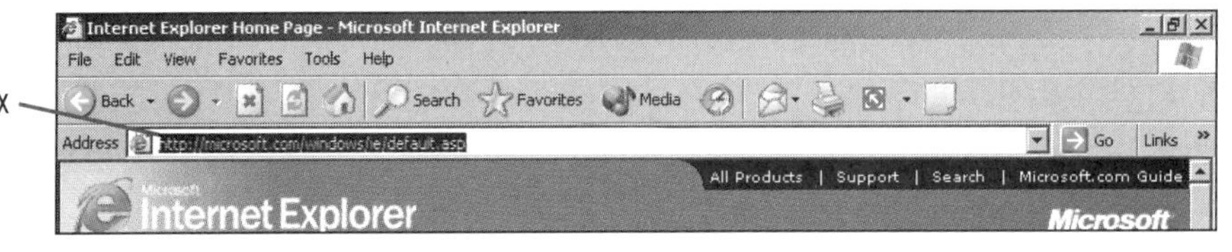

FIGURE D-14: Rowing Canada home page in Netscape

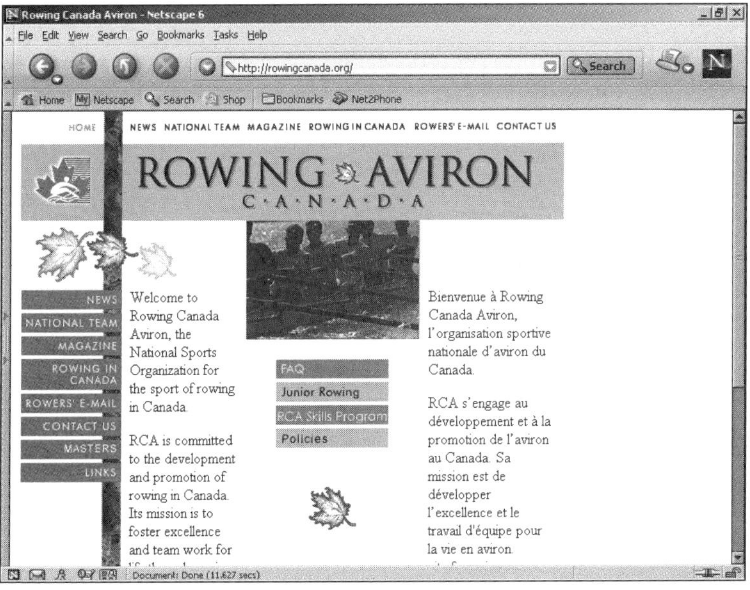

FIGURE D-15: row2K home page in Internet Explorer

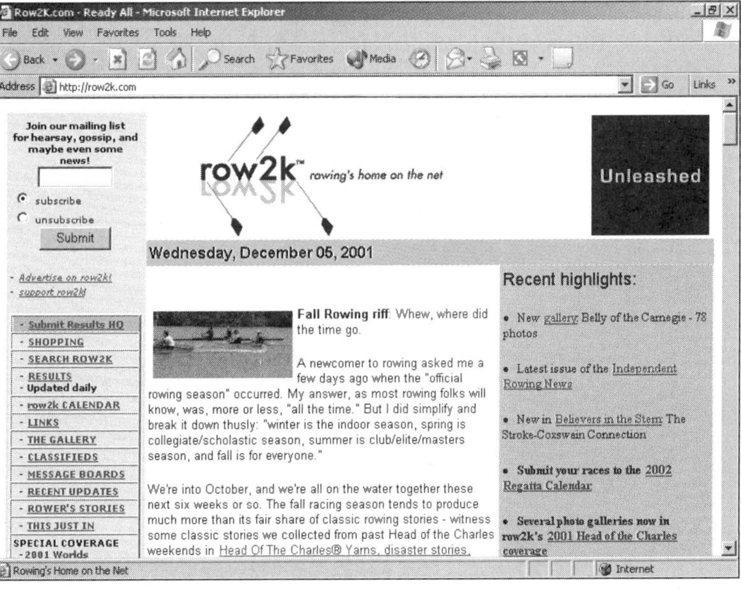

Navigating Through a Web Site

You can move from one Web page to a related one by clicking links. Thanks to links, you can browse through a Web site from Paris, France one minute and then look at a Web site in Tokyo, Japan, the next minute, simply by clicking links. Club members have expressed an interest in developing a Web site for the Riverview Rowing Club. Your boss has asked you to explore the Internet and find some examples of Web sites for other rowing organizations.

Steps

1. Select the **URL** in the Location text box in Netscape or the **URL** in the Address text box in Internet Explorer
2. Type **www.course.com/illustrated/internet3**, press **[Enter]**, click the **Unit D link**, then click the **Rowing Canada link** under Lesson 7
   Because you typed this domain name previously, the required URL appears before you finish typing it. You can click the URL instead of typing it in.
3. Point to the **National Team link** on the left side of the window
   Notice that your mouse pointer changes to as shown in Figure D-16.
4. Click the **National Team link**
   The National Team Web page appears. This Web page contains links to up-to-date information about the Canadian National Rowing Team.
5. Point to the **Home link** in the top left of the window
   Notice that the word Home is not underlined and formatted in a different color like the text links shown in Figure D-17. Although this appears to be a text link, it is an image.
6. Click the **Home link**
   You return to the home page for Rowing Canada.
7. Click the **Links link** on the left side of the window
   The Links Web page appears. This Web page contains links to other rowing Web sites, including the Web sites of several other clubs.
8. Scroll down the Web page, then click the link for St. Catharine's Rowing Club
   The St. Catharine's Rowing Club home page appears.
9. Click the **Back button** in Netscape or in Internet Explorer
   The Rowing Canada Web page reappears.
10. Click the **Forward button** in Netscape or in Internet Explorer
    The St. Catharine's Rowing Club Web page reappears.

Trouble?

Be sure to click the Home link to return to the Rowing Canada home page instead of the Home button on the toolbar (which will display the home page for your Web browser).

FIGURE D-16: Link in Netscape

FIGURE D-17: Image link that looks like a text link

Internet

Using the History Feature

In addition to using the Back and Forward buttons to move to and from previously visited Web pages, Netscape and Internet Explorer include a History feature. The **History** feature is a list of Web sites you've visited over the past days or weeks, which can help you locate Web sites you've visited in previous sessions on the Web. As you research equipment for the Riverview Rowing Club, you realize that you want to revisit some of the Web sites you visited yesterday. You use the History feature of your Web browser to find the desired Web sites.

Netscape History Window

1. **In Netscape, click Tasks on the menu bar, point to Tools, then click History**
   The History window opens. As shown in Figure D-18, previously visited Web sites are organized in folders by the day they were viewed.
2. **If necessary, double-click the Today folder to display its contents**
   The list of domain names for Web sites you visited today appears below the Today folder.
3. **Double-click the domain name for one of the rowing Web sites in the Today folder list, then double-click one of the URLs listed**
   The Web page opens in the Web browser.
4. **Click the History button on the taskbar, then click the Close button on the History window**
   The History window closes.

Internet Explorer History List

1. **In Internet Explorer, click the History button on the toolbar**
   The Explorer Bar opens on the left side of the document window, displaying the History list. Each folder indicates one Web site and contains links to individual Web pages you visited on that Web site.
2. **Click one of the Web site folders listed in the History list**
3. **Click one of the URLs listed in the Web site folder you clicked**
   The Web page for the URL you selected appears. Figure D-19 shows the History list. Notice that the folder for the row2k Web site is selected and that the URL visited via the row2k Web site is listed below the row2k folder.
4. **Click on the toolbar**
   The History list closes.

Trouble?

If an alert box opens, click OK.

FIGURE D-18: History window in Netscape

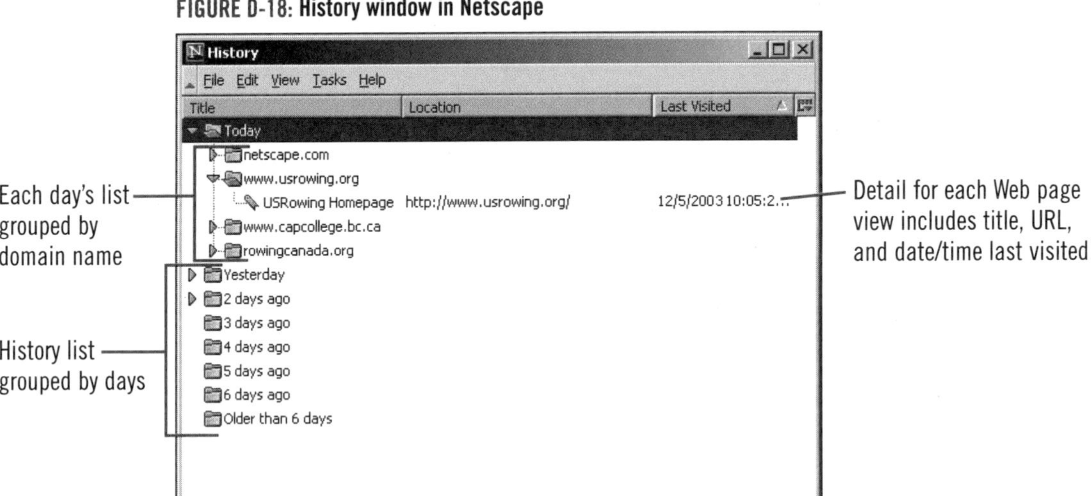

FIGURE D-19: History list in Internet Explorer

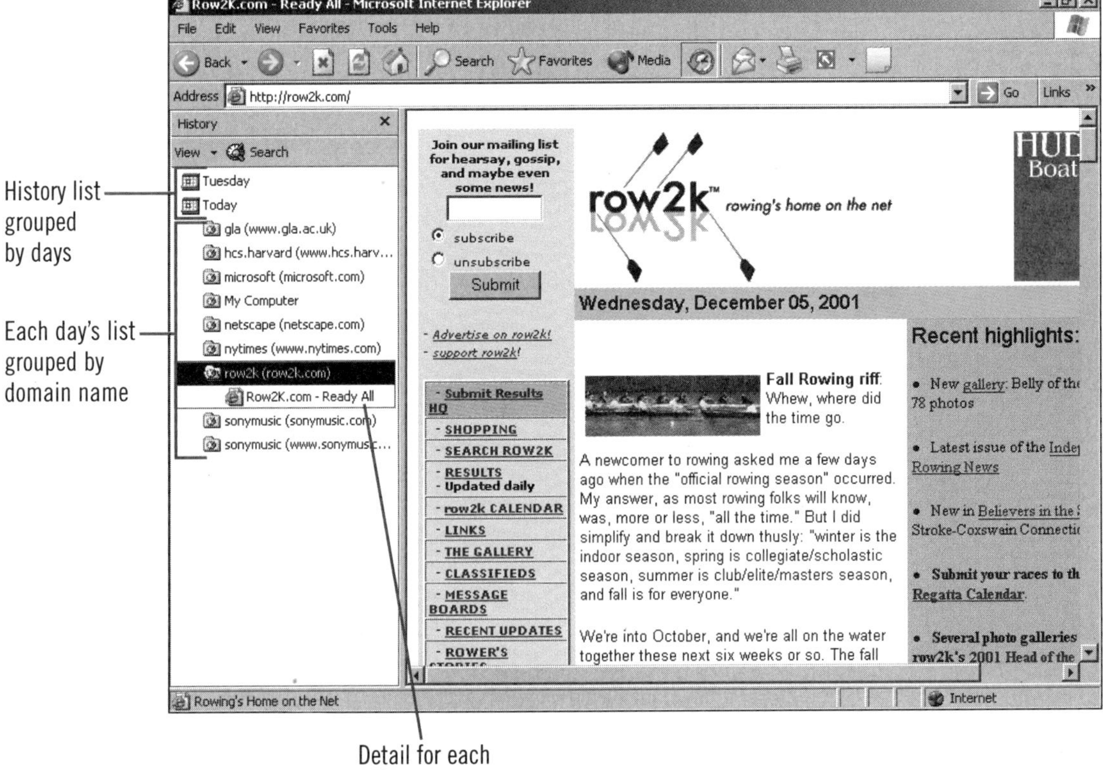

Internet

Creating Bookmarks or Favorites

Both Netscape and Internet Explorer allow you to create a customized menu in your Web browser containing shortcuts to Web sites you specify. In Netscape, these shortcuts are called **bookmarks**, and in Internet Explorer they're called **favorites**. You use bookmarks and favorites to store and organize the URLs of Web pages that you have visited so you can return to them easily. As business manager for the Riverview Rowing Club, you are hoping to take your team to compete in Europe. You start collecting information for the prospective trip by checking out a Web site that includes links to European rowing clubs. You create a bookmark or favorite for a Web site that contains useful information for planning the trip.

Netscape Bookmarks

1. Select the **URL** in the Location text box, type **www.course.com/illustrated/internet3**, press **[Enter]**, click the **Unit D link**, then click the **Rowing in Europe link** under Lesson 9
   A Web page containing a list of links to rowing clubs in Europe appears. As you can see, the URL is very long.
2. Click the **Bookmarks button** under the Location text box, then click **Add Bookmark**, as shown in Figure D-20
   You added the Web site to your list of bookmarks.
3. Click the **Home button**, click, then click the **Rowing Clubs bookmark**
   The Web page with the list of international rowing Web sites appears.

Internet Explorer Favorites

1. Click in the **Address text box**, type **www.course.com/illustrated/internet3**, press **[Enter]**, click the **Unit D link**, then click the **Rowing in Europe link** under Lesson 9
   A Web page containing a list of links to rowing clubs in Europe appears.
2. Click **Favorites** on the menu bar, then click **Add to Favorites**
   The Add Favorite dialog box opens, as shown in Figure D-21.
3. Click **OK**
   You added the Web site to your Favorites list.
4. Click the **Home button** on the toolbar, then click the **Favorites button** on the toolbar
   The Explorer Bar opens, displaying the Favorites list. You can open a list of your favorites by clicking either the Favorites button or Favorites on the menu bar.
5. Click the **Rowing Clubs link**
   The Web page with the list of European rowing Web sites appears in the right pane as shown in Figure D-22. (Your Favorites list might contain different favorites.)
6. Click on the toolbar
   The Favorites list closes.

Trouble?

Your Add Favorite dialog box might show more information than the dialog box in Figure D-21.

FIGURE D-20: Adding a bookmark in Netscape

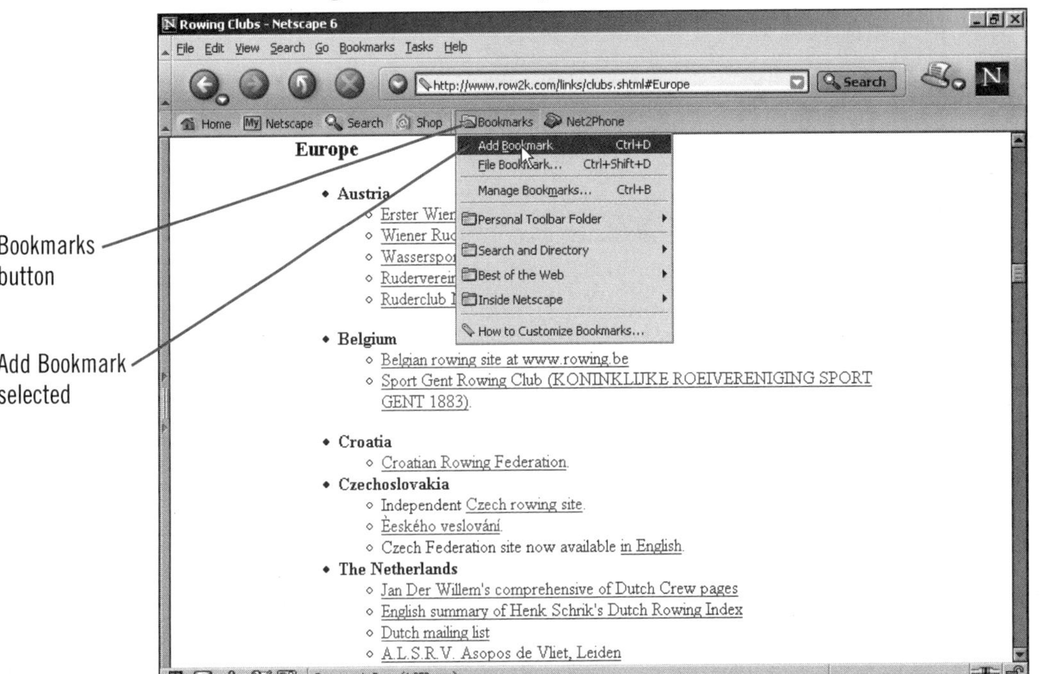

FIGURE D-21: Add Favorite dialog box in Internet Explorer

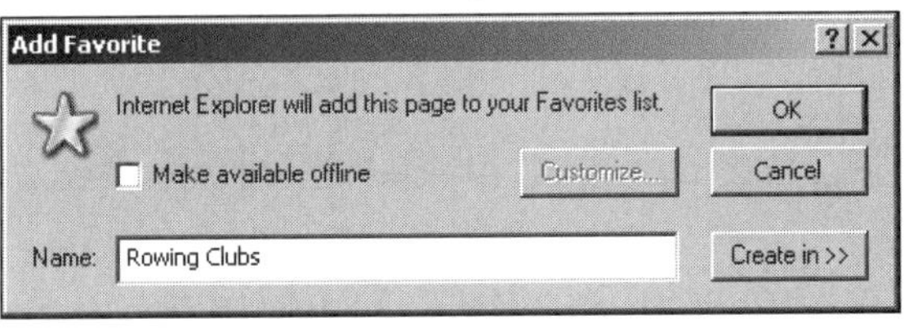

FIGURE D-22: Favorites list in Internet Explorer

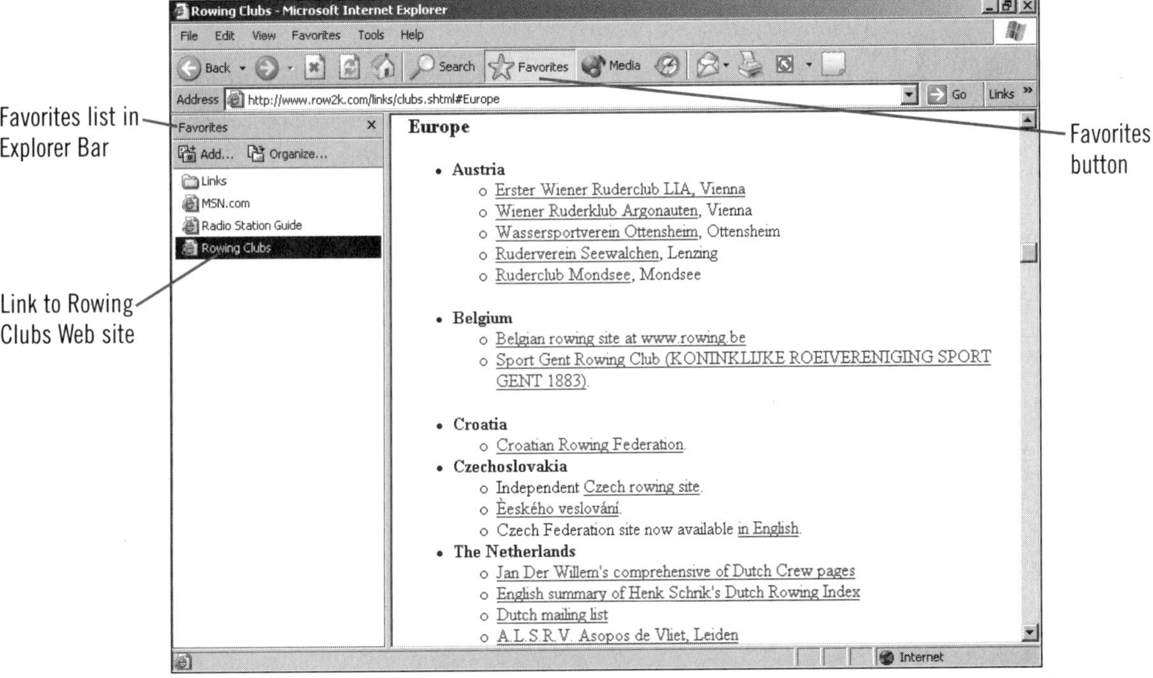

Internet

Managing Bookmarks in Netscape

As your bookmarks list grows large, it can become difficult to locate a bookmark when you need it. You can organize bookmarks into folders, so that you can group them by category. Your boss asked you to find a way to organize the bookmarks so that club members can quickly find the desired Web sites and visit them when they have time. You decide to create a folder called Rowing Bookmarks. You will save the bookmark of a rowing Web site to the Rowing Bookmarks folder.

Trouble?

If you are using Internet Explorer, go to the next lesson.

Trouble?

Depending on your Netscape settings, the Bookmarks window might display different folders from the ones shown in Figure D-23.

QuickTip

To delete a bookmark or bookmarks folder, click the Bookmarks button, click Manage Bookmarks, right-click the bookmark or folder, then click Delete.

1. In Netscape, click the **Bookmarks button** under the Location text box, then click **Manage Bookmarks**
2. Click **File** on the menu bar, then click **New Folder**
   The Create New Folder dialog box opens. The text "New Folder" appears in the Create a New Folder named text box.
3. Select the text **New Folder**, then type **Rowing Bookmarks**
   Figure D-23 shows the completed Create New Folder dialog box.
4. Click **OK**
   Notice that a new folder called Rowing Bookmarks is listed in the Bookmarks window.
5. Click the **Close button** on the Bookmarks window
   The Bookmarks window closes.
6. Select the **URL** in the Location text box, type **www.course.com/illustrated/internet3**, press **[Enter]**, click the **Unit D link**, then click the **Row2k.com link** under Lesson 10
   The row2k Web site appears.
7. Click , click **File Bookmark**, click **Rowing Bookmarks** in the Add Bookmark dialog box, then click **OK**
8. Click the **Back button** , click , point to **Rowing Bookmarks**, then point to **Row2K.com – Ready All**
   Figure D-24 shows the row2k Web site bookmark.
9. Click **Row2K.com – Ready All**
   The row2k Web site appears.

FIGURE D-23: Create New Folder dialog box in Netscape

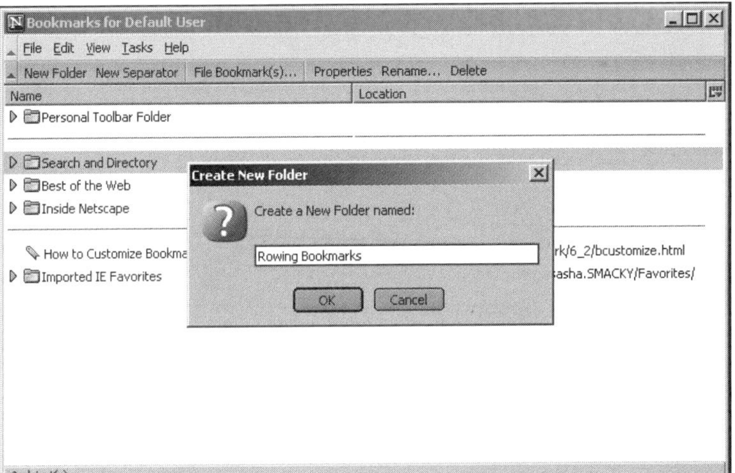

FIGURE D-24: Selecting the Row2k.com bookmark from the Rowing Bookmarks folder

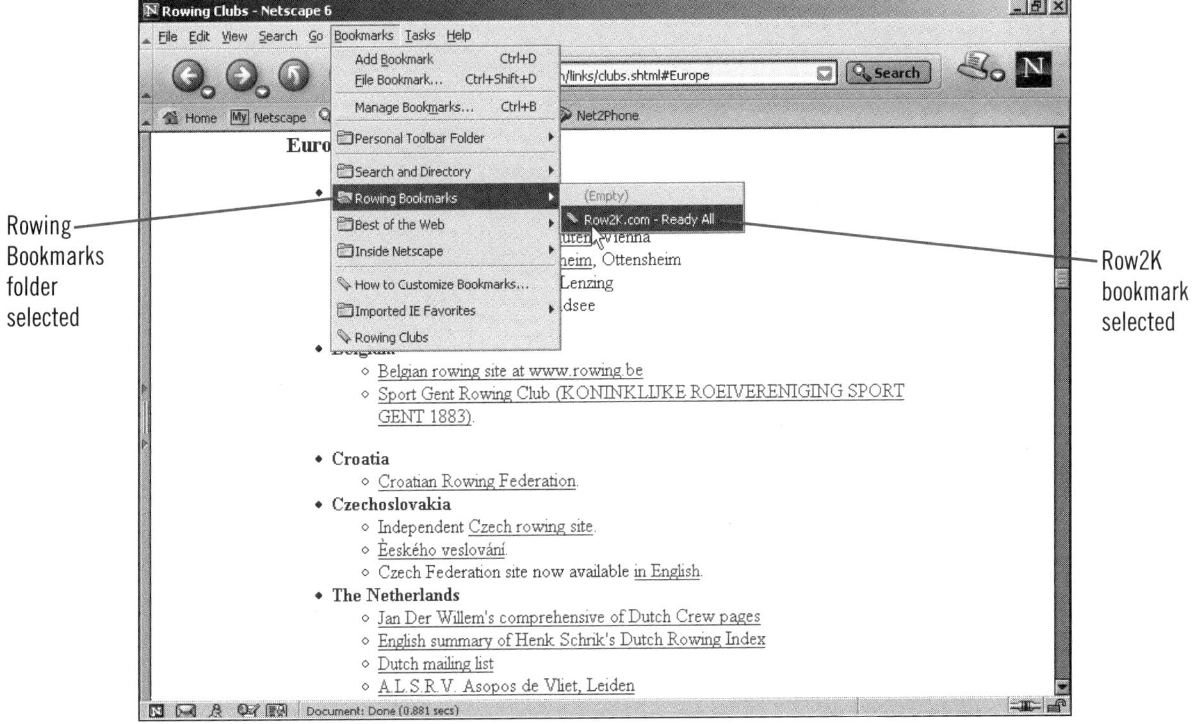

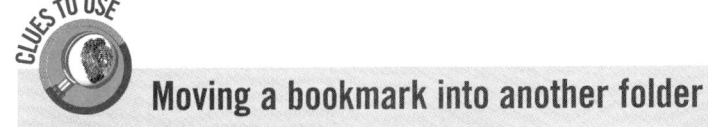

Moving a bookmark into another folder

To move a bookmark into another folder:

- Click the Bookmarks Button, then click Manage Bookmarks.
- Click the triangle next to the folder containing the bookmark you want to move so that you can view the folder contents.
- If you want to create a new folder, right-click in the area of the window where you want to create the folder, click New Folder on the shortcut menu, enter the name of the folder in the dialog box, then click OK.
- Drag the bookmark that you want to move into the new folder.
- Click the Close button.

Internet

Internet

Managing Favorites in Internet Explorer

As your Favorites list grows large, it can become difficult to locate a favorite when you need it. You can organize favorites into folders, so that you can group them by category. Your boss asked you to find a way to organize the favorites so that club members can quickly find the desired Web sites and visit them when they have time. You decide to create a folder called Rowing Information. You will save a rowing Web site to the Rowing Information folder.

Trouble?

If you are using Netscape, go to the next lesson.

1. In Internet Explorer, select the **URL** in the Address text box, type **www.course.com/illustrated/internet3**, press **[Enter]**, click the **Unit D link**, then click the **Row2k.com link** under Lesson 11
   The row2k Web site appears.
2. Click **Favorites** on the menu bar, then click **Add to Favorites**
   The Add Favorite dialog box opens.

Trouble?

If you collapsed the Add Favorite dialog box instead of expanding it, click Create in again.

3. Click **Create in**
   The Add Favorite dialog box expands to include a list of subfolders contained in your Favorites folder.
4. Verify that the **Favorites folder** is selected, then click **New Folder**
   The Create New Folder dialog box opens.
5. Type **Rowing Information**
   Figure D-25 shows the completed Create New Folder dialog box.
6. Click **OK**, verify that a new folder named Rowing Information is listed in Favorites, then click **OK** again
7. Click the **Back button** on the toolbar, click the **Favorites button** on the toolbar, then click **Rowing Information** in the Favorites list
   Figure D-26 shows the link in the Favorites list to the row2k.com Web page. You can change the width of the Explorer Bar where the Favorites list is displayed by moving the mouse pointer over the right border of the pane until it changes to a double-headed arrow, then dragging the border left or right to change the pane width.

QuickTip

To delete a favorite or favorites folder, right-click the favorite or folder in the Favorites list, click Delete, then click Yes.

8. Click the **Row2K.com link**
   The row2k Web page appears.
9. Click on the toolbar
   The Favorites list closes.

FIGURE D-25: Creating a new Favorites folder in Internet Explorer

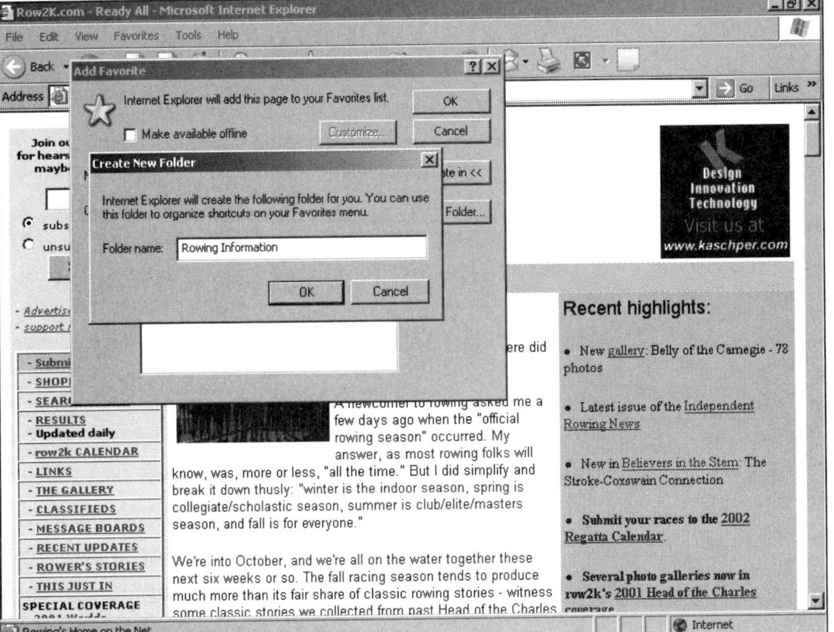

FIGURE D-26: Selecting the Row2K.com favorite from the Rowing Information folder in Internet Explorer

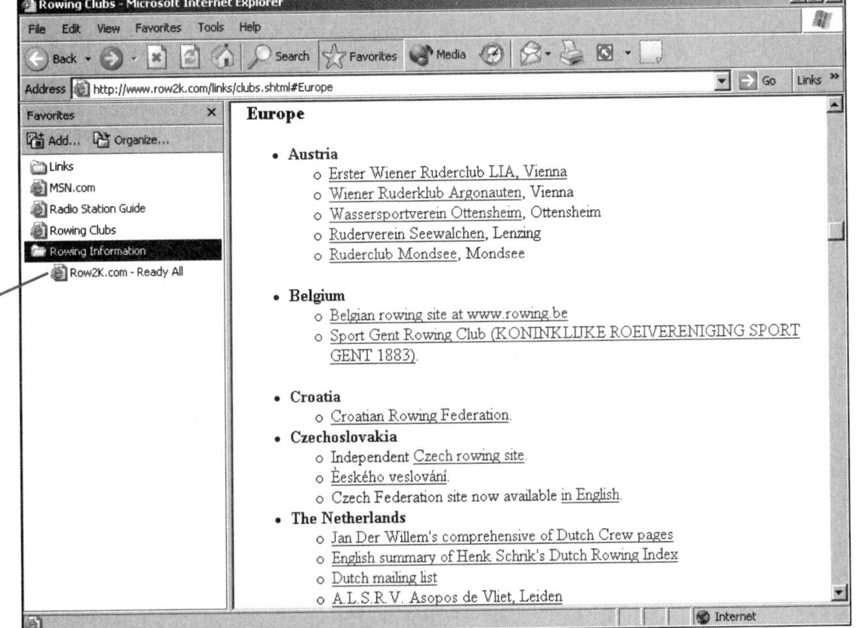

Row2K.com favorite filed in Rowing Information folder

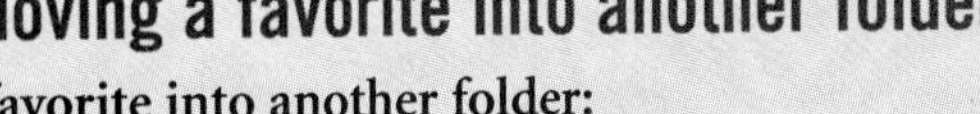

Moving a favorite into another folder

To move a favorite into another folder:

- Click Favorites on the menu bar, then click Organize Favorites. (The command on the Favorites menu might be Organize.)
- If you want to create a new folder, click Create Folder, type the name of the new folder, then press [Enter].
- If necessary, click the folder containing the favorite you want to move, then scroll until the favorite is visible in the list.
- Drag the favorite that you want to move onto the new folder.
- Click Close.

Internet

Checking Security Features

Encryption is a method of scrambling and encoding data transmissions to reduce the risk that any person who intercepts the Web page as it travels across the Internet will be able to decode and read the Web page's contents. Web sites use encrypted transmission to send and receive information such as credit card numbers, addresses, and phone numbers. You can check a Web page to determine if the Web page will be encrypted (also called secured) during its transmission from the Web server. Your rowing team will be attending a competition on Lake Mead, so your boss has asked you to make reservations at a hotel in Las Vegas. Before you enter the Riverview Rowing Club's credit card number, you need to determine whether the Web site is secure.

Steps

1. Select the **URL** in the Location text box in Netscape or the **URL** in the Address text box in Internet Explorer, type **www.course.com/illustrated/internet3**, press **[Enter]**, click the **Unit D link**, then click the **Luxor Hotel Reservations link** under Lesson 12
   The Web page for the Luxor Hotel in Las Vegas appears. Before you send your credit card number over the Internet, you should check the Web page's security features. In Netscape, an open lock in the lower-right corner of a Web page means the Web page is not secure. In Internet Explorer, the absence of a locked padlock in the status bar means that the Web page is not secure.
2. Click the **Online Reservations link**
3. If an alert box appears, click **OK** to close it
4. To view security information:
   - In **Netscape**, click the **Security button** in the lower-right corner of the status bar, as shown in Figure D-27
     The Page Info dialog box opens. The Web page you accessed is encrypted, meaning that you can safely enter and send your credit card number. You can click each tab in the dialog box to get additional security information.
   - In **Internet Explorer**, double-click the **Security button** on the status bar, as shown in Figure D-28
     The Certificate dialog box opens. You can click each tab in the dialog box to read security information.
5. Click the **Close button**
6. Close your Web browser

Trouble?

Sometimes, when you open a Web site, additional windows containing Web pages related to the Web site also open. These Web pages typically contain advertisements. If additional windows open after you click the Luxor Hotel Reservations link, close the windows.

FIGURE D-27: Netscape security information

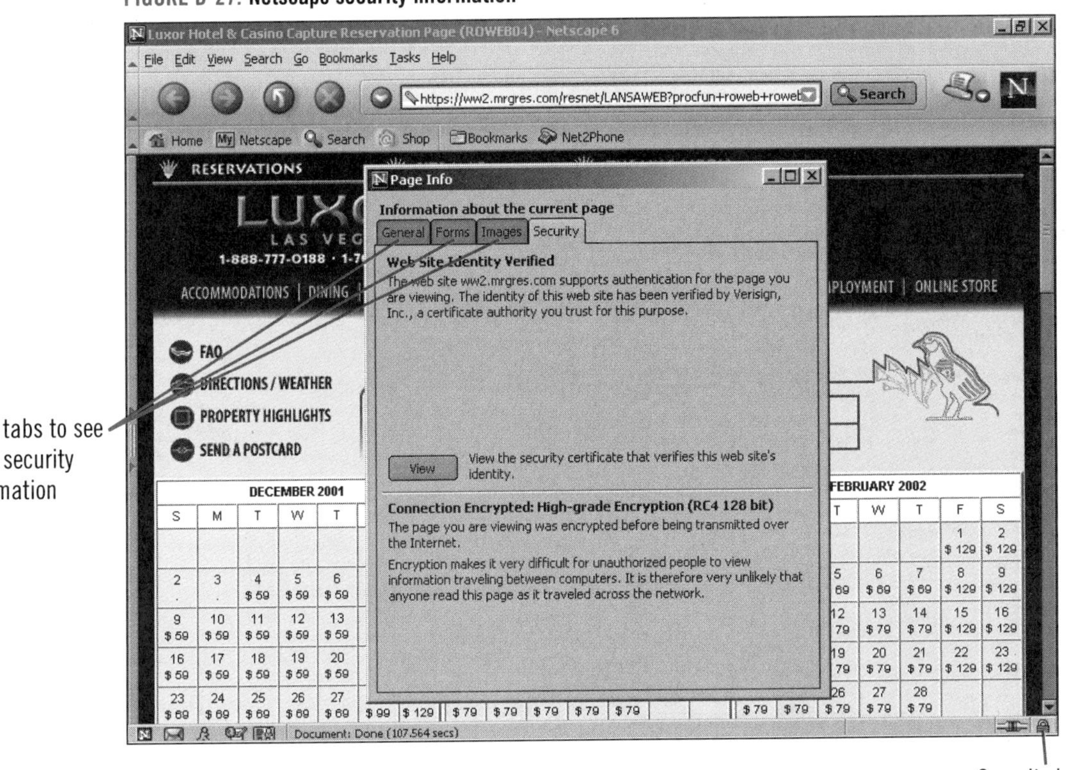

FIGURE D-28: Internet Explorer security information

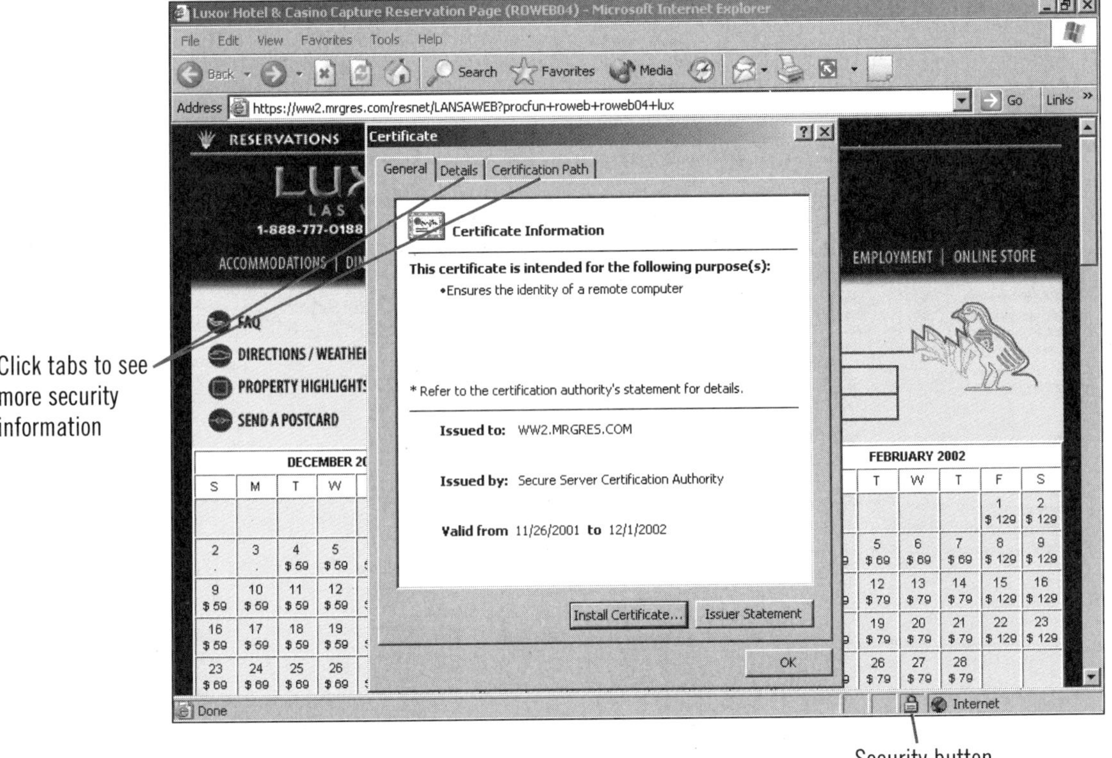

Internet

Internet

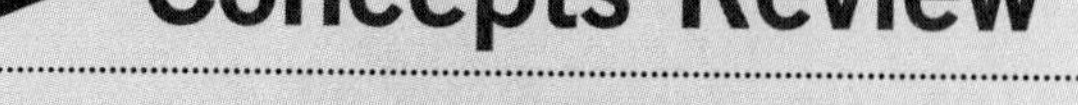

Practice

► Concepts Review

Identify each element of the Netscape window shown in Figure D-29.

FIGURE D-29

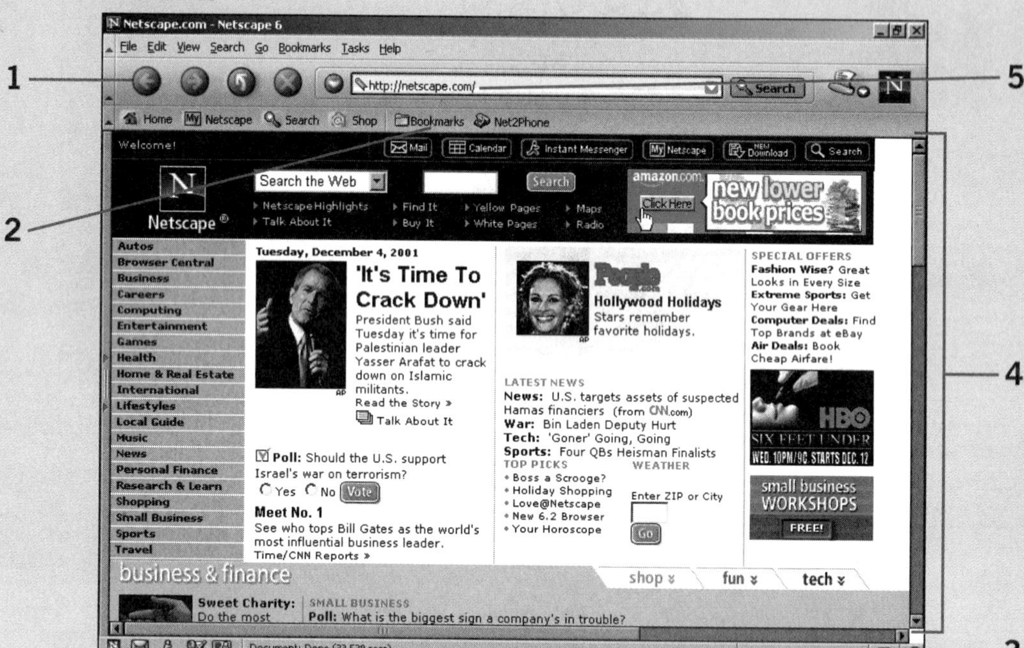

Identify each element of the Internet Explorer window shown in Figure D-30.

FIGURE D-30

Practice

Match each term with the statement that describes it.

11. Web browser	**a.** The first Web page that opens when a Web browser starts
12. HTML	**b.** The software that runs a computer to make it work as a Web client
13. Link	**c.** The four-part addressing scheme
14. Start page	**d.** The standard used to format Web page elements for display in Web browsers
15. URL	**e.** A reference to a Web page containing related information
16. Encryption	**f.** A security feature

Select the best answer from the list of choices.

17. Web page authors link HTML documents using:

a. HTML anchor tags.
b. Internet Explorer.
c. Netscape.
d. Encryption.

18. The numerical address that identifies each computer on the Internet is called the:

a. Domain name address.
b. Hierarchical address.
c. IP address.
d. URL.

19. Which of the following is an example of an "easy" domain name?

a. www.course.com
b. gphsrv1.geophys2.uni-bremen.de/~hherm/brv/rud_link/euro_rud_list.htm
c. 106.29.242.17
d. gsb.uchicago.edu

20. Which of the following is one of the recently introduced top-level domain names?

a. com
b. coop
c. ac
d. int

Internet

Skills Review

Note: To access the Skills Review Web sites, go to www.course.com/illustrated/internet3, click the Unit D link, then click the desired link under the appropriate Skills Review.

1. **Start a Web browser.**
   - **a.** Start your Web browser.
   - **b.** Wait for the home page to load.
   - **c.** Follow links on the home page to two or three Web sites that interest you.
   - **d.** Make a list of the Web sites you visited. Include the URL of each Web site and provide a brief description of each Web site.
   - **e.** Close the Web browser.

2. **Find a Web site.**
   - **a.** Start your Web browser.
   - **b.** Wait for the home page to load.
   - **c.** Type the URL for Course Technology: **course.com**.
   - **d.** On the Course Technology Web site, move the mouse pointer around the Web page to identify links.
   - **e.** Consider these questions: How are the links identified on the Web page? Are there any links that surprised you because they didn't look like links until you placed the mouse pointer over them?
   - **f.** Follow one link.
   - **g.** Consider these questions: What link did you follow? How did you identify the link on the Web page? Did the linked content relate to the link you followed?

3. **Navigate through a Web site.**
   - **a.** Go to the Surfer's Magazine Web site.
   - **b.** Follow the link to photos.
   - **c.** Follow one of the links to a particular photographer's photos.
   - **d.** Click one of the pictures to enlarge it.
   - **e.** Go back to the home page of Surfer's Magazine.
   - **f.** Go forward to the picture you enlarged.
   - **g.** Go back to the list of pictures.
   - **h.** Go to the home page of your Web browser.

4. **Use the History list.**
   - **a.** Open the History list.
   - **b.** Explore three links included in the History list.
   - **c.** Close the History list.

5. **Create bookmarks or favorites.**
   - **a.** Go to the New York Times Web site.
   - **b.** Add the Web site to your list of bookmarks or your list of favorites.
   - **c.** Go back to your Web browser's home page.
   - **d.** Test the New York Times bookmark or favorite to make sure it opens to the correct Web page.

6. Manage bookmarks in Netscape.

- **a.** Go to the Climbing Magazine Web site.
- **b.** Create a Bookmarks folder called **Climbing**.
- **c.** Add the Climbing Magazine Web site to the Climbing folder.
- **d.** Test the link you filed in the Climbing folder.

7. Manage favorites in Internet Explorer.

- **a.** Go to the Climbing Magazine Web site.
- **b.** Create a Favorites folder called **Climbing**.
- **c.** Add the Climbing Magazine Web site to the Climbing folder.
- **d.** Test the link you filed in the Climbing folder.

8. Check security features.

- **a.** Go to the Amazon Bookstore Web site.
- **b.** Perform a search or follow links to find a book that you want to purchase.
- **c.** After you have selected a book that you like, click the **Add to Shopping Cart link**.
- **d.** Click the **Proceed to Checkout link**.
- **e.** Click the **Sign in using our secure server link**.
- **f.** Check the security features of this Web page.
- **g.** List three ways you know this Web page is a secure Web site.
- **h.** Close your Web browser.

► Independent Challenge 1

The members of the St. Catharine's Rowing Club are interested in competing in countries outside North America. They asked you to find the Web sites of four rowing clubs in Europe, Asia, or South America.

- **a.** Start your Web browser. Go to **www.course.com/illustrated/internet3**, click the **Unit D link**, then click the link under Independent Challenge 1. Use this link as a starting point for your search.
- **b.** Find four rowing clubs located outside North America. Make sure the Web sites for these clubs include at least some English text.
- **c.** Create a bookmark or favorites folder called **Rowing Clubs**.
- **d.** Store the URLs of the four Web sites you have chosen in the Rowing Clubs folder.
- **e.** Test each URL from the folder.
- **f.** Close your Web browser.

Independent Challenge 2

You work for a small business and are learning about the Web as part of your job training. You are intrigued by the concept of "easy domain names" and think that your business would benefit from having such a domain name for its Web presence. You decide to see how many well-known organizations that you're familiar with use such domains.

a. Make a list of at least five large organizations that you would expect to have Web sites. Then list two possible easy domain names for each. For example, you might expect United Airlines to have a Web site at united.com or ual.com.

b. Start your Web browser. Enter each of your guesses in your Web browser's Address text box or Location text box.

c. Record the correct domain name for each organization, or write "not found" if both of your guesses were unsuccessful.

d. Identify a subject in which you are interested, and then try entering an easy domain name that might lead to a Web site connected with your interests. For example, if you are interested in skiing, see whether a Web site exists at www.skiing.com. If you are interested in Beethoven, check out www.beethoven.com. You might not find a Web site. You will know the domain name is invalid if your Web browser requires more than 10 or 20 seconds to find the Web site. If the Web browser takes too long, just click the **Stop button** and try another domain name. You might find all kinds of intriguing Web sites related to your interests just by entering a descriptive domain name.

e. Record the names of at least three subject-based domain names that produced the resources you were seeking.

f. Close your Web browser.

Independent Challenge 3

Business Web sites range from simple informational Web sites to comprehensive Web sites that offer information about the firm's products or services, history, current employment openings, and financial information. An increasing number of business Web sites offer products or services for sale via their Web sites. You have just landed a position on the public relations staff of Value City Central, a large chain of television and appliance stores. Your first assignment is to research and report on the types of information that similar large firms offer on their Web sites.

a. Start your Web browser. Go to **www.course.com/illustrated/internet3**, click the **Unit D link**, then examine the links for Independent Challenge 3. There you will find a list of appliance retailers.

b. Choose two of the business Web sites listed that you believe would be most relevant to your assignment.

c. Add each Web site to your list of bookmarks or favorites.

d. Spend about 10 minutes exploring each of the two Web sites you have chosen, then write a paragraph to compare the two Web sites in terms of the following characteristics:
- Overall presentation of the corporate image (clear? easy to understand? effective? attractive?)
- Description of products or services offered (easy to follow? engaging? non-threatening?)
- Security information (encrypted for credit card transactions?)

e. In your comparison, indicate which of the two Web sites you believe projects its image most effectively. Which of the two Web sites would encourage you to purchase the company's products? Why?

f. Close your Web browser.

► Independent Challenge 4

The Columbus Suburban Area Council is a charitable organization devoted to maintaining and improving the general welfare of people living in Columbus-area suburbs. As the director of the council, you are interested in encouraging donations and other support from area citizens and want to stay informed of grant opportunities that might benefit the council. You are especially interested in developing an informative and attractive presence on the Web.

a. Start your Web browser. Go to **www.course.com/illustrated/internet3**, click the **Unit D link**, then examine the links for Independent Challenge 4. There you will find a list of charitable organizations.

b. Follow the links to charitable organizations to find out more about what other organizations are doing with their Web sites.

c. Use the History feature to select two of the Web sites you visited. Save these Web pages to a folder named Charities. For each Web site, record a list of its contents. Note if each Web site includes financial information and if the Web site discloses how much the organization spent on administrative or non-program activities.

d. Identify which Web site you believe would be a good model for the council's new Web site. Explain why your chosen Web site would be the best example to follow.

e. Close your Web browser.

Visual Workshop

Many organizations update their Web sites on a daily basis. In this Visual Workshop, you will analyze the changes made to a Web site for a popular magazine. Go to the Sony Music Web site. Find four differences between the Sony Music home page on your screen and the Sony Music home page shown in Figure D-31. Make a list of these differences.

FIGURE D-31

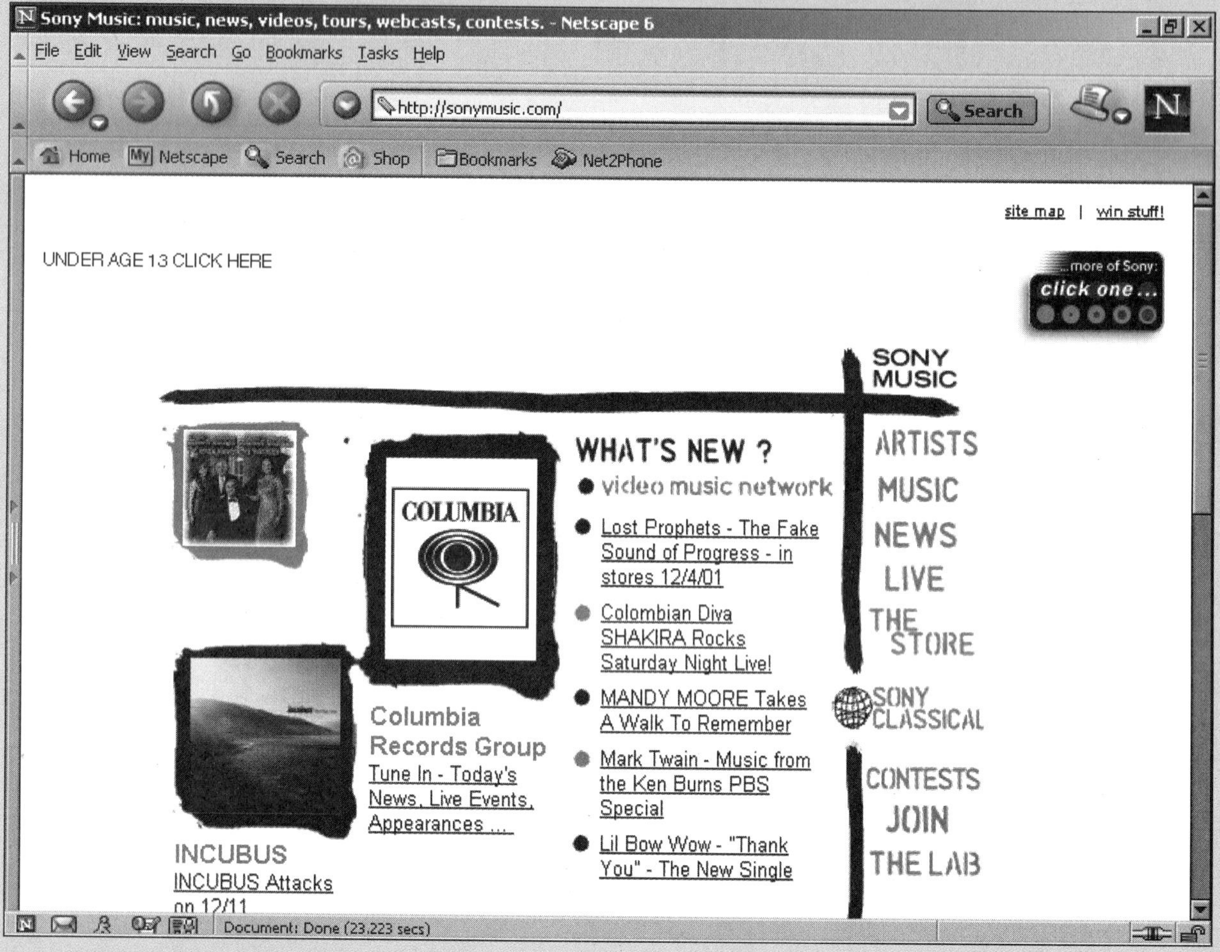

Searching the Web

Objectives

- Develop a Web search strategy
- Define search engines
- Use search engines
- Use directories
- Use meta-search engines
- Use a Web bibliography
- Use Boolean logic and filtering techniques
- Conduct advanced searches using AltaVista
- Conduct advanced searches using HotBot

You can use the Web to access millions of Web pages, which contain information on a virtually unlimited number of topics. To find the information you want among all these Web pages, you need to learn searching methods and tools. Nancy Shand and Ranjit Singh, staff writers at the Midland News, a top-rated daily newspaper that serves the Midland metropolitan area, have hired you as their assistant. They want you to use the Web to help them gather information for their stories.

Internet

Developing a Web Search Strategy

You can use the Web to quickly find answers to specific questions or as a resource to explore interesting concepts and ideas. Each of these question types, specific and exploratory, requires a different search strategy. Before you start accepting research requests from Nancy and Ranjit, you decide to spend some time familiarizing yourself with searching strategies.

► Specific Question

A **specific question** is a question that you can phrase easily and has only one answer. Specific questions might require you to start with broad categories of information and then gradually narrow the search until you find the answer to your question. Figure E-1 shows this process of sequential, increasingly focused questioning. As you narrow your search, you might find results that do not lead you to the answer of your question. If that happens, you need to choose the result (or path) that will lead you to the correct answer as shown in Figure E-1.

► Exploratory Question

An **exploratory question** starts with a general question that leads to other, less general questions, which result in multiple answers. The answers to the questions at each level should lead you to more information about the topic you are researching. This information then leads you to more questions and answers. Figure E-2 shows how this questioning process broadens the scope of results as you gather information pertinent to the exploratory question.

FIGURE E-1: Specific research question search process

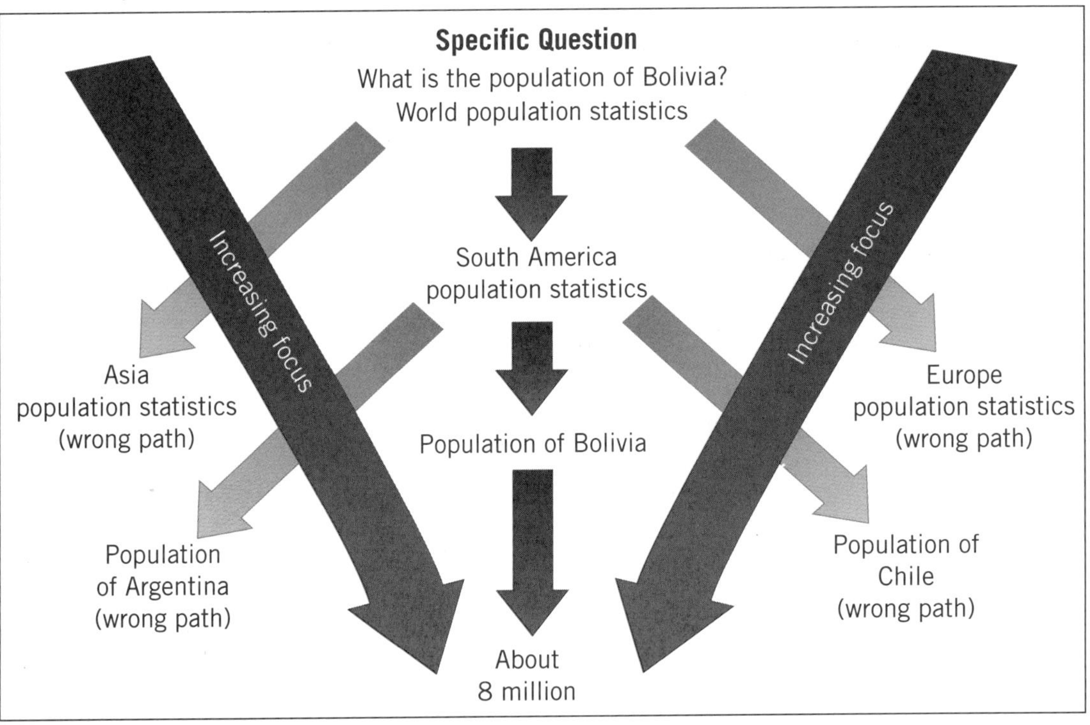

FIGURE E-2: Exploratory research question search process

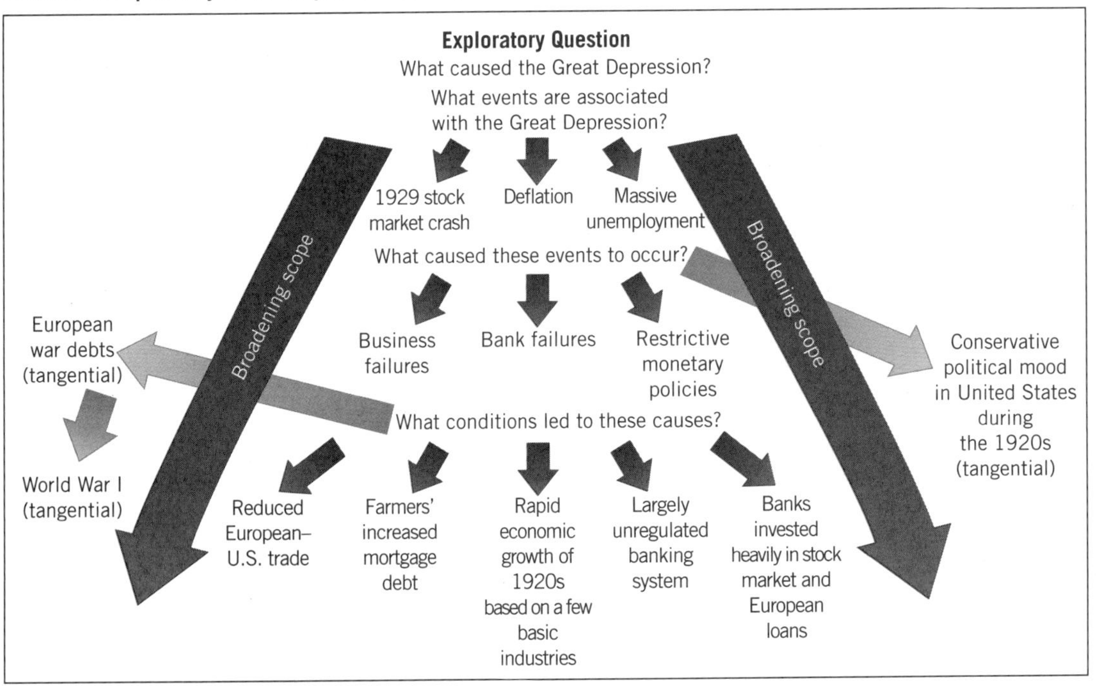

Internet

Internet

Defining Search Engines

A **search engine** is a special kind of Web site that finds Web pages containing the word or phrase you specify. For example, you could enter the word "Louisiana" into the appropriate location on a search engine and then click the Search button to get a long list of Web pages that might contain information about Louisiana. Before you accept your first research assignment from Ranjit and Nancy, you decide to learn some of the terms associated with Web searching and search engines in general.

► Search Expression

The words or phrases you enter when you are conducting a search are called **search expressions** or **queries.** A search expression can be composed of one or several words; each word in a search expression is called a **key term.** The word "Louisiana" when entered into a search engine is both a search expression and a key term. A search engine does not search the Web to find a match to the search expression you enter; it only searches its own database of Web content it has catalogued. Therefore, if you enter the same search expression into different search engines, you will get some results that are the same and some that are different because each search engine contains a different set of information in its database and each search engine uses different procedures to search its database. You get the best results by entering key terms that don't have multiple meanings and are not articles or prepositions.

► Hits

A **hit** is a Web page that is indexed in the search engine's database and contains text that matches your search expression.

► Results Pages

All search engines provide a series of **results pages,** which include links to Web pages that match your search expression. Figure E-3 shows a results page using the Google search engine for the search expression "modern art."

► Web Robot

Each search engine uses a Web robot to build its database. A **Web robot,** also called a **bot** or a **spider,** is a program that automatically searches the Web to find new Web sites and updates information about old Web sites that are already in the database. A Web robot also deletes information in the database when a Web site no longer exists. The main advantage of using an automated searching tool is that it can examine far more Web sites than a team of people. However, the Web changes every day and even the best search engine sites cannot keep their databases completely updated. When you click links on a search engine results page, you will find that some of the Web pages no longer exist.

FIGURE E-3: One search engine's results page for a search on "modern art"

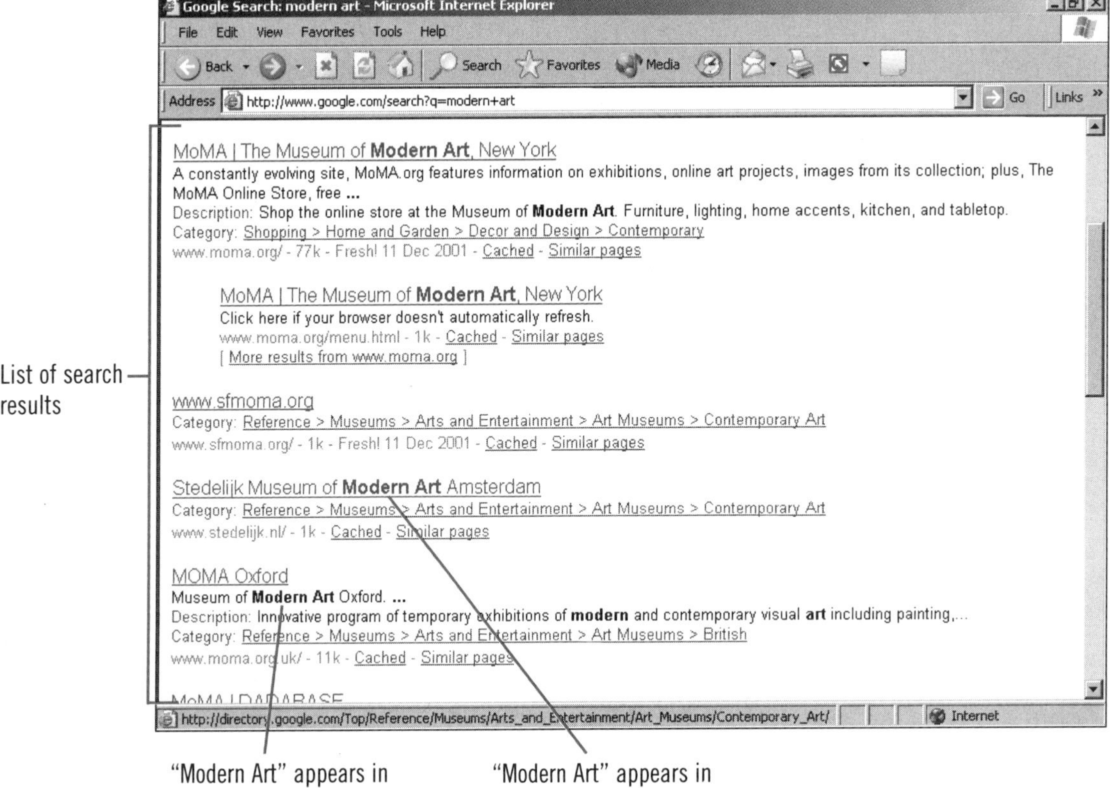

How search engines are financed

The organizations that operate search engines often sell advertising space on the search engine Web page and on the results pages to sponsors. An increasing number of search engine operators also sell paid placement links on results pages. For example, Toyota might want to purchase rights to the search term "car." When you enter a search expression that includes the word "car," the search engine creates a results page that has a link to Toyota's Web site at or near the top of the results page. Most, but not all, search engines label these paid placement links as "sponsored."

Search engine Web sites use the advertising revenue to generate profit after covering the costs of maintaining the computer hardware and software required to search the Web and create and search the database. The only price you pay for access to these tools is that you see advertising banners on many of the results pages and you might have to scroll through some sponsored links at the top of results pages; otherwise, your usage is free.

Using Search Engines

No one knows how many Web pages exist on the Web, but the number is now in the billions. Each of these Web pages might contain thousands of words, images, or links to downloadable files. Unlike the content of a library, the content of the Web is not indexed in any standardized way. Fortunately, you can use search engines to help you find the information you need. Nancy needs to know the amount of average rainfall in Belize for a story that she is writing. This search question is a specific question, not an exploratory question because you are looking for one specific answer. Table E-1 lists the tasks required to find information on the Web. You apply these tasks to find the average annual rainfall in Belize.

1. Start your Web browser, go to **www.course.com/illustrated/internet3**, click the **Unit E link**, then click the **AltaVista link** under Lesson 3
   The AltaVista home page opens.
2. Type **Belize annual rainfall** in the Search for text box
   Figure E-4 shows the search expression entered in the Search for text box.
3. Click **Search**
   The search results appear on a new results page, which states that there are hundreds of Web pages that might contain the answer to your query.
4. Scroll down the results page, examine your search results, then click links until you find a Web page that provides the average annual rainfall for Belize
   The annual rainfall in Belize ranges from 50 inches in the north to 170 inches in the south.
5. Go to **www.course.com/illustrated/internet3**, click the **Unit E link**, then click the **HotBot link** under Lesson 3
   The HotBot home page opens.
6. Type **Belize annual rainfall** in the Search Smarter text box
   Figure E-5 shows the search expression entered in the Search Smarter text box.
7. Click **SEARCH**
   The search results appear on a new results page.
8. Scroll down the results page, examine your search results, then click links until you find the average annual rainfall for Belize
   Once again, you should find that the average rainfall in Belize ranges from 50 inches in the north to 170 inches in the south. Some Web sites might report a different average. Always check the Web page source just as you would with printed material before accepting the validity of the information presented.

Trouble?

If you receive a message about a "cookie," click OK.

Trouble?

If you do not find any useful links on the first page of search results, click the numbers at the bottom of the results page to open additional results pages.

CLUES TO USE

Why search results differ

The HotBot search engine, by default, returns hits only for Web pages that include *all* of the words you enter in a search expression. The AltaVista search engine's default is to return hits for Web pages that include any of the words. AltaVista ranks each document it finds to determine how many of the search terms it contains, the location of the terms in the document, and a term's proximity to another term. For example, AltaVista would probably rank a document containing the phrase "rainfall in Belize" higher than a document containing the words "rainfall" and "Belize" in separate sentences.

FIGURE E-4: Search expression entered in the AltaVista search engine

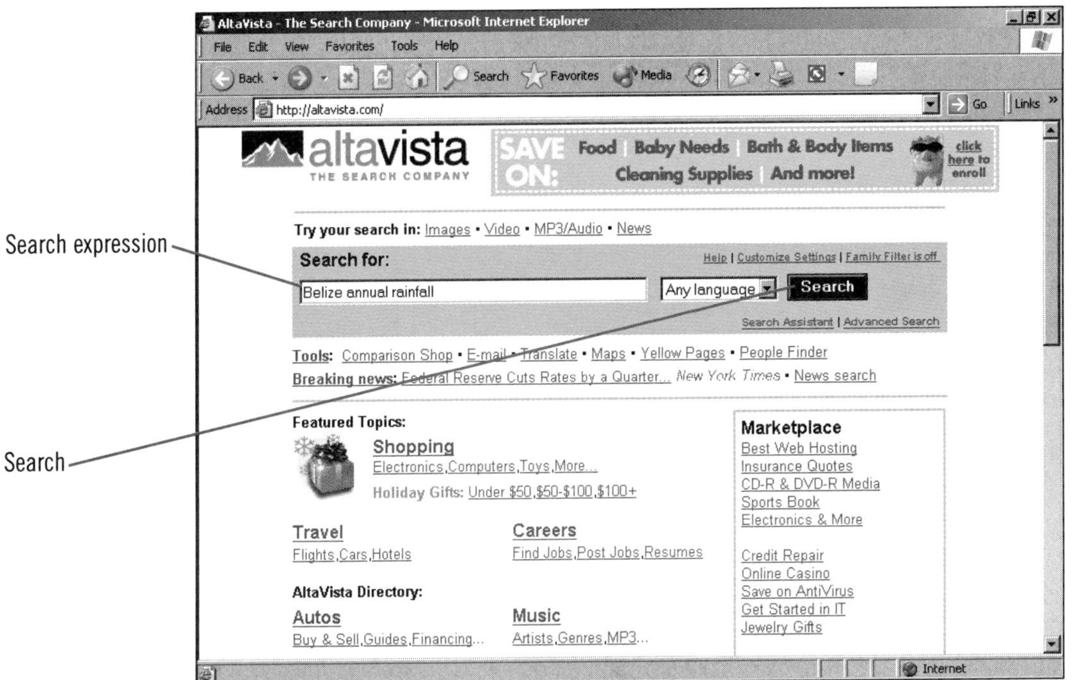

FIGURE E-5: Search expression entered in the HotBot search engine

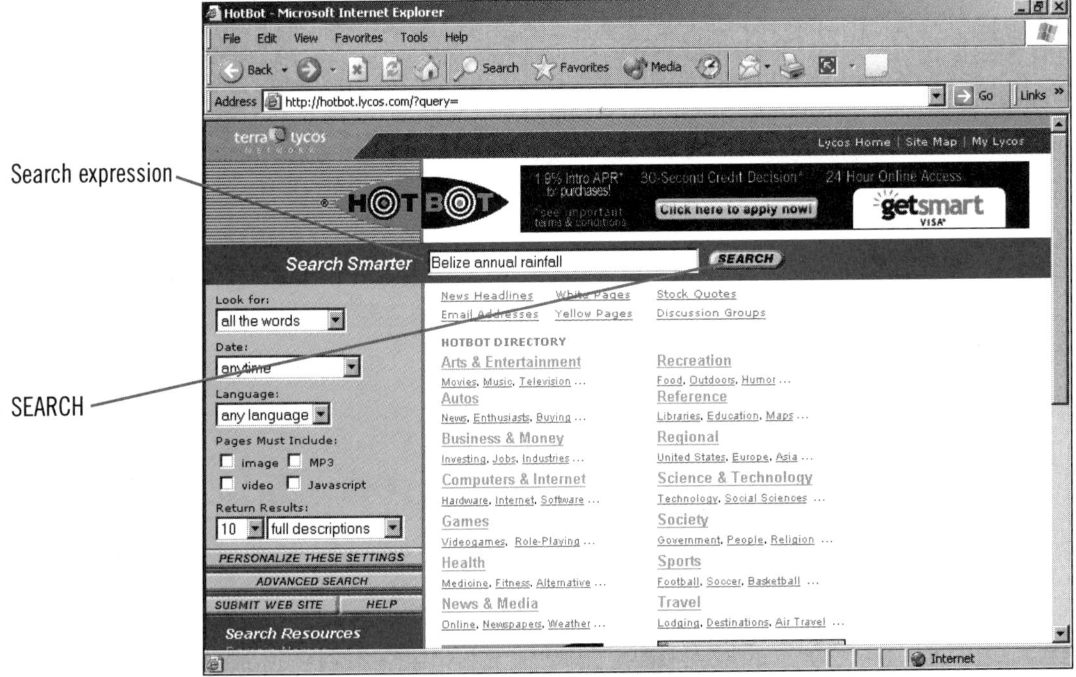

TABLE E-1: Tasks required for a specific search

task	description
1.	Formulate and state the question (for example, "What is the average annual rainfall in Belize?")
2.	If the question is a specific question, rather than an exploratory one, identify key search terms in the question that you will use in your search expression (for example, "Belize," "rainfall," and "annual")
3.	Enter the key terms in a search engine
4.	Use the search engine results page to identify the information you were seeking, or to reformulate the question, key terms, or method

Internet

Using Directories

A **Web directory** is a list of links to Web pages that is organized into hierarchical categories. Most Web directories are part of Web sites that also include search engines. Web directories and search engines both use a database of links to Web pages to enable users to search for information in different ways. Rather than using a database compiled by Web bots, however, a Web directory lists Web pages selected by people. Users can browse for information by general categories, rather than by using specific search terms. Ranjit wants to know the latest news and information about his profession. He asks you to provide him with a set of links to Web sites about the media industry. You use the Yahoo! directory to identify Web sites based on the category of information that Ranjit needs.

1. Go to **www.course.com/illustrated/internet3**, click the **Unit E link**, then click the **Yahoo! link** under Lesson 4
   The Yahoo! home page opens. Below the search area, the page lists the main categories in the Yahoo! directory, as shown in Figure E-6.
2. Click the **News & Media link**
   The News & Media page opens, showing links to lower levels in the hierarchy and to other points in the hierarchies of other categories. New categories and categories that include new Web pages are indicated by a "NEW!" icon.
3. Examine the categories listed, then click the **Industry Information link**
   The Industry Information page opens, listing more links to subcategories.
4. Click the **Media Industry News link**
   The Yahoo! Directory page for Media Industry News opens, displaying a link to a Yahoo! Web page, additional categories, and links to other Web sites, as shown in Figure E-7.
5. Examine the links on the Media Industry News page
6. Click one of the links in the Site Listings section and examine the Web page
7. Navigate back to the Media Industry News page, click a different link in the Site Listings section, then examine the Web page

FIGURE E-6: Yahoo! directory categories

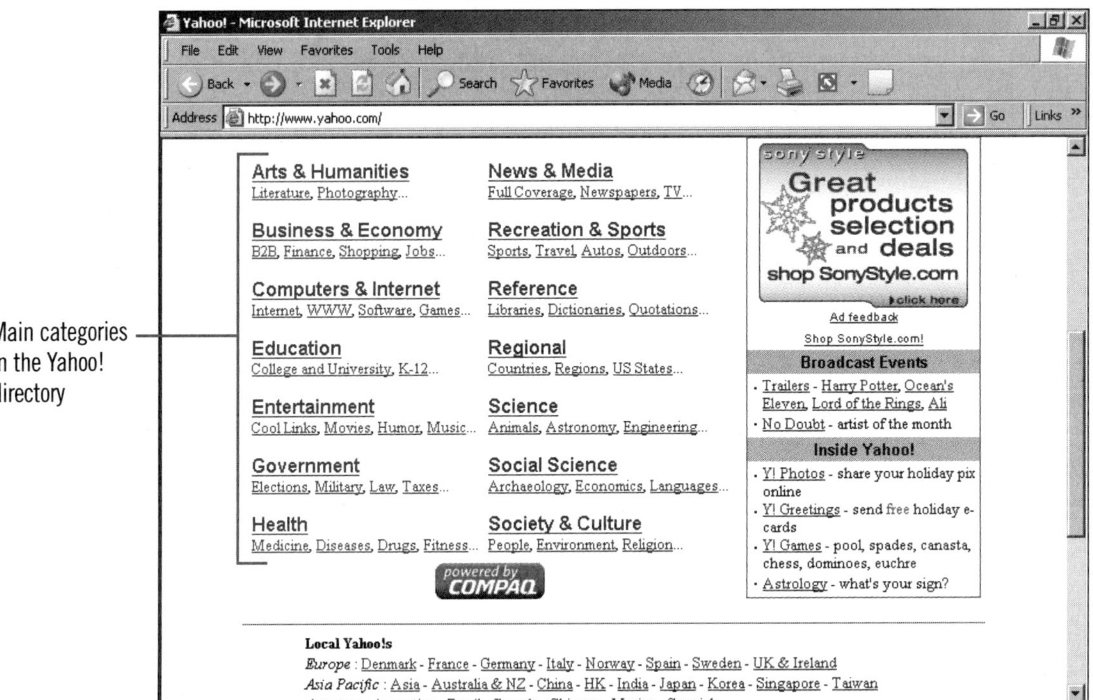

FIGURE E-7: Yahoo! Media Industry News directory page

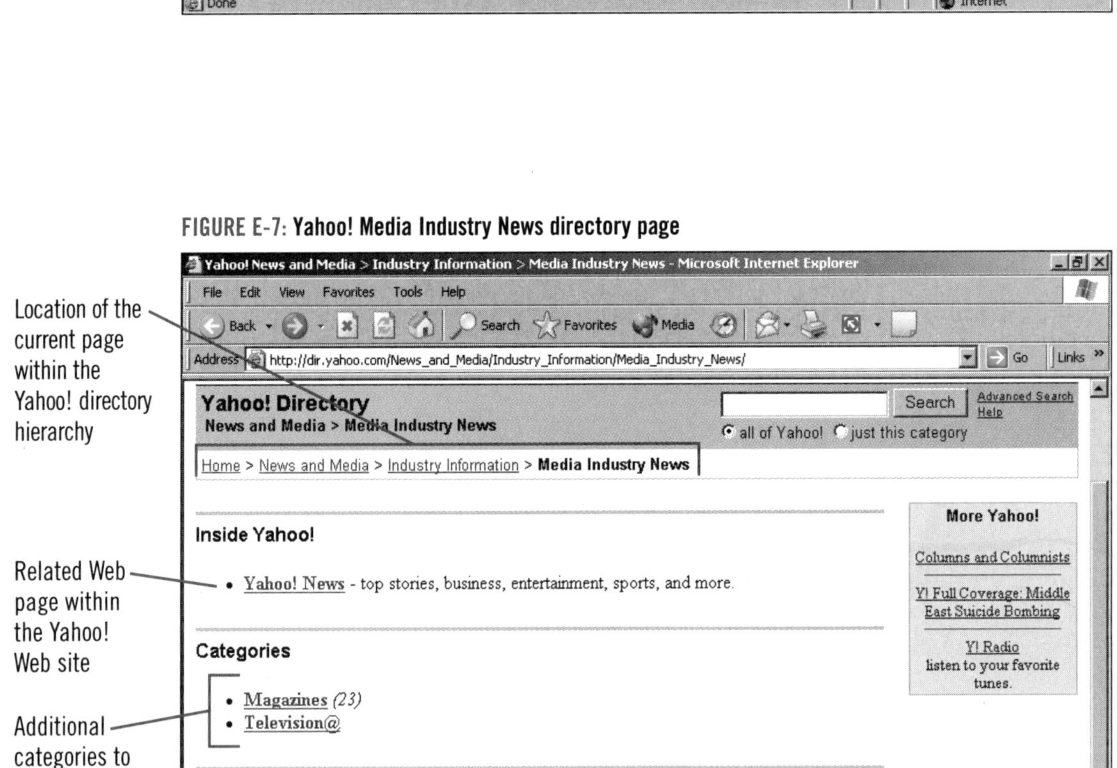

Internet

Using Meta-Search Engines

A **meta-search engine** is a tool that uses multiple search engines. Using a meta-search engine, you can search several search engines simultaneously, so you don't have to conduct the same search in different search engines. After a meta-search engine sends your search expression to several search engines, the search engines compare the search expression against their databases of Web page information and return results to the results page of the meta-search engine for you to view. Dogpile is one of the more comprehensive meta-search engines available; it forwards your queries to more than a dozen major search engines and directories, including About.com, AltaVista, FindWhat, LookSmart, Open Directory, Overture, Yahoo!, and several others. You want to learn how to use meta-search engines so that you can access information more quickly. You decide to use Nancy's rainfall question to test the Dogpile meta-search engine.

1. Go to **www.course.com/illustrated/internet3**, click the **Unit E link**, then click the **Dogpile link** under Lesson 5
   The Dogpile meta-search engine page opens.
2. Type **Belize annual rainfall** in the Fetch text box
   Figure E-8 shows the search expression entered in the Dogpile meta-search engine.
3. Click **Fetch**
   A results page appears, similar to the one shown in Figure E-9. The results page shows the hits for each search engine.
4. Examine your search results, then click appropriate links to find the average rainfall in Belize

Analyzing the search results of a meta-search engine

As you scroll through the results pages, you might see a wide variation in the number and quality of the results provided by each search engine or directory. You might see many hits, but no links. Although most of the Web pages returned by one search tool will not be returned by any other search tool, you also might notice duplicate hits. You can click the Next button that appears at the bottom of the results page to see the hits returned by other search tools.

FIGURE E-8: Search expression entered in the Dogpile meta-search engine

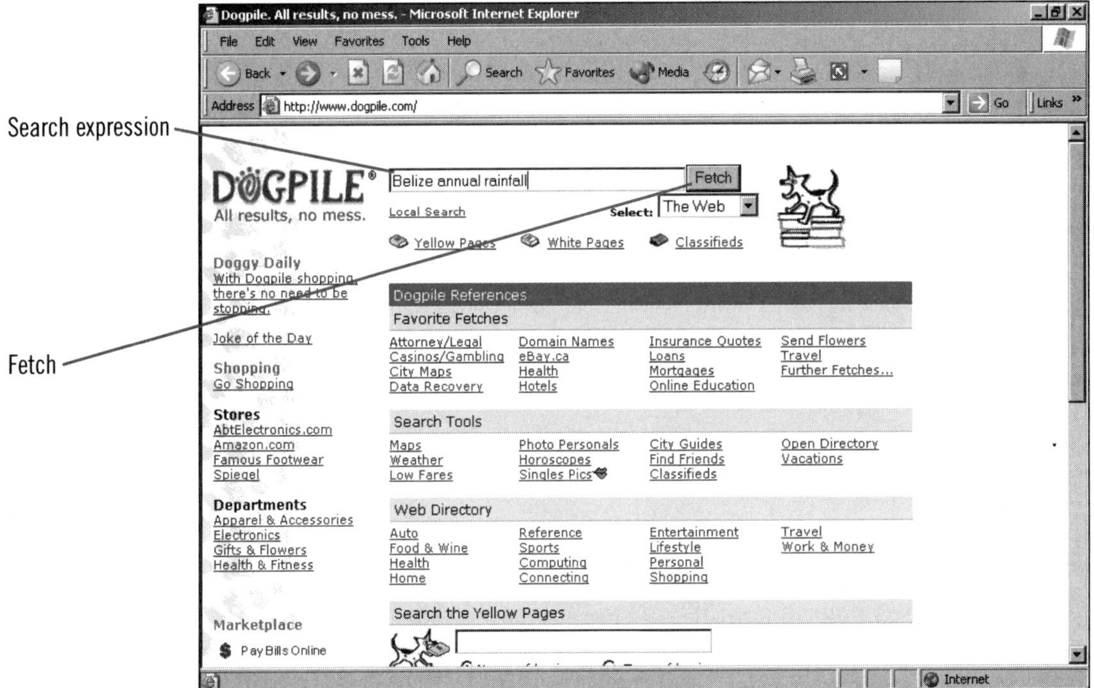

FIGURE E-9: Dogpile meta-search engine results

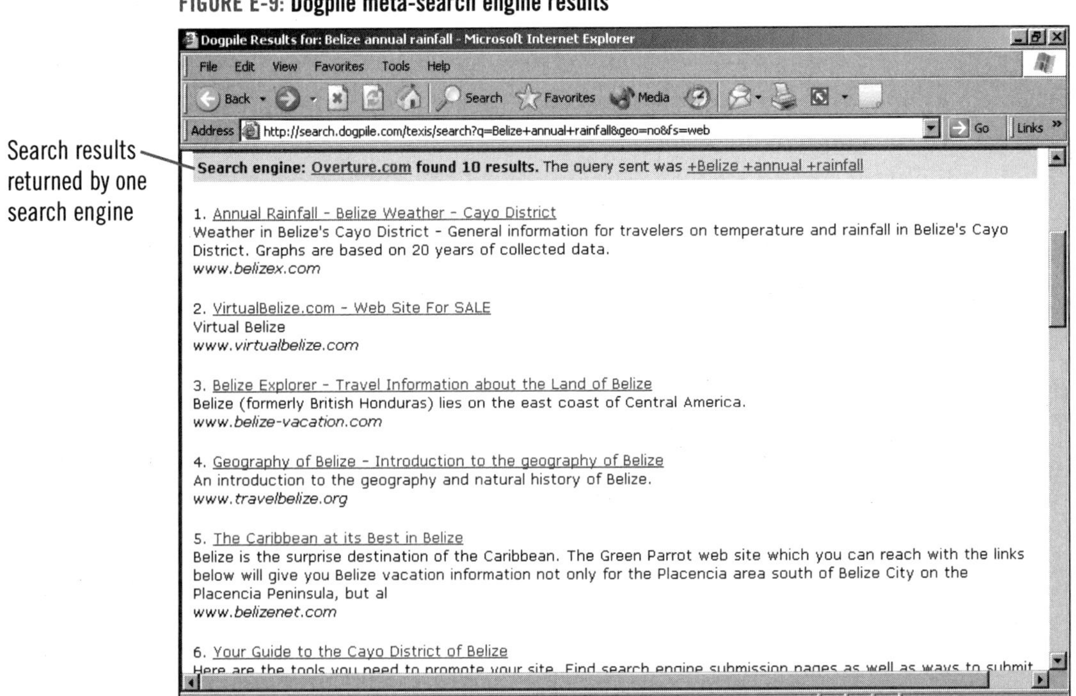

Using a Web Bibliography

A **Web bibliography** organizes information into categories and subcategories just like a printed bibliography. In a Web bibliography, each reference is a link to a Web page. Just as some printed bibliographies are annotated, many Web bibliographies include summaries or reviews of Web pages. Web bibliographies can be very useful when you want to obtain a broad overview or a basic understanding of a complex subject area. Ranjit informs you that he needs information about the business and economic effects of current trends in biotechnology and the potential effects of genetic engineering research. He asks you to find some Web sites that he can explore to learn more about biotechnology trends in general and genetic engineering research in particular. You know that biotechnology is a branch of the biological sciences, so you identify three category terms, *biotechnology*, *genetic engineering*, and *biology*, to use as your search categories. You decide to use the Argus Clearinghouse Web bibliography, which reviews and provides links to subject guides.

Steps

1. Go to **www.course.com/illustrated/internet3**, click the **Unit E link**, click the **Argus Clearinghouse link** under Lesson 6, then scroll down the Web page and read the category links
   Notice that biotechnology, genetic engineering, and biology are not listed on the Argus Clearinghouse home page. Science, however, is listed.
2. Click the **Science & Mathematics link**
   A list of subcategories opens.
3. Click the **biology link**
   A list of keywords in the selected subcategory appears. Notice that the navigation path on the left changes as you click through the Web site. Both biotechnology and genetic engineering are listed on the biology page.
4. Click the **biotechnology link**
   A list of guides appears, as shown in Figure E-10. The five red check marks next to the National Biotechnology Information Facility link identify this Web site as the most highly rated Web site.
5. Click the **National Biotechnology Information Facility link**
   The Guide Information page for the Web site opens, as shown in Figure E-11. The Guide Information page includes a link to the Web site, indexing keywords, information about the author of the Web site, and detailed ratings.
6. Click the **biology link** that appears in the Navigation path on the left side of the Web page
   The list of keywords for the biology subcategory reappears.
7. Scroll down the Web page, then click the **genetic engineering link**
   The Guides page displays three entries. One of these entries is the Biotechnology - WWW Virtual Library page, which also appeared on the Guides page shown in Figure E-10.
8. Click the **Biotechnology - WWW Virtual Library link**, then explore the resources at that Web site

Trouble?

If an alert box appears warning that the Web page is busy or inaccessible at this time, click OK, wait a few seconds, then try again. If you still can't access the Web page, skip to Step 7.

FIGURE E-10: Biotechnology subcategory in Argus Clearinghouse

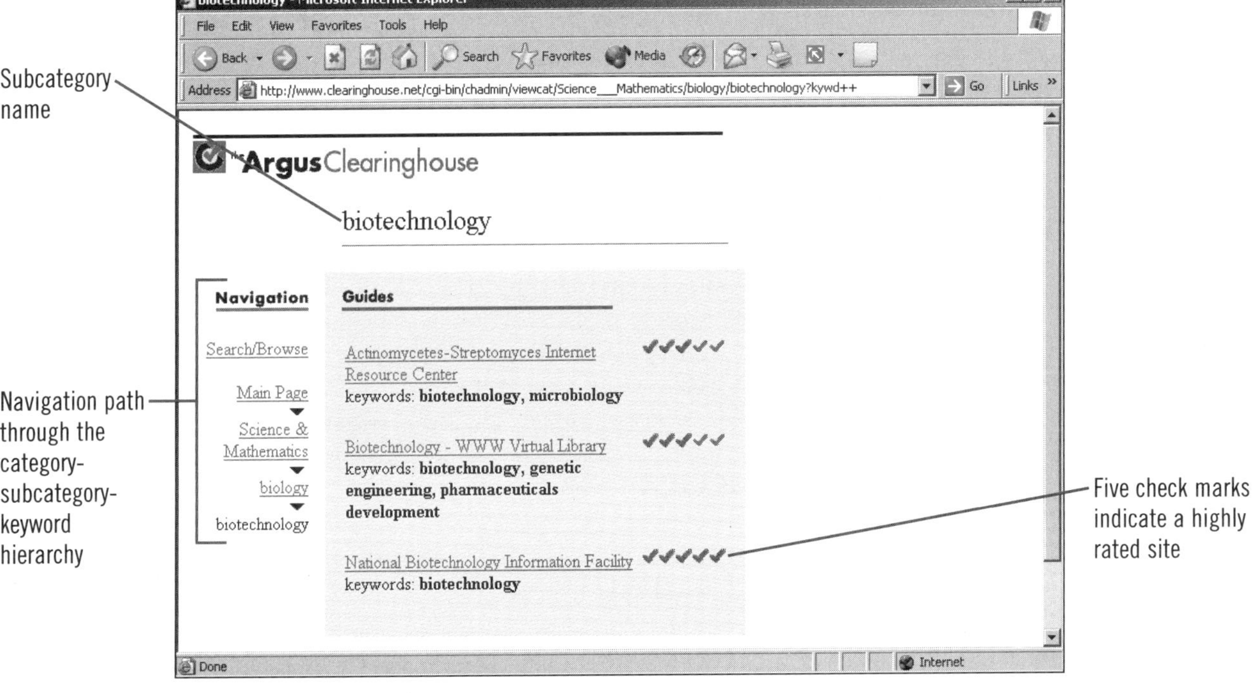

FIGURE E-11: Information about the National Biotechnology Information Facility Web site

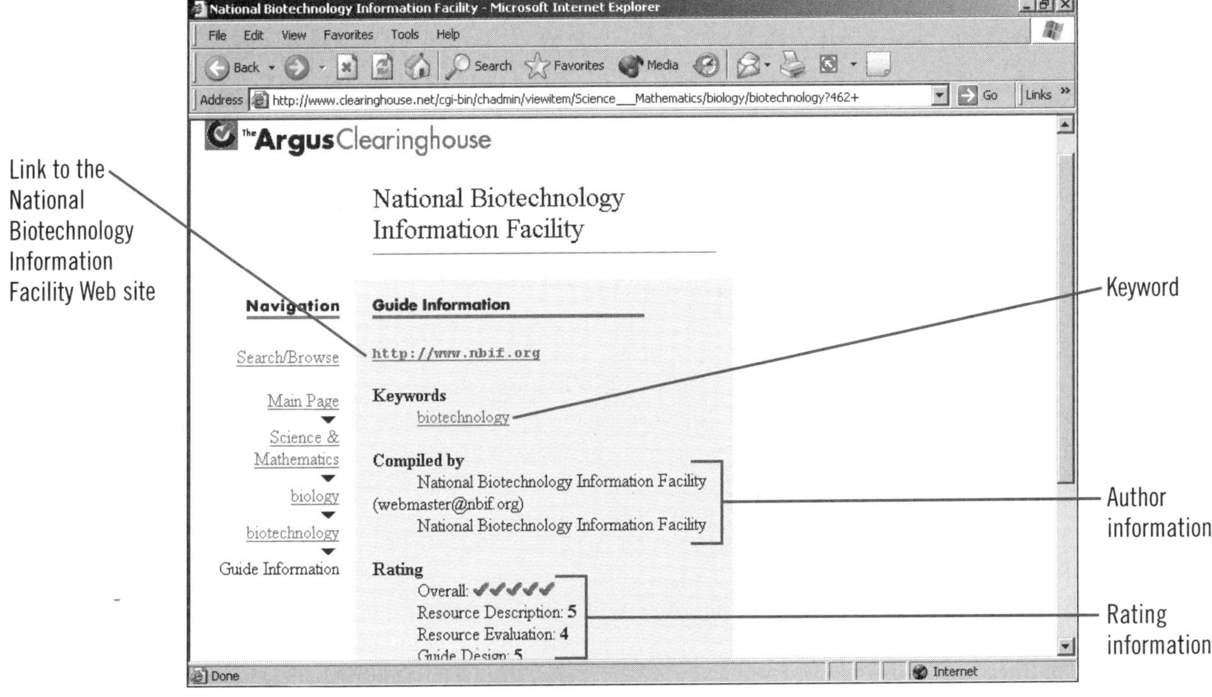

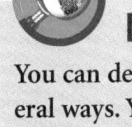

Delivering Web information

You can deliver information from Web pages in several ways. You can print copies of Web pages with the URLs appearing as a header or footer. You can send the URLs as links in an e-mail message. You can send a Web page in an e-mail message as an attachment.

You can also save the Web pages as favorites or bookmarks, which you can annotate if you like, and then save to your hard disk. You then can share your favorite or bookmark files with others.

Internet

Using Boolean Logic and Filtering Techniques

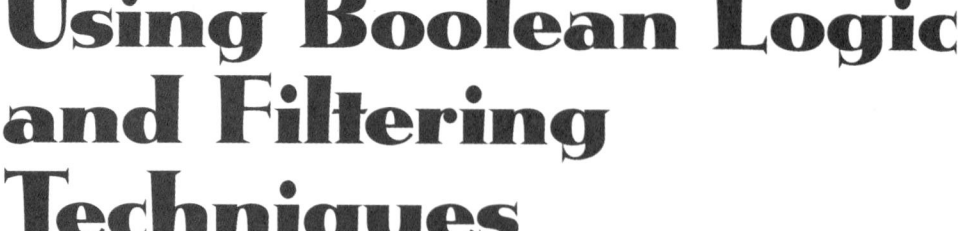

To get good results from a search engine or a meta-search engine, you must select your search terms carefully. When the objective of your search is straightforward, you can choose one or two words that will work well. More complex search questions require more complex queries to broaden or narrow your search expression. To perform advanced searches, you can use **Boolean operators** (which are terms that denote the relationship between words in a search phrase), special characters, such as the asterisk (*), and search filters. Some of the questions Ranjit and Nancy ask require you to conduct quite complicated searches. You decide to learn about the techniques for formulating complex queries.

► Boolean Operators

Boolean operators, also called **logical operators**, specify the logical relationship between the elements they join, just as the plus sign specifies the mathematical relationship between the two elements it joins. Most search engines recognize at least three basic Boolean operators: AND, OR, and NOT. You can use these operators in many search engines by simply including them with search terms. Figure E-12 shows several ways to use Boolean operators in more complex search expressions that contain the words *exports*, *France*, and *Japan*. A search engine returns the matches shown in the figure if it interprets the Boolean operators correctly.

► Precedence Operators

When you join three or more search terms with Boolean operators, you can easily become confused by the expression's complexity. To reduce the confusion, you can use precedence operators along with the Boolean operators. A **precedence operator**, also called an **inclusion operator** or a **grouping operator**, clarifies the grouping within a complex expression and is usually indicated by the parentheses symbols. Figure E-13 shows several ways to use precedence operators with Boolean operators in search expressions.

► Location Operators

A **location operator**, or **proximity operator**, lets you search for terms that appear close to each other in the text of a Web page. The most common location operator offered in search engines is the NEAR operator. For example, if you are interested in French exports, you might want to find only Web pages in which the terms *exports* and *France* are close to each other, so to perform this search you would type exports NEAR France.

► Wildcard Characters

A **wildcard character** allows you to omit part of the search term or terms so that you can search for related words or variations on a word that might be used in a Web page. Many search engines recognize the asterisk (*) as the wildcard character. For example, the search expression *export** might return Web pages that contain the terms *exports*, *exporter*, *exporters*, and *exporting*.

► Search Filters

A **search filter** eliminates Web pages from a search. You can access search filter options for a search engine on its advanced search page. (Search engines usually include a link such as "Advanced" or "More Options" on the main page to open the advanced search page.) You can use the filter to specify a language, date, domain, host, or page component (such as a URL, link, image tag, or title tag). For example, you could search for a term, such as *exports*, in Web page titles and ignore Web pages in which the term appears in other parts of the Web page.

FIGURE E-12: Use of Boolean operators in search expressions

SEARCH EXPRESSION	SEARCH RETURNS WEB PAGES THAT INCLUDE	USE TO FIND INFORMATION ABOUT
exports AND France AND Japan	All of the three search terms	Exports from France to Japan or from Japan to France
exports OR France OR Japan	Any of the three search terms	Exports from anywhere, including France and Japan, and all kinds of information about France and Japan
exports NOT France NOT Japan	Exports, but not if the Web page also includes the terms France or Japan	Exports to and from any countries other than France or Japan
exports AND France NOT Japan	Exports and France, but not Japan	Exports to and from France to anywhere else, except exports shipped to and from Japan

FIGURE E-13: Use of Boolean and precedence operators in search expressions

SEARCH EXPRESSION	SEARCH RETURNS WEB PAGES THAT INCLUDE	USE TO FIND INFORMATION ABOUT
exports AND (France OR Japan)	Exports and either France or Japan	Exports from or to either France or Japan
exports OR (France AND Japan)	Exports or both France and Japan	Exports from anywhere, including France and Japan, and all kinds of other information about France and Japan
exports AND (France NOT Japan)	Exports and France, but not if the Web page also includes Japan	Exports to and from France, except exports to and from Japan

CLUES TO USE

Understanding the origins of Boolean operators

George Boole was a nineteenth-century British mathematician who developed **Boolean algebra**, the branch of mathematics and logic that bears his name. In Boole's algebra, all values are reduced to one of two values. In most practical applications of Boole's work, these two values are true and false. Although Boole did his work many years before practical electrically powered computers became commonplace, his algebra has proved useful to computer engineers and programmers.

Internet

Internet

Conducting Advanced Searches Using AltaVista

AltaVista provides an advanced search page that you can use to conduct Boolean queries and specify other search criteria, such as language type and Web page publication date ranges. Nancy needs information in English about the German perspective on trade issues related to agriculture. You recognize this request as an exploratory question and decide to use the advanced query capabilities of the AltaVista search engine to conduct a complex search for Web pages that Nancy can use for her research.

1. Go to **www.course.com/illustrated/internet3**, click the **Unit E link**, then click the **AltaVista link** under Lesson 8
2. Click the **Advanced Search link** on the right side of the Web page
3. Type **Germany AND (trade OR treat*) AND agricult*** in the Boolean query text box
   This query instructs the search engine to look for Web pages containing the following characteristics: the word "Germany"; the word "trade" *or* a word starting with "treat"; and a word starting with "agricult."
4. Click the **Any language list arrow**, then click **English**
   Figure E-14 shows the completed advanced search entry.
5. Scroll down the advanced search page, then click **Search**
6. Scroll down to the bottom of the results page to see the number of results pages, then examine some of the descriptions of the first 10 results
   The search returns 20 results pages with 10 links per page. Notice that some of the descriptions include information about fertilizer treatments, which is unnecessary information.
7. Scroll to the top of the results page, then click the **Help link**
8. Click the **Advanced Cheat Sheet link**
   An explanation of various search terms appears, as shown in Figure E-15. As explained next to the keyword domain, the filter "domain:" followed by the name of the domain to which you want to limit your search limits the search to URLs with the domain you specify. The domain name for Germany is "de" (for "Deutschland").
9. Navigate back to the AltaVista Advanced Search page
10. In the Boolean query text box, click after agricult*, press **[Spacebar]**, type **AND NOT treatment AND domain:de**, then click **Search** to narrow the search to Web pages matching the earlier query, but not containing the word "treatment" and located on a Web site in the .de domain
    AltaVista returns a much smaller number of hits this time. If necessary, you could revise the search further.

FIGURE E-14: Complex search using AltaVista

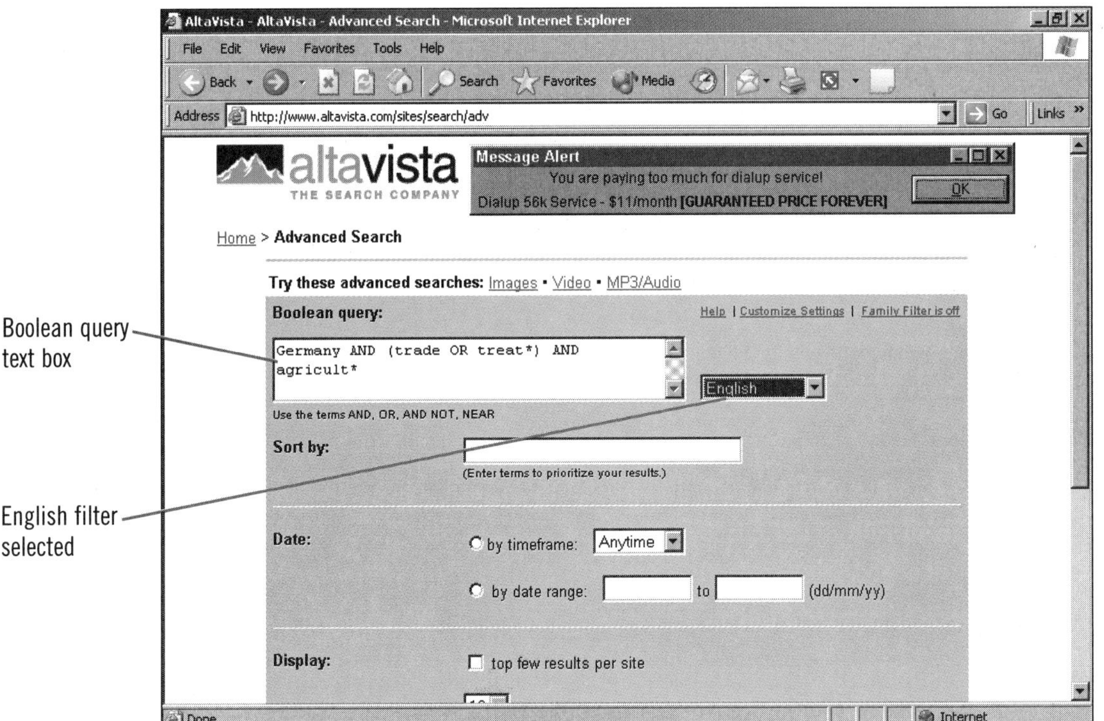

FIGURE E-15: Information on AltaVista's Advanced Search Cheat Sheet

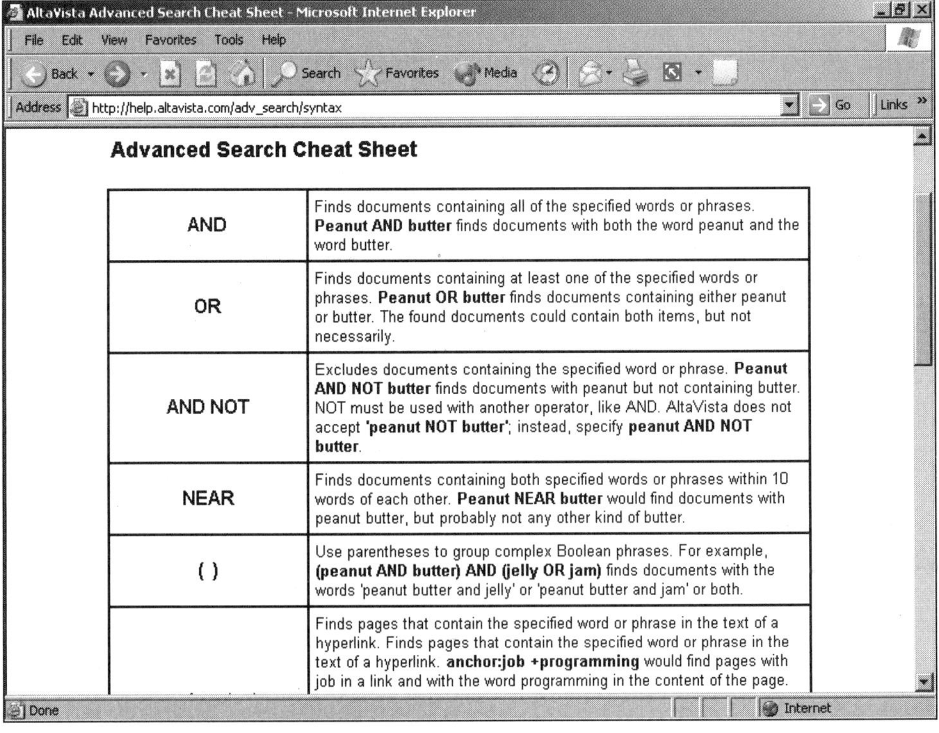

Advanced Search Cheat Sheet

AND	Finds documents containing all of the specified words or phrases. **Peanut AND butter** finds documents with both the word peanut and the word butter.
OR	Finds documents containing at least one of the specified words or phrases. **Peanut OR butter** finds documents containing either peanut or butter. The found documents could contain both items, but not necessarily.
AND NOT	Excludes documents containing the specified word or phrase. **Peanut AND NOT butter** finds documents with peanut but not containing butter. NOT must be used with another operator, like AND. AltaVista does not accept **'peanut NOT butter'**; instead, specify **peanut AND NOT butter**.
NEAR	Finds documents containing both specified words or phrases within 10 words of each other. **Peanut NEAR butter** would find documents with peanut butter, but probably not any other kind of butter.
( )	Use parentheses to group complex Boolean phrases. For example, **(peanut AND butter) AND (jelly OR jam)** finds documents with the words 'peanut butter and jelly' or 'peanut butter and jam' or both.
	Finds pages that contain the specified word or phrase in the text of a hyperlink. Finds pages that contain the specified word or phrase in the text of a hyperlink. **anchor:job +programming** would find pages with job in a link and with the word programming in the content of the page.

CLUES TO USE

Getting help on a search engine

Each search engine follows different rules and offers different features. To obtain help for a particular search engine, examine its home page and look for a link to help pages. The AltaVista Advanced Search page includes a link titled Help.

Internet

Conducting Advanced Searches Using HotBot

HotBot provides a step-by-step process for conducting an advanced search. You use list arrows with drop-down menus and text boxes to enter keywords and search expressions. Nancy asks you for information about the effect of unusual weather patterns and recent rainstorms on Southeast Asian rice crops during the past six months. You decide to use the HotBot search engine to run a complex query about the weather patterns in Southeast Asia.

Steps

1. Go to **www.course.com/illustrated/internet3**, click the **Unit E link**, then click the **HotBot link** under Lesson 9
   The HotBot home page opens.
2. Click **Advanced Search** on the left side of the Web page
3. Click the **Look For list arrow**, then click **boolean phrase**
4. Click the first **Date list arrow** (next to anytime), then click **in the last 6 months**
5. Scroll down the advanced search page, click the first **Location/Domain list arrow** under the Region option button, then click **Southeast Asia**
6. Scroll to the top of the advanced search page, then type **rice AND (weather OR season) AND production** in the text box under the HotBot logo
   Your screen should appear similar to Figure E-16.
7. Click **SEARCH** to perform a search on the effect of weather on Asian rice crops during the past six months
   The search results page opens, similar to the one shown in Figure E-17.
8. Close your Web browser

QuickTip

HotBot does not recognize wildcard characters, but it does allow you to set precedence operators.

FIGURE E-16: Advanced search using HotBot

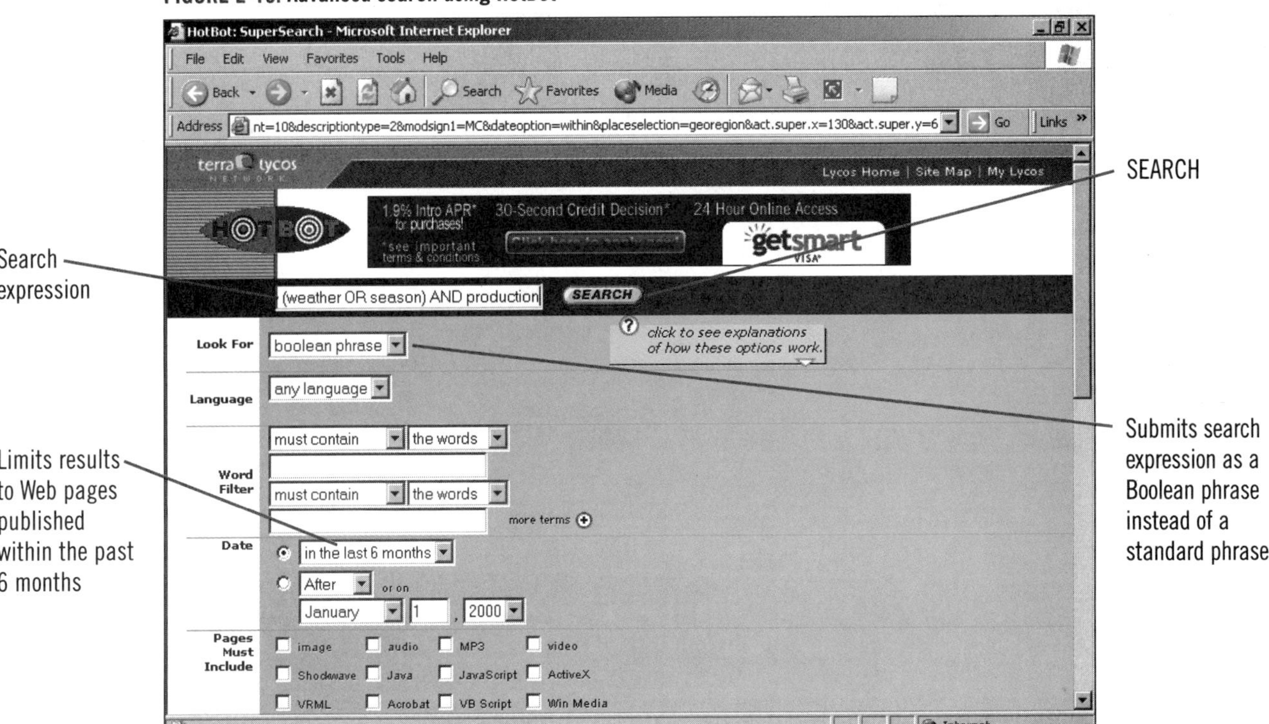

FIGURE E-17: HotBot search results page

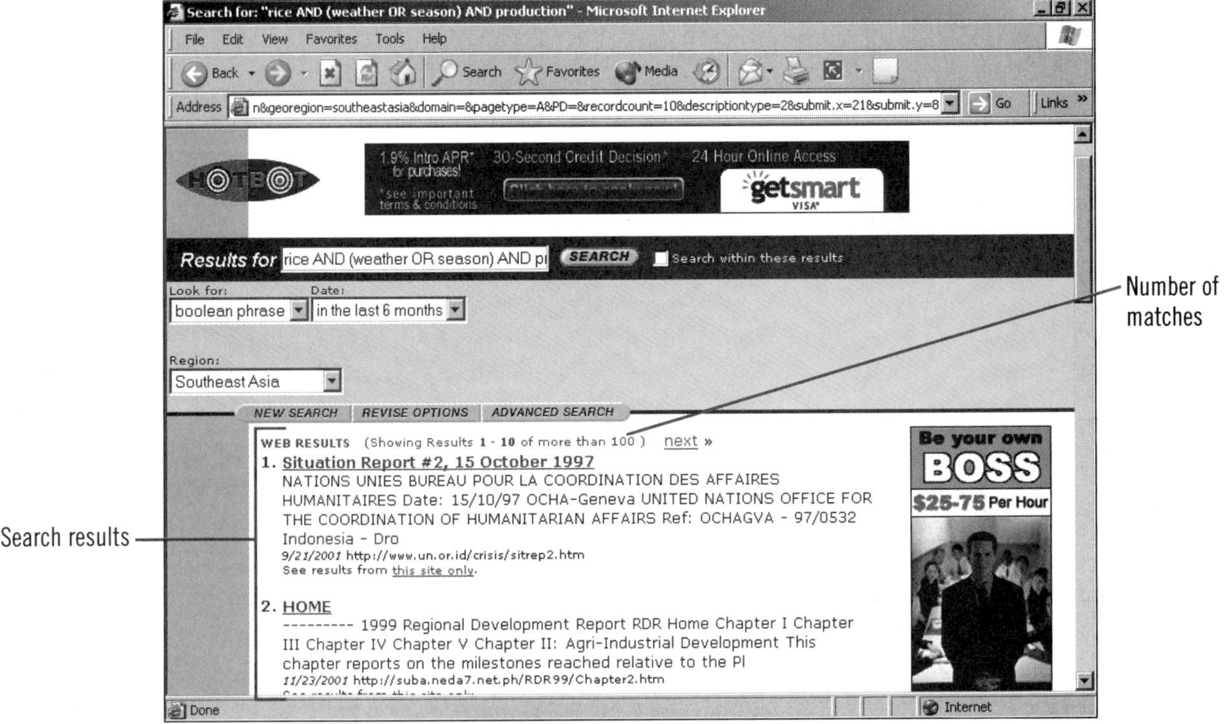

Internet

Practice

▶ Concepts Review

Describe the function of each element in the HotBot Web page window shown in Figure E-18 for searching the Web.

FIGURE E-18

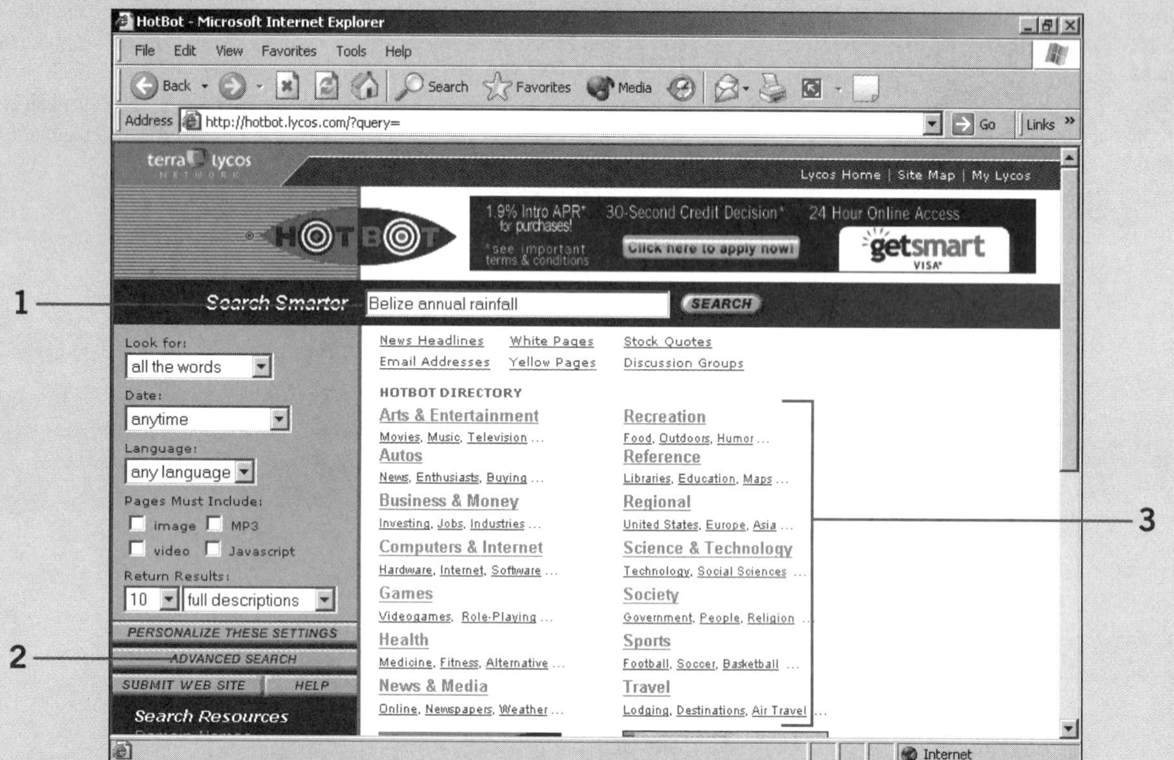

Match each term with the statement that describes it.

4. Search filter	**a.** A Web site that finds other Web pages containing the word or phrase you specify
5. Web robot	**b.** A list of links to Web pages that is organized into hierarchical categories
6. Search engine	**c.** Describes the relationship between words in a search expression
7. Boolean operator	**d.** Often called a spider
8. Meta-search engine	**e.** Provides search results from several search engines
9. Boolean expression	**f.** Japan AND (food OR sushi)
10. Web directory	**g.** Eliminates Web pages from a search

Practice

Select the best answer from the list of choices.

11. Which of the following is not a Web search tool?
- **a.** Directory
- **b.** Multisearch engine
- **c.** Argus Clearinghouse
- **d.** Search engine

12. Dogpile is an example of a:
- **a.** Web spider.
- **b.** Meta-search engine.
- **c.** Search engine.
- **d.** Boolean operator.

13. Which of the following are basic Boolean operators?
- **a.** AND, NOR
- **b.** NEAR, OR
- **c.** AND, OR, NOT
- **d.** PLUS, NOT

14. Which of the following characters is recognized as a wildcard character by many search engines?
- **a.** Plus sign (+)
- **b.** Tilde (~)
- **c.** Asterisk (*)
- **d.** Exclamation mark (!)

15. Which of the following search techniques is not recognized by HotBot?
- **a.** Wildcard characters
- **b.** Precedent operators
- **c.** Boolean operators
- **d.** Boolean phrase

Skills Review

Note: To access the Skills Review Web sites, go to **www.course.com/illustrated/internet3**, click the **Unit E link**, then click the desired link under the appropriate Skills Review.

1. Use search engines.
- **a.** Open the AltaVista search engine.
- **b.** Use **capital Bulgaria** as a search expression.
- **c.** Perform the search.
- **d.** Examine the search results to find the capital of Bulgaria.
- **e.** Record the time required to find the answer to the question.
- **f.** Use the HotBot search engine to search for the same information.
- **g.** Record the time required to find the answer to the question.
- **h.** Determine which of the two search engines allowed you to find the answer more quickly.

2. Use directories.
- **a.** Open the Yahoo! directory.
- **b.** Follow the Arts & Humanities link.
- **c.** Follow the Museums, Galleries, and Centers link.
- **d.** Click the link for a subcategory of interest.
- **e.** Examine two links in this subcategory.

3. Use meta-search engines.
- **a.** Open the Dogpile meta-search engine.
- **b.** Use **Olympics 2000 gymnastics gold men** as a search expression, then perform the search.
- **c.** Scroll through the results from the first five search engines (for example, GoTo, Excite, Infoseek).
- **d.** Read the descriptions of the links returned. You are looking for the name of the man who won the all-around gymnastics gold medal at the 2000 Sydney Summer Olympics.
- **e.** Follow the links to find the winner's name.
- **f.** Keep a list of the links you follow.
- **g.** When you find the gold-medal winner, record his name. Did you go down any wrong paths? Were you surprised at any of the hits that resulted from your search expression?

4. **Use other Web resources.**
   a. Open the Argus Clearinghouse home page.
   b. Starting from the Health & Medicine link, follow the appropriate links to find the list of fitness links shown in Figure E-19.
   c. Explore the FitnessLink link.
   d. Record the URL of the FitnessLink Web site.

FIGURE E-19

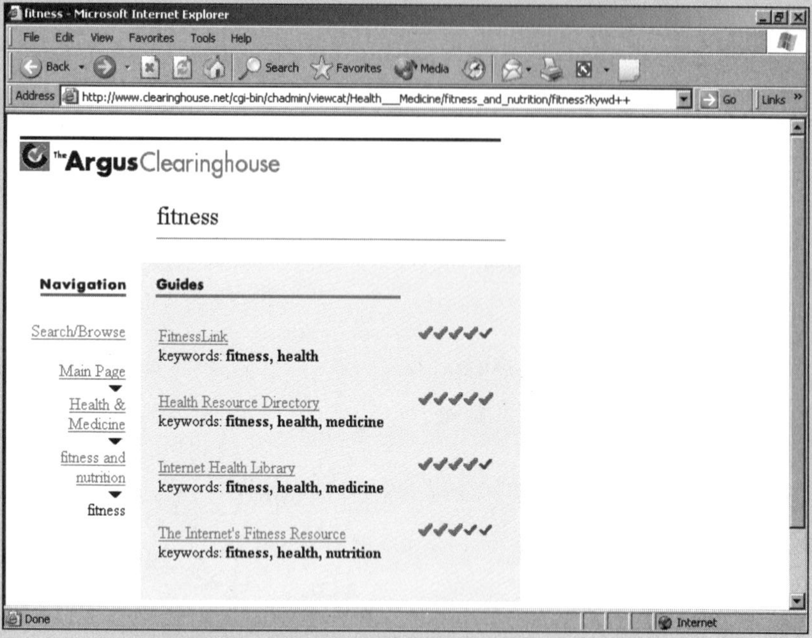

5. **Conduct advanced searches using AltaVista.**
   a. Open the AltaVista search engine.
   b. Follow the Advanced Search link.
   c. Select English as the language.
   d. Use the following Boolean expression to search for information about Scotland, Edinburgh and/or Glasgow, and bagpipes, and folk groups: **Scotland AND (Edinburgh OR Glasgow) AND bagpipes AND folk groups**
   e. Refine the search further by specifying no words with the letters "accomm" (for accommodations) and the "com" domain. Use the following Boolean expression: **Scotland AND (Edinburgh OR Glasgow) AND bagpipes AND folk groups AND NOT accomm* AND domain:com**
   f. Find a Web page listing Scottish folk groups and folk bands.
6. **Conduct advanced searches in HotBot.**
   a. Open the HotBot search engine.
   b. Perform an Advanced Search.
   c. Specify that you want to use a Boolean phrase.
   d. Specify **in the last 3 months** as the search time frame.
   e. Specify **Oceania** as the region.
   f. Enter **marsupials AND NOT numbats** as the search expression.
   g. Perform the search.
   h. Record how many hits your search turned up (even if it's zero).

► Independent Challenge 1

A friend is putting together a Web site on rural living. She wants you to help her find additional Web sites on rural living so she can create a page of links to these Web sites as a resource to her visitors. You use Web search tools to find Web sites on this topic and select a small number of links that seem particularly useful.

a. Go to **www.course.com/illustrated/internet3**, then click the **Unit E link**. The links under Independent Challenge 1 are for search engines, directories, and meta-search engines. Use these links as a starting point for your search.
b. Choose at least one search tool from each category and conduct a search using the keywords **rural** and **living**.
c. Extend or narrow your search using each tool until you find five Web sites that you believe are comprehensive guides or directories that your friend should link to on her Web site.
d. For each Web site, record the URL and note why you believe the Web site would be useful to someone looking for information and resources on rural life. Identify each Web site as a guide, directory, or other resource.

Independent Challenge 2

A friend who's never used the Web finds it hard to believe that you can find information about almost anything on the Web. You show him some of the resources that are available on the Web. To put the Web to the test, he asks five specific questions that he wants answers to during your session together.

a. Go to **www.course.com/illustrated/internet3**, click the **Unit E link**, click the **AltaVista link** under Independent Challenge 2.

b. Ask questions and perform searches to find the following pieces of information:
- The current temperature in Varberg, Sweden
- A picture of the flag of the state of Washington
- The telephone area code for New Orleans, Louisiana
- The number of miles in 30 kilometers
- The capital of British Columbia in Canada (*Hint:* Include the word "city" in your question.)

c. Note that you might need to refine your questions to get the required answers.

d. When you have found the answer to a question, record the question you asked, the URL of the Web site that contained the answer, and the answer to the question.

Independent Challenge 3

You are a manager at Key Consulting Group, a firm of geological and engineering consultants who specialize in earthquake-damage assessment. When an earthquake strikes, Key Consulting Group sends a team of geologists and structural engineers to the quake's site to examine the damage to buildings and determine what kinds of reconstruction will be needed. In some cases, the buildings must be demolished. Because an earthquake can occur without warning in many parts of the world, Key Consulting Group needs quick access to information about local conditions in various parts of the world, including the temperature, rainfall, and currency exchange rates. It is early July when you receive a call that an earthquake has just occurred in Japan. You decide to use the Web to obtain information about local midwinter conditions there.

a. Use a search engine to search for information on weather conditions in Japan in July and current exchange rates.

b. Record the daily temperature range, average annual rainfall, and current exchange rate for your currency to Japanese currency.

Independent Challenge 4

You work as a marketing manager for Lightning Electrical Generators, Inc., a firm that has built generators for more than 50 years. The generator business is not as profitable as it once was, and John Delaney, the firm's president, asked you to investigate new markets for the company. John mentioned the fuel cell business, and explained that a fuel cell creates energy from gasoline through a chemical reaction, rather than burning it like a car does. John wants you to study the market for fuel cells in the United States. He wants to know which firms currently make and sell these products, and he wants to get some idea about the power ratings and prices for individual units.

a. Use one of the search tools to search for information about fuel cells. Design your searches to find the manufacturers' names and information about the products they offer.

b. Prepare a short report that describes the information you have gathered, including the manufacturer's name, model number, product features, and suggested price for at least three fuel cells.

▶ Visual Workshop

Go to **www.course.com/illustrated/internet3**, click the **Unit E link**, then click the **HotBot link** under Visual Workshop. Set up the HotBot advanced search page so that it appears similar to the search page shown in Figure E-20. (*Hint:* Scroll up and down the search page if necessary so that you have the same information in the text boxes.) After you have set up the search page to search for Web pages related to coffee production in Costa Rica or Nicaragua, run the search and record the number of hits you receive. Determine how you would refine the search so that you can easily find Web pages that describe coffee production in Costa Rica and Nicaragua.

FIGURE E-20

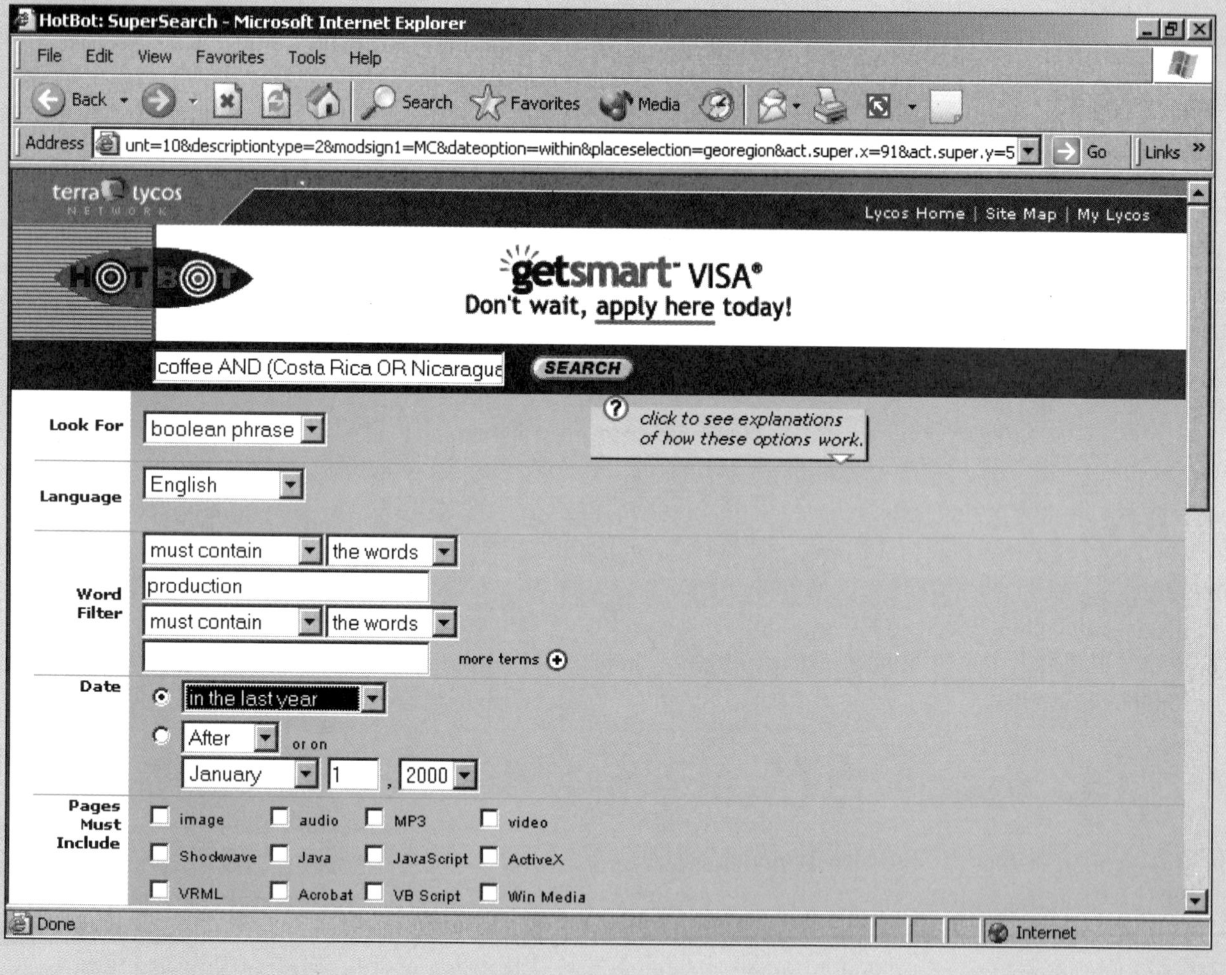

Getting Information from the Web

Objectives

- Save a Web page in Netscape
- Save a Web page in Internet Explorer
- Print a Web page
- Copy text from a Web page
- Get the news
- Obtain weather reports
- Obtain maps and city guides
- Find businesses and people
- Understand graphics and multimedia
- Evaluate Web resources
- Understand e-commerce
- Understand cookies

For both businesses and individuals, the Web can be a valuable source of up-to-date information. You can get the latest news, print a map of your neighborhood, find a local business, and even reconnect with long-lost friends. In this unit, you will learn how to save Web information, search the Web for current information, and identify graphics and multimedia formats. Finally, you will learn how to evaluate Web pages.

You have just been hired by Cosby Promotions, a public relations firm. You are responsible for helping staff members stay current on news items and for providing up-to-date travel information to staff and clients.

Internet

Saving a Web Page in Netscape

If you travel with a laptop or if you want to decrease the time you are connected to the Internet, you might want to save a Web page on a floppy or hard disk to view the Web page offline. Marti Cosby, the president of Cosby Promotions, will be flying to Chicago on business, and wants access to a Web page that lists upcoming Chicago music events while she's traveling. She asks you to save the list of concerts from a local Web site so that she can view it on her laptop even when she does not have an Internet connection.

Steps

1. Start **Netscape**, go to **www.course.com/illustrated/internet3**, click the **Unit F link**, then click the **Chicago music events link** under Lesson 1
   A Web page that contains a list of upcoming music events in Chicago appears.
2. Click **File** on the menu bar, then click **Save As**
   The Save File dialog box opens. The name in the File Name text box matches the filename in the URL. The file is saved as an HTML file by default.
3. Click the **Save in list arrow**, navigate to the drive and folder where your Project Files are stored, then click **Save**
   The Web page is saved as concerts.htm.
4. Click the **Back button** on the toolbar
5. Click **File** on the menu bar, click **Open File**, then click **concerts.htm**
   Figure F-1 shows the completed Open File dialog box.
6. Click **Open**
   Figure F-2 shows the newly saved Web page. Graphics do not appear in Web pages saved in Netscape; the heading at the top of the Web page is actually a graphic. The content of the Web page in your Web browser might differ from the content shown in Figure F-2.
7. Go to **www.course.com/illustrated/internet3**, click the **Unit F link**, click the **Chicago music events link** under Lesson 1, right-click the graphic of the skyline, then click **Save Image**
   See Figure F-3. The filename of the image in Figure F-3 might differ from the filename on your screen. The file type format of the image is GIF. See the Understanding Graphics and Multimedia lesson in this unit for more information about images.
8. Click **Save**
9. Click the **Back button** on the toolbar, then repeat Steps 5 and 6 to reopen the saved Web page
   The saved Web page still appears without the heading graphic. However, you have a saved copy of the graphic for reference.

QuickTip

GIF is a commonly used file format for images.

QuickTip

If you open a saved Web page without an Internet connection, the links on the Web page will not work.

FIGURE F-1: Open File dialog box

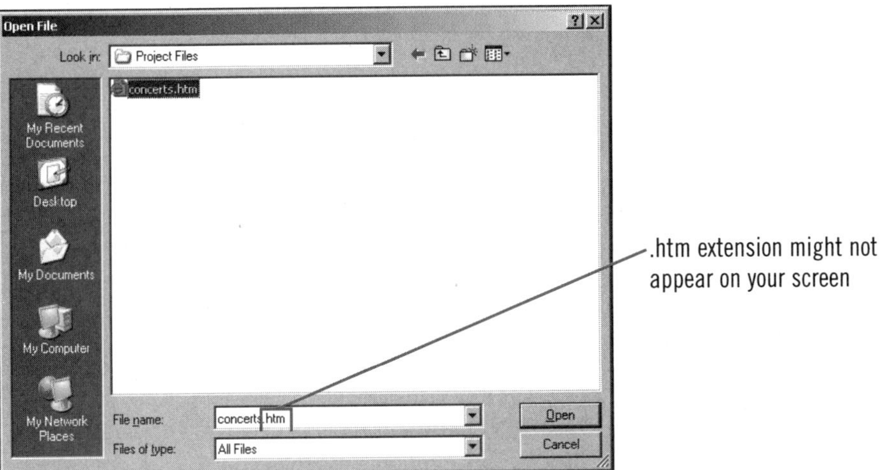

FIGURE F-2: Saved Web page without graphics

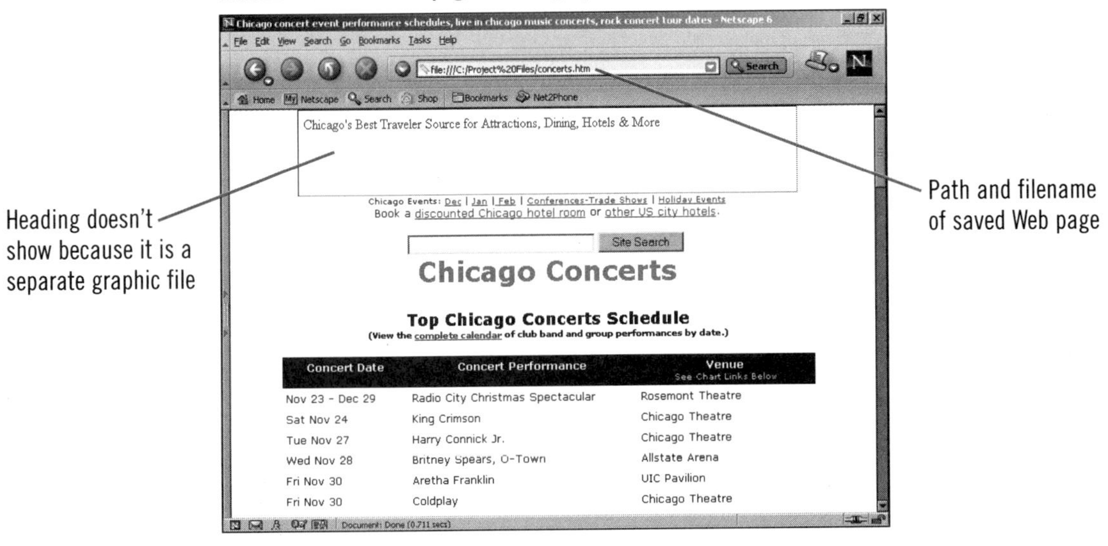

FIGURE F-3: Shortcut menu with Save Image command selected

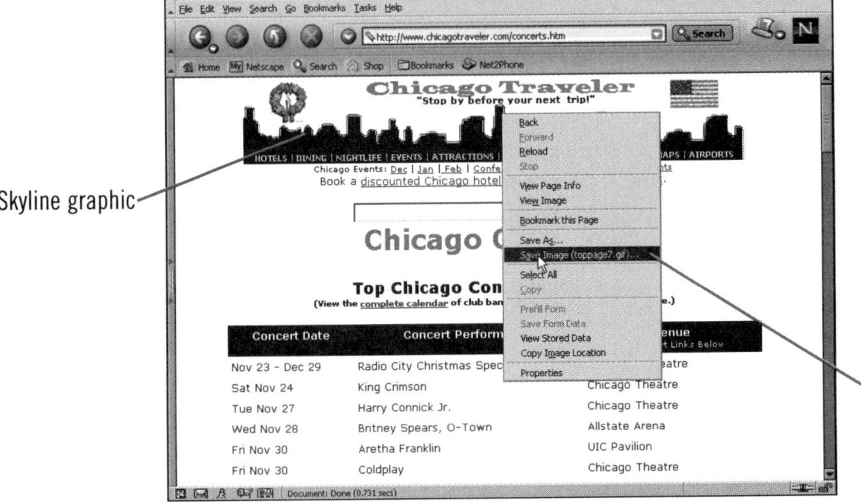

Internet

Internet

Saving a Web Page in Internet Explorer

If you travel with a laptop or if you want to decrease the time you are connected to the Internet, you might want to save a Web page on a floppy or hard disk to view the Web page offline. Marti Cosby, the president of Cosby Promotions, will be flying to Chicago on business, and wants access to a Web page that lists upcoming Chicago music events while she's traveling. She asks you to save the list of concerts from a local Web site so that she can view it on her laptop, even when she does not have an Internet connection.

Steps

1. Start **Internet Explorer**, go to **www.course.com/illustrated/internet3**, click the **Unit F link**, then click the **Chicago music events link** under Lesson 2
   A Web page that contains a list of upcoming music events in Chicago appears.
2. Click **File** on the menu bar, then click **Save As**
   The Save Web Page dialog box opens. The filename that appears in the File name text box is the Web page's title, which appears in the Internet Explorer title bar. Notice that the file type is Web Page, complete, which means the Web page will be saved as an HTML document, along with any associated files, such as graphics.
3. Type **Chicago music events** in the File name text box
4. Click the **Save in list arrow**, then navigate to the drive and folder where your Project Files are stored
   Your screen should look similar to Figure F-4.
5. Click **Save**
   The Web page is saved as Chicago music events.htm. The .htm extension identifies this file as an HTML file. The associated files are saved in a folder called Chicago music events_files.
6. Click the **Back button** on the toolbar
7. Click **File** on the menu bar, click **Open**, click **Browse**, click **Chicago music events.htm**, then click **Open**
   Figure F-5 shows the completed Open dialog box. When you save a Web page and open it without an Internet connection, links that are linked to Web pages other than the saved Web page will not work. To use links on a saved Web page that are linked to other Web pages, you must be connected to the Internet.
8. Click **OK**
   Figure F-6 shows the newly saved Web page.

Trouble?

Make sure you click the file Chicago music events.htm instead of the folder named Chicago music events_files.

FIGURE F-4: Save Web Page dialog box

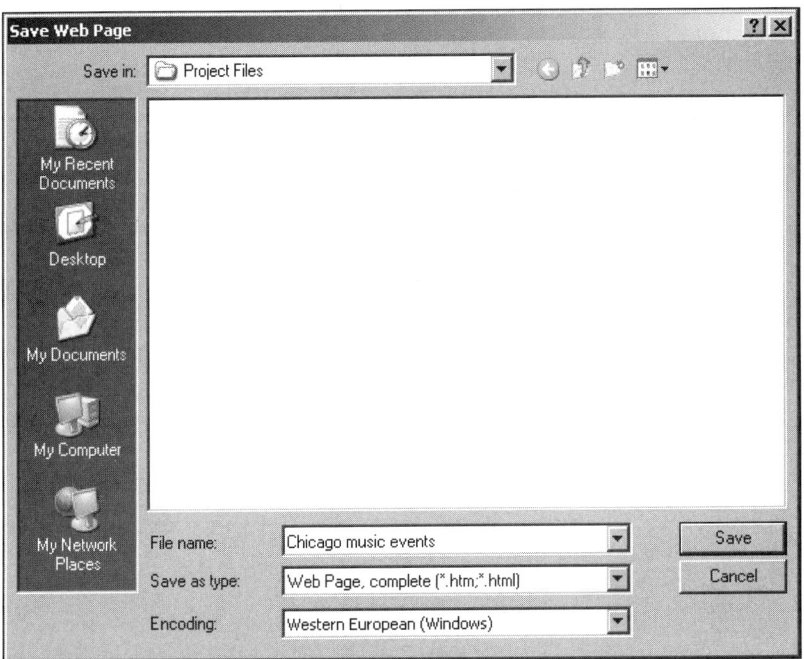

FIGURE F-5: Open dialog box

FIGURE F-6: Saved Web page

Unit F

Internet

Steps

Printing a Web Page

You can easily print the contents of a Web page so that you can view the information when you are not at your computer. When you print a Web page, the Web site source and the date on which the Web page was printed also appear. In addition to the saved version of the Web page on her laptop, Marti wants a printed copy of the Web page.

Printing in Internet Explorer

1. Go to **www.course.com/illustrated/internet3**, click the **Unit F link**, then click the **Chicago music events link** under Lesson 3
2. In Internet Explorer, click **File** on the menu bar, then click **Page Setup** to view page setup options
   The Page Setup dialog box opens, as shown in Figure F-7. This dialog box allows you to set options for paper, headers and footers, page orientation, and margins.
3. Click **Cancel**
   Clicking Cancel instead of OK ensures that if you accidentally change any settings, the changes aren't implemented.
4. Click **File** on the menu bar, then click **Print Preview** to preview how the printer will print the Web pages
   The Web page appears in the Print Preview window as shown in Figure F-8. In this window, you can determine the number of sheets of paper on which the Web page will print. The current page number and the total number of pages appear on the toolbar.
5. Click **Close** on the Print Preview toolbar
6. Click **File** on the menu bar, click **Print**, click the **Pages option button**, verify that 1 appears in the Pages text box, then click **Print**
   The first page of the Web page prints.

Trouble?

The options in your Page Setup dialog box might vary depending on the type of printer you are using.

Trouble?

The number of pages in the Print Preview window might change depending on the length of the Web page content.

QuickTip

You can also print directly from the Print Preview window by clicking Print on the toolbar.

Printing in Netscape

1. Go to **www.course.com/illustrated/internet3**, click the **Unit F link**, then click the **Chicago music events link** under Lesson 3
2. Click **File** on the menu bar, click **Print**, click the **Pages option button** in the Print dialog box, type **1** in the from text box, then click **OK**
   The first page of the Web page prints.

CLUES TO USE

Printer-friendly Web pages

Sometimes a Web page is wider than a standard sheet of paper. On some Web pages, most of the space is occupied by Web site navigation elements, with the main page content occupying only a narrow column in the center of the Web page. This can cause part of the Web page to be cut off on the printout, which can result in the use of many sheets of paper for a relatively small amount of information. To make Web page printouts as practical as possible, some Web pages include a **printer friendly link**. This link opens a Web page containing the same information as on the original Web page, but it's formatted like a printed page, rather than a Web browser window. You should get in the habit of looking for a printer friendly link on Web pages you want to print to ensure that you get a practical printout.

FIGURE F-7: Page Setup dialog box in Internet Explorer

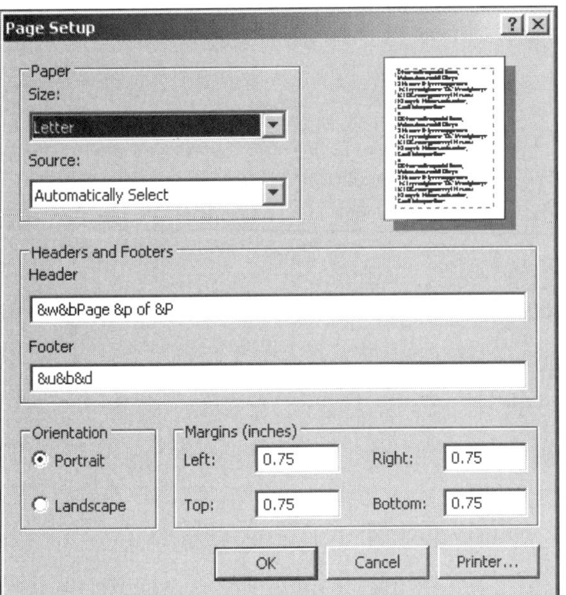

FIGURE F-8: Print Preview in Internet Explorer

Internet

Copying Text from a Web Page

If you use the Web as a resource, you might want to use portions of Web page text as support for a topic in a research or business document. When you copy text from a Web page, you need to be aware of copyright restrictions. If you want to use the text you copy to supplement your document, you must treat it like any other written source. Document the Web source if you quote the text directly or rewrite the text in your own words to avoid plagiarism. Marti is planning a trip to Europe where she will visit clients in Paris, Venice, and Barcelona. She asks you to find information about hotels in Paris.

1. Go to **www.course.com/illustrated/internet3**, click the **Unit F link**, then click the **Paris link** under Lesson 4
   The home page of the Paris Web site appears.
2. Click the **Tourist Information link**, click the **Hotels link**, scroll down if necessary, then click **06** under the Arrondissements section
   A Web page listing hotels in the 6th Arrondissement of Paris appears. (An arrondissement is a neighborhood or district.)
3. Scroll down the Web page, then click the **ABBAYE SAINT-GERMAIN link**
   A description and review of the Hotel Abbaye Saint-Germain appears.
4. Select the name of the hotel and all the text down to the end of the comments
   The Web page scrolls down as you select text. Figure F-9 shows the hotel information selected.
5. Press **[Ctrl][C]**
   The text is copied to the Windows Clipboard.
6. Click the **Start button** on the taskbar, point to **Programs** or **All Programs**, point to **Accessories**, then click **WordPad**
   The WordPad program opens in a new window.
7. Press **[Ctrl][V]**
   The text is pasted into the WordPad document window, as shown in Figure F-10. Your text layout might be different depending on your settings.
8. Press **[Enter]** twice in WordPad, redisplay your Web browser, click the **Back button**, scroll down the Web page if necessary, click the **CRYSTAL link**, select the hotel information including the comments, repeat Step 5 to copy the text, click the **WordPad button** on the taskbar, then repeat Step 7 to paste the text into the WordPad document
   You have information about two hotels in the WordPad document.
9. In WordPad, click **File** on the menu bar, click **Save**, type **hotels** in the File name text box, click the **Save in list arrow**, navigate to the drive and folder where your Project Files are stored, click **Save**, then close WordPad

QuickTip

Web page text can be copied into any word-processing program.

FIGURE F-9: Hotel information selected

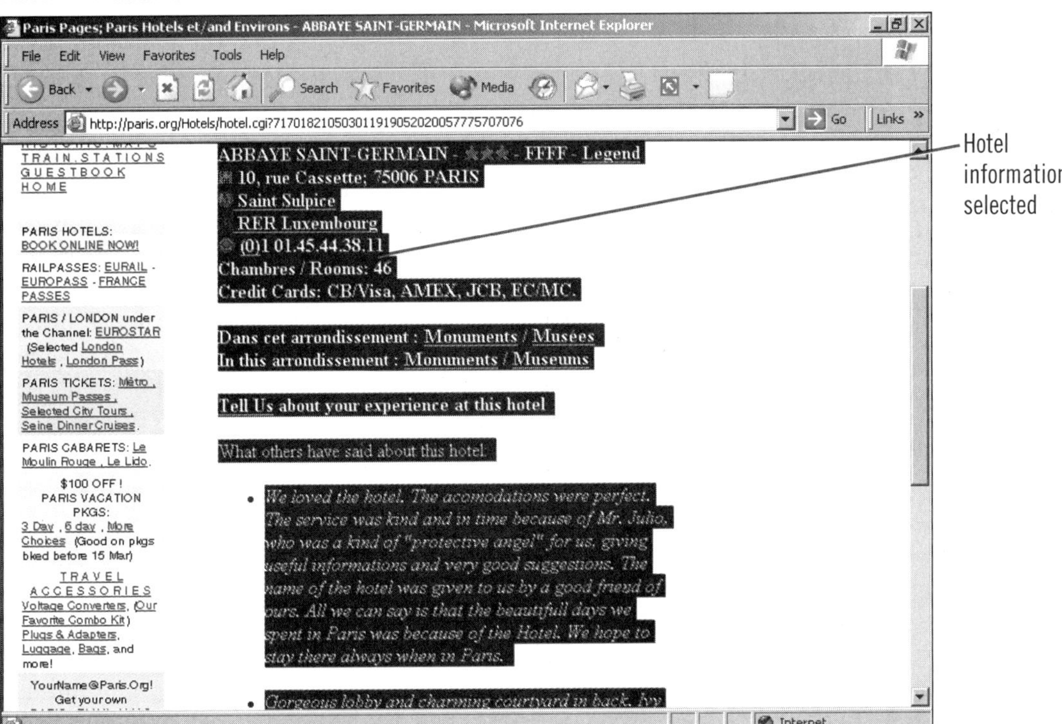

FIGURE F-10: Text copied to WordPad

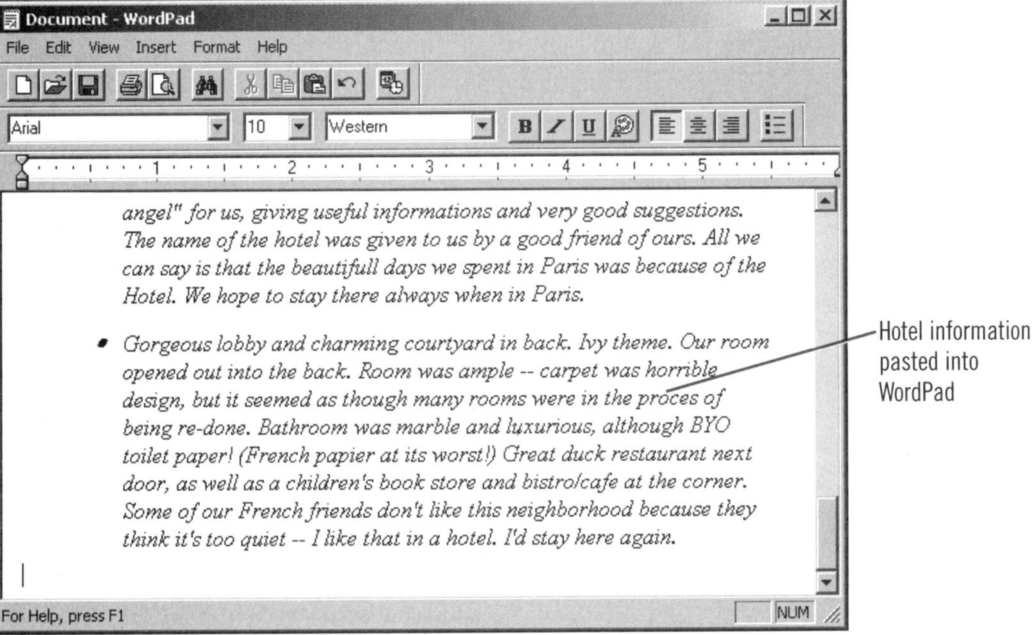

Internet

Getting the News

You can easily find current news stories on the Web. Almost every search engine and directory includes a list of current news links to broadcast networks, wire services, and newspapers. All the major U.S. broadcasters, including ABC, CBS, CNN, Fox, MSNBC, and National Public Radio (NPR) maintain Web sites that carry news features. Broadcasters in other countries, such as the BBC, also provide news reports on their Web pages. Major newspapers, such as *The New York Times*, *Washington Post*, and *London Times*, offer Web sites that include current news and many other features from their print editions. Susan Zhu, Cosby Promotions' research director, wants you to find recent news stories about NASA because a technical company heavily involved with the space program might become a client of Cosby Promotions. Before she meets with Marti about this potential client, Susan needs to know as much as possible about the latest news associated with NASA. You use two news search sites to look for recent news articles that mention NASA.

Steps

1. Go to **www.course.com/illustrated/internet3**, click the **Unit F link**, then click the **Yahoo! news link** under Lesson 5
2. Type **nasa** in the Search text box, then click **Search**
   The search results page returned by the Yahoo! news search lists articles related to NASA.
3. Explore two links that you believe will provide interesting information about NASA
4. Go to **www.course.com/illustrated/internet3**, click the **Unit F link**, then click the **Dogpile link** under Lesson 5
5. Click the **Select list arrow**, then click **News** in the drop-down menu
6. Type **nasa** in the Fetch text box, then click **Fetch**
   A results page appears, similar to Figure F-11. Your results might be different from the figure. Notice that each news report entry includes a link to the Web site that contains the item, the news report's source, and a brief summary.
7. Click the link to read one of the stories listed in the search results
   A story opens from the publication's Web site, similar to the one shown in Figure F-12.

Trouble?

If you get too far from the search results page, use your Web browser's Back button or use the History feature to return to the search results page.

FIGURE F-11: Dogpile news search results

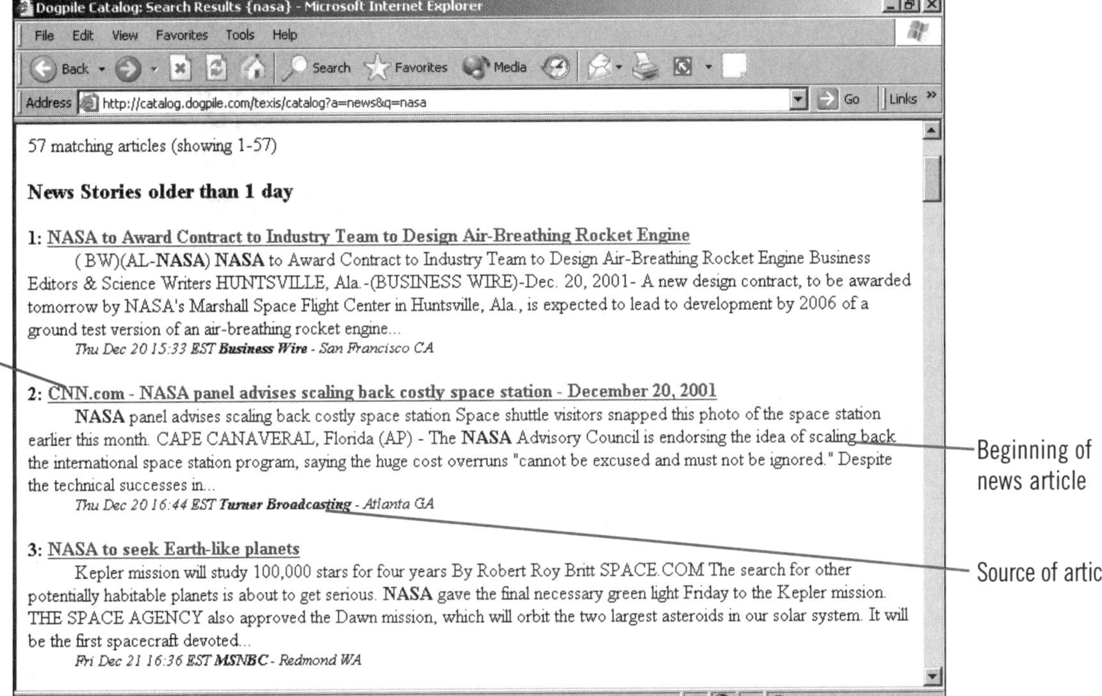

FIGURE F-12: NASA-related news story on the CNN Web site

Internet

Obtaining Weather Reports

You can obtain up-to-the-minute weather reports in destinations all over the world. This information is particularly useful for travelers. Suppose you are planning a trip to Sydney, Australia, in December. Do you take sandals or snow boots? You can check the weather report on the Web to find out. Marti's first stop on her European trip is Venice, so she asks you to check the local weather conditions. She heard that Venice receives quite a bit of rain and wants to know what to expect this time of year. You decide to check two sources of information because you know that meteorology is not an exact science; forecasts from different sources can differ.

1. Go to **www.course.com/illustrated/internet3**, click the **Unit F link**, then click the **weather.com link** under Lesson 6
2. Type **Venice** in the Enter city or US zip code text box, then click **GO**
   A list of cities named Venice appears.
3. Click the **Venice, Italy link**, then examine the Web page that opens
   A Web page similar to Figure F-13 appears, showing current weather conditions as well as a 10-day forecast.
4. Go to **www.course.com/illustrated/internet3**, click the **Unit F link**, then click the **Weather Underground link** under Lesson 6
5. Type **Venice** in the Fast Forecast text box, then click **Fast Forecast**
   A Web page opens showing summarized weather forecasts for all cities named Venice.
6. Click the **Venice, Italy link**, then explore the Web page that opens
   The Weather Underground page for Venice, Italy opens, similar to the one shown in Figure F-14. The temperatures shown should be quite close to the temperatures displayed on weather.com.

FIGURE F-13: Weather.com results for Venice, Italy

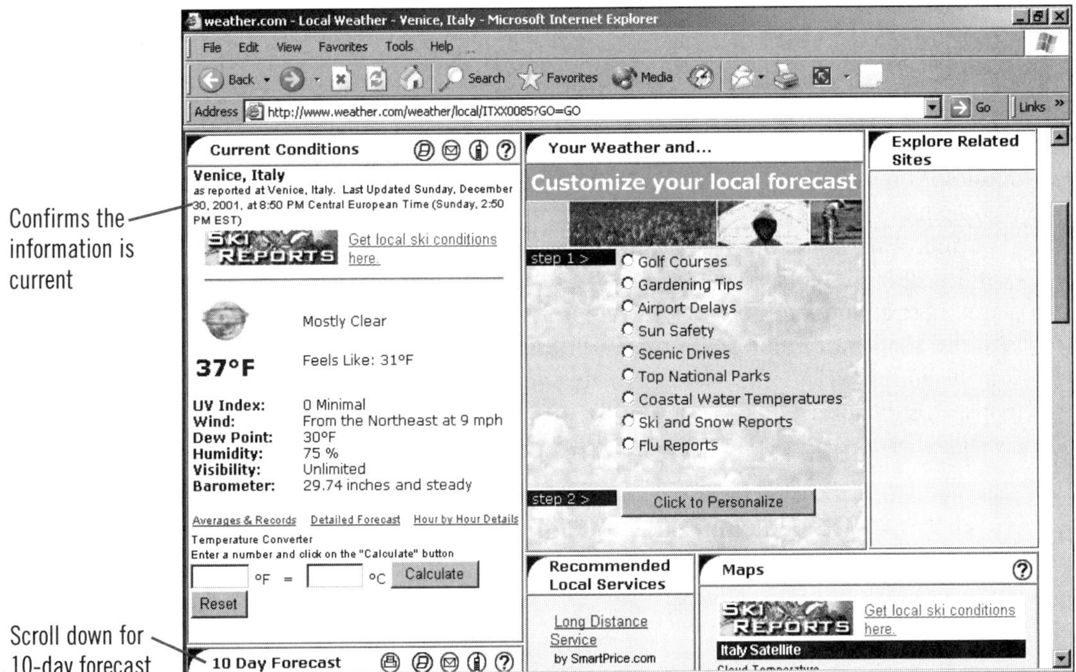

FIGURE F-14: Weather Underground results for Venice, Italy

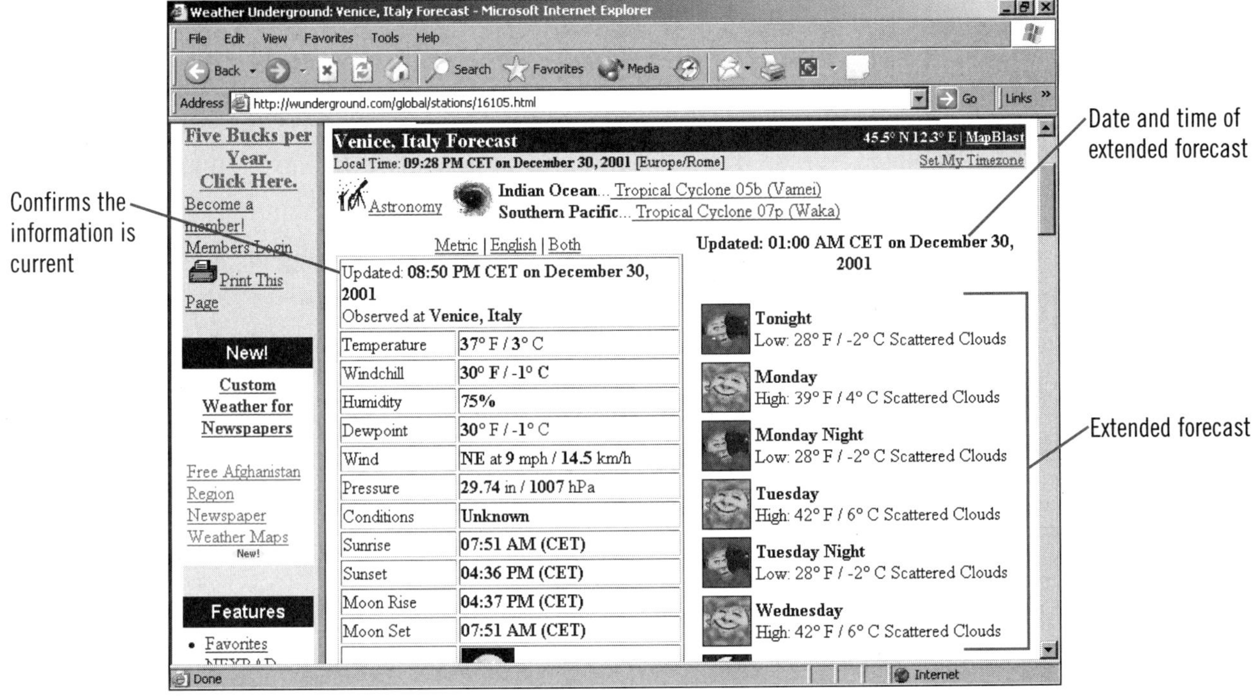

Internet

Internet

Obtaining Maps and City Guides

Suppose you need to find a friend who has moved to a city you've never visited. Fortunately, the Web includes Web sites designed to help you find addresses in even the most convoluted city plan. You can also use the Web to find a wealth of travel information, such as hotel and restaurant listings and sightseeing guides. Franco Devries, Cosby Promotions' Webmaster, is planning to attend a conference on Web page design in Nashville, Tennessee. While in Nashville, he wants to include a stop at Ryman Auditorium, the home of the Grand Ole Opry. Franco gives you the address, 116 Fifth Avenue North, and asks you to find a map of Nashville on the Web that shows the location of Ryman Auditorium. You also look for a city guide to get information about restaurants and other things to do in Nashville.

1. Go to **www.course.com/illustrated/internet3**, click the **Unit F link**, then click the **MapQuest link** under Lesson 7
   The MapQuest Web page appears.
2. In the find a U.S. map section, click in the **Address or Intersection text box**, then type **116 Fifth Avenue North**
3. Press **[Tab]**, type **Nashville** in the City text box, press **[Tab]**, then type **TN** in the State text box
   The MapQuest Web page appears similar to the Web page shown in Figure F-15.
4. Click **MAP IT!**
   The map appears for the address you entered, as shown in Figure F-16. It identifies Ryman Auditorium with a red star.
5. Go to **www.course.com/illustrated/internet3**, click the **Unit F link**, then click the **Excite Travel link** under Lesson 7
6. Scroll down to the Destination Guides section, click the **North America link**, then on the Web page that opens, click the **USA link**
7. On the Web page that opens, click the **Other destinations in USA link**, then on the Web page that opens, click the **Nashville link**
   Figure F-17 shows the Destination Nashville Web page, which provides links to information about different things to do in Nashville. The Web page displayed in your Web browser might look slightly different.
8. Click links to explore the Web site

QuickTip

You can also get detailed driving directions to an address by clicking the Driving Directions link and entering a starting address and destination address in the appropriate text boxes.

Trouble?

If you get too far from the city guide Web page for Nashville, use your Web browser's Back button or the History feature to return to Excite Travel.

FIGURE F-15: Address entered in MapQuest

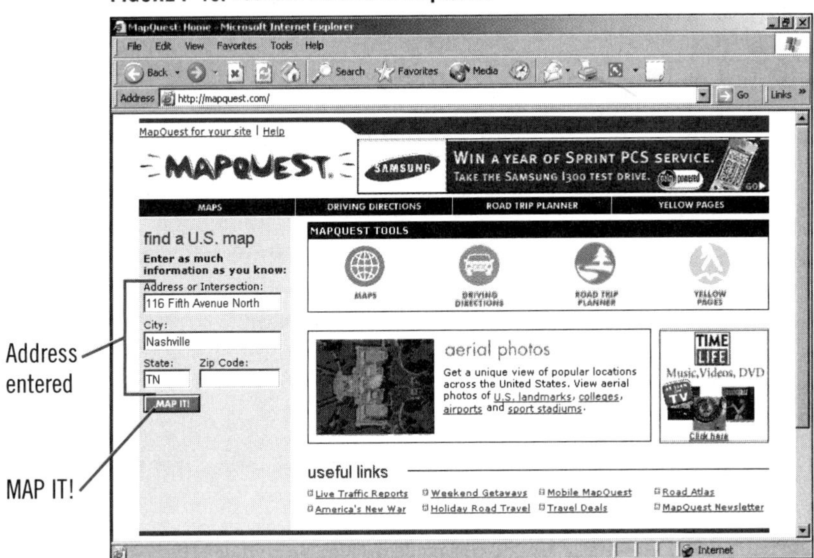

FIGURE F-16: MapQuest map showing the location of Ryman Auditorium

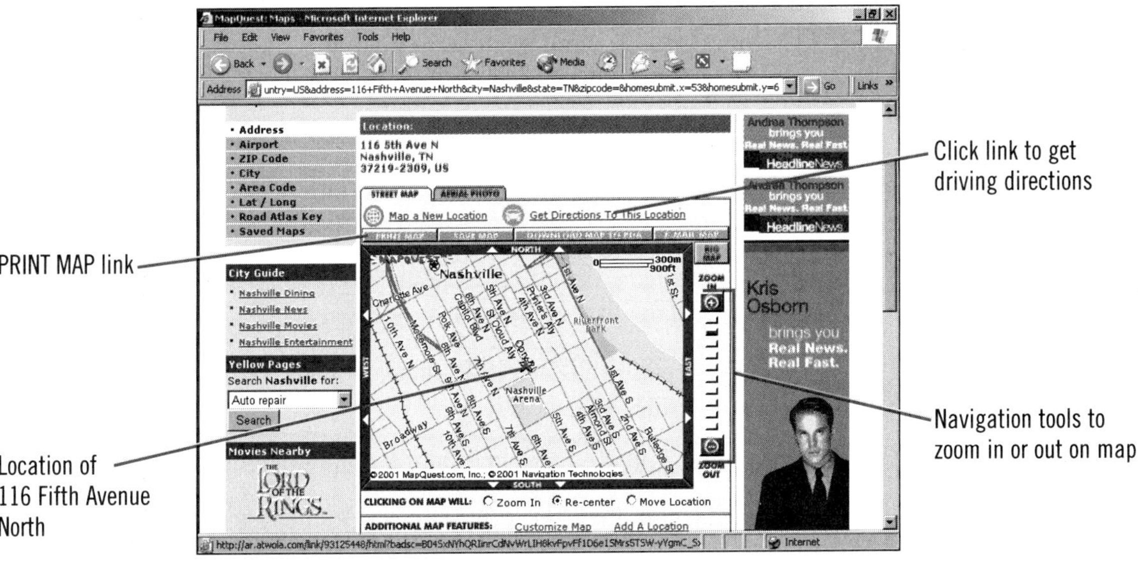

FIGURE F-17: Excite Travel city guide for Nashville, Tennessee

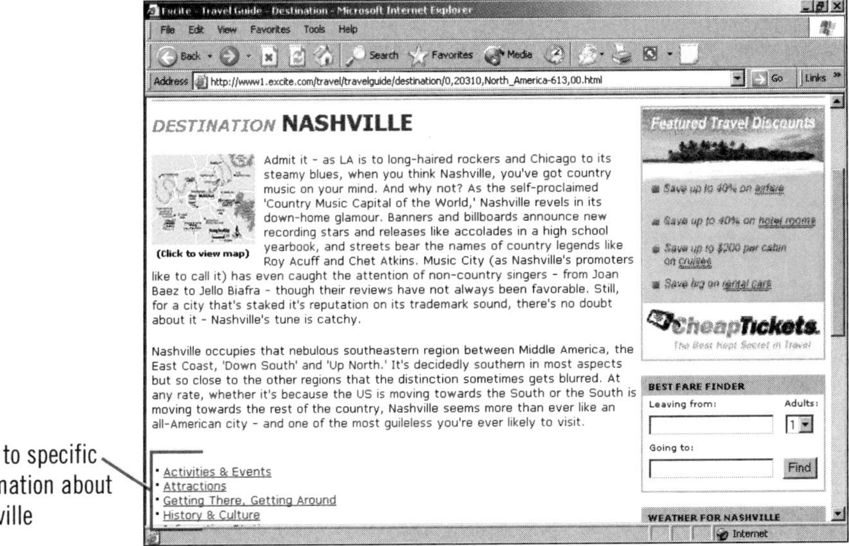

Internet

Finding Businesses and People

A number of search engines on the Web specialize in finding businesses; the businesses are grouped by type and location like the yellow pages phone book. In addition, many Web sites enable you to search for addresses and telephone numbers for individuals as you would in a white pages phone book. Marti is interested in developing reciprocal relationships with public relations firms in Nashville. She asks you to search the Web to find a list of public relations firms in Nashville. She also asks you to check your listing on the WorldPages Web site to familiarize yourself with this resource.

1. Go to **www.course.com/illustrated/internet3**, click the **Unit F link**, then click the **SuperPages link** under Lesson 8
2. Type **public relations** in the Category text box
3. Press **[Tab]** twice, then type **nashville** in the City text box
4. Click the **State list arrow**
5. Scroll down, click **TN**, then click **Find It**
   A Web page opens displaying the categories that most closely match the one you entered.
6. Click **Public Relations Counselors**
   Figure F-18 shows the results page with many business listings from the SuperPages Public Relations Counselors category. The listings include a name, address, telephone number, and link to a map and driving directions for each firm. SuperPages also provides links to the Web sites of firms (if the firm has one).
7. Go to **www.course.com/illustrated/internet3**, click the **Unit F link**, then click the **WorldPages link** under Lesson 8
8. On the WorldPages home page, click the **Find a Person link**
9. Click in the **Last Name text box**, type your last name, press **[Tab]**, then complete the remaining text boxes
   Your screen appears similar to Figure F-19, except your information will appear in place of "A Student."
10. Click **Search**
    Your name might appear in the first results page. If it does not appear, click the Next Page link to go to the next results page.

QuickTip

You can also click the browse link to select a category from a list.

Trouble?

To search listings for Canada, click the Search Canada link; to search other countries, click the International link.

Trouble?

If you do not find your listing, try searching for a friend's listing or for your parents' listing.

FIGURE F-18: Results page for SuperPages search

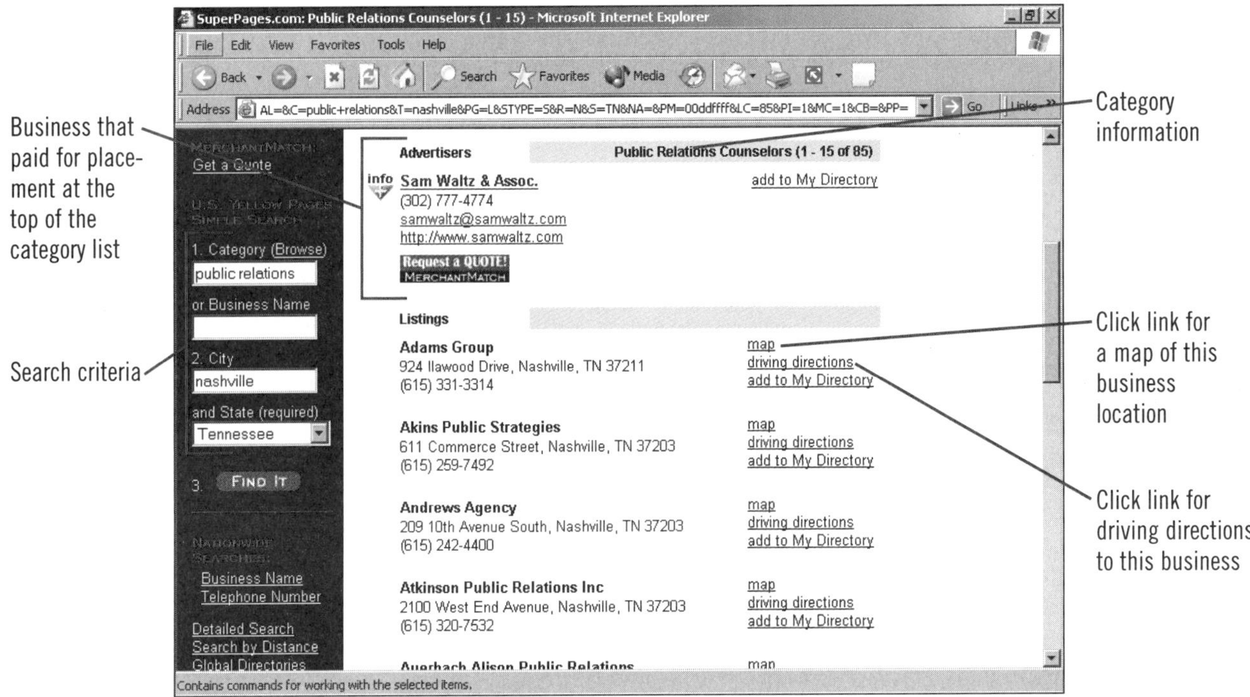

FIGURE F-19: Personal information entered in WorldPages

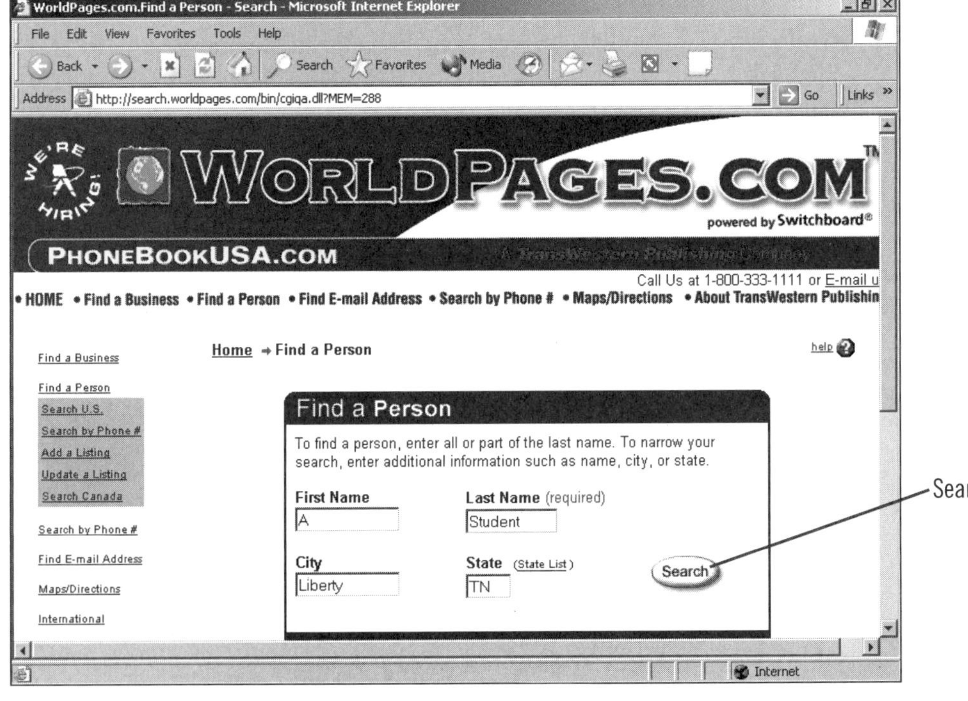

Privacy concerns

Many people expressed concerns about privacy violations when "white pages" information became easily accessible on the Web. In some cases, Web sites made unpublished and unlisted telephone numbers available for public use. Some Web sites even grouped individual listings by religious or political affiliations.

In response to these privacy concerns, most white pages sites now offer individuals ways to remove their listings. If you want to remove your listing from a white pages site, check out the Web site's Help or FAQs (Frequently Asked Questions) links.

Internet

Understanding Graphics and Multimedia

In addition to basic text, most Web sites incorporate images or art, known as **graphics**, into their designs. Graphics can help Web site users find information more easily, and can strongly influence the Web site's mood. Some Web sites also incorporate sound, animation, and video, known collectively as **multimedia**. Web pages can communicate information by playing music, including animated images, or showing a video. You're preparing to research how other promotional agencies are promoting their clients on the Web. You've been asked to focus on the prevalence of graphics and multimedia in such promotions. You start by asking Franco, the company's Webmaster, to give you an overview of graphical and multimedia elements in Web pages.

► Graphics File Formats

Most graphics on the Web are saved in one of two file formats:

- **GIF**, an acronym for **Graphics Interchange Format**, is a file format that compresses small or medium-size images. A GIF file can contain no more than 256 colors. An **animated GIF** file combines several images into a single GIF file so that the images can be displayed one after the other to simulate movement.
- **JPEG**, an acronym for **Joint Photographic Experts Group**, is a file format that can store over 16 million colors. The JPEG format is particularly useful for photographs.

► Finding Image Files

A collection of individual icons, shapes, and other graphics is known as **clip art**. Clip art is available for free use or for purchase on many Web sites. Some Web sites, such as the one shown in Figure F-20, offer clip art or tools for helping you find clip art. Often you can browse clip art by subject category or search for images associated with a keyword you specify.

► Sounds, Music, and Video Clips

Many Web site designers include sound or video clips to enhance the information on their Web pages. Unlike graphics files, sound and video files appear on the Web in many different formats and often require that you install additional software that works with your Web browser. These programs, known as **plug-ins**, are typically available as free downloads. In order for your computer to play sounds, it must also be equipped with a sound card and either speakers or earphones.

► Sound and Video File Formats

Many different file formats are used for sound and video on the Web. **RealAudio** and **MP3** are common formats used for audio, and **AVI**, **MPEG**, and **QuickTime** are common formats used for video. Some file types, including RealAudio and Quicktime files, use a proprietary format, which requires special software to play them. MP3, AVI, and MPEG are all public domain formats, and can be played using the same software that plays many other multimedia file types, including the player that comes with Windows.

► Streaming

In the past, to play an audio and video file from a Web site, you would have to first download the multimedia file and then play it using media software. Currently, another technique known as streaming is being used more widely. When **streaming** a multimedia file, the Web server sends the first part of the file to the Web browser, which begins playing the file. While the Web browser plays the file, the server continues sending the next segment of the file. Streaming transmission allows you to access very large audio or video files in much less time than traditional transmission, because you start playing the file before you finish downloading it. Streaming is a popular method for making radio stations available live on the Web. Figure F-21 shows the Web page for a radio station that streams both RealAudio and MP3 versions of its programming.

FIGURE F-20: Web site offering free clip art

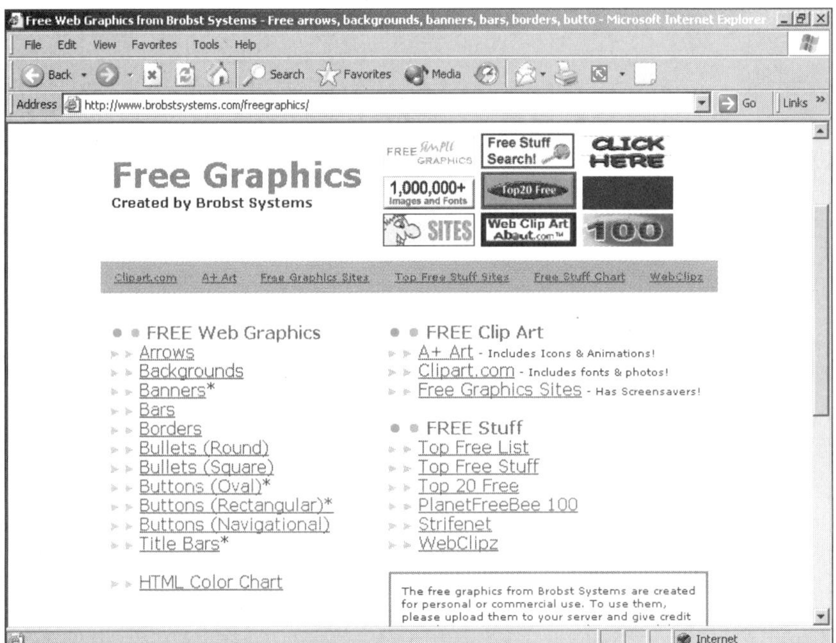

FIGURE F-21: Radio station Web site offering streaming

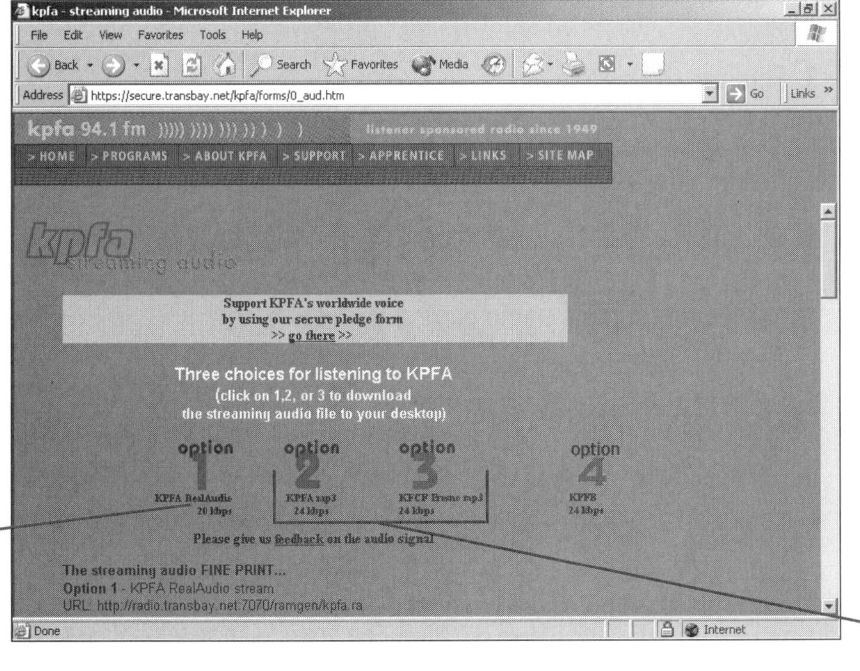

CLUES TO USE

Copyright issues

When you use graphics that you download from a Web site, you need to be very careful not to violate the image owner's rights. You should check for copyright notices and conditions-of-use statements. Fortunately, some Web sites provide graphics files that are in the public domain, which means that you can freely copy the files without requesting permission from the source. Even though you can use public domain information without obtaining permission, you should check the Web site carefully for requirements that you acknowledge the source of the material when you use it. Acknowledging a source can be especially important when you use public domain material in school or business projects. If you cannot find a clear statement of copyright terms or a statement indicating that the files are in the public domain, you should not use them.

Internet

Evaluating Web Resources

Like a library, the Web makes a huge variety of information readily available without a failsafe standard for differentiating reliable data from less reliable data. As a result, it's important to evaluate and verify the information you view. Table F-1 summarizes how you can evaluate the three major components of any Web page: authorship, content, and appearance. A client of Cosby Promotions is a nonprofit group that is concerned about global warming. While doing research for this organization, you have found a Web site that appears to contain relevant information. Before you pass along your findings, you need to evaluate the quality of the Web site.

Steps

1. **Go to www.course.com/illustrated/internet3, click the Unit F link, then click the PSR Environment and Health link under Lesson 10**
   A Web page opens, similar to Figure F-22.

2. **Evaluate the three components of a Web page: authorship, content, and appearance**
   The Web page shown in Figure F-22 has a simple, clear design. The .org domain in the URL verifies that the publisher is a not-for-profit organization. The grammar and spelling are correct, and the content is clearly presented. In addition, the text cites such authorities as the U.S. Department of Energy. The reputable references and the consistent style of the Web page suggest that this Web site is a quality resource. However, the author or publisher of the Web page is identified only as "PSR."

3. **Scroll to the bottom of the Web page**
   As you can see, "PSR" is an acronym for Physicians for Social Responsibility. The organization's address, telephone number, and e-mail address are listed along with contact information for key individuals in PSR's Environment and Health Program.

4. **Click in the Address text box or Location text box, click to the right of the URL, then press [Backspace] as many times as necessary to delete all of the text to the right of the .org/ domain name portion of the URL**
   The URL should appear similar to *http://www.psr.org/*.

5. **Press [Enter]**
   The PSR home page appears. This Web page includes links to information about the organization, including its goals, activities, directors, and membership.

6. **To view an additional resource, go to www.course.com/illustrated/internet3, click the Unit F link, then click the LibrarySpot link under Lesson 10**
   The LibrarySpot includes many of the same things you would expect to find in a public or school library. This library is, however, open 24 hours a day and seven days a week. The LibrarySpot Web site lets you access reference materials, electronic texts, and other library Web sites from one central Web page.

Citing Web research resources

For academic research, the two most widely followed standards for citing Web resources are those of the American Psychological Association (APA) and the Modern Language Association (MLA). You can use a search engine to find Web pages that describe how to cite Web resources using both standards.

FIGURE F-22: PSR Web site

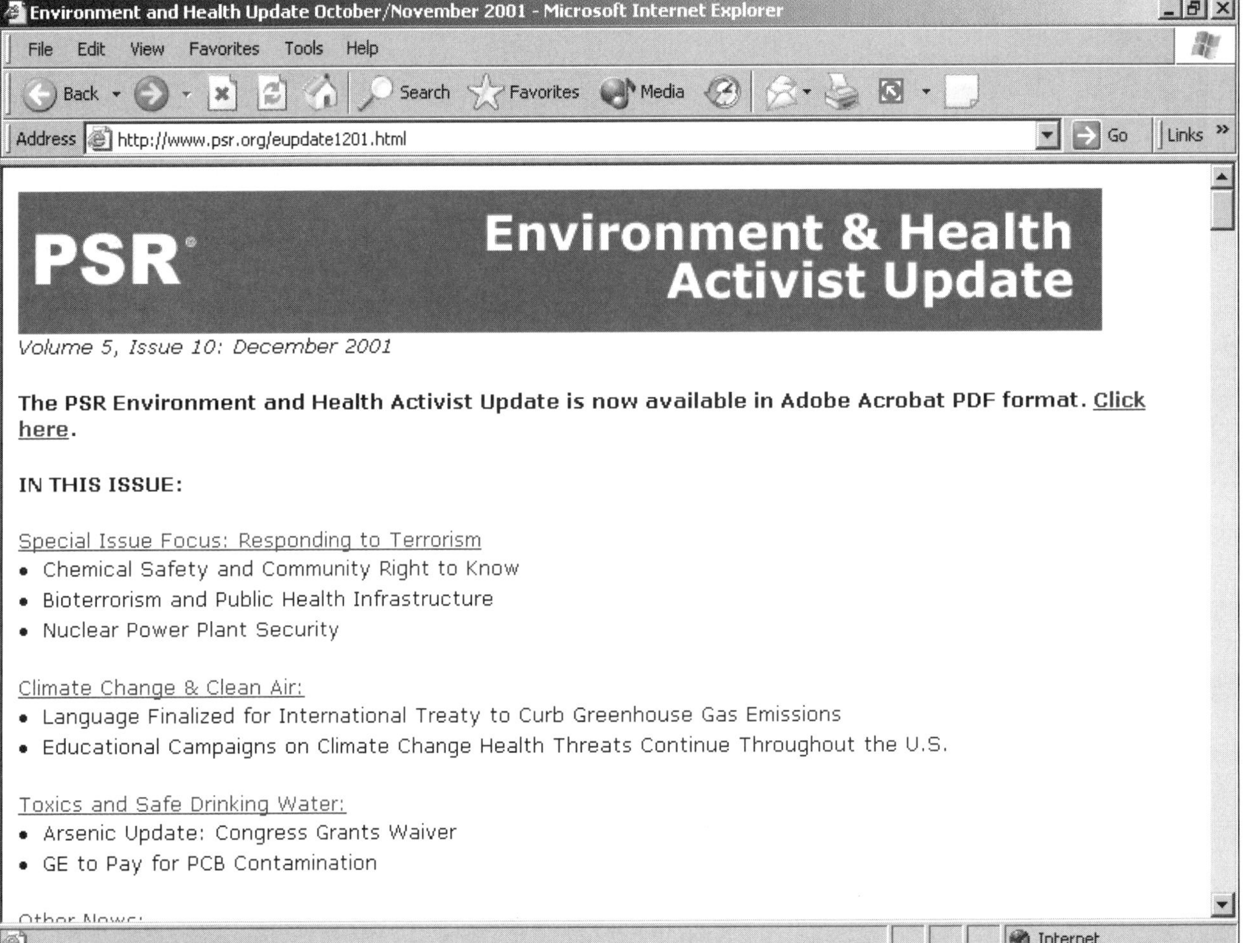

TABLE F-1: Web page evaluation guidelines

component	evaluation
Authorship	*Author contact information*: Make sure you can telephone or e-mail the author directly
	Author affiliations: Check universities or companies associated with the author to verify a relationship
	Domain identifier: Examine the domain identifier in the URL. If the Web site claims affiliation with an educational or research institution, then the domain should be .edu or .ac for educational or academic institution. A not-for-profit organization would most likely use the .org domain, and a government unit or agency would use the .gov domain
	Author qualifications: Determine if the author's qualifications relate to the material that appears on the Web site
Content	Read the content critically and evaluate if the included topics are relevant to the Web site
Appearance	Look at the design critically; Web page design elements that often suggest low quality include loud colors that distract the user, graphics that serve no purpose, flashing text, and grammatical and spelling errors

Internet

Understanding E-Commerce

Electronic commerce, or **e-commerce**, takes place when two parties engage in a business transaction over various kinds of networks instead of in person. E-commerce is growing rapidly as more people discover how easy it is to buy items and conduct business over the Internet. Many types of businesses provide secure Web sites where people can safely pay for items or services with a credit card or have money debited directly from their bank accounts. Franco is considering ways that Cosby Promotions might use e-commerce. He asks you to investigate the types of Web sites that use e-commerce.

Details

► Catalog Retailing

A number of businesses that have traditionally sold goods through catalogs using mail and telephone orders have now established e-commerce Web sites. These businesses already have functioning product-delivery systems and know how to anticipate their customers' needs to stock the right merchandise. They have simply converted their printed catalogs and telephone order-takers into properly designed Web pages. One example of this type of Web site is the Lands' End Web site, shown in Figure F-23.

► Book and Music Retailing

Businesses that sell books and music on the Web want to offer their customers a wide selection of titles. Customers can search for books and music by topic, title, and author or artist. In most cases, these Web sites have the title the customer wants. Amazon.com started as a book retailer, but has since expanded to include music, electronics, toys and games, and even an auction page. A national book store chain, Barnes & Noble, also set up its own Web site, bn.com. Cdnow is also an example of a Web site that specializes in music and videos.

► Cost-Reduction Features

Many firms have set up Web sites to reduce their costs. For example, Federal Express Corporation, better known as FedEx, set up a Web site to reduce customer service phone calls. Using the Web site, customers can get information about rates, shipping services, and drop-off locations, as well as track packages.

► News, Information, and Advertising

Traditional news media raise revenues by charging a subscription fee, accepting paid advertisements, or by doing some combination of the two activities. News sites on the Web follow the same model. Most news sites that receive revenue from displaying an advertisement banner on their Web site are free to visitors; however, some allow visitors to view a few stories, but require the visitor to pay a subscription or pay-per-item fee to view more content. For example, The Wall Street Journal Interactive Edition Web site provides free access to items like the classified job ads and the annual report service, but to access the rest of the Web site, a visitor must pay a subscription fee.

► Online Auctions

Online auctions represent an innovative use of e-commerce. They display items for sale, and customers are allowed to bid on those items for a specific amount of time, usually a few days to a week. Some Web sites, such as the Onsale Auction Supersite, offer merchandise that is the property of the Web site owner. Other auction sites, such as eBay, auction the property of others, much like an auctioneer would do at a public auction. Figure F-24 shows the home page of eBay.

FIGURE F-23: Lands' End Web site

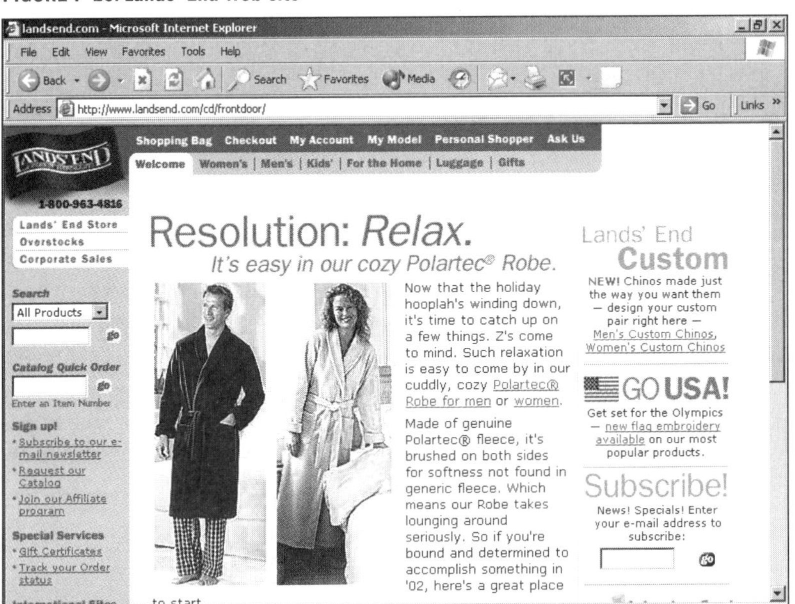

FIGURE F-24: eBay Web site

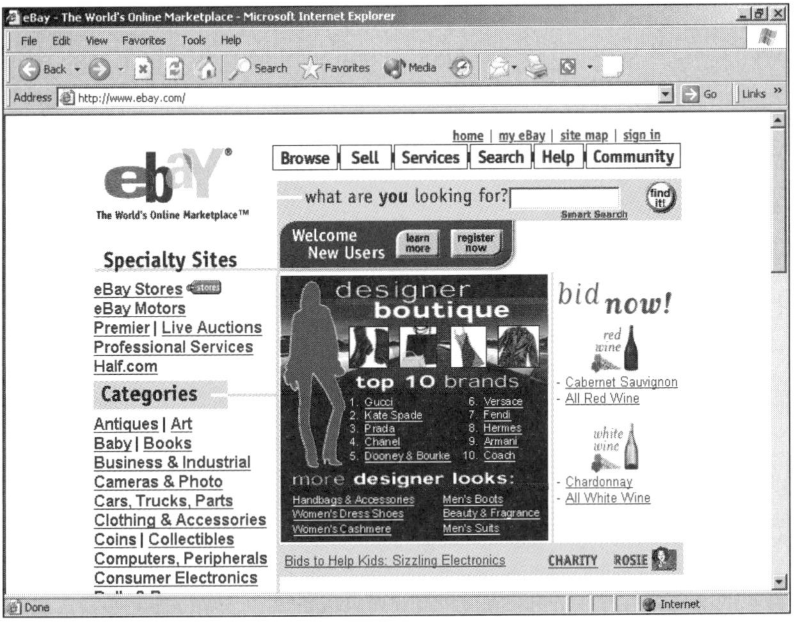

CLUES TO USE

Addressing transaction security and privacy concerns

Participants in e-commerce have two major concerns: transaction security and privacy. To address users' security concerns, many Web sites used in e-commerce use the Secure Socket Layer (SSL) protocol to protect sensitive information as it travels over the Internet. A consortium of firms, including Visa International and MasterCard International, has created a standard known as the Secure Electronic Transaction (SET) protocol. SET is more complex and considerably more secure than the SSL protocol. As SET or other higher-security protocols become widely adopted on e-commerce sites, Web transactions will become safer.

Potential customers of Web-based businesses are also concerned about their privacy. Web sites can collect a great deal of information about customers' preferences, even before they place an order. No general standards currently exist for maintaining confidentiality regarding such information. Although many business Web sites include statements of their customer privacy policies, no laws exist requiring such statements or policies. Web site owners can purchase assurance certifications that certify the Web site as meeting some criteria for conducting business in a secure and privacy-preserving manner.

Internet

Understanding Cookies

When getting information from the Web, you will often encounter cookies. A **cookie** is a small text file that a Web site stores on your computer. Cookies contain information that makes your Web-browsing experience simpler and more personalized. For example, an online bookstore might store your book preferences in a cookie. When you revisit the bookstore, the Web site will inform you of new books available by the same author as the one whose book you purchased previously. Sometimes cookies are intrusive and are created without your consent. Fortunately, you can set your Web browser to warn you when a Web site is attempting to create a cookie file, or you can block storing cookie files altogether. Figure F-25 shows a sample cookie warning. As you surf the Web, you frequently receive cookie warnings. You decide to change your Web browser preferences relating to cookies.

Netscape Users

1. Click **Edit** on the menu bar, then click **Preferences**
2. Click the **triangle** next to Privacy & Security, then click **Cookies**
   Your screen should look similar to Figure F-26. You can select options to accept all cookies or disable cookies. A check mark in the Warn me before storing a cookie check box means that a cookie alert box will appear each time a cookie is sent, which then allows you to accept or reject the cookie.
3. Click **Cancel**
4. Close Netscape

Internet Explorer Users

1. Click **Tools** on the menu bar, then click **Internet Options**
   The Internet Options dialog box opens.
2. Click the **Privacy tab**
   Your screen should look similar to Figure F-27. The Privacy tab contains a slider bar, which allows you to customize your Web browser's privacy level. You can also click the Edit button to set rules for cookies from specific Web sites.
3. Click **Cancel**
4. Close Internet Explorer

FIGURE F-25: Cookie alert box

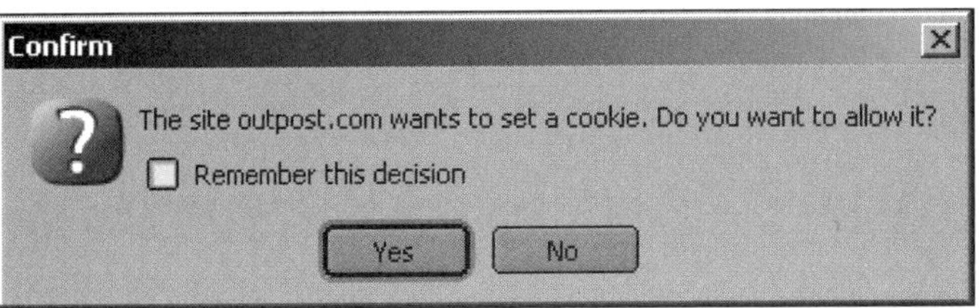

FIGURE F-26: Cookie preferences in Netscape

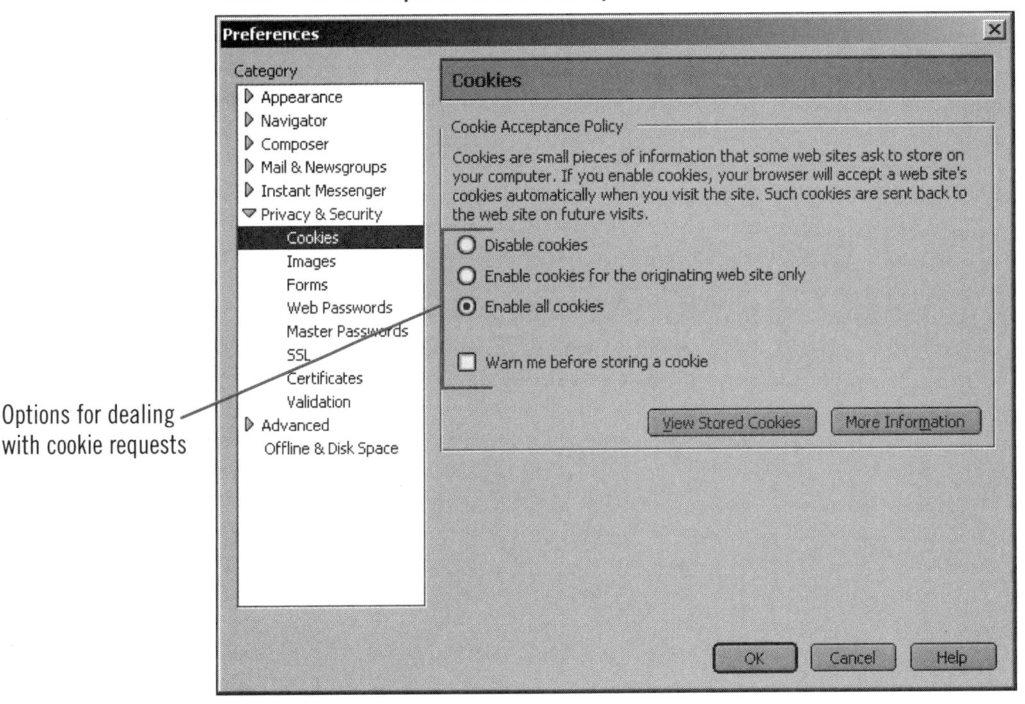

FIGURE F-27: Cookie preferences in Internet Explorer

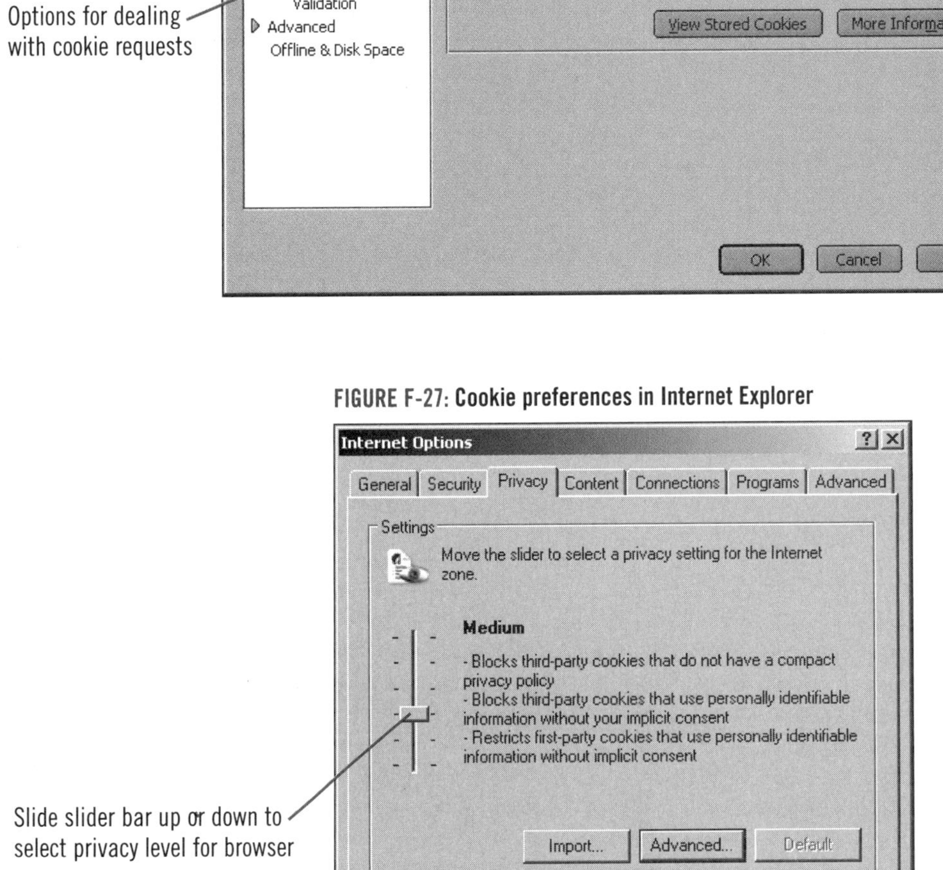

Internet

Practice

▶ Concepts Review

Identify the purpose of each Web page shown in Figures F-28 through F-31.

FIGURE F-28

1

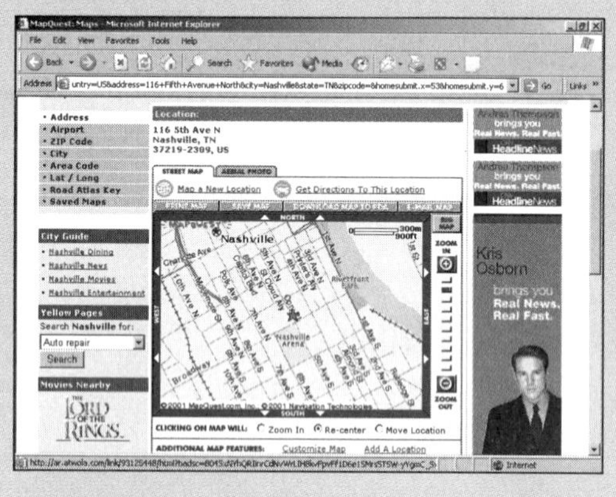

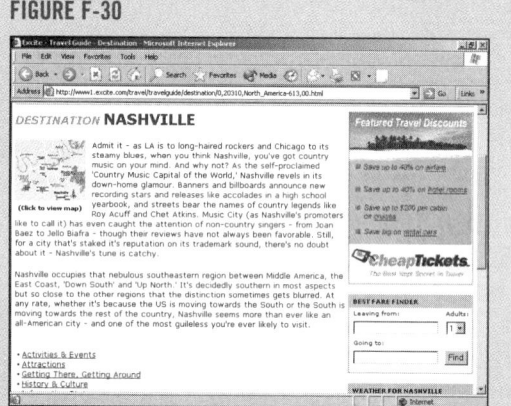

FIGURE F-29

2

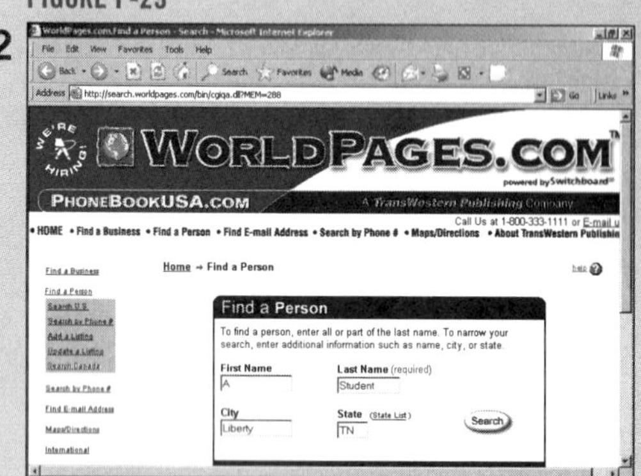

FIGURE F-30

3

FIGURE F-31

4

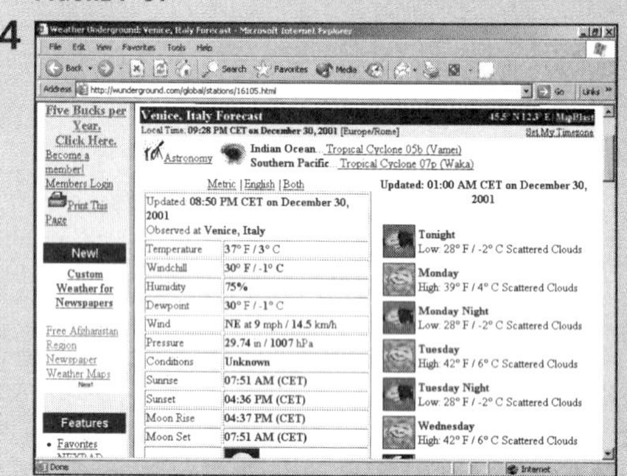

Match each term with the statement that describes it.

5. Streaming	**a.** A news search tool
6. QuickTime	**b.** A sound file format
7. Dogpile	**c.** A graphics file format
8. WorldPages	**d.** Playing a sound or video file before it is fully downloaded
9. GIF	**e.** A directory of personal information such as address and phone number
10. MP3	**f.** A video file format

Select the best answer from the list of choices.

11. Which of the following elements appears when you save a Web page in Netscape?
- **a.** Background texture
- **b.** GIF
- **c.** Graphic image
- **d.** Text

12. Which of the following file extensions is not related to sound or video?
- **a.** .avi
- **b.** .ra
- **c.** .mpg
- **d.** .gif

13. Which of the following characteristics might identify a Web page as unreliable?
- **a.** Use of the .org domain
- **b.** Spelling errors
- **c.** Author's e-mail address
- **d.** References

14. A small text file that a Web site stores on your computer is called a:
- **a.** Cookie.
- **b.** Password.
- **c.** Portable file.
- **d.** User file.

Skills Review

1. Save a Web page in Netscape.
- **a.** Go to **www.course.com/illustrated/internet3**, click the **Unit F link**, then click the **Chicago event calendar link** under Skills Review 1 through 3.
- **b.** Save the Chicago event calendar Web page where your Project Files are stored with the filename **chicago.htm**.
- **c.** Display your Web browser's home page.
- **d.** Open the file you saved to check the Web page. Notice that the images do not appear.
- **e.** Check the path and filename to be sure you are viewing the Web page you saved.
- **f.** Go to **www.course.com/illustrated/internet3**, click the **Unit F link**, then click the **Chicago event calendar link** under Skills Review 1 through 3.
- **g.** Save the Ferris wheel graphic where your Project Files are stored.

Practice

2. **Save a Web page in Internet Explorer.**
   - **a.** Go to **www.course.com/illustrated/internet3**, click the **Unit F link**, then click the **Chicago event calendar link** under Skills Review 1 through 3.
   - **b.** Save the Chicago event calendar Web page where your Project Files are stored.
   - **c.** Display your Web browser's home page.
   - **d.** Open the Web page file you saved to check the Web page.
   - **e.** Check the path and filename in the address text box to be sure you are viewing the Web page you saved.

3. **Print a Web page.**
   - **a.** Go to **www.course.com/illustrated/internet3**, click the **Unit F link**, then click the **Chicago event calendar link** under Skills Review 1 through 3.
   - **b.** If you are using Internet Explorer, view the page in Print Preview.
   - **c.** Set the print options to print only one page.
   - **d.** Print one page.

4. **Copy text from a Web page.**
   - **a.** Go to **www.course.com/illustrated/internet3**, click the **Unit F link**, then click the **Auckland restaurants link** under Skills Review 4.
   - **b.** Explore the restaurant listings for Auckland, New Zealand, to find two restaurants that appeal to you.
   - **c.** Copy the descriptions of the two restaurants you have chosen to WordPad.
   - **d.** Save the document where your Project Files are stored with the filename **auckland.rtf**.
   - **e.** Close WordPad.

5. **Get the news.**
   - **a.** Go to **www.course.com/illustrated/internet3**, click the **Unit F link**, then click the **Yahoo! news link** under Skills Review 5.
   - **b.** Search for recent news stories about Russia.
   - **c.** Go to **www.course.com/illustrated/internet3**, click the **Unit F link**, then click the **Dogpile link** under Skills Review 5.
   - **d.** Search for recent news stories about Russia.

6. **Obtain weather reports.**
   - **a.** Go to **www.course.com/illustrated/internet3**, click the **Unit F link**, then use the weather.com and Weather Underground links under Skills Review 6 to find and enter the current temperatures for each of the cities listed in the following table:

	Stockholm, Sweden	Tokyo, Japan	Santiago, Chile	Cairo, Egypt
weather.com				
Weather Underground				

7. **Obtain maps and city guides.**
   a. Go to **www.course.com/illustrated/internet3**, click the **Unit F link**, then click the **MapQuest link** under Skills Review 7.
   b. Find a map of Howard University in Washington, DC. The address is 2400 Sixth St. NW.
   c. Print a copy of the map.
   d. Go to **www.course.com/illustrated/internet3**, click the **Unit F link**, then click the **Excite Travel link** under Skills Review 7.
   e. Open the city guide to Washington, DC.

8. **Find businesses and people.**
   a. Go to **www.course.com/illustrated/internet3**, click the **Unit F link**, then click the **SuperPages link** under Skills Review 8.
   b. Conduct a search for art in New Orleans, Louisiana.
   c. When prompted, select the Art Galleries Dealers & Consultants category.
   d. Find maps to two of the art galleries.
   e. Print the maps.

9. **Evaluate Web resources.**
   a. Go to **www.course.com/illustrated/internet3**, click the **Unit F link**, then click the **About.com link** under Skills Review 9.
   b. Click the **Health & Fitness link**, then click the **Diabetes link**.
   c. Click the **Causes link**, then follow links in that category.
   d. Explore two of the Web sites, then evaluate them using the following table:

	author contact	author affiliation	.edu, .org or .gov domain	reputable references
Web site 1 URL:	Yes/No	Yes/No	Yes/No	Yes/No
Web site 2 URL:	Yes/No	Yes/No	Yes/No	Yes/No

Note: To access the Web sites listed in the Independent Challenges, go to the Student Online Companion at www.course.com/illustrated/internet3, click the Unit F link, then click the desired link(s) under the appropriate Independent Challenge.

Internet

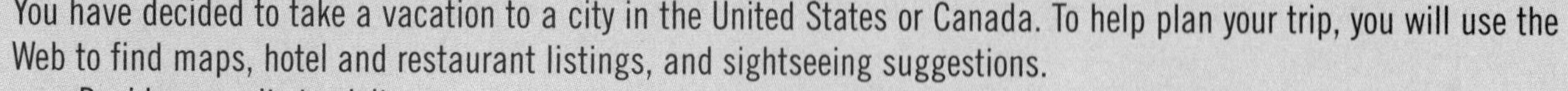

Independent Challenge 1

You have decided to take a vacation to a city in the United States or Canada. To help plan your trip, you will use the Web to find maps, hotel and restaurant listings, and sightseeing suggestions.

- **a.** Decide on a city to visit.
- **b.** Use the Excite Travel Web site to find links to information about the city you plan to visit.
- **c.** Copy information to WordPad about two restaurants in the city you plan to visit.
- **d.** Save the list as **restaurants.rtf**.
- **e.** Find a Web page with information about two hotels in the city you plan to visit.
- **f.** Save the Web page where your Project Files are stored.
- **g.** Print the first page of the Web page. Be sure to include the URL in the header or footer information.
- **h.** Check Weather.com to find the current temperature in the city you plan to visit.
- **i.** Summarize the information you have found about the city you plan to visit. Include the names and addresses of the two restaurants, the URL for the Web page with information about two hotels, and a brief description of the current weather conditions.

Independent Challenge 2

You are a sales representative for Portland Concrete Mixers, a company that makes replacement parts for concrete mixing equipment. You have been transferred to the Olympia area in Washington and want to plan your first sales trip there. Because you plan to drive to Olympia, you need information about the best route as well as a map of the city. You hope to generate some new customers and, therefore, need to identify sales-lead prospects in the Olympia area. Companies that manufacture ready-mixed concrete are good prospects for you.

- **a.** Open the MapQuest home page, then click the **DRIVING DIRECTIONS link**.
- **b.** Type **Portland, OR** as your starting address, then type **Olympia, WA** as your destination address.
- **c.** Click the **GET DIRECTIONS link**.
- **d.** Click the **ZOOM IN link** to the right of the map to obtain a more detailed map of the route from Portland to Olympia, then print the map.
- **e.** Scroll down to the bottom of the Web page to view the map of Olympia.
- **f.** To identify sales leads in Olympia, open the SuperPages Web site.
- **g.** Search for information about ready-mixed concrete in Olympia.
- **h.** Select three companies that you think would be good prospects.
- **i.** Outline your travel plans and list the names and addresses of the three companies you've identified.

Independent Challenge 3

You are the owner of a popular nightclub, Ragtime Tonight, which is located near a convention center. An increasing number of your patrons are travelers who make airline, hotel, and car-rental reservations using the Web, and you want to create a Web site that reaches them. While designing the Web site, you'd like to add some ragtime audio clips that play when the Web site is opened using a Web browser. However, you need to know more about allowable usage, copyright restrictions, and licensing before proceeding.

a. In the Student Online Companion, explore the links under Independent Challenge 3 to learn about allowable use and limitations of copyrighted work.

b. Write a summary of the information you find. Describe what you can do, what you can't do, and ideas for how you might legally include ragtime music on your Web site at the lowest cost.

Independent Challenge 4

You are conducting research on politics in Mexico. Currently, you are studying the history of land ownership in this country. In your report, you want to tie this history together with relevant recent events.

a. In the Student Online Companion, use the links under Independent Challenge 4 to find recent news articles mentioning land ownership issues in Mexico.

b. Print the first page from two of these articles.

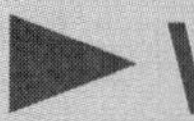

Visual Workshop

Use MapQuest to find the map illustrated in Figure F-32. The address entered in MapQuest is 25 Thomson Place, Boston, Massachusetts. When you have found the map, print a copy.

FIGURE F-32

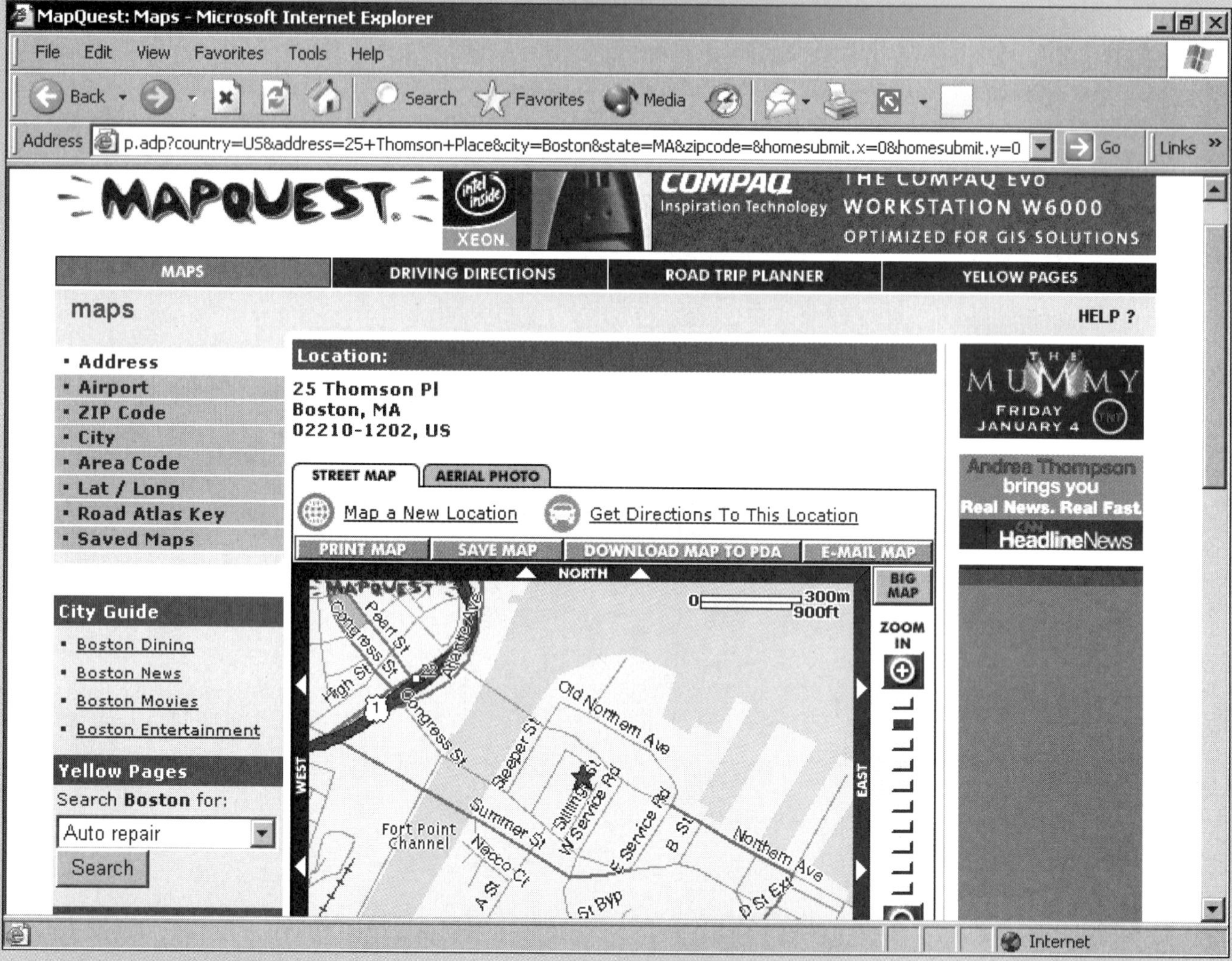

MapQuest: Maps - Microsoft Internet Explorer
File Edit View Favorites Tools Help
Back Search Favorites Media
Address p.adp?country=US&address=25+Thomson+Place&city=Boston&state=MA&zipcode=&homesubmit.x=0&homesubmit.y=0 Go Links
MAPQUEST
COMPAQ Inspiration Technology
THE COMPAQ EVO WORKSTATION W6000
OPTIMIZED FOR GIS SOLUTIONS
MAPS
DRIVING DIRECTIONS
ROAD TRIP PLANNER
YELLOW PAGES
maps
HELP ?
Address
Airport
ZIP Code
City
Area Code
Lat / Long
Road Atlas Key
Saved Maps
Location:
25 Thomson Pl
Boston, MA
02210-1202, US
STREET MAP
AERIAL PHOTO
Map a New Location
Get Directions To This Location
PRINT MAP
SAVE MAP
DOWNLOAD MAP TO PDA
E-MAIL MAP
NORTH
WEST
EAST
BIG MAP
ZOOM IN
300m
900ft
Congress St
Pearl St
High St
Old Northern Ave
Sleeper St
Summer St
Fort Point Channel
Nacco Ct
A St
W Service Rd
E Service Rd
B St
Northern Ave
D St Ext
City Guide
Boston Dining
Boston News
Boston Movies
Boston Entertainment
Yellow Pages
Search Boston for:
Auto repair
Search
THE MUMMY
FRIDAY JANUARY 4
Andrea Thompson brings you
Real News. Real Fast.
HeadlineNews
Internet

Using Web-Based Tools

- Set up Web-based e-mail
- Send and read messages using Hotmail
- Reply to and forward messages using Hotmail
- File and delete messages using Hotmail
- Understand Web portals
- Customize a Web portal
- Create a Web calendar
- Customize a Web calendar
- Print a Web calendar
- Create a Web address book
- Maintain a Web address book
- Use a Web address book

Web-based e-mail allows you to use a Web browser to send and receive messages on any computer connected to the Internet. Web-based e-mail is often incorporated into a **Web portal**, which is a Web site offering customized news along with features, such as a calendar and an address book. You're planning to travel abroad for several months. You want to set up Web-based e-mail and an address book to keep in touch with friends and family. You also want to customize a Web portal with news and other information from back home and create a Web calendar to keep track of your travels.

Internet

Setting Up Web-Based E-Mail

Many companies and organizations, such as Yahoo! and MSN Hotmail offer Web-based e-mail. To use Web-based e-mail, you open the company's Web page and log in. To log in, you first need to establish a user account. A **user account** sets up your e-mail address and account with the Web-based e-mail company. After you have a user account, you can then receive, view, compose, and send e-mail messages. No matter where you are in the world, if you can connect to the Internet, you can access a Web-based e-mail account. You decide to set up a Hotmail account for your Web-based e-mail.

1. Go to **www.course.com/illustrated/internet3**, click the **Unit G link**, then click the **Hotmail link** under Lesson 1
   The Hotmail page opens in your Web browser. If the Hotmail page displays "Welcome" followed by a user name (not yours), click Sign Out to end the previous user's session.

Trouble?
If you already have a Hotmail account, log in to your account, then skip to the next lesson.

2. In the New to Hotmail? section, click the **Sign Up link**
   The Hotmail Registration page shown in Figure G-1 opens. The Web page changes occasionally, so your Web page might look different from Figure G-1.
3. In the First Name text box, type your first name, press **[Tab]** to move to the Last Name text box, then type your last name

Trouble?
If you live outside the United States, a new Web page might open in which you select information relevant to your country. Follow the on-screen instructions.

4. Complete the remaining fields in the Profile Information section with information about yourself, finishing with Occupation
5. If necessary, scroll down to view the Account Information section shown in Figure G-2, then type a user name in the Sign-In Name text box
   A **sign-in name**, or **user name**, is the name that uniquely identifies you in Hotmail. Your sign-in name is the first part of your Hotmail e-mail address, followed by @hotmail.com. Your sign-in name must begin with a letter. It can contain letters, numbers, and underscore characters (_), but it cannot contain spaces. Try to come up with a sign-in name that is likely to be unique, such as your first and last names together, or one or two words (without spaces) along with a number.

Trouble?
If a new Web page opens telling you about a registration error, follow the instructions on the Web page to correct the error and submit the new information; if a Confirm dialog box opens and asks if you want to remember your logon, click No.

6. Complete the remaining fields in the Account Information section, then click **Sign Up**
   The Sign Up Successful! page opens, displaying your new Hotmail e-mail address along with information about your account.
7. Click **Continue at Hotmail**, read the Terms of Use page, click **I Accept**, then scroll down and click the **Click here link** (if the WebCourier FREE Subscriptions page does not open after you click I Accept)
   The WebCourier FREE Subscriptions page opens.
8. Without making any selections, scroll to the bottom of the Web page, then click **Continue**
   The Special Offer Newsletters page opens.
9. Without making any selections, scroll to the bottom of the Web page, then click **Continue to E-mail**
   The Hotmail home page opens.

FIGURE G-1: Profile Information section of Hotmail Registration page

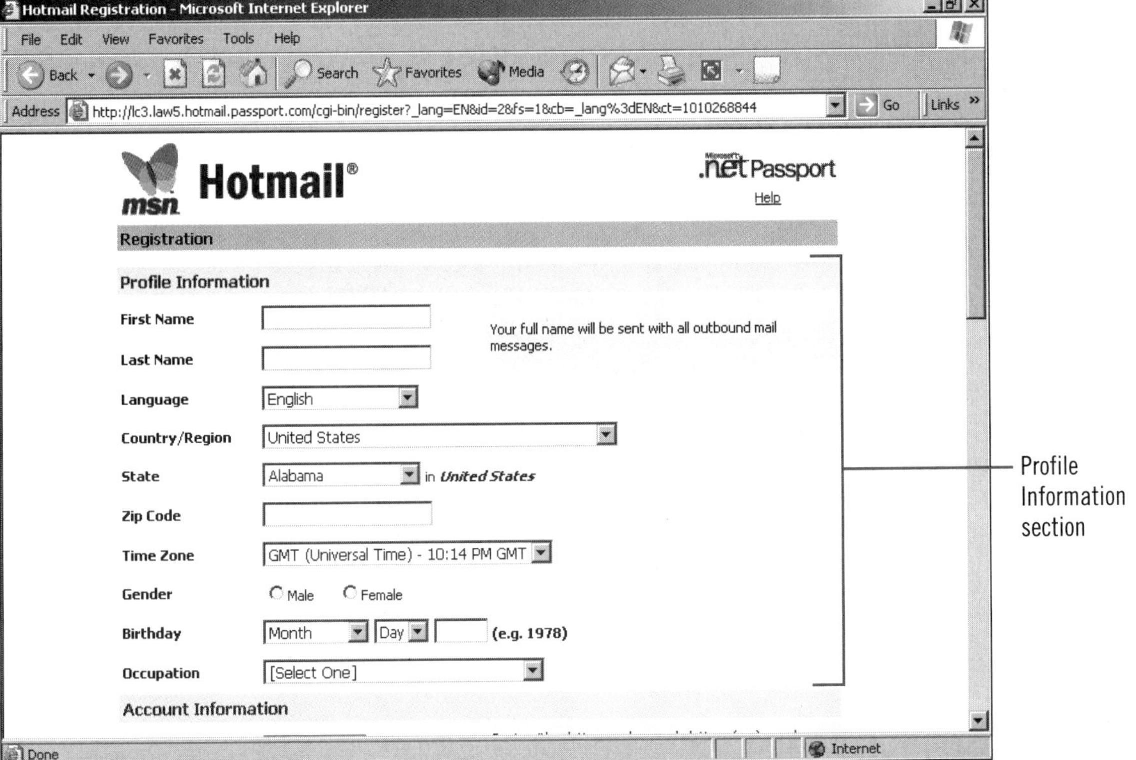

FIGURE G-2: Account Information section of Hotmail Registration page

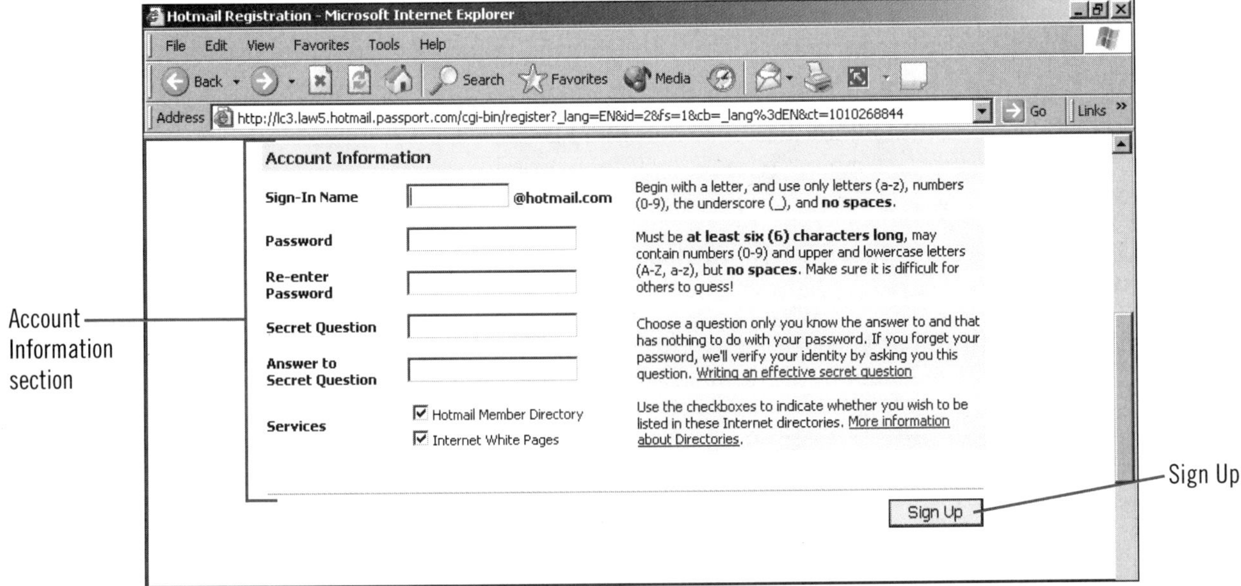

Internet

Sending and Reading Messages Using Hotmail

As shown in Figure G-3, the Hotmail home page displays four tabs for your Hotmail account: Home, Inbox, Compose, and Address Book. The **Home tab** shows links to news, shopping opportunities, and general links to other MSN Web sites. In addition, the Home tab displays the **Message Summary section**, which shows you how many messages are stored in your e-mail folders. Clicking a folder name opens that folder and displays its contents. The **Inbox tab** displays the list of messages you have received, aside from those that Hotmail suspects are **junk mail**, or unsolicited e-mail; these messages are stored in the Junk Mail folder. The **Compose tab** contains options for creating a new message. The **Address Book tab** contains options for managing your list of contacts. You can click the Options and Help links from any tab to open Web pages containing program options and help for Hotmail users, respectively. You send a message to a friend to let her know you plan to visit her and send a copy to yourself to verify that your account is working properly. You then check for new messages to verify that your message was sent successfully.

Trouble?

Check your Web browser's status bar to make sure that a Web page has fully loaded before using it.

1. On the Hotmail home page, click the **Compose tab**
   A form opens containing options for creating a new message. "Hotmail Staff" will send a welcome message to you when you first access your Hotmail account.
2. In the To text box, type **sharonkikukawa@yahoo.com**, press **[Tab]**, then type your e-mail address in the Cc text box
3. Press **[Tab]** twice, type **Visit** in the Subject text box, then click at the top of the message area
4. Type **Sharon**, press **[Enter]** twice, type **I'm planning to travel for several months and hope to visit you in Hawaii. I expect to be there around April. Let me know if you'll be home then.**, press **[Enter]** twice, then type your full name
   Figure G-4 shows the completed Compose tab.
5. Click **Send**
   The Sent Message Confirmation page opens and shows that your message has been sent.
6. Click **OK**
   The Inbox tab opens, displaying e-mail messages you have received. A copy of the message you sent appears in the Inbox, along with a Welcome message from Hotmail if your account is new.
7. Click your name in the From column to open the message you sent
   The contents of your message appear, as shown in Figure G-5.
8. Click the **Inbox tab**
   A list of your messages appears. The background color of the message header summary for the message you sent yourself has changed from tan to white, indicating that you have read this message.

QuickTip

You can add an e-mail address to the Address Book, by selecting its check box on the Sent Message Confirmation page.

Trouble?

If no message from yourself appears in your Inbox, click the Inbox tab to check for new messages until the message appears.

FIGURE G-3: Hotmail home page

Tabs for working with your account

Number of messages you've received

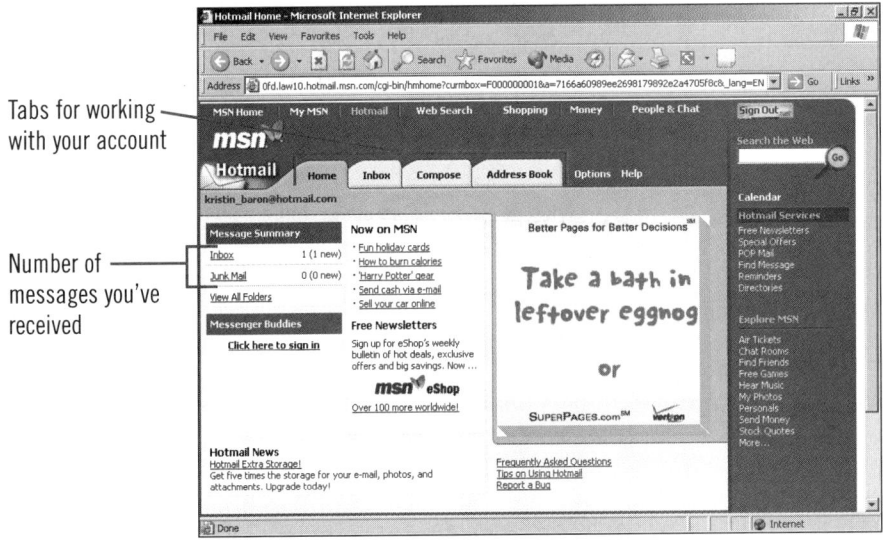

FIGURE G-4: Completed message to Sharon

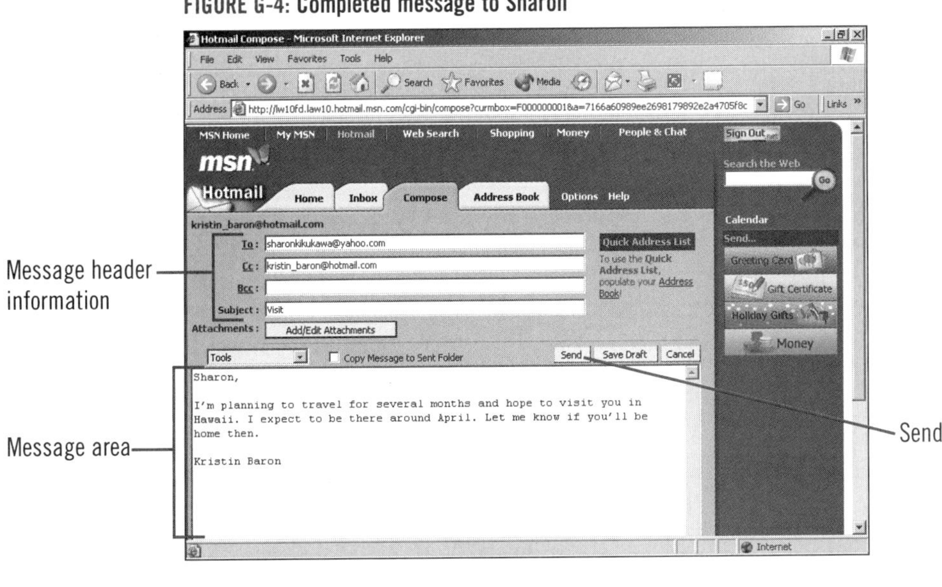

FIGURE G-5: Copy of message received

Internet

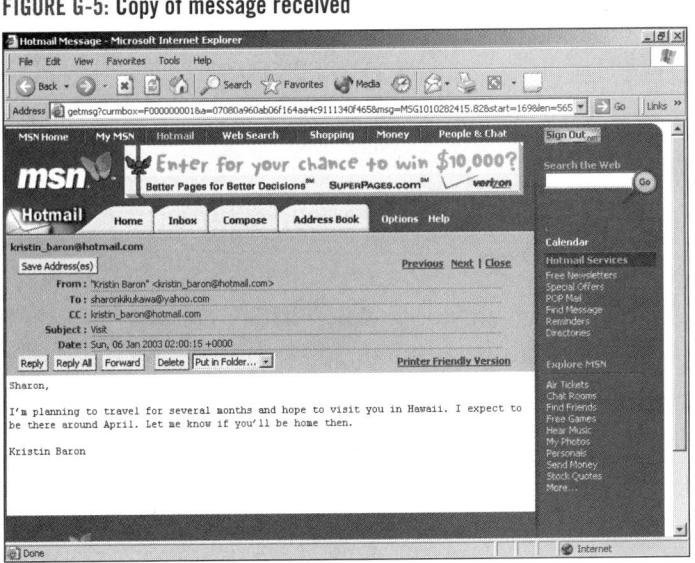

Internet

Replying to and Forwarding Messages Using Hotmail

You can use the Reply option in Hotmail to respond to the sender of a message quickly and efficiently. When you reply to an e-mail message, the sender's name is automatically placed in the To text box, and the text of the original message appears in the body of the new message for reference. You can also send any message you receive to someone else, which is called **forwarding**. When you use the Forward option, the original message appears on the Compose tab. Forwarding is similar to replying, except that a forwarded message is not automatically addressed to the original sender; you must address the message to the desired recipient(s). You practice using the Reply and Forward options by replying to and forwarding the e-mail message you sent to your friend.

1. On the Inbox tab, click your name in the From column for the Visit message
2. Click **Reply**
   The Compose tab opens and the original sender's address appears in the To text box. "Re:" appears at the beginning of the original subject text, indicating that this message is a response to the original message. If you want, you can replace this subject line with new text. The original message appears in the message area. A greater-than sign (>) appears to the left of each line from the original message.
3. In the message area, type **I created this message using the Reply option in Hotmail.**, press **[Enter]** twice, then type your full name
   The Compose tab should appear similar to the one in Figure G-6.
4. Click **Send**, click **OK** on the Sent Message Confirmation page, then click the **Inbox tab**
   The message you replied to appears in your Inbox.
5. Click your name in the From column for the Visit message
   The contents of your message appear.
6. Click **Forward**
   The Compose tab opens and displays the text of the message to forward. Notice that the Subject text box includes Fwd: and the original subject text. The Fwd: indicates that the message is being forwarded. Just like when you reply to a message, you can edit the subject line if you want to clarify the subject of the message. Like in a reply, a greater-than sign (>) appears to the left of each line from the original message in the message area.
7. Type **sharonkikukawa@yahoo.com** in the To text box, then type your e-mail address in the Cc text box
8. In the message area, type **Sharon,** press **[Enter]** twice, type **I used the Forward option to send this message.**, press **[Enter]** twice, then type your full name
   Your screen should appear similar to Figure G-7.
9. Click **Send**, click **OK** on the Sent Message Confirmation page, then click the **Inbox tab**
   A copy of the message you forwarded appears in your Inbox.

QuickTip

You can reply to only the sender by clicking the Reply button or to the sender and all recipients of the original message by clicking the Reply All button.

QuickTip

To send a file along with your messages, click Add/Edit Attachments, click Browse, navigate to the drive and folder that contains the file that you want to send, click Open, click Attach, then click OK.

FIGURE G-6: Replying to a message

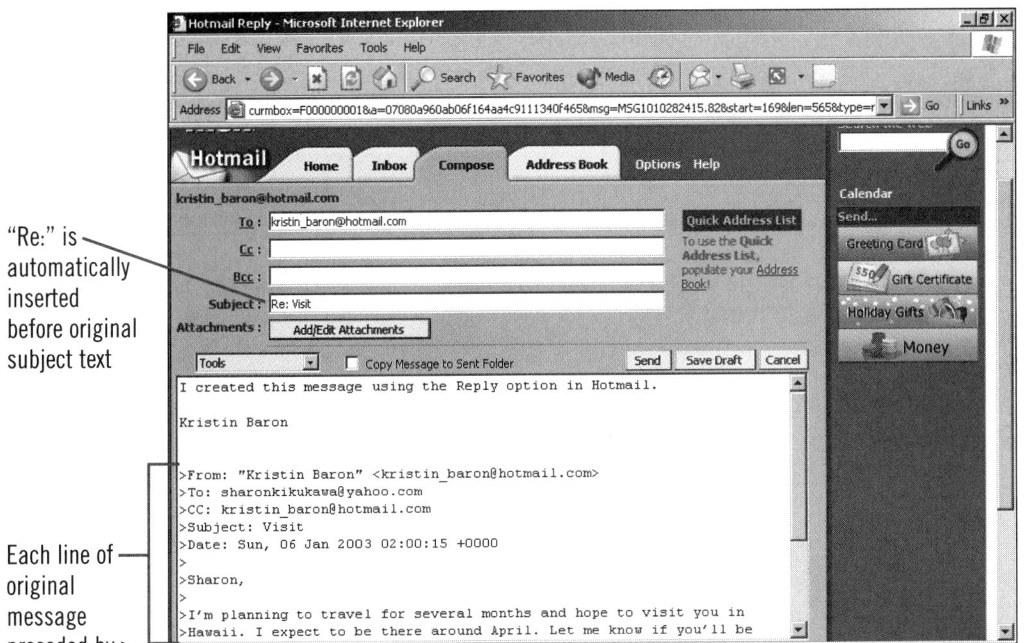
"Re:" is automatically inserted before original subject text
Each line of original message preceded by >

FIGURE G-7: Forwarding a message

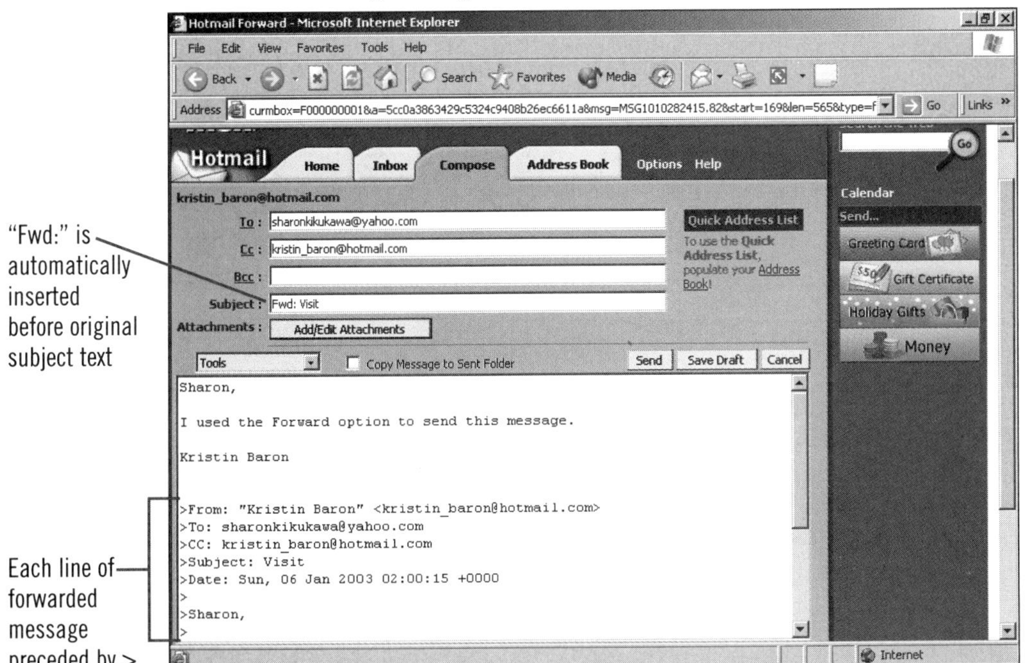
"Fwd:" is automatically inserted before original subject text
Each line of forwarded message preceded by >

CLUES TO USE

Maintaining a Hotmail account

Hotmail, like most Web-based e-mail providers, regularly deletes accounts that are no longer being used to free up disk space on its servers. Hotmail's terms of use require that you sign into your Hotmail account at least once in the first 10 days after you create it. After that, you must access the account at least once every 30 days for it to remain active. If you use your Web-based e-mail account frequently, you should have no problem meeting these requirements. However, if you don't use e-mail regularly and only check for messages from time to time, you need to make sure you follow these guidelines to avoid having your Hotmail account closed.

Internet

Internet

Filing and Deleting Messages Using Hotmail

By default, Hotmail includes five folders: Inbox, Sent Messages, Drafts, Trash Can, and Junk Mail. The **Inbox folder** stores your new messages. The **Sent Messages folder** stores messages that you have sent (if you change your account settings to enable this function). The **Drafts folder** stores messages that you have written and saved but have not yet sent. The **Trash Can folder** stores messages that you have deleted. The **Junk Mail folder** stores messages from senders that you specify as bulk mailers, advertisers, or any Web site from which you don't want to receive e-mail. In addition to these folders, you can create other folders for filing your e-mail messages. When you file a message, you move it to another folder. You can create folders for different categories of e-mail that you want to keep. For example, you might save messages from friends in a folder called Friends, or save messages from your boss in a folder called Work. You create a folder named Notification to keep track of all the friends who you've contacted about your upcoming trip. You file the copy of the Visit message in the Notification folder, and delete some of the test messages in your Inbox.

Steps

1. On the Hotmail home page, click the **Home tab**, then click the **View All Folders link** in the Message Summary section
   The Folders page opens.
2. Click **Create New**
   The Create New Folder page opens.
3. In the New Folder Name text box, type **Notification**, then click **OK**
   The Notification folder you created appears in the list of folders, as shown in Figure G-8.
4. Click the **Inbox tab**
5. Click your name in the From column for the Visit message
6. Click the **Put in Folder list arrow**, then click **Notification**
   The message moves to the Notification folder.
7. Click the **Inbox tab** (if it's not already displayed), then click the **Notification link** in the list of folders
   The Visit message appears in the Notification folder, as shown in Figure G-9.
8. Click the **Inbox tab**
9. Select the check boxes for the messages with the subjects **Fwd: Visit** and **Re: Visit**, then click **Delete**
   The messages move to the Trash Can folder. All of the messages you created in this unit are removed from your Inbox.

Trouble?

The number and size of messages on your screen might differ from those shown in Figure G-8, depending on other messages you might have received.

QuickTip

You can also file a message by selecting the check box next to its message header summary, clicking the Put in Folder list arrow, then clicking the folder name.

FIGURE G-8: New folder on Folders page

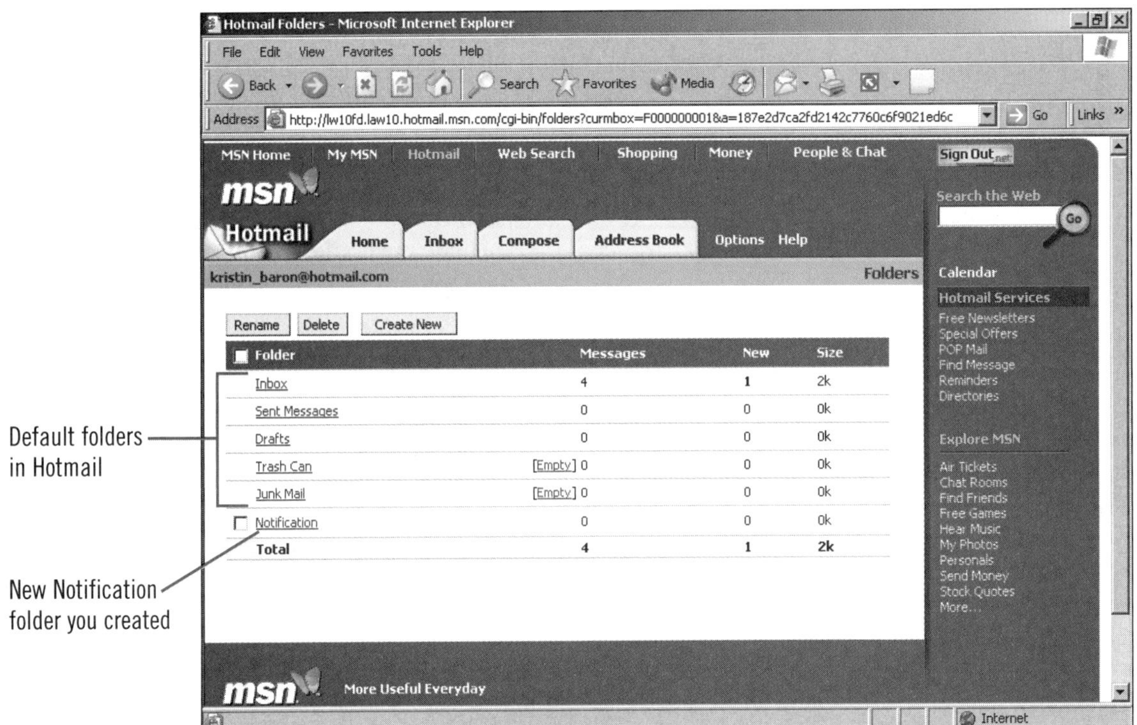

FIGURE G-9: Visit message filed in Notification folder

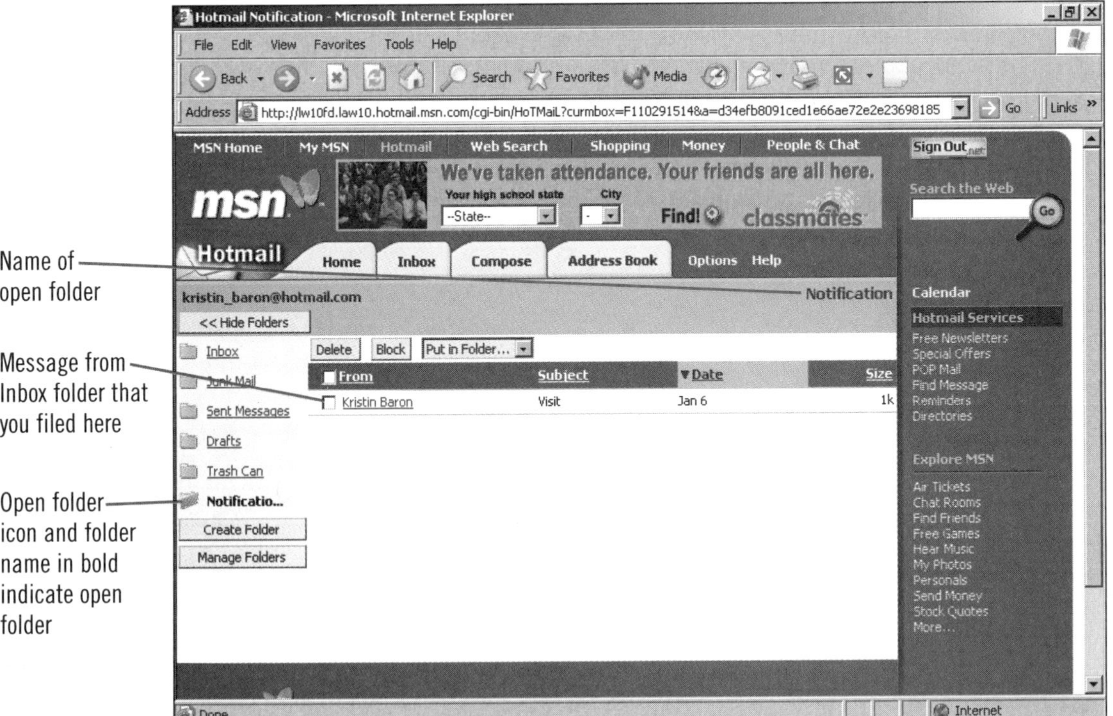

Internet

Understanding Web Portals

Web portals supply users with current, customized information. They serve as doorways to the Web, because they usually include general interest information and can help users find just about anything on the Web. Popular Web portals include the Excite, InfoSpace, MSN, Netscape, and Yahoo! Web sites. Web portals share some common characteristics, including free e-mail, links to search engines, Web directories, membership services, news headlines and articles, discussion groups, chat rooms, links to virtual shopping malls, calendars, and address books. Because you use an e-mail account on Hotmail, which is part of the MSN Web site, you decide to explore the MSN Web portal. If it contains the Web calendar and news features that you want access to while traveling, you can use a single Web portal for all of your basic information and communication needs while on the road.

1. **Click MSN Home at the top of the Hotmail home page**
   The home page opens for the MSN Web site, as shown in Figure G-10. Because Hotmail is part of the MSN Web site, you don't need to sign out of Hotmail.

2. **Scroll down to explore all the sections of this Web page**
   The home page includes a link to your Hotmail account, as well as a set of links to common Web sites, such as Expedia.com to shop for a plane ticket, or barnesandnoble.com to shop for a book. It also includes areas that display information and highlight pages for given subject areas, such as general news, financial news, and shopping.

3. **Click the My MSN tab**
   As shown in Figure G-11, the My MSN Web page looks similar to the MSN Home page.

4. **Scroll down to explore all the sections of this Web page**
   Like the MSN Home page, the My MSN page also contains lists of links, along with highlighted pages for different subjects. However, the My MSN page displays your name, and includes links that enable you to customize Web page contents, layout, and color, as well as the content of each subject area. It also includes a set of links for additional personalized features, including a calendar. Notice that the Local News & Weather section shows news and weather for the area you live in, which you entered when signing up for Hotmail.

Web portals and personal information

Web portals are available for free use because the companies running them make money from selling advertisements on their Web pages, and from collecting and selling information about the browsing habits of Web portal users. User information can be sold to other companies for marketing purposes, and can result in you receiving unsolicited e-mail. If privacy is a concern to you, or if you want to avoid the inconvenience of receiving e-mail you don't want, it's important to understand the information that a Web portal might collect about you. The company that owns the Web portal generally specifies how it can use this information in a document known as the **terms of use**. The terms of use is available for you to read when you sign up to use a Web portal. Additionally, you can generally open it by clicking a link on any Web page in the Web portal. For example, on the MSN Web site, the link TERMS OF USE appears at the bottom of every Web page. Knowing how the Web portal's owner plans to use information it collects about you can help you make an informed choice about how much you want to use the Web portal, and in what ways.

FIGURE G-10: MSN home page

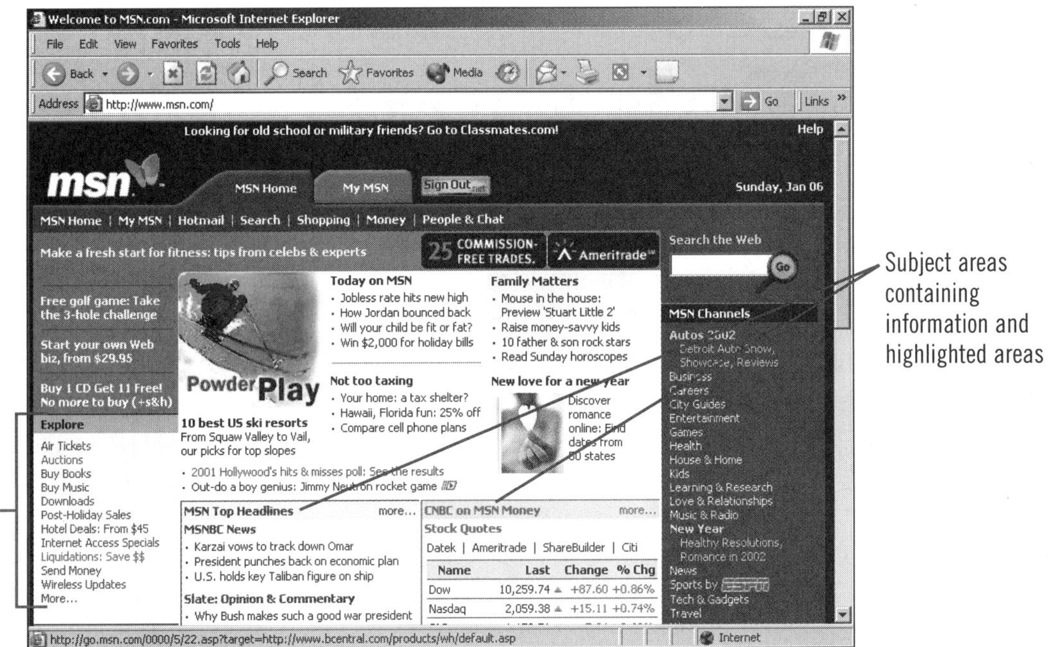

FIGURE G-11: My MSN page

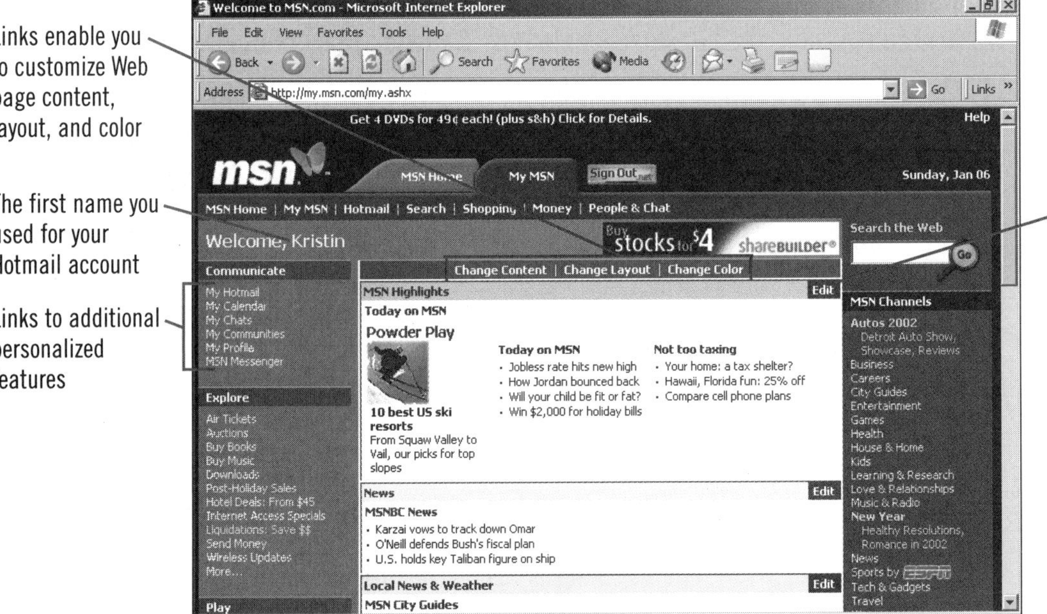

Internet

Internet

Customizing a Web Portal

A popular feature of most Web portals is the ability to customize the information on and layout of the Web pages on the Web portal. You can use the My MSN page to save your preferences and deliver current information to your PC each time you visit the MSN Web site. MSN allows you to customize the content, layout, and appearance of your personalized Web page. You can customize the content by choosing categories of information that most suit your interests, and by removing default categories that you're not interested in. You can change the Web page's layout by changing the order in which categories appear. You can also alter the Web page's appearance by picking a color scheme. You remove the default Web page content that won't be important while you're on the road, and add content that will be useful. You also put the Web page element you're most interested in at the top, and change the Web page's color scheme.

Trouble?

Because Web pages change frequently, the My MSN page might show slightly different options than those in these steps; if so, go to *www.course.com/illustrated/internet3*, click the Unit G link, then use the replacement steps under Lesson 6.

1. On the My MSN page, click the **Change Content link**
   The Personalize My MSN page opens, as shown in Figure G-12. U.S. users can enter or change their ZIP code on this Web page. Additionally, all users can click the content links to edit the category content appearing on the customized My MSN page.
2. Click the **MSN Highlights link** in the Change Content section
   The Change Content: MSN Highlights page opens, allowing you to select or deselect options in the MSN Highlights section of the My MSN Web page.
3. Deselect the **Today on MSN check box**
   The Today on MSN information will no longer appear on your My MSN page.
4. Click the **Local News & Weather link** in the Change Content section, deselect the **MSN City Guides check box**, scroll down, click the **Shopping link** in the Change Content section, then deselect the **eShop Sales & Deals check box**
5. Click the **Personal Finance link** in the Change Content section, deselect the **CNBC on MSN Money Stock Quotes check box**, scroll down, click the **Travel link** in the Change Content section, then select the **Expedia.com Travel Deals check box**
6. Click **Update My MSN**, then scroll down to explore the Customized My MSN page
   Your My MSN page now contains only items relevant for a traveler: news headlines, local news and weather from back home, and information on travel deals.
7. Click the **Change Layout link**
8. Click **Travel** in the Select item to change list box, then click **Move Up** twice to move it to the top of the list
9. Click the **Change Color link**, click the **Green option button**, then click **Update My MSN**
   The updated My MSN page opens, similar to the one shown in Figure G-13. Your customization changed the color scheme as well as the order of the highlighted items.

FIGURE G-12: Personalize My MSN page

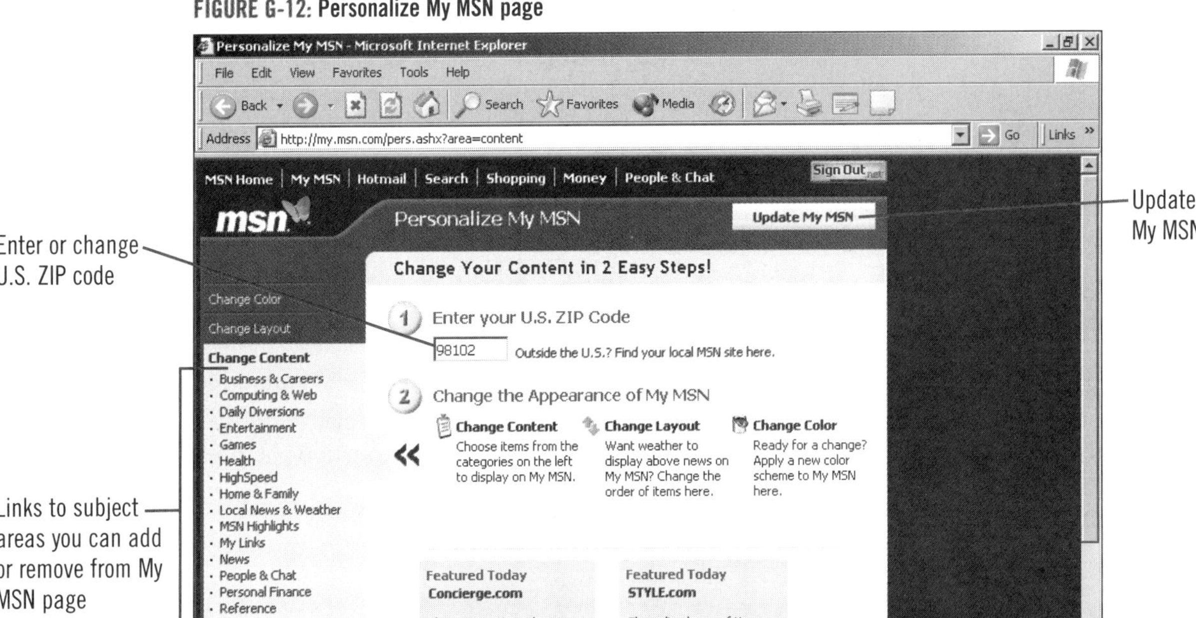

FIGURE G-13: Customized My MSN page

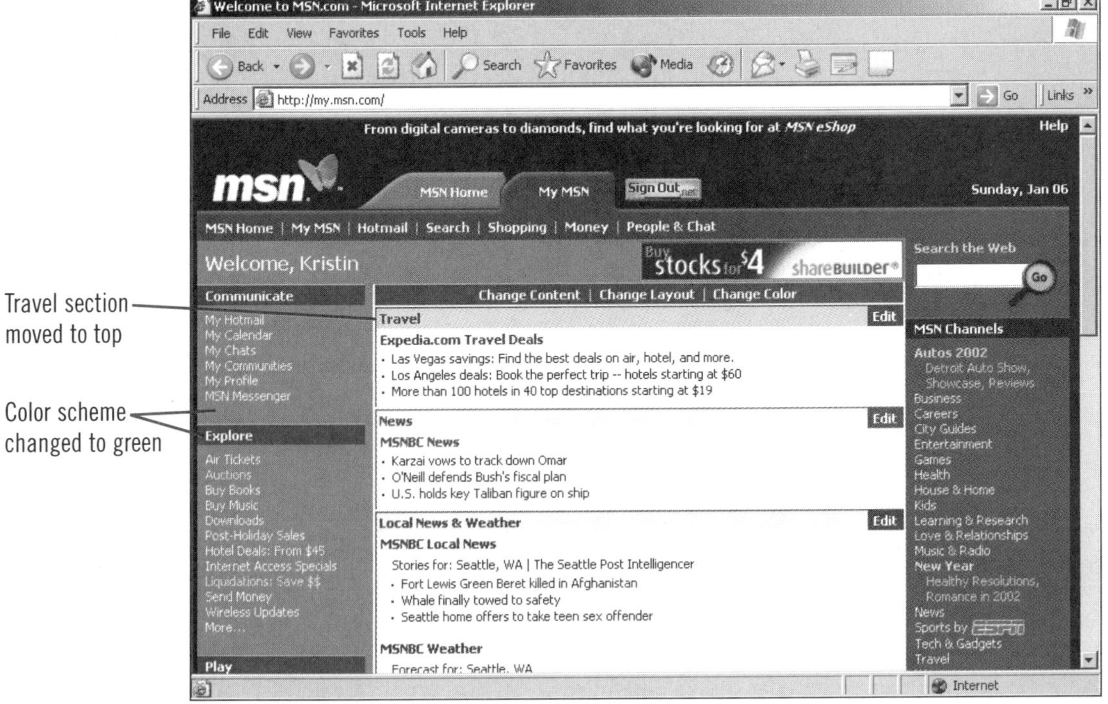

Creating a Web Calendar

A common feature on a Web portal is a **Web calendar**, which allows you to record details about upcoming events as you would in a planner book or calendar, and store them on the Web. You can view and modify your Web calendar from any computer connected to the Internet. You set up a Web calendar to keep track of your travel plans.

Trouble?
If you have already signed up for MSN Calendar, skip to Step 4.

1. On the My MSN page, click the **My Calendar link** in the Communicate section
   The MSN Calendar - Registration Web page opens. Your e-mail address and time zone information is already entered in the form, based on the information you provided when signing up for a Hotmail account.
2. Type your first name in the First Name text box, then type your last name in the Last Name text box
3. Make sure your correct e-mail address is entered in the Primary e-mail address text box and your correct time zone is selected in the Specify a time zone list box, then click **I Accept**
   The Terms of Use are the same ones you agreed to when setting up your Hotmail account. The MSN Calendar Web page opens displaying the Today tab. The Today tab shows an overview of features available in MSN Calendar. When your calendar contains appointments, tasks, and reminders, they are summarized on the Today tab.
4. Click the **Calendar tab**
   The Calendar tab opens, as shown in Figure G-14. The Calendar tab displays your appointments. By default, it shows appointments for the current day. You use the Week, Month, and Year tabs for other views of the MSN Calendar. The Calendar tab also shows a calendar of the current month; each day is a link that you can click to display the day's appointments.
5. Click the **Add New Appointment link** in the Appointments section
   The Add New Appointment page opens.
6. Type **Fly to Mexico City** in the Description text box, then click the list arrows in the Dates section to enter the Start Date **January 6, 2003**, Start Time **6:30 PM**, and Duration **9 hours 30 minutes**
7. Click **Save and Add Another**
   The appointment you entered is saved, and the Add New Appointment page reopens.
8. Type **Meet Reinaldo** in the Description text box, type **Oaxaca** in the Location text box, click the list arrows in the Dates section to enter the Start Date **January 25, 2003** and Start Time **5:00 PM**, then click **Save**

QuickTip
You can also display a different month by clicking the month and year links listed in the third section on the left side of the Web page.

9. Click the **Month tab**, then if necessary, click the triangles to the left and right of the current month and year above the calendar to display **January 2003**
   The January 2003 calendar appears on the MSN Calendar Web page, displaying the appointments you entered as shown in Figure G-15. The Fly to Mexico City appointment appears on two dates because it begins in the evening and ends the next day.

FIGURE G-14: MSN Calendar's Calendar tab

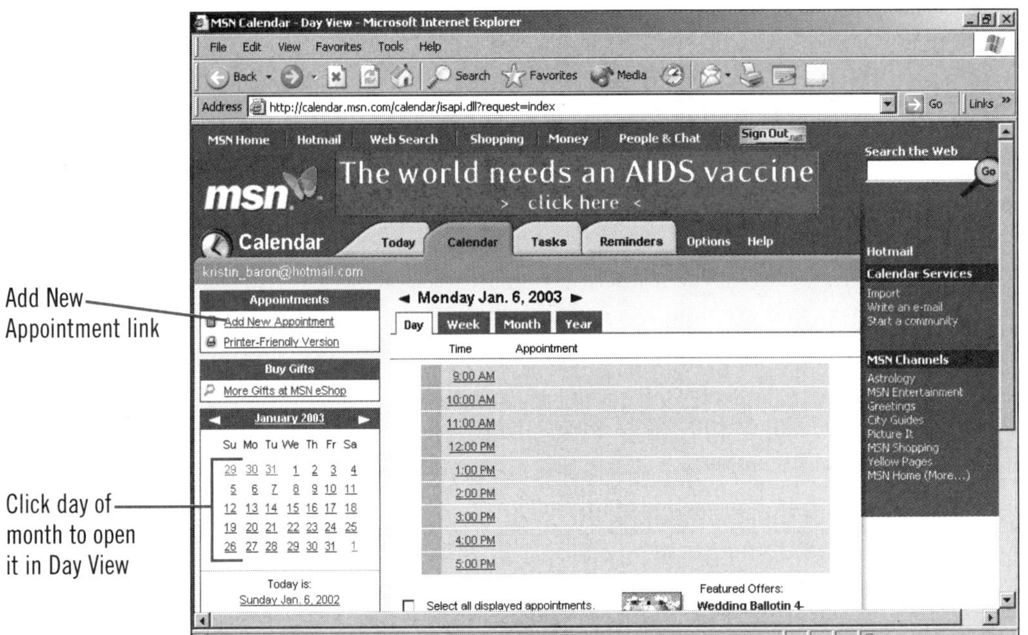

FIGURE G-15: Appointments in Month View

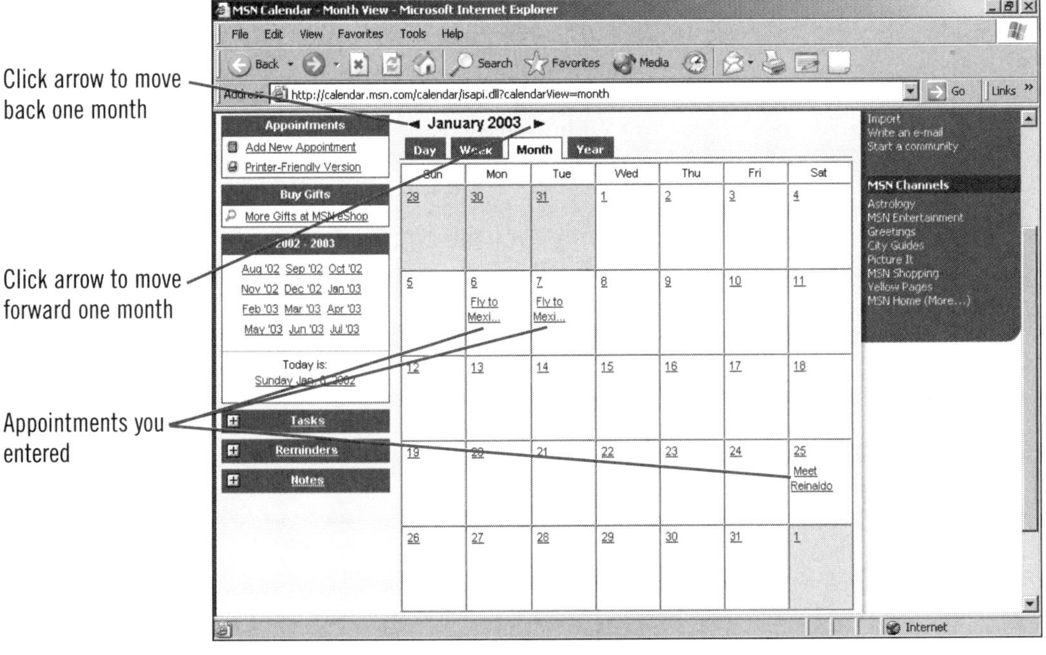

Creating tasks and reminders

In addition to appointments, MSN Calendar includes forms for two other types of entries. A **task** allows you to set up a long-term project, including start and end dates. The form is similar to the Appointments form, but allows you to set a priority for the project, as well as to record its status, such as Not Started, In Progress, or Completed. You can also use MSN Calendar to set up **reminders**, which are events that trigger an automatic e-mail message to you just before they happen. For example, you could set up a reminder for your sister's birthday (June 12), which would send you an e-mail June 5 to remind you to send a card.

Internet

Customizing a Web Calendar

Just as you can modify aspects of your home page for a Web portal, you can also customize a Web portal calendar. For example, you can specify the calendar view (such as Day, Week, or Month) that you want to view when you first open MSN Calendar. You format your calendar to display holidays automatically. Because you're traveling, you also make sure that any holidays appear that are unique to each country you're visiting. Because Mexico and Central America are predominantly Christian, you also add Christian religious holidays to the calendar.

1. Scroll to the top of the MSN Calendar page if necessary, then click **Options**
   The Options page opens.
2. Click the **Calendar Options link**
   The Calendar Options page opens.
3. Scroll down (if necessary) to view all the options available
   Figure G-16 shows the options available on the Calendar Options page.
4. Click the **plus sign (+)** next to Holidays
   The Calendar Options page reopens, displaying a list of countries and religious holidays.
5. Select the check boxes for **Christian Religious Holidays**, **Costa Rica**, and **Mexico**
6. Click **Save and Return**
   Your selections are saved and the Options page reopens.
7. Click the **Calendar tab**, then click the **Month tab**
8. Use the triangles to the left and right of the current month and year to navigate to **January 2003**, then scroll down (if necessary) to view the holidays added to this month's calendar
   As shown in Figure G-17, this month includes two holidays specific to the countries you selected and two Christian religious holidays.

FIGURE G-16: Calendar Options page

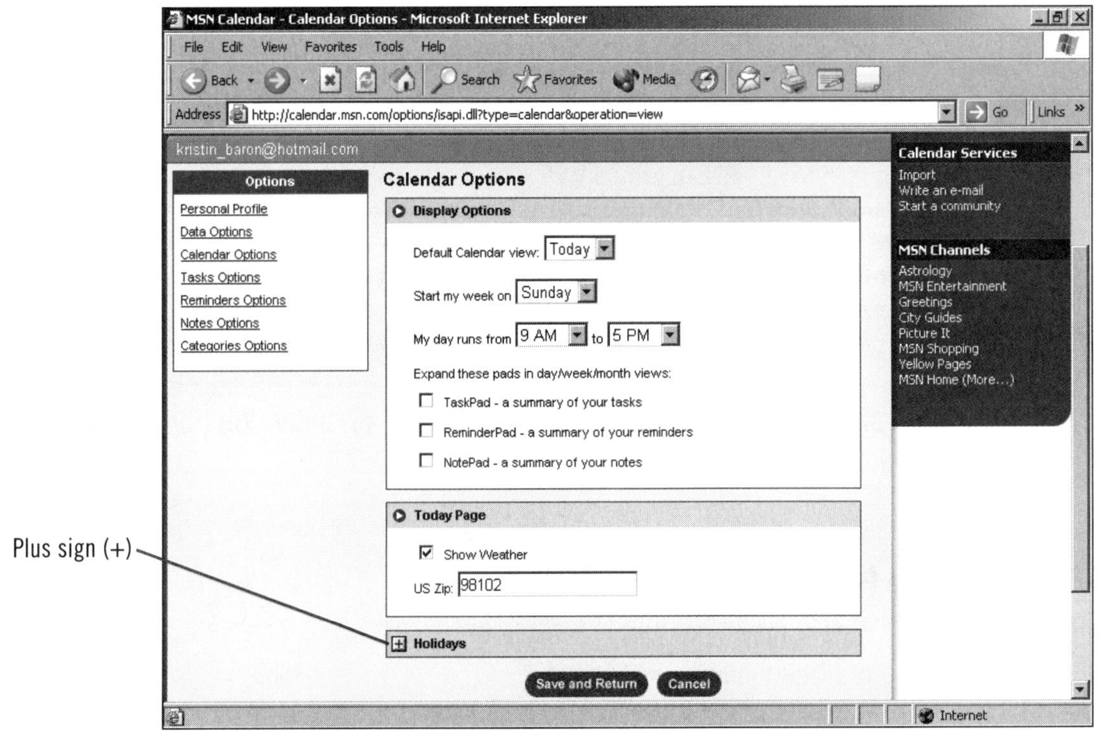

FIGURE G-17: Calendar in Month View showing holidays

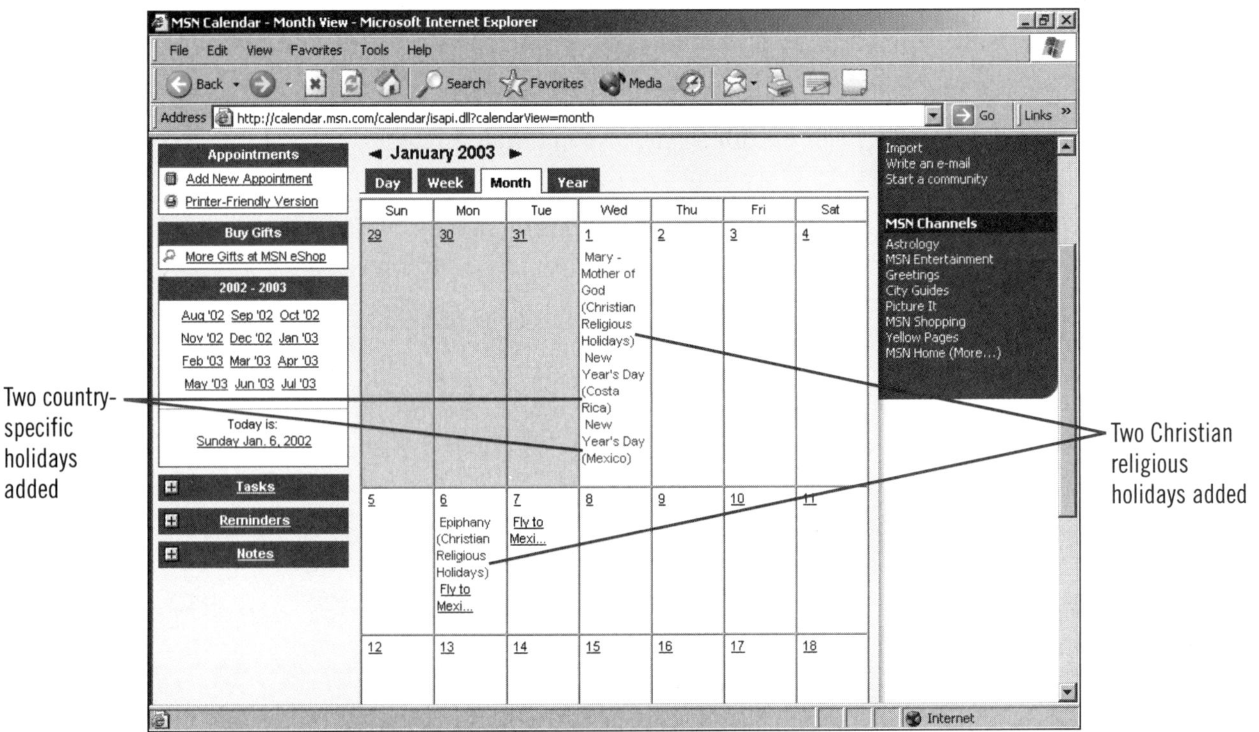

Internet

Internet

Printing a Web Calendar

Like any other Web page, you can print a Web calendar. However, because Web portal Web pages contain numerous links and options, a calendar Web page might not fit entirely on a printed page, or might break oddly between two pages. Web portals like MSN address this situation by including **printer-friendly pages**, which are Web pages that contain the information you want to print and are specially formatted to fit on a printed page. As you continue planning your trip, you print your Web calendar for reference when you're away from a computer.

1. On the MSN Calendar page, click the **Printer-Friendly Version link** in the Appointment section
   A new Web browser window opens, displaying the month calendar without menus or tabs, as shown in Figure G-18.
2. Click the **Print button** on your Web browser's toolbar
   The January 2003 calendar prints.
3. Close the printable month view window
4. If necessary, display the MSN Calendar – Month View Web page
5. Click the **Week tab**, then click the **left triangle** next to the date to display the calendar for January 5, 2003 – January 11, 2003
6. Scroll down (if necessary) to see the calendar for the entire week
7. Click the **Printer-Friendly Version link** in the Appointments section
   A new Web browser window opens, displaying the week calendar without menus or tabs, as shown in Figure G-19.
8. Click the **Print button** on your Web browser's toolbar
   The January 5, 2003 – January 11, 2003 calendar prints.
9. Close the printable week view window, then if necessary display the MSN Calendar – Week View Web page

FIGURE G-18: Printer-friendly version of month calendar

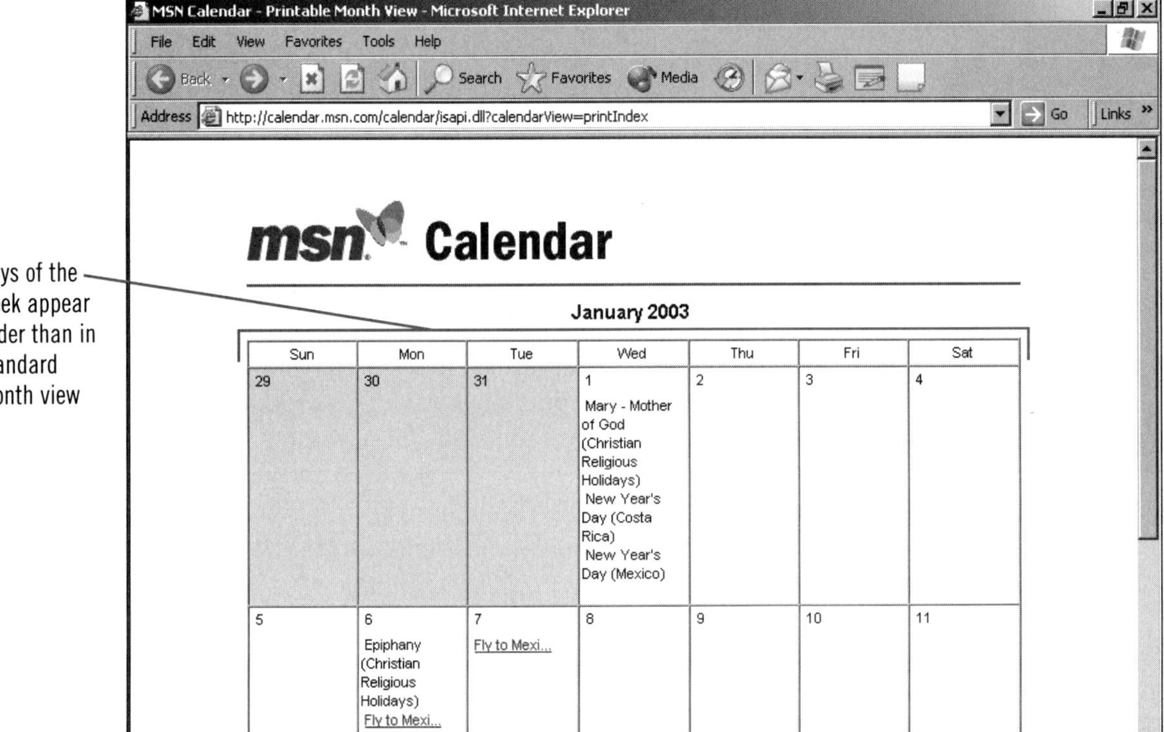

FIGURE G-19: Printer-friendly version of week calendar

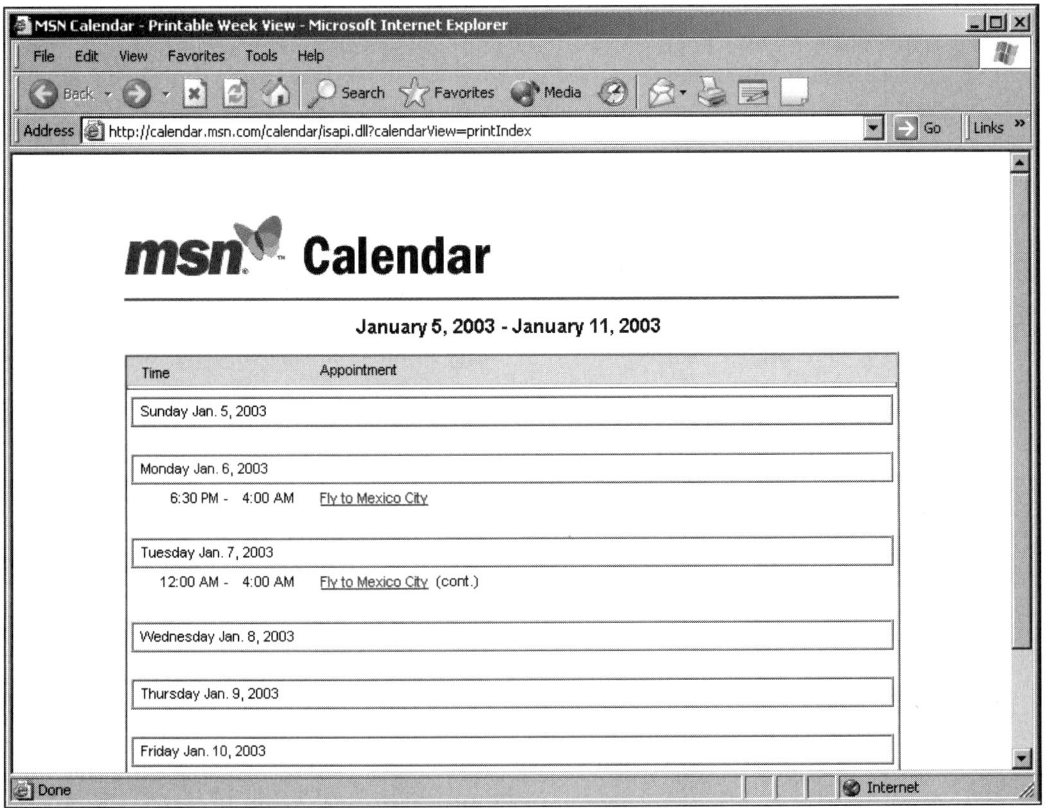

Internet

Creating a Web Address Book

Hotmail, like almost every Web-based e-mail system, enables you to save contact information for friends and colleagues in an address book. You can save each person's e-mail address as part of their contact information, which enables you to address e-mail messages by typing names rather than requiring you to remember and type e-mail addresses each time you create a message. You can also send messages to a group of people, by creating a **mailing list**, which assigns a name to a group of e-mail addresses. You can e-mail each person in the group simply by typing the mailing list name. You begin entering contact information for friends who you want to keep updated on your travels. You also create a mailing list of friends who will receive regular travel updates via e-mail.

1. Click **Hotmail** at the top of the MSN Calendar page
   The Hotmail home page opens. Because Hotmail is part of the MSN Web site, you don't need to sign in.
2. Click the **Address Book tab**
   The Address Book opens.
3. Click **Create New**
   The Create New Individual page opens. This Web page allows you to add a person's contact information to the Address Book.
4. Type **David** in the Quickname text box, press **[Tab]**, type **David** in the First text box, press **[Tab]**, then type **Golkin** in the Last text box
   You use a quickname to quickly address an e-mail to a contact. As long as the quickname for each contact in the Address Book is unique, you can address messages without typing both first and last names.
5. Type **dgolkin@cavco.com** in the Personal text box in the E-mail Address section, scroll down, then type **602.555.6141** in the Personal text box in the Phone Numbers section
6. Click **OK** at the bottom of the Web page
   The Address Book tab reopens, displaying the entry for David Golkin.
7. Use Steps 3 through 6 as a model to add the following contacts to the Address Book:

James	**James**	**Garcia**	**jgarcia@roanoke.com**	**703.555.1909**
Lin	**Lin**	**Choong**	**choong@lilly.com**	**317.555.6762**
Sharon	**Sharon**	**Kikukawa**	**sharonkikukawa@yahoo.com**	**808.555.9157**

   All four contacts appear in the Address Book, as shown in Figure G-20.
8. Click the **Groups tab**, then click **Create New**
   The Create New Group page opens.
9. Type **updates** in the Group Name text box, type **david,james,lin,sharon** in the Group Members text box, then click **OK**
   The updates group, including David, James, Lin, and Sharon, appears in the Address Book, as shown in Figure G-21.

FIGURE G-20: Address Book

Contact information added for four people

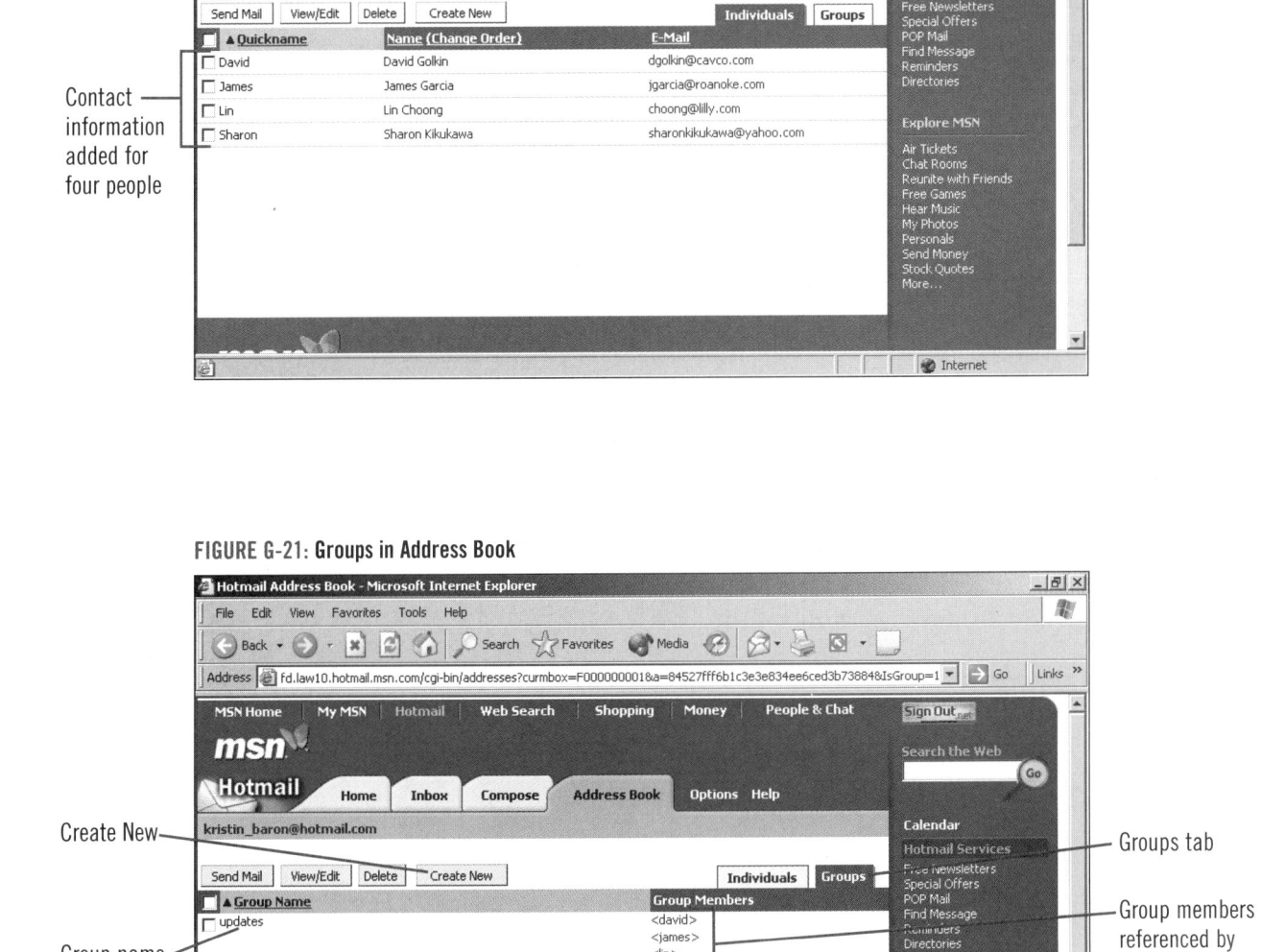

FIGURE G-21: Groups in Address Book

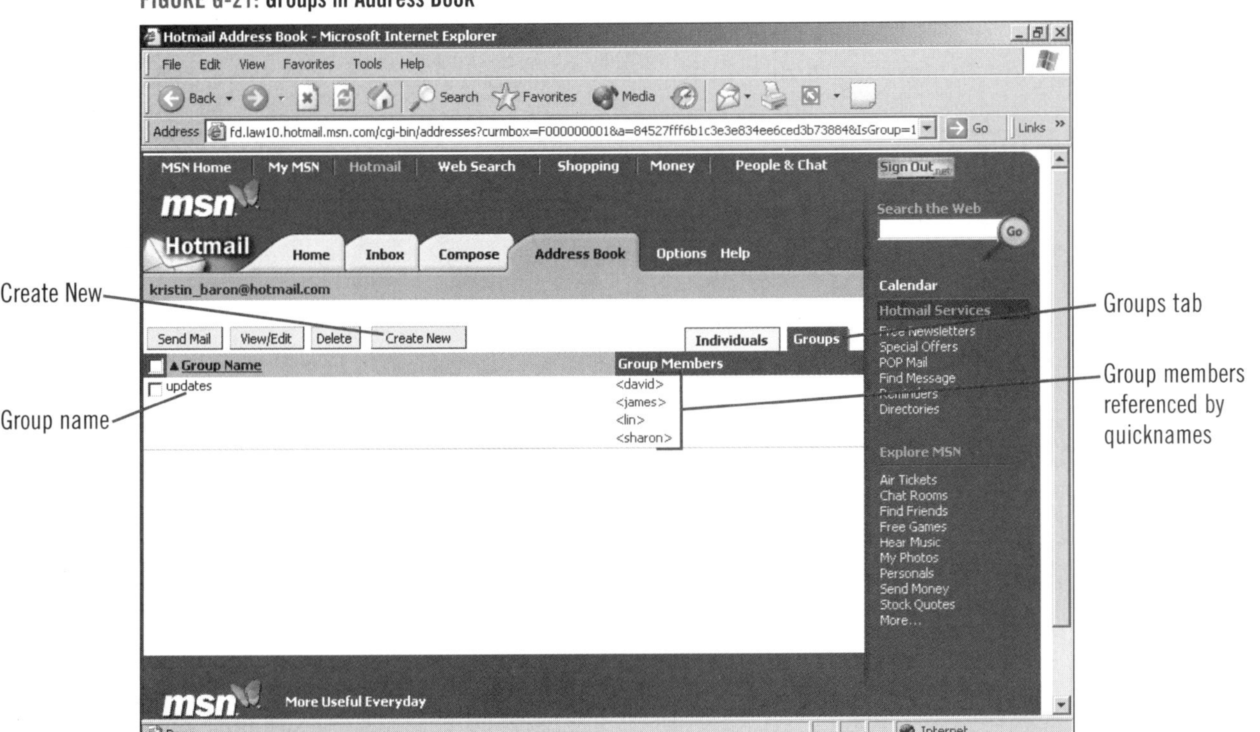

Maintaining a Web Address Book

Because contact information tends to change, you need to be able to edit your address book. In Hotmail, you can enter new or change existing contact information in the Address Book. You can also sort contacts in the Address Book by column heading to help you quickly find a contact's information. You experiment with changing the order of contacts in the Address Book. You also update the e-mail address for one of your friends.

1. On the Address Book page, click the **Individuals tab**
   The contacts list opens.
2. Click the **Quickname column heading**
   The Web page reopens, displaying the contacts in reverse alphabetical order by quickname, as shown in Figure G-22. When you're working with a large list of contacts and want to quickly locate one whose quickname is at the end of the alphabet, reordering the column can speed up your search.
3. Click the **E-Mail column heading**
   The Web page reopens, displaying the contacts in reverse alphabetical order by e-mail address. When you're working with a large list of contacts and are looking for a contact with a specific e-mail address, reordering on this column can help you search more efficiently.
4. Select the **check box** next to James in the contacts list
   The background color for this line changes to blue.
5. Click **View/Edit**
   The View/Edit Individual page opens, displaying the form you originally used to enter James's information.
6. Select the contents of the **Personal text box** in the E-mail Address section, then type **jamesgarcia@nomad-ltd.com**
7. Scroll to the bottom of the Web page, then click **OK**
   The list of contacts reopens, displaying the e-mail address change you made, as shown in Figure G-23.

QuickTip

You can switch between ascending order (a to z) and descending order (z to a) by clicking the column heading again for the column on which the Address Book is sorted.

FIGURE G-22: Reordered contacts list

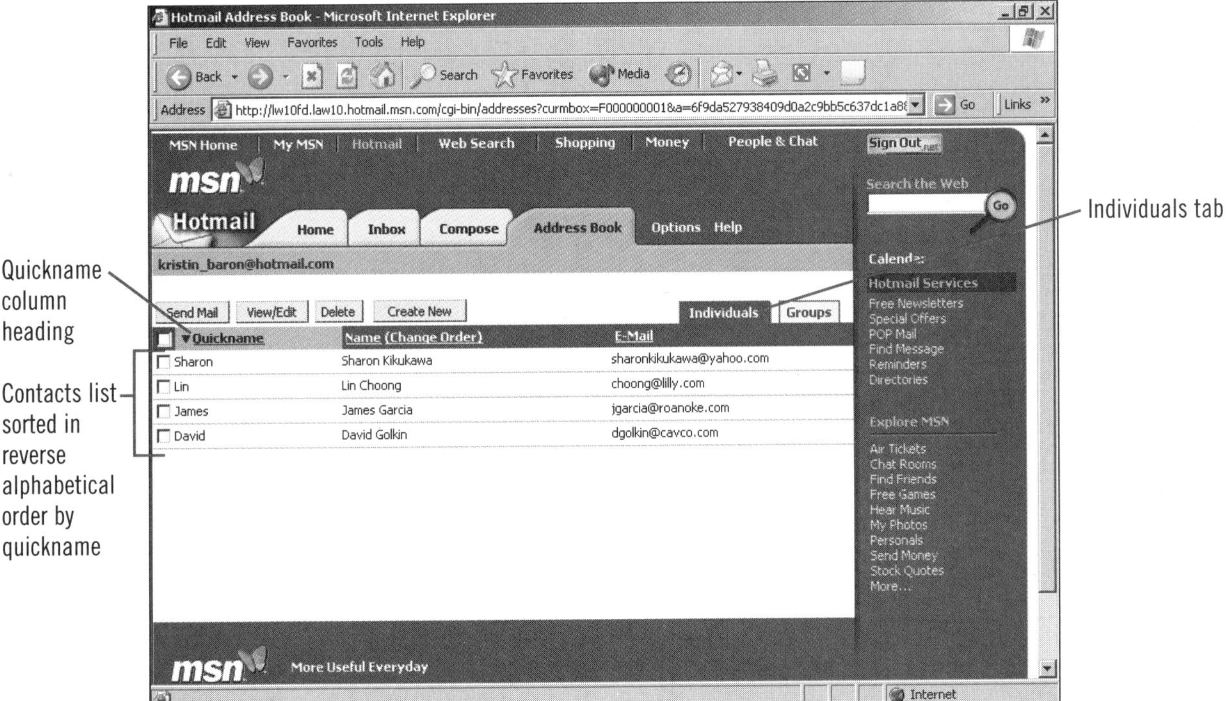

FIGURE G-23: Updated Address Book

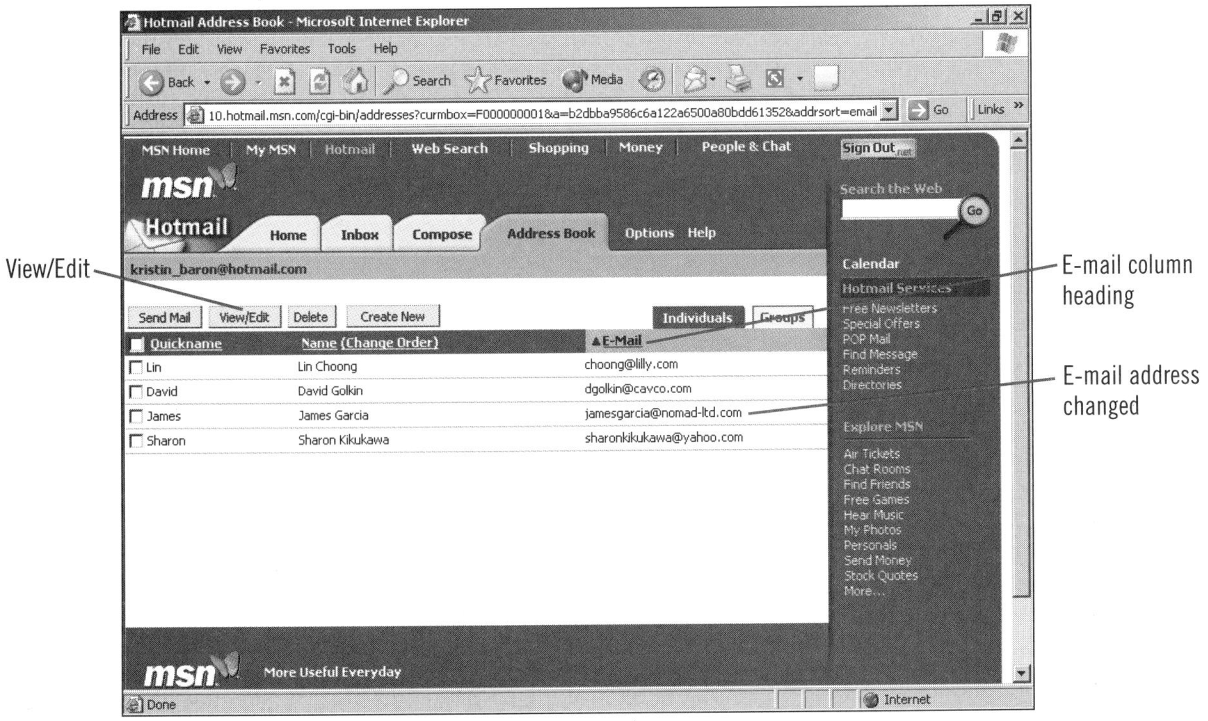

View/Edit

E-mail column heading

E-mail address changed

Internet

Internet

Using a Web Address Book

Unlike written address books, which require you to look up and transcribe names and contact information when you use them, Web address books include features for automating addressing. For example, in Hotmail, you can use the Address Book to automatically address a new e-mail message. In addition to saving you time, automated addressing ensures that you don't mistype an e-mail address. You experiment with creating a new message from your Hotmail account using the Address Book. Then you sign out of MSN.

1. In the Address Book, select the **check box** next to Sharon, then click **Send Mail**
   The Compose tab opens displaying Sharon as the addressee for the new message, as shown in Figure G-24. You can also use the Quick Address List on the Compose tab to easily add addressees to a message.
2. Click in the **Cc text box**
3. Click the **triangle** next to James in the Quick Address List
   James's e-mail address appears in the Cc text box.
4. Click in the **Bcc text box**
5. Click the **triangle** next to updates in the Quick Address List
   The group name updates appears in the Bcc text box.
6. Click **Cancel**
7. Click **Sign Out** in the top-right corner of the Web page
   You sign out of the MSN Web site. The MSN.com home page opens. Signing out ensures that no one will have access to your personalized Web pages or account at the computer you used until you sign back in.
8. Click the **My MSN tab**
   The My MSN page opens as shown in Figure G-25, prompting you to sign in. Your personalized content no longer appears on this Web page because you signed out. You can sign in on any computer to verify your identity to MSN and access your personalized Web pages, along with your Hotmail account, calendar, and Address Book.
9. Close your Web browser

Trouble?

The Connect to my.msn.com dialog box might open instead of the My MSN page.

FIGURE G-24: Hotmail Compose tab containing address selected from Address Book

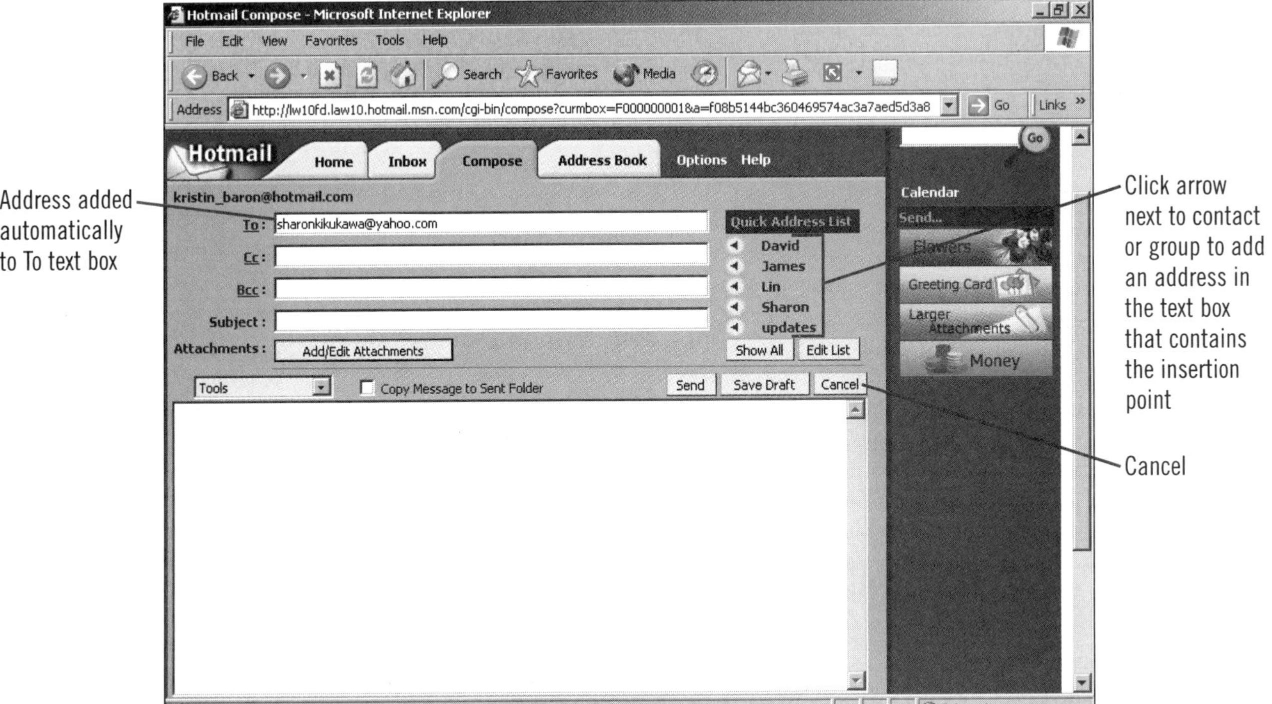
Address added automatically to To text box
Click arrow next to contact or group to add an address in the text box that contains the insertion point
Cancel

FIGURE G-25: My MSN page prompting you to sign in

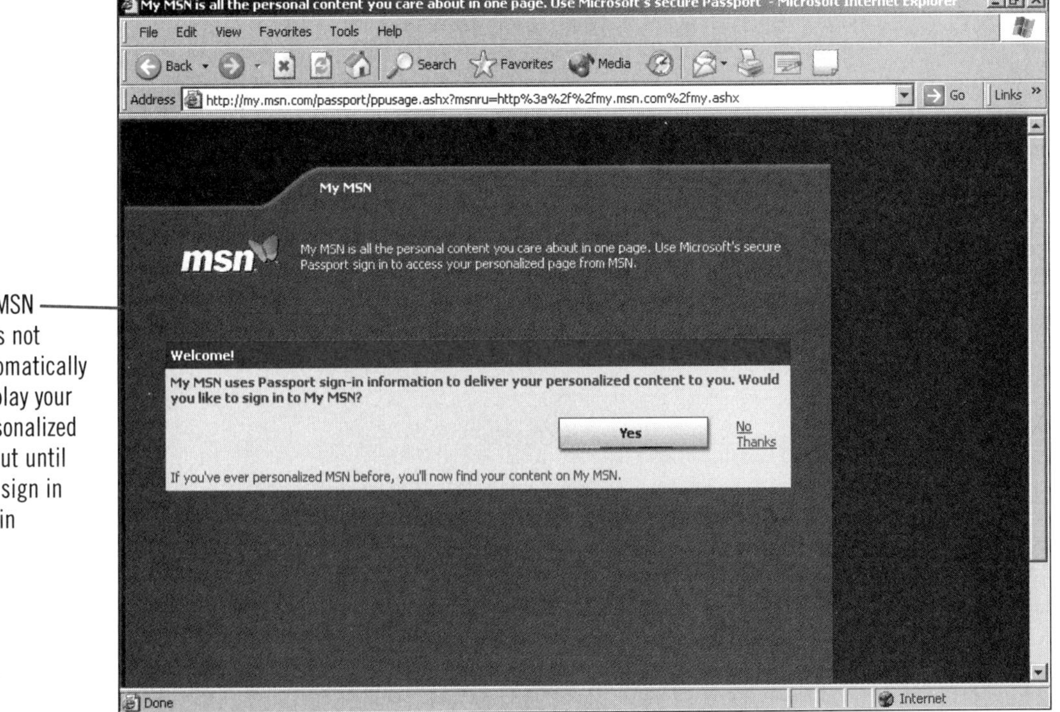
My MSN does not automatically display your personalized layout until you sign in again

Internet

Practice

▶ Concepts Review

Describe the function of each link shown in Figure G-26.

FIGURE G-26

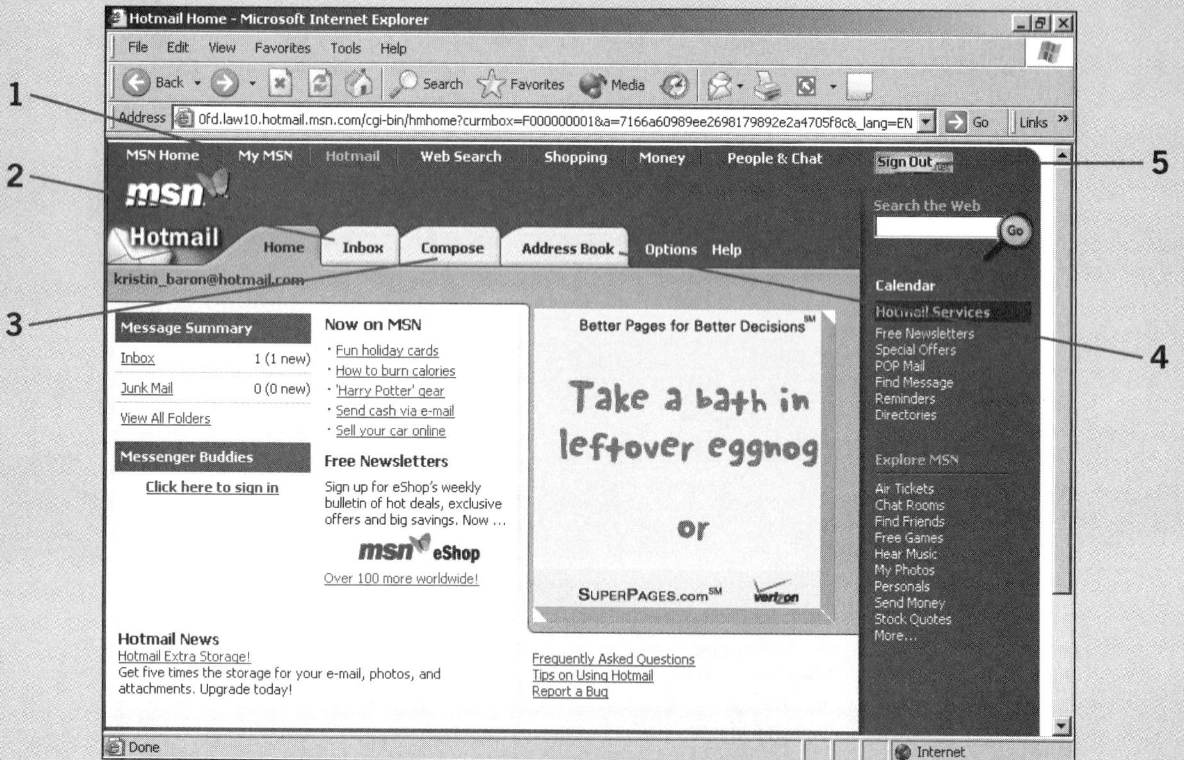

Match each term with the statement that describes it.

6. **Web portal**
7. **Sign-in name**
8. **Forwarding**
9. **Printer-friendly page**
10. **Mailing list**

a. Sending a message you receive to someone else

b. A Web page containing information you want to print and is specially formatted to fit on a printed page

c. A Web site offering customized news and features, such as a calendar and an address book

d. A shortcut for sending e-mail that assigns a name to a group of e-mail addresses

e. A name that uniquely identifies you on a Web-based e-mail system

Practice

Select the best answer from the list of choices.

11. Which of the following would you use if you wanted to regularly view a Web page that displays customized weather information for your location when you open it?
- **a.** Web-based e-mail
- **b.** Web portal
- **c.** Web calendar
- **d.** Web address book

12. Which of the following would you use if you wanted to create a personal schedule that you could access from any computer connected to the Internet?
- **a.** Web-based e-mail
- **b.** Web portal
- **c.** Web calendar
- **d.** Web address book

13. Which of the following would you use if you wanted to create a list of the names and contact information of your friends, which you could access from any computer connected to the Internet?
- **a.** Web-based e-mail
- **b.** Web portal
- **c.** Web calendar
- **d.** Web address book

14. Another word for a sign-in name is a(n):
- **a.** Password.
- **b.** Quickname.
- **c.** User name.
- **d.** E-mail address.

15. What is the difference between forwarding and replying to e-mail messages?
- **a.** When you reply to an e-mail message, the original sender's name is automatically placed in the To text box
- **b.** When you forward an e-mail message, the original sender's name is automatically placed in the To text box
- **c.** The text of the original message appears in the body of a reply only
- **d.** The text of the original message appears in the body of a forward only

16. Which of the following aspects of the MSN Web portal can you NOT change?
- **a.** Content
- **b.** Layout
- **c.** Font
- **d.** Color

Skills Review

1. Send and read messages using Hotmail.
- **a.** Go to **www.course.com/illustrated/internet3**, click the **Unit G link**, then click the **Hotmail link** under Skills Review 1.
- **b.** Open the form for creating a new e-mail message.
- **c.** Address the message to **sharonkikukawa@yahoo.com**, then Cc the message to yourself.

- **d.** Enter **Arriving soon** as the subject, then type the following message: **I'll be in Hawaii next week. Can't wait to see you!**
- **e.** Press **[Enter]** twice after the end of the message, then type your full name.
- **f.** Send the message.
- **g.** Check for new messages in your Inbox.

2. Reply to and forward messages using Hotmail.

- **a.** Open the Arriving soon message.
- **b.** Start a reply to this message.
- **c.** Enter the following reply: **This is a reply.**
- **d.** Send the reply, then view the contents of your Inbox.
- **e.** Open the Re: Arriving soon message.
- **f.** Forward this message to the address **sharonkikukawa@yahoo.com** and to yourself, adding the message **This is a forward.**
- **g.** Send the forward, then open your Inbox.

3. File and delete messages using Hotmail.

- **a.** Display all the folders for your Hotmail account.
- **b.** Create a new folder named **Itinerary**.
- **c.** Open your Inbox, open the Arriving soon message, then move it into the Itinerary folder.
- **d.** Open the Itinerary folder and verify that the message you filed appears in it.
- **e.** Open your Inbox, then delete the Fwd: Re: Arriving soon and Re: Arriving soon messages.

4. Customize a Web portal.

- **a.** Open the My MSN page.
- **b.** Follow the Change Content link to the Personalize My MSN page.
- **c.** Follow the Health link, and select **MSN Health**.
- **d.** Follow the Local News & Weather link, and deselect **MSNBC Local News**.
- **e.** Update your content settings, then verify that your My MSN page appears correctly.
- **f.** Follow the Change Layout link to the Personalize My MSN page.
- **g.** Move Local News & Weather to the top of the list.
- **h.** Follow the Change Color link, select **Purple**, then update your settings.

5. Create a Web calendar.

- **a.** Open the MSN Calendar, then click the **Calendar tab**.
- **b.** Add a new appointment with the following characteristics:
  Description: **Arrive in Hawaii**
  Start Date: **July 14, 2003**
  Start Time: **2:00 PM**
  Duration: **1 hour 00 minutes**
- **c.** Save your appointment, then add the following as a new appointment:
  Description: **Dinner with Sharon**
  Start Date: **July 14, 2003**
  Start Time: **6:00 PM**
  Duration: **3 hours 00 minutes**
- **d.** Save your appointment, then open your calendar for the month of July 2003.

Practice

6. **Customize a Web calendar.**
   a. View the MSN Calendar options.
   b. Display the holiday categories.
   c. Select **Islamic Religious Holidays**, **Jewish Religious Holidays**, and **Puerto Rico (USA)**.
   d. Save your changes, then open your calendar.
   e. Display the MSN Calendar in Month View, then examine the holidays on the calendar until you find one from one of the categories you just added.

7. **Print a Web calendar.**
   a. Open a printer-friendly version of the currently displayed month.
   b. Print the printer-friendly version of this calendar, then close the Web browser window for the printer-friendly version only.
   c. If necessary, display the MSN Calendar - Month View Web page.
   d. Display the calendar for the week of July 20, 2003 - July 26, 2003.
   e. Print the printer-friendly version of this week's calendar, then close it.

8. **Create a Web address book.**
   a. Open the home page for your Hotmail account.
   b. Open the Address Book.
   c. Add the following contacts to the Address Book:

Clyde	**Clyde**	**Hankey**	**hankey@spinc.net**	**303.555.5950**
Jose	**Jose**	**Salgado**	**jes@spinc.net**	**303.555.0082**

   d. Create a new group named **colleagues**, and add Clyde and Jose to this group.

9. **Maintain a Web address book.**
   a. Display the list of individual contacts in the Address Book.
   b. Reorder the list by Quickname.
   c. Change Jose's e-mail address to **jose@nomad-ltd.com**.

10. **Use a Web address book.**
   a. Use the Address Book to open a new message automatically addressed to Clyde.
   b. Use the Quick Address List to add Jose's e-mail address to the Cc text box.
   c. Use the Quick Address List to add the colleagues list to the Bcc text box.
   d. Cancel the e-mail message.
   e. Sign out of MSN.
   f. Open the My MSN tab to verify that you have successfully signed out.
   g. Close your Web browser.

Internet

▶ Independent Challenge 1

You are the office manager for Grand American Appraisal Company, a national real-estate appraisal company that handles real-estate appraisal requests from all over the United States and maintains a large list of approved real-estate appraisers located throughout the country. Your supervisor asks you to start using e-mail to send out appraisal requests to affiliated appraisers instead of the current fax system.

- **a.** Start your Web browser and log in to your Hotmail account.
- **b.** Obtain the e-mail address of a classmate who will assume the role of an approved appraiser.
- **c.** Add your classmate's full name, quickname, and e-mail address to the Address Book.
- **d.** Add your instructor's full name, quickname, and e-mail address to the Address Book.
- **e.** Create a new message addressed to your classmate with you and your instructor listed in the Cc text box.
- **f.** Enter **Request for appraisal** as the subject.
- **g.** Type a short message asking if the appraiser is available for an assignment.
- **h.** Send the message, then check your Inbox.
- **i.** Delete the Request for appraisal message from your Inbox.
- **j.** Sign out of Hotmail and close your Web browser.

▶ Independent Challenge 2

You're working a part-time job while going to school. Because your hours change from week to week, you need to keep close track of each week's schedule. You want to create a calendar that you'll have easy access to at school, work, and home, but you don't want to worry about forgetting a planner book. You decide to start recording your work schedule on a Web-based calendar.

- **a.** Start your Web browser and log in to your Hotmail account.
- **b.** Open the My Calendar page, then open the current week.
- **c.** Enter the following appointments, using **Work** as the description for each:
  Monday: 12:00 PM – 6:00 PM
  Wednesday: 2:00 PM – 6:00 PM
  Thursday: 3:00 PM – 7:00 PM
  Friday: 9:00 AM – 2:00 PM
- **d.** Open the printer-friendly version of the current week, then print it.
- **e.** Sign out of MSN and close your Web browser.

Independent Challenge 3

Bridgefield Engineering Company (BECO) is a small engineering firm in Somerville, New Jersey, that manufactures and distributes heavy industrial machinery for factories worldwide. To facilitate contact with clients around the world in different time zones, the company is relying more on e-mail. You've just received e-mail contact information for a few new clients. You send them an introductory e-mail message to ensure that they have BECO's e-mail address, and to verify that you have the correct address for each client.

- **a.** Start your Web browser and log in to your Hotmail account.
- **b.** Add the full name, quickname, and e-mail address of your instructor and two classmates to the Address Book.
- **c.** Create a mailing list for the two classmates you added to the Address Book in Step b using the group name **clients**.
- **d.** Create a new message addressed to the clients list and to yourself, using the subject **Welcome to BECO**.
- **e.** In the message area, type a short note thanking the clients for choosing BECO and asking them to respond to you when they receive your message, then add your full name to the message.
- **f.** Send the message, wait a few seconds, and then view the contents of your Inbox.
- **g.** Reply to the Welcome to BECO message.
- **h.** Forward the Welcome to BECO message to yourself.
- **i.** Create an e-mail folder named **clients**, and then file the Welcome to BECO message in the clients folder.
- **j.** Delete the Re: Welcome to BECO and Fw: Welcome to BECO messages.
- **k.** Sign out of Hotmail and close your Web browser.

Independent Challenge 4

You've started using a popular Web portal, and enjoy receiving customized information and features. However, your friends who use other Web portals say that their Web portals have specific features that make them better than others. Compare a few popular Web portals to decide if there's actually a significant difference between Web portals.

- **a.** Start your Web browser.
- **b.** Go to **www.course.com/illustrated/internet3**, then click the **Unit G link**.
- **c.** Use the links under Independent Challenge 4 to open at least three popular Web portals. Examine each Web portal's main page and customizable features, and compare features and content between Web sites. You might also want to create a login name for each service and explore how easy the Web site is to personalize.
- **d.** Write two paragraphs comparing and contrasting the three Web portals you examined. You might also include the MSN portal in the discussion for reference. Be sure to state if you think some Web portals are better than others, and provide evidence to support your conclusion.
- **e.** Close your Web browser.

▶ Visual Workshop

Go to **www.course.com/illustrated/internet3**, click the **Unit G link**, then click **Hotmail** under Visual Workshop. Use the skills you learned in this unit to display the calendar view shown in Figure G-27. Be sure your calendar includes the same appointments; the title for the appointment on July 13 should be your name. Print a copy of the calendar.

FIGURE G-27

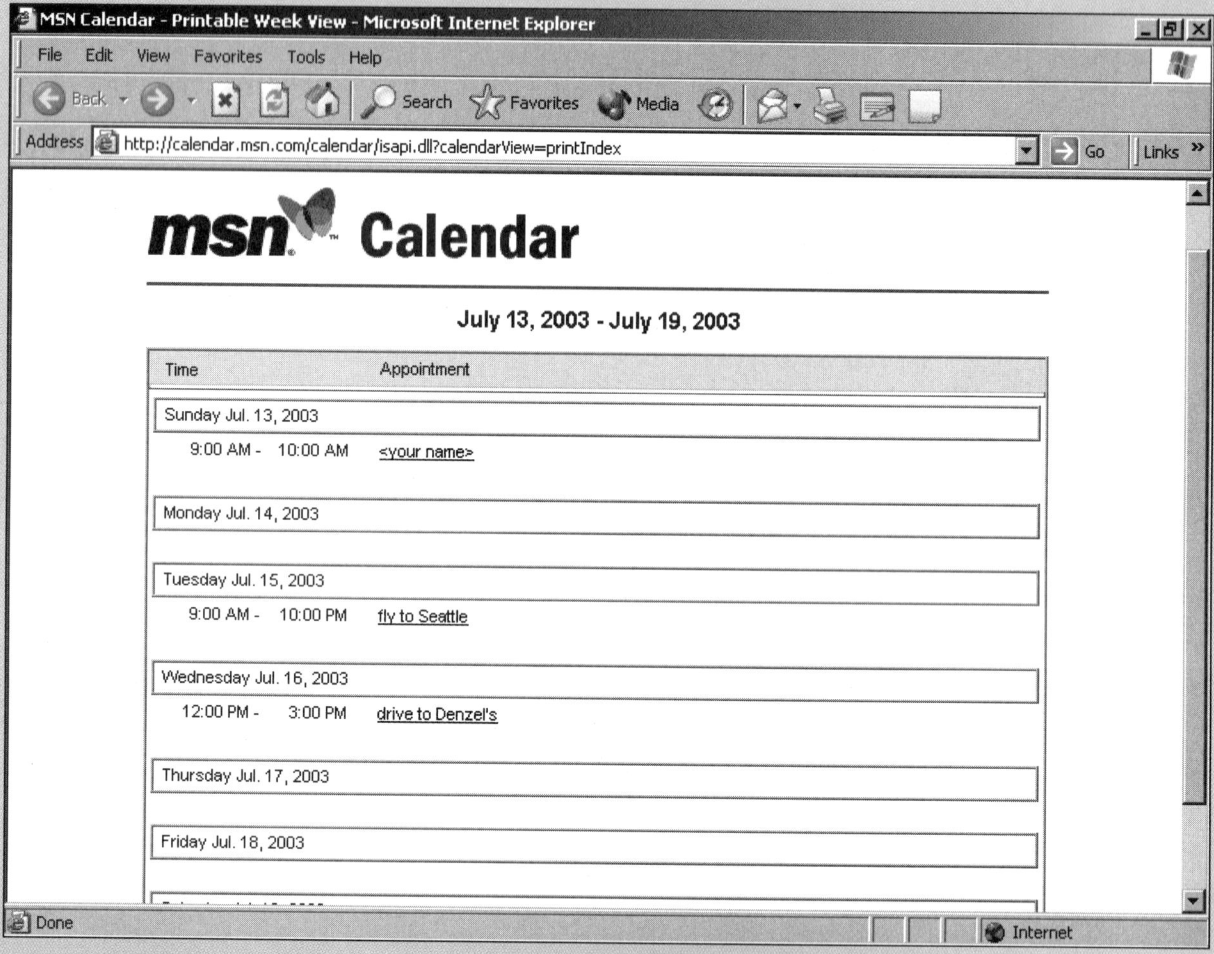

Using Advanced E-Mail and Communication Tools

- Define mailing lists
- Locate mailing lists
- Subscribe to mailing lists
- Monitor mailing lists
- Leave mailing lists
- Understand chat
- Participate in chat sessions
- Find newsgroups

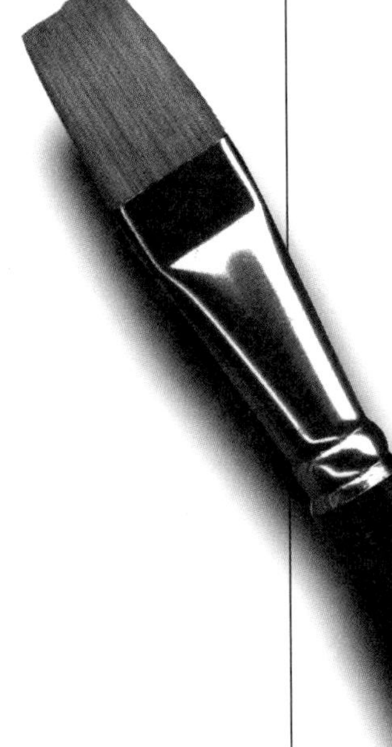

You can build on your Internet knowledge by taking advantage of more advanced Internet communication tools, such as mailing lists, chat groups, and newsgroups. These tools enable you to easily exchange ideas and information with other people interested in common topics or areas. Lincoln Art Glass Company (LAG) is a small art glass company located in Nebraska. From its combined showroom and studio, LAG sells stained glass, glass supplies, and books to the public. Your job is to investigate how your boss, Mike DeMaine, can use mailing lists, chat groups, and newsgroups to learn about new industry techniques and trends, as well as to make contact with colleagues in the industry and potential customers.

Internet

Defining Mailing Lists

An Internet **mailing list**, or **e-mail list**, is a system that allows a group of people to communicate via e-mail about a subject of interest, such as gardening in Alaska. An Internet server that runs mailing list software maintains a database containing the e-mail addresses for all members. Each member receives all messages sent to the mailing list. You want to find out if mailing lists provide information about art glass and art glass dealers. You start your research by learning some common terms associated with mailing lists.

Details

► Mailing List Server Software

Each mailing list is administered by mailing list server software that runs on an Internet server. This software manages each user's request to join or leave a mailing list, receives e-mail messages posted to the list, and sends mailing list messages to list members.

► Subscribing

Traditional mailing list servers enable you to join a mailing list, or **subscribe** to it, by sending an e-mail message to the server. This message usually contains a command that the server understands, such as "subscribe," along with the name of the mailing list and your e-mail address. Today, many mailing lists are administered by more user-friendly servers that also accept user input via a Web page rather than requiring e-mailed commands. Figure H-1 shows a sample Web page from the Yahoo! Groups Web site, which accepts user input.

► Posting

A message sent to a mailing list is called a **posting**, or a **post**. Mailing list server software sends out posts submitted by list members to all members of the list.

► Moderated and Unmoderated Lists

Posts sent to a **moderated mailing list** are read and evaluated by a list moderator before they are sent to all members in the mailing list. The list moderator is responsible for discarding any messages that are inappropriate for or irrelevant to the list's members. All members of an **unmoderated mailing list** automatically receive all messages, regardless of content. Most mailing lists are unmoderated because of the time required to read and evaluate the contents of the many messages that members post each day.

► Frequently Asked Questions (FAQ)

A **Frequently Asked Questions** (**FAQ**) document contains the answers to common questions that users ask about a mailing list and its subject. Users who want information about a mailing list, or potential members who want to find out if the mailing list seems appropriate for their interests, can find answers in the mailing list's FAQ. Figure H-2 shows the FAQ Web page for a mailing list.

CLUES TO USE

A warning about mailing lists

Mailing lists are essential tools for receiving current and useful information. However, if you subscribe to a mailing list, you need to check your e-mail regularly. Depending on a mailing list's activity, you might receive many messages every day. In fact, some mailing lists can generate hundreds of messages each week. By checking your e-mail frequently, you can respond to, file, or delete messages in a timely fashion.

FIGURE H-1: Yahoo! Groups Web page

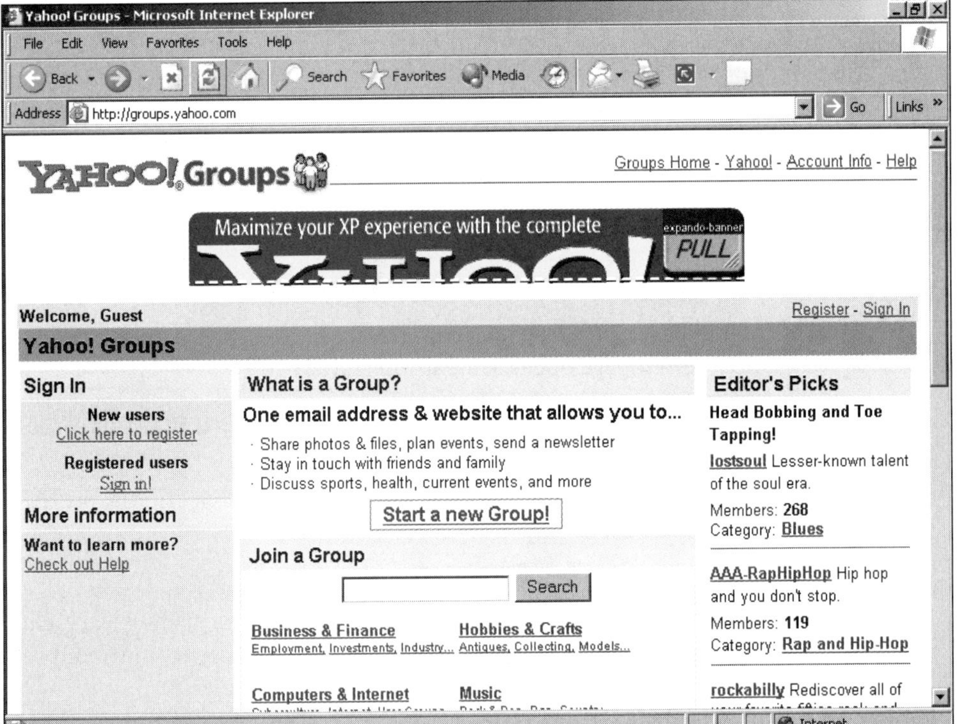

FIGURE H-2: Mailing list FAQ Web page

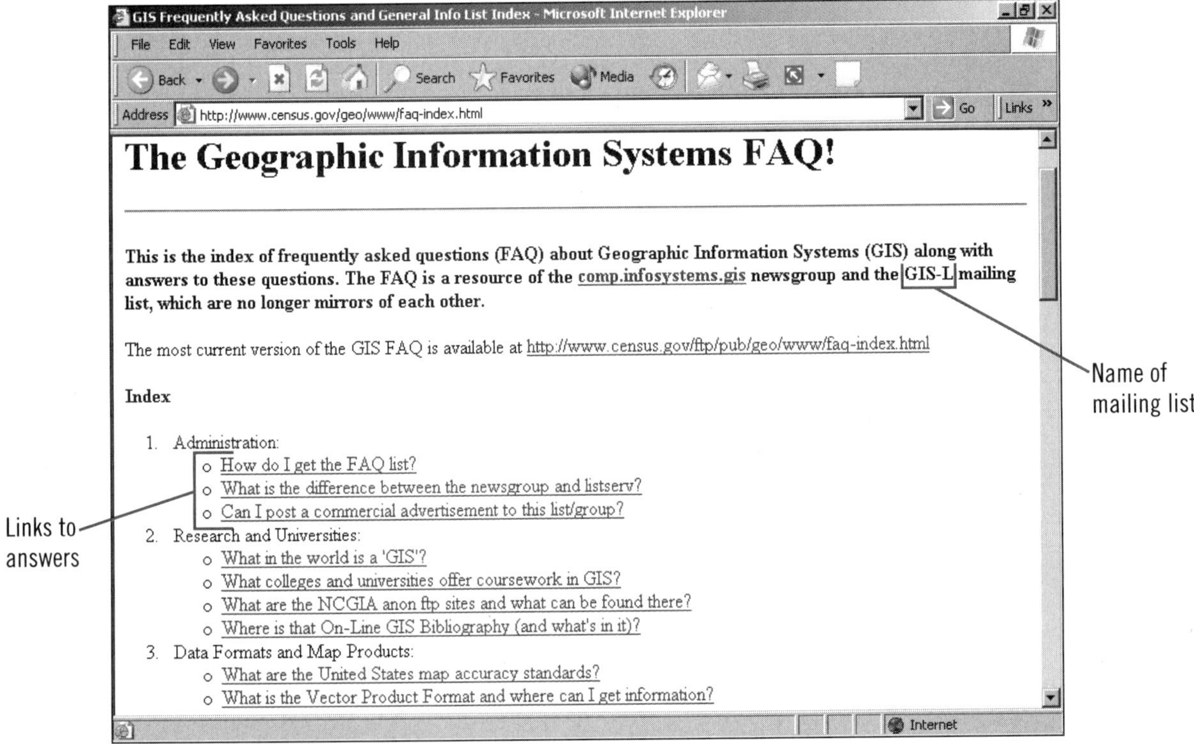

Internet

Unit H

Internet

Locating Mailing Lists

Thousands of mailing lists on many different topics are maintained on the Internet. To find a mailing list, you can use search engines to search for mailing lists by subject. In addition to search engines, several Web sites index mailing lists and can help you locate mailing list resources. Now that you understand the basic terms used when discussing mailing lists, you begin working on Mike's request. You start by searching for mailing lists related to art glass.

1. Start your Web browser, go to **www.course.com/illustrated/internet3**, click the **Unit H link**, then click the **PAML link** under Lesson 2
   The PAML search page opens, similar to Figure H-3.
2. Scroll down the Web page, click in the **Enter keyword text box**, type **art glass**, then click **Search**
   PAML returns a list of mailing lists that match your search criteria. A brief description and link for each mailing list appears.
3. Click one of the mailing list links
   The Web page that opens provides information about the mailing list, including the mailing list's name, host, contact person, and description, and information about or links to instructions for subscribing and unsubscribing.
4. Go to **www.course.com/illustrated/internet3**, click the **Unit H link**, then click the **Topica link** under Lesson 2
   The Topica home page opens, similar to Figure H-4.
5. Scroll down the Web page, then click in the **Search text box**
6. Type **art glass**, then click **Search**
   A results page for the search expression "art glass" appears.
7. Scroll down the results page and review the results

FIGURE H-3: PAML search page

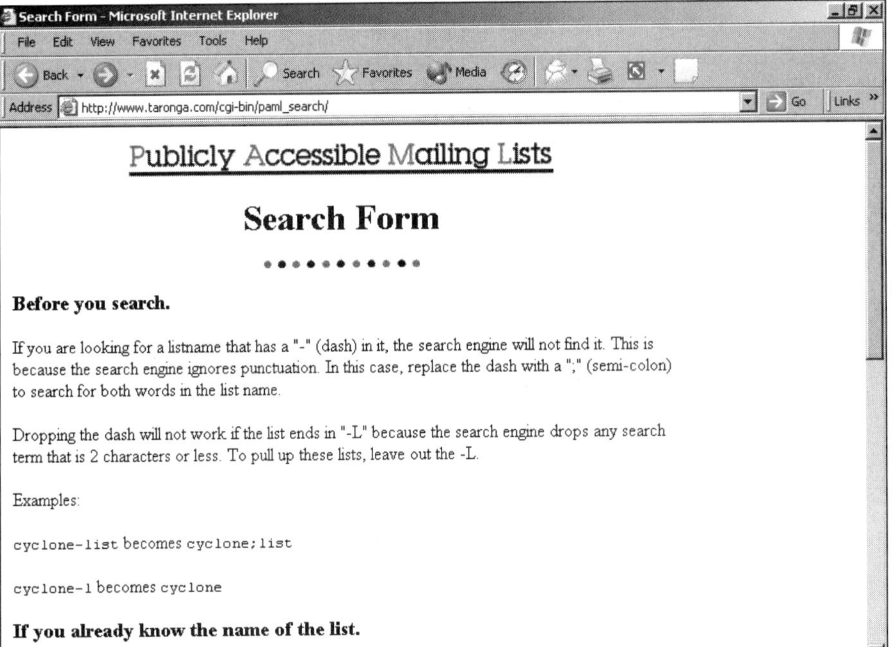

FIGURE H-4: Topica home page

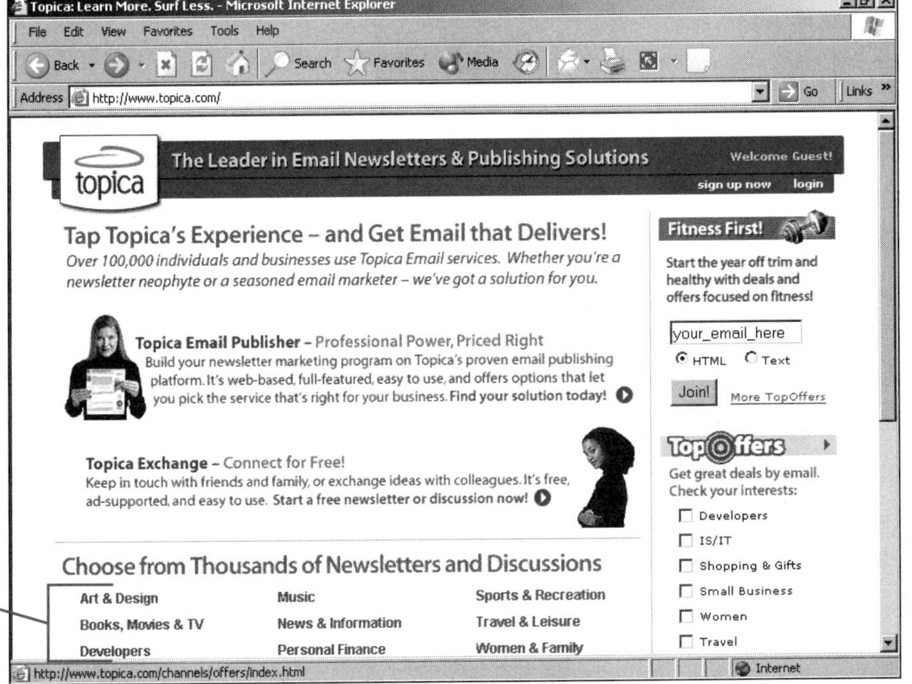

Internet

Subscribing to Mailing Lists

You subscribe to a mailing list by sending an e-mail message to the mailing list server with a request to join the list's membership. When you subscribe to a moderated mailing list, the list's moderator must accept you as a member before you can send and receive messages; when you subscribe to an unmoderated mailing list, your acceptance is automatic as long as you have formatted the e-mail request properly. While Mike checks with colleagues on which art glass mailing lists would be the best to join, you join a mailing list for practice.

1. Start your e-mail program or log in to your Web-based e-mail account, then start a new message
2. Address the message to **listserv@listserv.classroom.com**
   This address is the administrative e-mail address for the NEW-LIST mailing list, which announces new mailing lists. Only administrative tasks, such as member subscriptions, are handled through this e-mail address.
3. Enter **subscribe** as the message subject
   Although the mailing list server software doesn't read the message subject, using a subject can make it easier to identify messages that you have sent.
4. In the message body, type **subscribe new-list**, press **[Spacebar]**, then type your full name
   Your message should appear similar to Figure H-5.
5. Send your message, wait a few minutes, check for new messages, then open the message from **L-Soft list server**
   After the mailing list server has accepted and processed your subscription request, you receive a message to confirm your membership to the mailing list, similar to the one shown in Figure H-6. You might have to wait several minutes before you receive a reply from the server.
6. Read the subscription information, create a reply to the current message, delete the original message contents, then type **ok**
7. Send your message, wait a few minutes, then check for new messages
   The mailing list server responds with two messages, similar to the message header summaries shown in Figure H-7.
8. Read each new message
   The welcome message like the one shown in Figure H-8 contains important information that will help you participate in the mailing list. It's a good idea to file the message in an e-mail folder for future reference.

Trouble?

If the mailing list server returns your subscription request without processing it, make sure that you spelled the word "subscribe" correctly, you typed your first and last names, you did not include a signature file, and you did not type any other information in the message body.

FIGURE H-5: Request for mailing list subscription

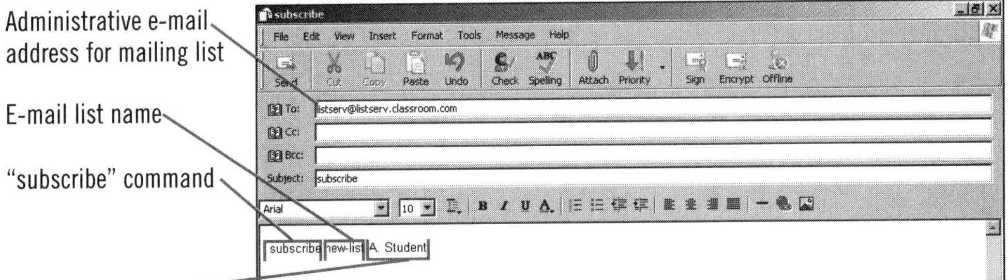

FIGURE H-6: Confirmation of mailing list subscription

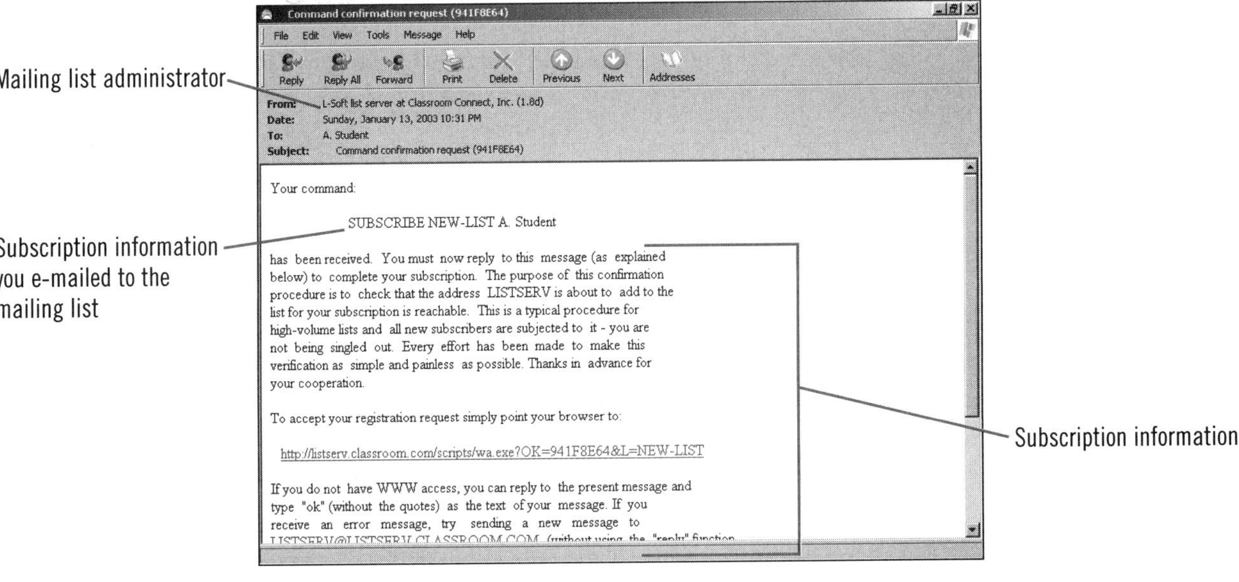

FIGURE H-7: Message header summaries for confirmation and welcome messages

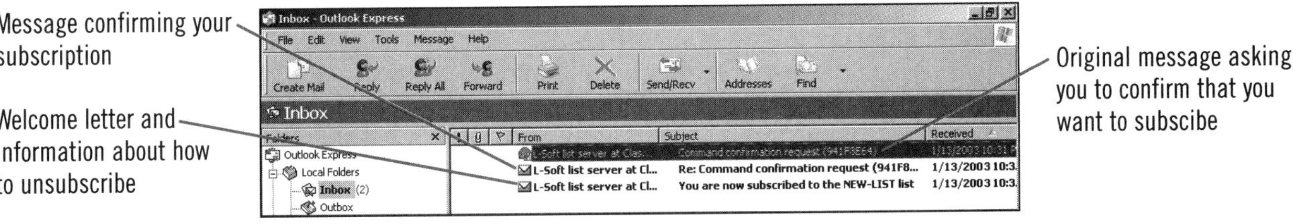

FIGURE H-8: Welcome message

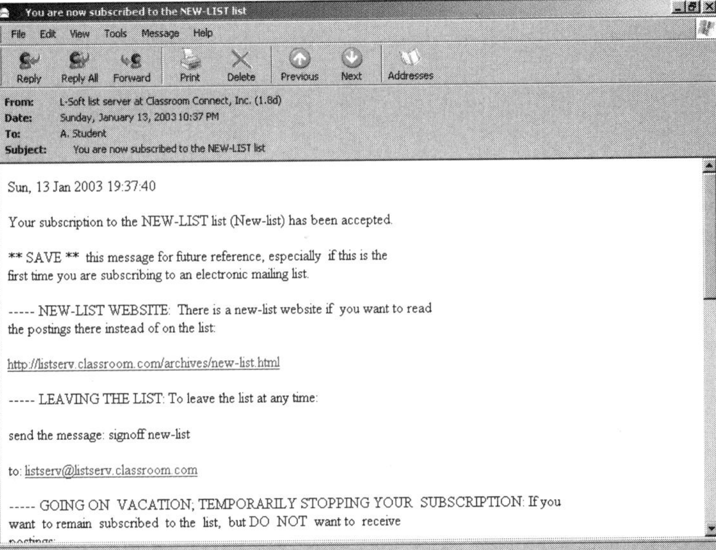

Internet

Internet

Monitoring Mailing Lists

You contribute to a mailing list by sending (or posting), messages to the mailing list. Figure H-9 shows a sample post. Before you post your first message to a mailing list, you should spend some time reading the postings of other list members. Participating in a mailing list in this way, known as **lurking**, allows you to become familiar with the list's culture and to research any basic questions in the list's FAQ to avoid filling up other members' e-mail boxes with questions that you might be able to answer yourself. In addition to lurking, you might also want to review past messages from the list. The mailing list server stores past messages in a file called an **archive**. To access an archive, you can send a command to the mailing list server that requests messages from a particular time frame. You continue to work with mailing lists by requesting and viewing archived messages for the NEW-LIST mailing list.

1. Address a new e-mail message to **listserv@listserv.classroom.com** (which is the system administrator's address)
   You are sending this message to the system administrator because you are sending a command rather than posting a message. You post messages to the mailing list address listed in the welcome message you receive after you subscribe.
2. Enter **index request** as the subject, then enter **index new-list** in the message body
   Make sure that nothing else appears in the message body. The word "index" is the command that you use to ask the mailing list server to send the list of archives for the NEW-LIST mailing list. Each mailing list's basic commands are usually summarized in the welcome message you receive after you subscribe.
3. Send your message, wait a few seconds, then check for new messages
   The mailing list server sends an e-mail message that contains a list of archive filenames. If the message doesn't arrive after a few seconds, wait a minute and check for messages again. It might take several minutes to receive a reply.

QuickTip

In addition to the archive message, you might receive other messages from the mailing list server. You can review or delete these messages.

4. Open the message with the subject **File: "NEW-LIST FILELIST"**
   Figure H-10 shows an archive list. The list in your e-mail message will probably be different. The message lists weekly archives for all e-mail messages posted to the NEW-LIST mailing list.
5. Address a new e-mail message to **listserv@listserv.classroom.com**, then enter **Week of 10/14/01 list** as the subject
   Again, you are sending this message to the system administrator because you are sending a command.
6. Type **get new-list LOG0110C** in the message body
   Note that the first three characters of LOG0110C are letters, and the next four are numbers. This command retrieves the messages sent to the mailing list during the week of October 14, 2001. These messages are contained in an archive named LOG0110C. To retrieve the file, you use the get command followed by the filename.

QuickTip

Make sure you type a space after "get" and after "new-list" so that the server will correctly handle your command to retrieve the file.

7. Send your message, wait a few seconds, then check for new messages
8. Open the message with the subject **File: "NEW-LIST LOG0110C"**
   This message contains the text of all messages sent to the list during the week of October 14, 2001.

FIGURE H-9: Mailing list post

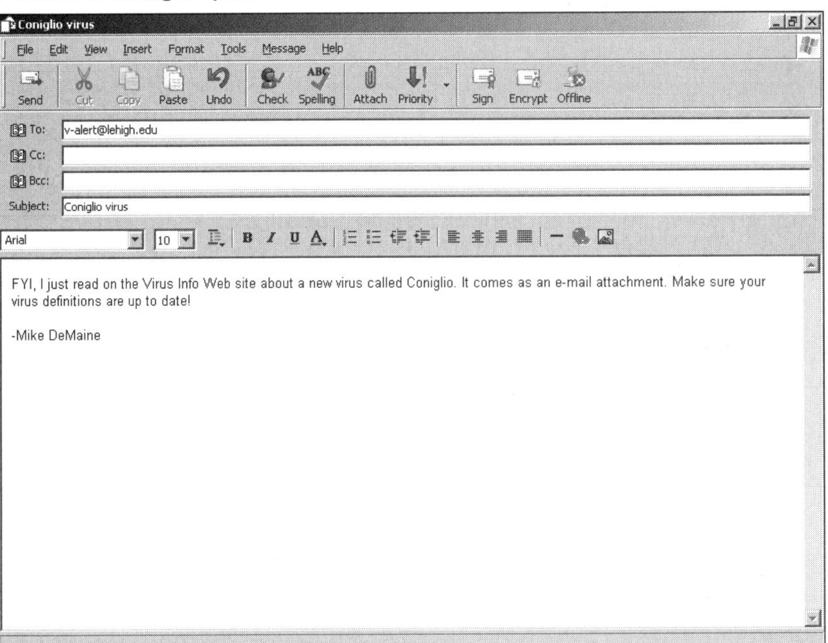

FIGURE H-10: List of available archive files

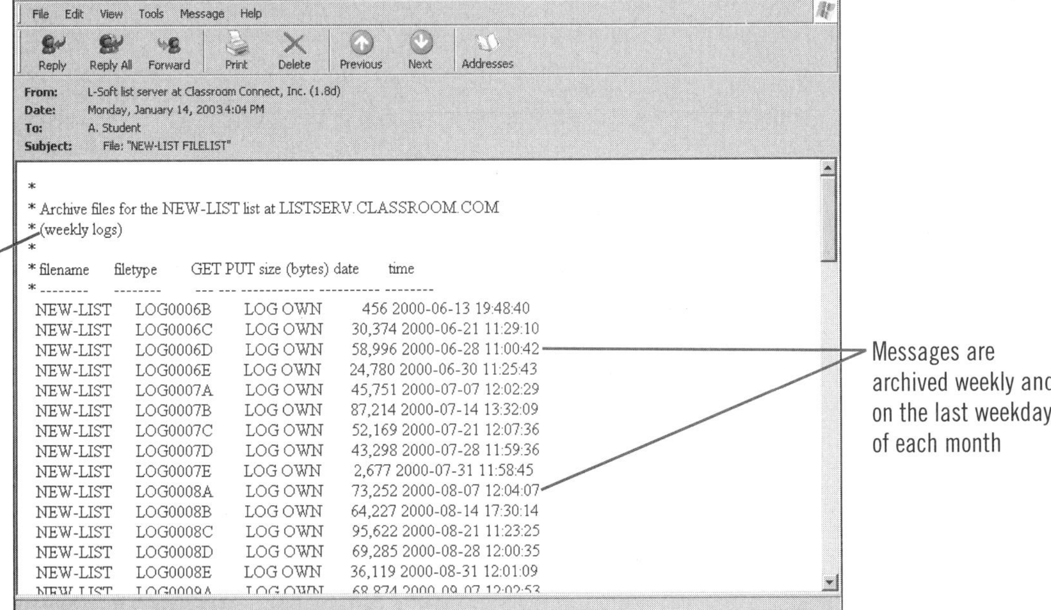

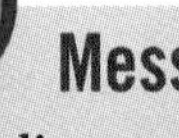

Messages and commands

Mailing list programs manage two types of e-mail: messages and commands. **Messages** are e-mail messages that express ideas or ask questions that each member of the mailing list receives. **Commands** request the mailing list server to take a prescribed action. The most common commands are subscribe and unsubscribe. Most of the programs that run mailing lists, such as LISTSERV, ListProc, Mailbase, or Majordomo, process the same commands. Thus, after you know a few commands for one program, you will know the basic command set for several programs. You post messages to the mailing list address (for example, new-list@listserv.classroom.com), and you send commands to the administrative address (for example, listserv@listserv.classroom.com).

Internet

Internet

Leaving Mailing Lists

When you remove your name from a mailing list (or **unsubscribe** from or **drop** the mailing list), you stop receiving messages. Typically, the command to leave a mailing list is either **unsubscribe** or **signoff** followed by the mailing list's name. As with all administrative requests, you send your unsubscribe or signoff message to the mailing list's administrative address. Now that you've learned how to join and use mailing lists, you leave the NEW-LIST mailing list to reduce the number of e-mail messages that you receive each day. The welcome message that you received when you initially subscribed instructs you to use the signoff command to leave the NEW-LIST mailing list.

Steps

1. Create a new e-mail message addressed to **listserv@listserv.classroom.com**
2. Enter **signoff** as the subject
3. Enter **signoff new-list** in the message body
   Figure H-11 shows the signoff message.
4. Send the message, wait a few seconds, then check for new messages
5. Open the message with the subject **Re: signoff**
   The message confirms your removal from the NEW-LIST mailing list, similar to the one shown in Figure H-12. If the message you receive does not contain any text but does contain an attachment, then double-click the attachment to open it. The attachment confirms your removal.

Trouble?

If you receive an error message, then you were not removed from the mailing list. Try sending a new signoff message. Make sure that you type "signoff" correctly and that you leave a space between signoff and new-list.

FIGURE H-11: Signoff message

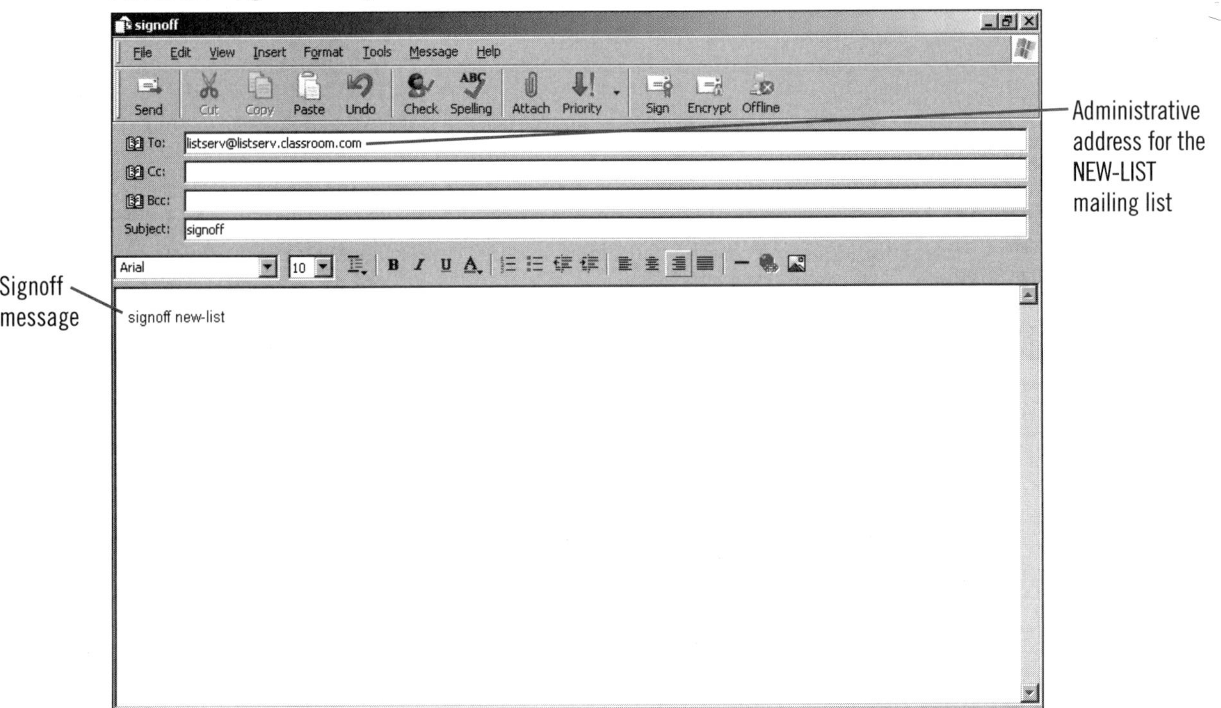

FIGURE H-12: Signoff confirmation

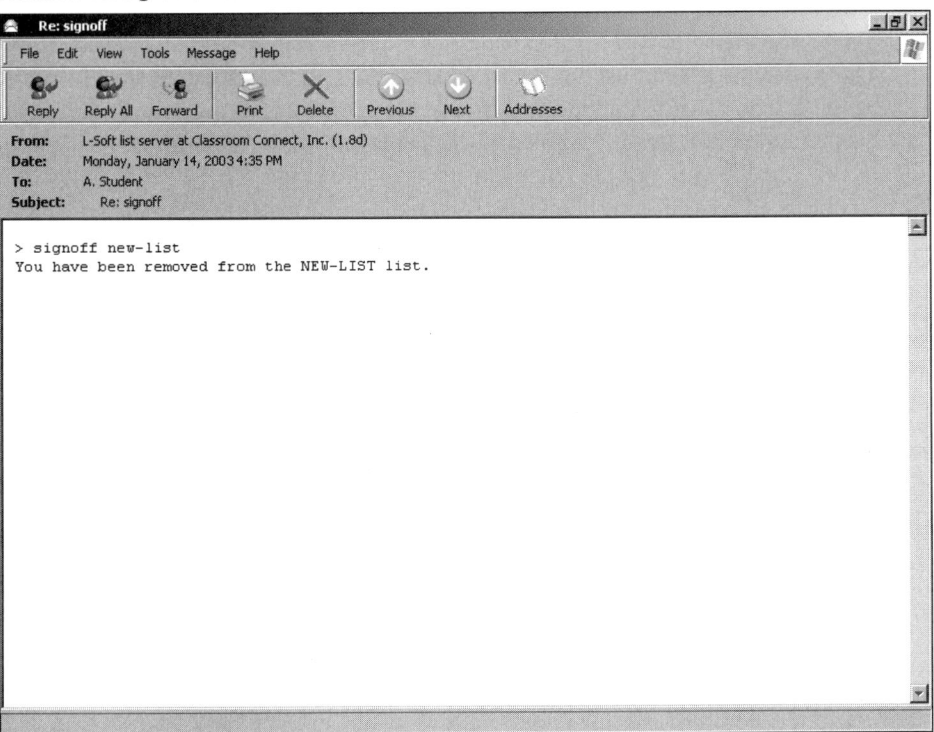

Internet

Internet

Understanding Chat

Chat is instantaneous (or **real-time**) communication on the Internet or on the Web. Chats can be continuous, with participants entering and leaving ongoing discussions, or they can be planned to occur at a specific time and to last for a specific duration. Some chats are open to discussion of any topic, whereas other chats are focused on a specific topic or category of participants. Some chats feature participation by a celebrity or an authority on the chat topic. Mike has recently heard about chat from some colleagues at an art glass conference. He asks you to learn how to use Web-based chat facilities to communicate live with individuals or groups of people. You begin by reviewing basic chat terms.

Details

Public and Private Chats

A **private chat** occurs between two individuals. Often, the two individuals participating in a private chat meet while chatting in a group, or **public chat**.

Internet Relay Chat

Internet Relay Chat (**IRC**) is a communications program that was developed by Jarkko Oikarinen of the University of Oulu in Finland in 1988. IRC is popular with businesses, which use it for virtual meetings with clients and employees at worldwide branch offices. You use IRC client software to connect to an IRC server.

ICQ Chat

ICQ ("I seek you") is an Internet chat client. This software was created by a small Israeli company, Mirabilis, in 1996. To use ICQ, each person in the chat group must have a copy of the program. Figure H-13 shows the ICQ Tips and Tricks page on the CNET Web site. You can click links on this Web page to learn how to download, install, and use ICQ. To view this Web page, go to *www.help.com*, search on ICQ, then click ICQ Tips and Tricks.

Web Chat Sites

Web chat sites offer the same capabilities as text-based IRC chat networks. However, a Web chat site is often easier to use. In addition to making chats more accessible to users, Web chat sites allow participants to include multimedia elements, such as pictures, audio clips, video clips, and links in their messages. A Web chat page loads into your Web browser just as any other Web page does. The Web chat page is then constructed and reconstructed continually by Web chat server software in response to the messages that the Web chat site accepts from chat participants. The Web chat server software actually re-creates the Web chat page every time it accepts a message.

Chat Acronyms

Chatting requires participants to type quickly, even in the enhanced graphical environment of the Web. Therefore, chat participants often omit capitalization and do not worry about proper spelling and grammar. They frequently use icons composed of standard typed characters, known as **emoticons** or **smileys**. Like e-mail users, some chat users find these icons, such as :) and :-(, helpful to display humor and emotions in their messages. In addition, chat participants use some of the acronyms listed in Table H-1 as shortcuts for common expressions. Most chat participants type everything in lowercase letters, because typing in all capital letters is usually interpreted as shouting.

FIGURE H-13: ICQ Tips and Tricks page

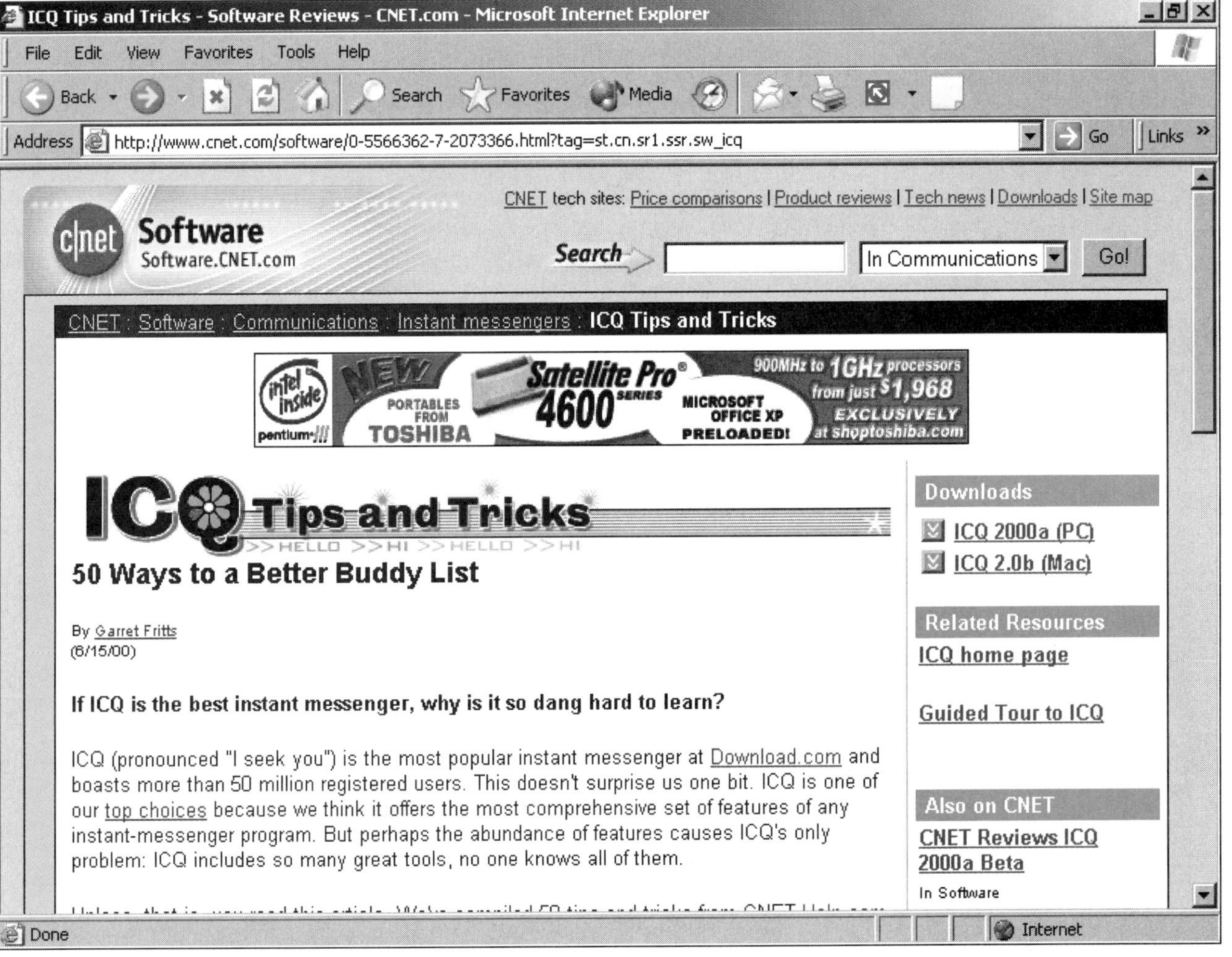

TABLE H-1: Commonly used chat acronyms

acronym	meaning	acronym	meaning
afk	Away from keyboard	irl	In real life (contrasted with one's online existence)
atm	At the moment	jk	Just kidding
bbl	Be back later	lol	Laughing out loud
brb	Be right back	np	No problem
btw	By the way	oic	Oh, I see
cul8r	See you later	rotfl	Rolling on the floor laughing
c-ya	See you	eg	Evil grin
ttfn	Ta-ta (goodbye) for now	wb	Welcome back
imho	In my humble opinion		

Internet

Participating in Chat Sessions

You can find chat groups at many Web sites. After you find a Web chat site, you typically need to register before you can use the Web chat facilities. You should carefully consider whether to provide detailed personal information when you register because most current laws do not require a Web site administrator to maintain confidentiality of your information. If one Web chat site requires information that you do not want to disclose, you can simply look for another Web chat site with a less intrusive registration page. To evaluate a chat session, you sign on to a popular Web chat site and try using chat.

1. Start your Web browser, go to **www.course.com/illustrated/internet3**, click the **Unit H link**, then click the **Yahoo! Chat link** under Lesson 7
   The Yahoo! sign in page opens.

QuickTip

If you already have a Yahoo! ID, enter your ID and password, click Sign In, then skip to Step 5.

2. Click the **Sign up now link**
   A form opens.
3. Complete the form, then click **Submit This Form**
   Yahoo! processes your information, and then a welcome message appears. If messages appear asking you to reenter information, follow the directions, then resubmit the form. Sometimes, you will be asked to choose a different user name if the name you have chosen has already been used.
4. Click **Continue to Yahoo!**
   The Yahoo! Chat Web page appears, similar to Figure H-14.
5. Click the link to a subject area of your choice
   From this Web page, you can select a general chat topic and then enter the chat room for that topic.

Trouble?

If you get a warning that you need to download and run Yahoo! Chat, you need to click Yes or you won't be able to participate in a chat. If you get warnings about any other programs, check with your instructor or technical support person before downloading them.

6. Click the link for the topic of your choice, then click the desired chat room on the menu that appears
7. If necessary, click **Start Chat Now**
   The chat screen opens for the room you picked, similar to Figure H-15. The text on your screen will differ from Figure H-15. If you want to join in a chat, you can type a message in the Message text box, then click Send. If you want to change chat rooms, click Change Rooms.
8. Click the **Exit link**, then click the **Home link**
   The main Yahoo! Chat Web page appears.
9. Click the **Sign Out link**

FIGURE H-14: Yahoo! Chat Web page

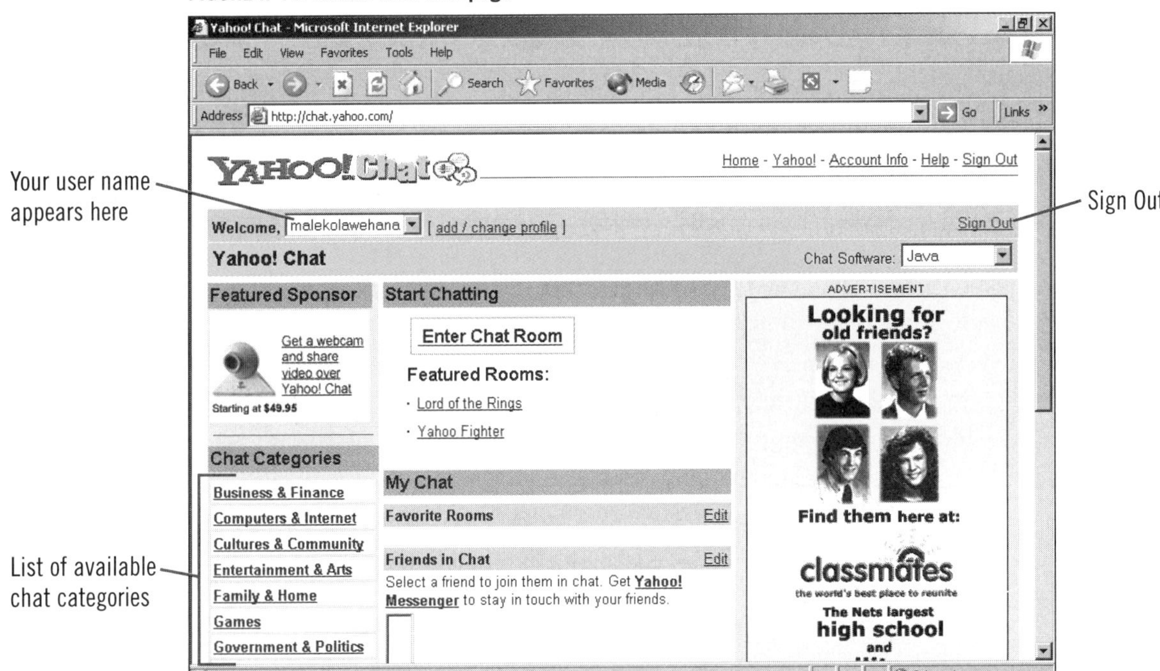

FIGURE H-15: Yahoo! Chat in progress

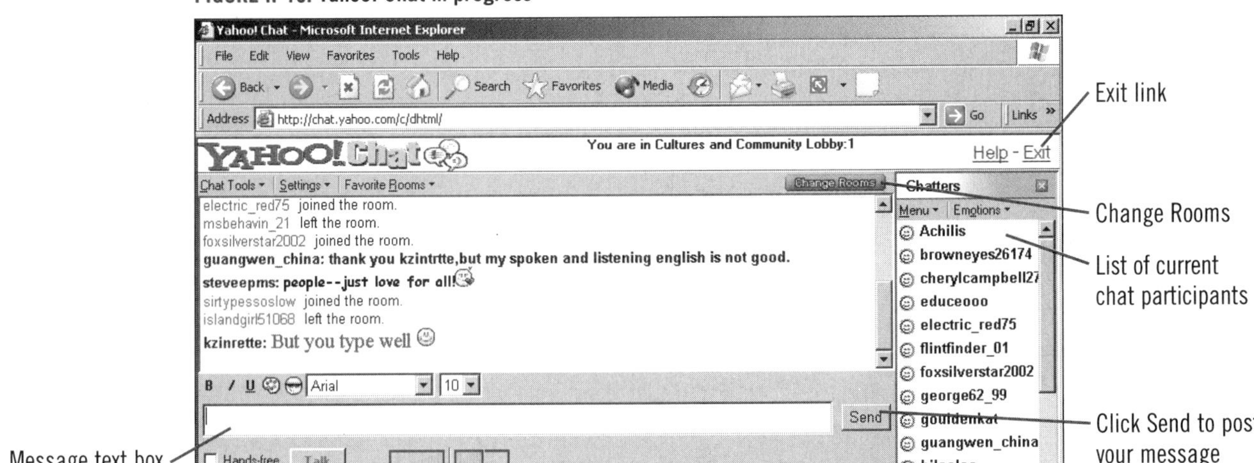

Internet

Finding Newsgroups

A **newsgroup**, sometimes called an Internet discussion group or **Usenet**, is a system like a mailing list that creates a forum for participants to discuss a topic. Unlike a mailing list, in which messages are sent to participants via e-mail, a newsgroup's posts are stored on Internet servers, sorted by topic. Each participant chooses when to view and post to a newsgroup. Most Internet service providers offer access to current postings in most or all available newsgroups. Additionally, several Web sites archive newsgroup articles and provide search engines that help you quickly find past articles on specific topics. You start learning about newsgroups by investigating newsgroup archives on the Web.

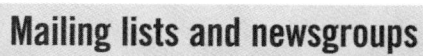

1. Go to **www.course.com/illustrated/internet3**, click the **Unit H link**, then click the **Tile.net link** under Lesson 8
   The home page for the Tile.net directory opens. Tile.net maintains a directory of mailing lists and newsgroups, as well as other types of resources on the Internet.
2. Click the **Category list arrow**, then click **news**
3. Type **glass** in the Text To search for text box, then press **[Enter]**
   The search engine returns a Web page with hyperlinks to newsgroups containing the key term "glass."
4. Click the **rec.crafts.glass link**
   A Web page opens providing some information about this newsgroup, as shown in Figure H-16. The description indicates that users exchange information about glassworking and glass in this newsgroup.
5. Go to **www.course.com/illustrated/internet3**, click the **Unit H link**, then click the **Google Groups link** under Lesson 8
   The home page for Google Groups opens. The Google Groups directory stores more than 100 million newsgroup articles dating from 1995 in its database and plans to continue adding older articles going all the way back to Usenet's origin in 1979. The Google Groups site also includes a search engine that allows you to query its newsgroup article database by subject, newsgroup name, or article author.
6. Type **art glass** in the Google Search text box, then click **Google Search**
   A Web page similar to the one shown in Figure H-17 opens. Google Groups returns a list of suggested newsgroups, as well as links to individual news articles. The newsgroup to which each article was originally posted is included at the end of each article summary.

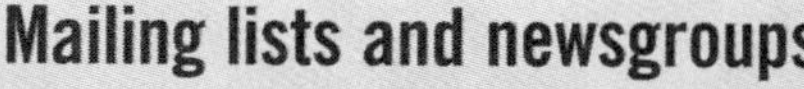

Mailing lists and newsgroups

Although newsgroups seem similar to mailing lists, here are some important differences:

- An e-mail program is used to create a mailing list, and only members of the mailing list receive messages sent to the mailing list. Any information sent to a mailing list is delivered automatically to every e-mail address on the list and must be retrieved through each member's e-mail account.
- A newsgroup can be accessed directly from the Web. When you send a message to a newsgroup, anyone with Internet access can read it.

FIGURE H-16: **rec.crafts.glass page at Tile.net**

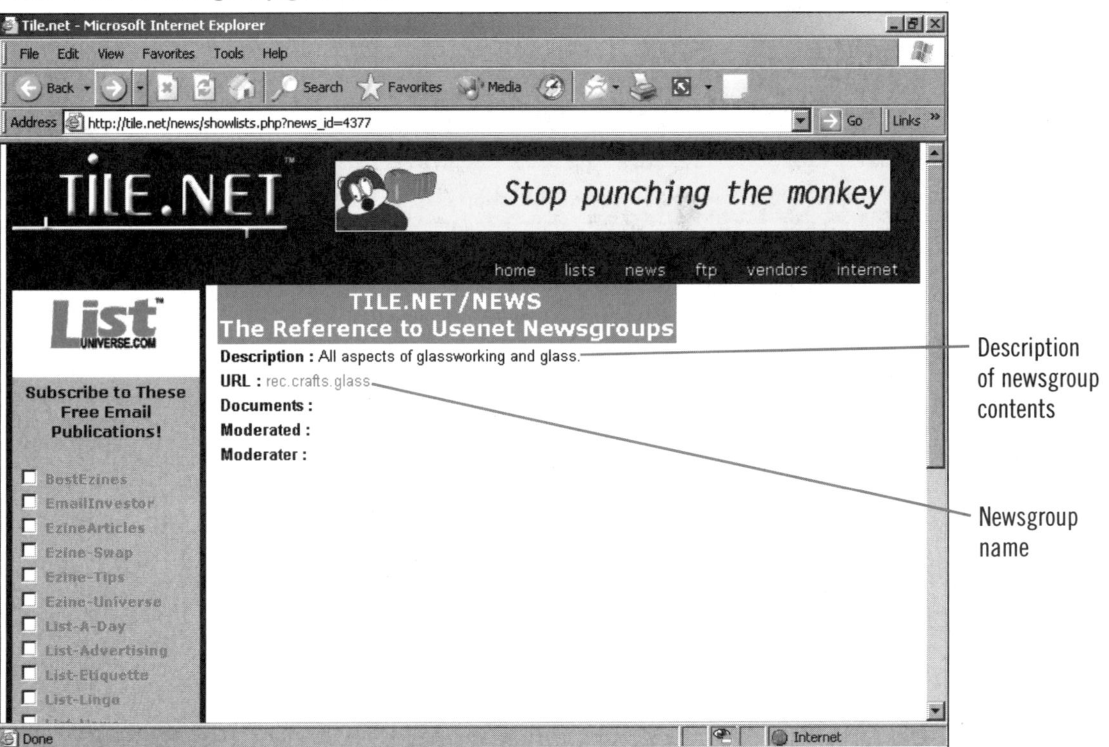

FIGURE H-17: **Google Groups search results**

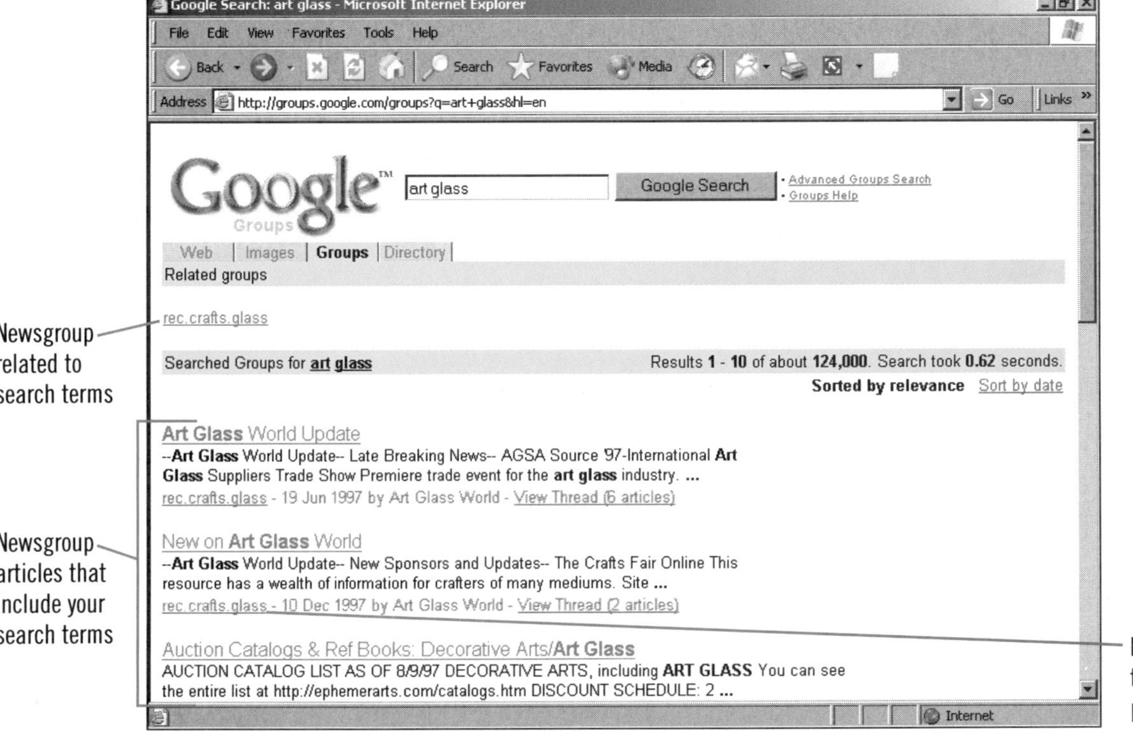

Internet

Practice

▶ Concepts Review

Identify the communication tool in use in each of the following figures.

FIGURE H-18

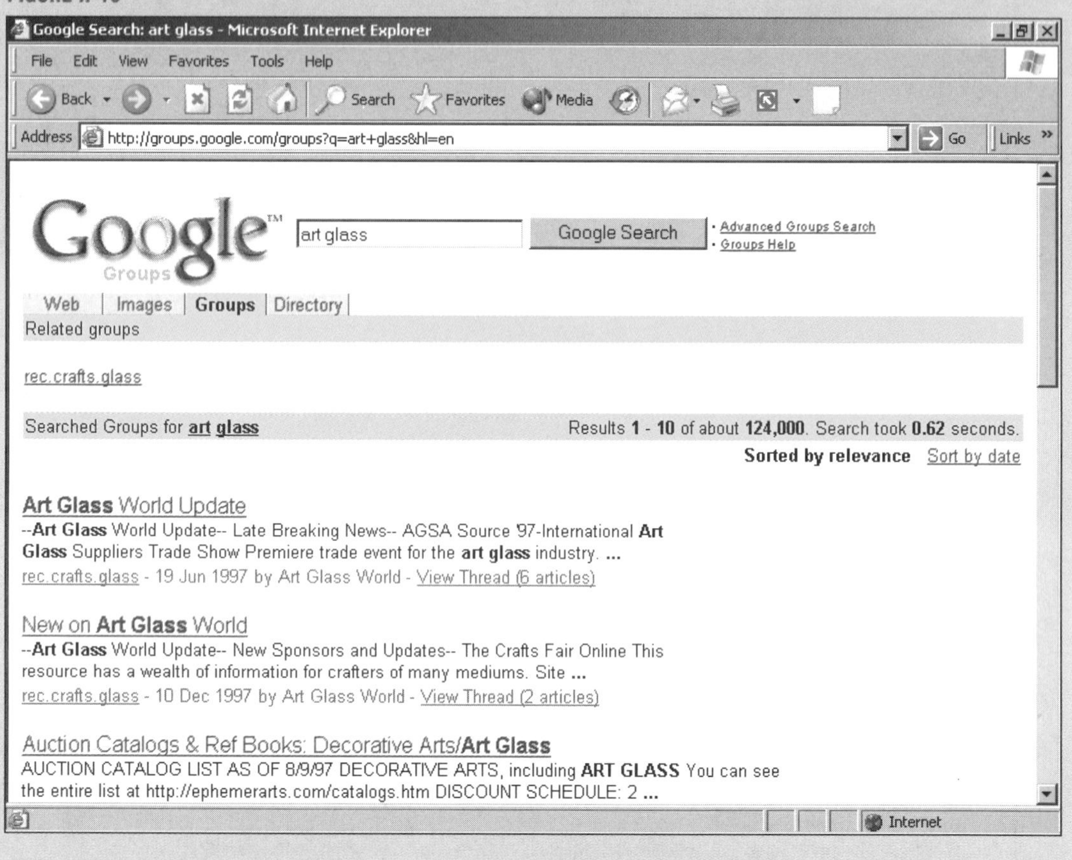

Practice

FIGURE H-19

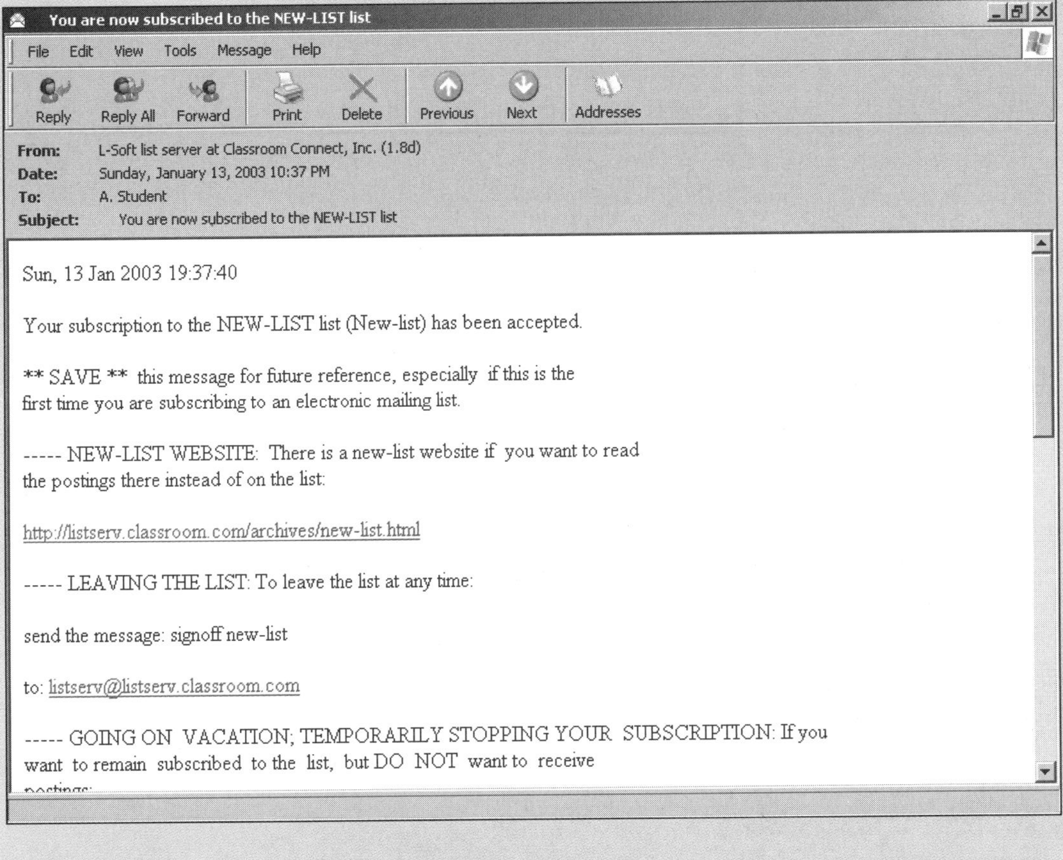
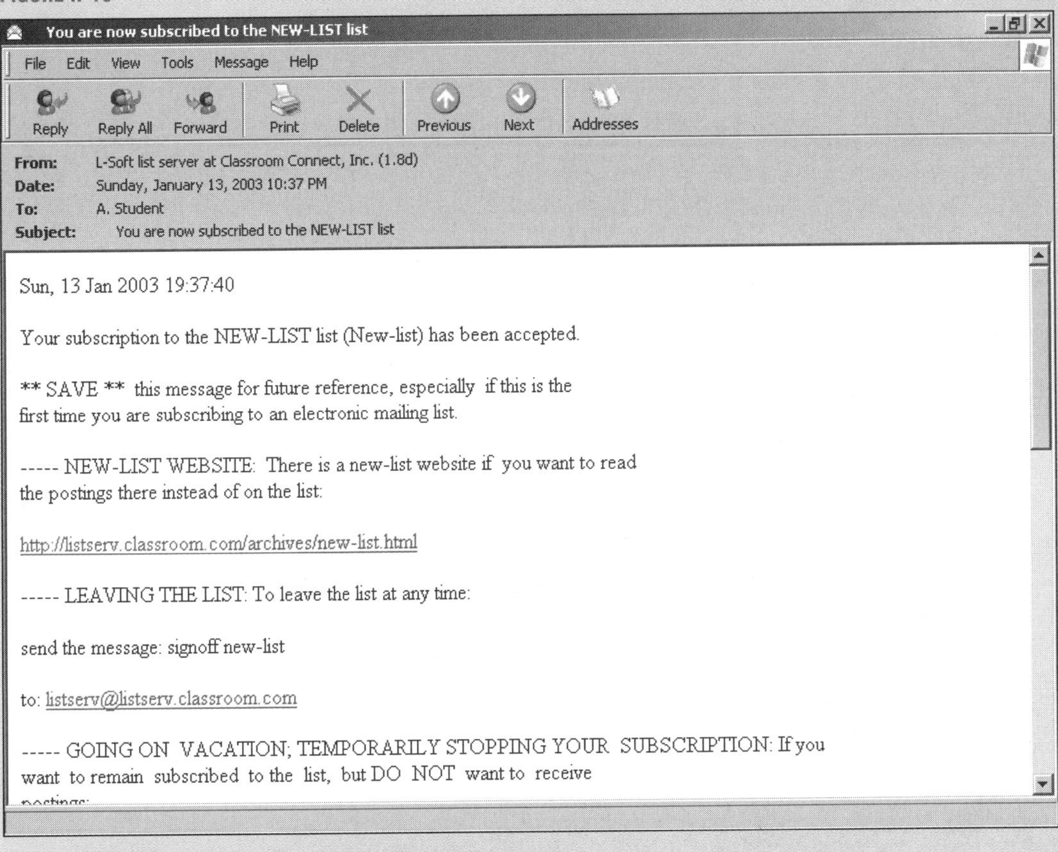

You are now subscribed to the NEW-LIST list

File Edit View Tools Message Help

Reply | Reply All | Forward | Print | Delete | Previous | Next | Addresses

From: L-Soft list server at Classroom Connect, Inc. (1.8d)
Date: Sunday, January 13, 2003 10:37 PM
To: A. Student
Subject: You are now subscribed to the NEW-LIST list

Sun, 13 Jan 2003 19:37:40

Your subscription to the NEW-LIST list (New-list) has been accepted.

** SAVE ** this message for future reference, especially if this is the first time you are subscribing to an electronic mailing list.

----- NEW-LIST WEBSITE: There is a new-list website if you want to read the postings there instead of on the list:

http://listserv.classroom.com/archives/new-list.html

----- LEAVING THE LIST: To leave the list at any time:

send the message: signoff new-list

to: listserv@listserv.classroom.com

----- GOING ON VACATION; TEMPORARILY STOPPING YOUR SUBSCRIPTION: If you want to remain subscribed to the list, but DO NOT want to receive

FIGURE H-20

Internet

Practice

Match each term with the statement that describes it.

4. Mailing list server	**a.** A program that manages mailing lists
5. Posting	**b.** An emoticon
6. SUBSCRIBE VALERT-L	**c.** A real-time communication program
7. :)	**d.** Sending a message to a mailing list
8. IRC	**e.** A command that mailing list server software can read
9. Newsgroups	**f.** Another term for Usenet groups

Select the best answer from the list of choices.

10. In what type of mailing list are messages reviewed before being distributed?
- **a.** Public mailing list
- **b.** Unmoderated mailing list
- **c.** Administered mailing list
- **d.** Moderated mailing list

11. You post mailing list messages using which type of mailing address?
- **a.** Mailing list address
- **b.** Majordomo address
- **c.** Administrative address
- **d.** LISTSERV address

12. Mailing list programs manage which two types of e-mail?
- **a.** Articles and requests
- **b.** Postings and receivings
- **c.** Messages and commands
- **d.** Searches and FAQs

13. Silently observing postings on a mailing list is called:
- **a.** Lurking.
- **b.** Peeking.
- **c.** Watching.
- **d.** Observing.

14. __________ chat happens between two people.
- **a.** Emoticon
- **b.** Public
- **c.** Private
- **d.** ICQ

15. Newsgroup messages:
- **a.** Are e-mailed to group participants.
- **b.** Are stored on an Internet server.
- **c.** Require a subscription.
- **d.** Are not archived.

Skills Review

1. Locate mailing lists.

- **a.** Start your Web browser, go to **www.course.com/illustrated/internet3**, click the **Unit H link**, then click the **PAML link** under Skills Review 1.
- **b.** Search for mailing lists related to literature.
- **c.** Scroll through the results and explore links.
- **d.** Go to **www.course.com/illustrated/internet3**, click the **Unit H link**, then click the **Topica link** under Skills Review 1.
- **e.** Search for mailing lists related to literature.
- **f.** Follow links to find a mailing list that interests you.

2. Subscribe to mailing lists.

- **a.** Choose a literature mailing list based on your search results to which you want to subscribe.
- **b.** Follow links to a Web page describing the literature mailing list that interests you.
- **c.** Read the requirements for joining the list.
- **d.** Start your e-mail program and create a new message.
- **e.** Use the administrative address of the mailing list you chose to address the message.
- **f.** Enter the required subscribe message in the message body.
- **g.** Send the message.
- **h.** Retrieve your messages.
- **i.** If necessary, send a confirmation message.

3. Monitor mailing lists.

- **a.** Create a new e-mail message.
- **b.** Read the welcome message from your mailing list to find the required command for getting an index of the mailing list's archives.
- **c.** Use the mailing list's administrative address to address the message.
- **d.** Type the command required to get an index of the mailing list's archive (for example, index LISTNAME) in the message body.
- **e.** Send the message.
- **f.** Wait several minutes, then retrieve your messages.
- **g.** If necessary, send another message to request the archives for a particular week or month.
- **h.** Open the message that contains the index, and scroll down to read some of the messages that have been sent to the mailing list.

4. Leave mailing lists.

- **a.** Read the welcome message from your mailing list to find the command required to leave the mailing list you have joined.
- **b.** Create a new e-mail message.
- **c.** Use the administrative address of the mailing list server to address the message.
- **d.** Enter the required command to leave the mailing list in the message body.
- **e.** Send the message.
- **f.** Wait several minutes, then retrieve your messages.
- **g.** Read the messages from the mailing list server to confirm that you have been removed from the mailing list.

5. **Participate in chat sessions.**
   a. Go to **www.course.com/illustrated/internet3**, click the **Unit H link**, then click the **Lycos Chat link** under Skills Review 5.
   b. Click the link for a category that interests you, then follow links to open a chat room on a topic you choose.
   c. If necessary, complete the registration form to join the Lycos chat rooms.
   d. Participate in the chat session, if you want.
   e. Exit the Lycos chat room.

6. **Find newsgroups.**
   a. Go to **www.course.com/illustrated/internet3**, click the **Unit H link**, then click the **Tile.net link** under Skills Review 6.
   b. Search for newsgroups related to landscape design.
   c. Explore the links to find articles related to landscape design.
   d. Go to **www.course.com/illustrated/internet3**, click the **Unit H link**, then click the **Google Groups link** under Skills Review 6.
   e. Search for newsgroups related to landscape design.
   f. Explore the links in some of the articles that appear to find other related articles about setting up a landscape design business.

Independent Challenge 1

Big Island Coffee Company (BICC) grows and ships coffee beans to many of the Hawaiian Islands and parts of mainland North America. Manoa Kileahu, BICC's owner, wants to find mailing lists that might be relevant to a coffee bean supplier's marketing efforts. You will send a message to a mailing list to retrieve the names of other known mailing lists.

a. Start your e-mail program, then create a new message.
b. Type **listserv@listserv.net** in the To text box.
c. Type **global marketing** in the Subject text box.
d. In the message area, type **list global marketing**. You are requesting a list of all known lists with the word marketing in their titles or names.
e. Send the message. The mailing list server will return mailing list names that include the word marketing.
f. When you receive an answer from the mailing list server, scan the list of mailing list names and note which ones related to marketing look interesting.
g. Print a copy of the message.
h. Close your e-mail program.

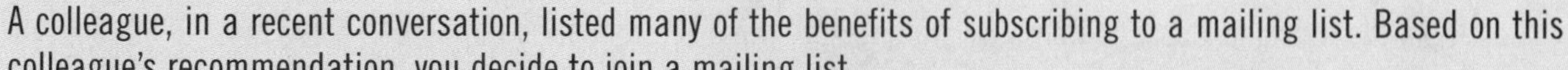

Independent Challenge 2

A colleague, in a recent conversation, listed many of the benefits of subscribing to a mailing list. Based on this colleague's recommendation, you decide to join a mailing list.

a. Start your Web browser, go to **www.course.com/illustrated/internet3**, click the **Unit H link**, then click the **L-Soft link** under Independent Challenge 2. The L-Soft International organization's Web page appears. L-Soft produces and licenses the LISTSERV mailing list software.
b. Click the **CataList link** on the left side of the Web page, then scroll down the Web page until you see the List information section. Click the View lists **with 10,000 subscribers or more link**. A Web page appears that lists hundreds of mailing lists. Each mailing list is accessible via a link.

c. Scroll down the list of mailing lists and locate one that interests you. Click the link of a list you want to join. A new Web page appears displaying information about the list.
d. Scroll down until you can see a line describing how to subscribe to the list or a link to subscription information. The line will read, in part, "To subscribe, send mail to . . ." Make a note of the list's name and the administrative address.
e. Click the e-mail link to the administrative address. If the address does not appear as a link, start your e-mail program, then create a new message addressed to the list's administrative address.
f. Compose the message to subscribe to the list, then send the message.
g. If the mailing list server has any specific instructions, follow its requests.
h. When the mailing list server sends you a welcome message, forward it to your instructor.
i. Read the messages on the list for a few days. After you have read several messages, unsubscribe from the list.
j. When you receive the confirmation of your removal from the list, forward it to your instructor.
k. Close your Web browser and e-mail program.

► Independent Challenge 3

Laura Jensen is president of Rockin' Tees, a small manufacturer of printed t-shirts that specializes in creating designs using images of famous rock bands. Rockin' Tees must either purchase the rights to use band names and likenesses or agree to pay negotiated per-shirt royalties to the bands. Laura needs to estimate the demand for t-shirt designs before she negotiates with the bands' agents and agrees to payment terms. She wants you to check out chat rooms related to rock music to find out which rock bands are mentioned most frequently.

a. Start your Web browser, go to **www.course.com/illustrated/internet3**, click the **Unit H link**, then click the **Yahoo! Chat link** under Independent Challenge 3.
b. Examine the chat topics on the Yahoo! Chat Web page and explore some of the chat rooms to which they lead. Remember that you are collecting information for Laura, so stay focused on her research question: Which rock bands are mentioned most frequently in the chats?
c. Send an e-mail message to your instructor that lists three of the most frequently mentioned bands.
d. Close your Web browser.

► Independent Challenge 4

Dan Rivetti is the director of Triangle Research, a small laboratory that tests metal parts and assemblies using physical and computer models. Usually, Dan knows enough about the general design of the parts and assemblies to be able to develop the testing procedures. Sometimes, however, he wants to conduct background research and contact experts in the field before designing his testing procedures. Dan heard that newsgroups offer such information and the opportunity to post inquiries, but he has also heard that some newsgroups are more reliable than others. Dan asks you to help him evaluate the quality of some newsgroups.

a. Start your Web browser, go to **www.course.com/illustrated/internet3**, click the **Unit H link**, then click the **Google Groups link** under Independent Challenge 4.
b. Click the **sci. link**, then examine and follow some of the links.
c. Look for two newsgroups in a similar topic area, one moderated and one unmoderated.
d. Examine a sample of messages from each type of newsgroup devoted to the same topic.
e. Describe the differences you found between the postings in the moderated and unmoderated newsgroups. Explain which type of newsgroup would best serve Dan's needs.
f. Close your Web browser.

▶ Visual Workshop

Go to **www.course.com/illustrated/internet3**, click the **Unit H link**, then click the **Topica link** under Visual Workshop. Conduct a search on this Web site to display information similar to the information shown in Figure H-21.

FIGURE H-21

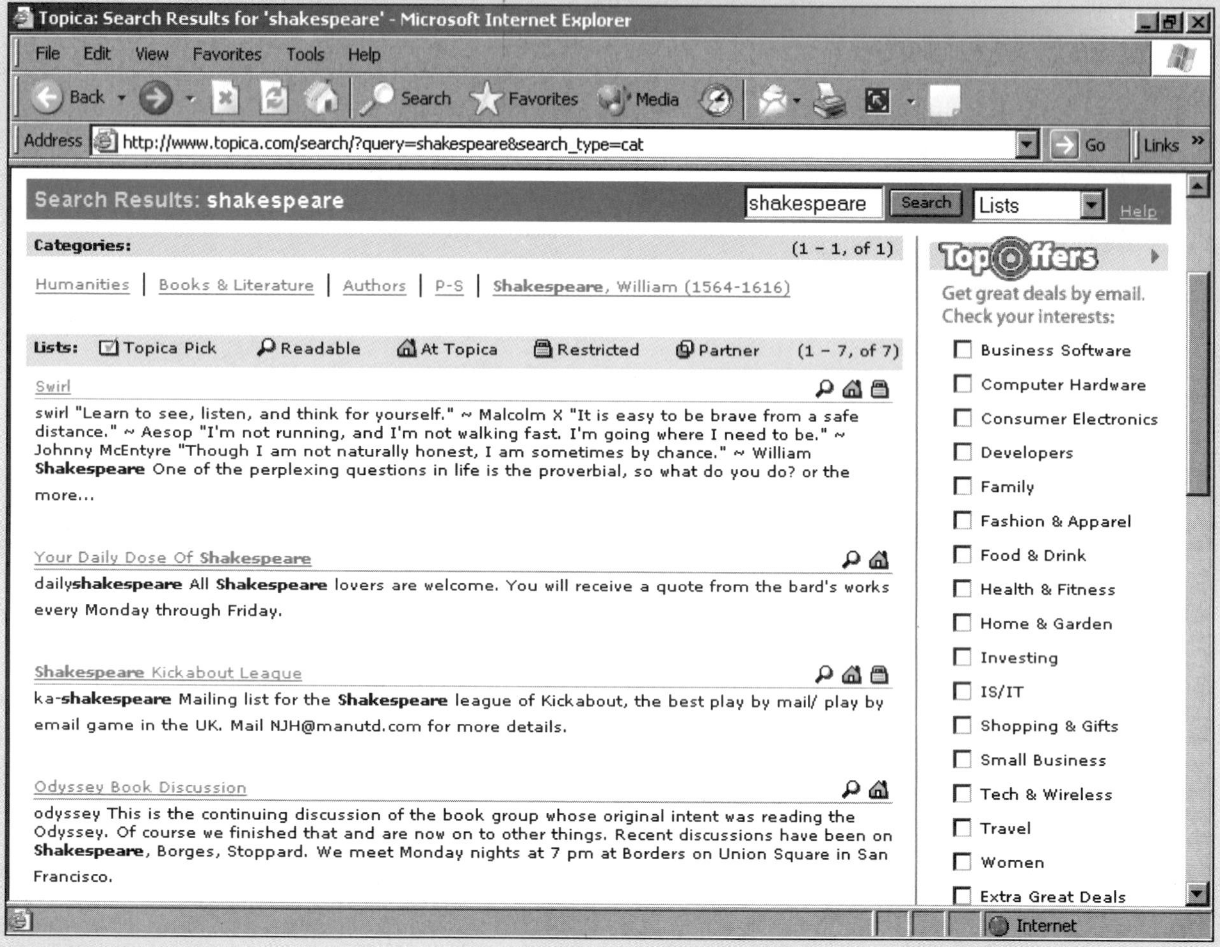

Topica: Search Results for 'shakespeare' - Microsoft Internet Explorer

File Edit View Favorites Tools Help

Back Search Favorites Media

Address http://www.topica.com/search/?query=shakespeare&search_type=cat Go Links

Search Results: **shakespeare** shakespeare Search Lists Help

Categories: (1 - 1, of 1)

Humanities | Books & Literature | Authors | P-S | **Shakespeare**, William (1564-1616)

Lists: Topica Pick Readable At Topica Restricted Partner (1 - 7, of 7)

Swirl

swirl "Learn to see, listen, and think for yourself." ~ Malcolm X "It is easy to be brave from a safe distance." ~ Aesop "I'm not running, and I'm not walking fast. I'm going where I need to be." ~ Johnny McEntyre "Though I am not naturally honest, I am sometimes by chance." ~ William **Shakespeare** One of the perplexing questions in life is the proverbial, so what do you do? or the more...

Your Daily Dose Of **Shakespeare**

daily**shakespeare** All **Shakespeare** lovers are welcome. You will receive a quote from the bard's works every Monday through Friday.

Shakespeare Kickabout League

ka-**shakespeare** Mailing list for the **Shakespeare** league of Kickabout, the best play by mail/ play by email game in the UK. Mail NJH@manutd.com for more details.

Odyssey Book Discussion

odyssey This is the continuing discussion of the book group whose original intent was reading the Odyssey. Of course we finished that and are now on to other things. Recent discussions have been on **Shakespeare**, Borges, Stoppard. We meet Monday nights at 7 pm at Borders on Union Square in San Francisco.

Top Offers

Get great deals by email. Check your interests:

- Business Software
- Computer Hardware
- Consumer Electronics
- Developers
- Family
- Fashion & Apparel
- Food & Drink
- Health & Fitness
- Home & Garden
- Investing
- IS/IT
- Shopping & Gifts
- Small Business
- Tech & Wireless
- Travel
- Women
- Extra Great Deals

Internet

Internet

Downloading

Programs and Files

- ► **Understand FTP**
- ► **Locate software download sites**
- ► **Download an FTP client program**
- ► **Install an FTP client program**
- ► **Set up an FTP session**
- ► **Use FTP to download a program**
- ► **Download a .zip file**
- ► **Open a .zip file**

When you use the Internet, you sometimes need to transfer files between your computer and other computers on the Internet. Although you can transfer files in several ways, the most common and widely used method is **File Transfer Protocol** (**FTP**). A common use of FTP is to transfer small program files from the Internet to your computer. After the transfer is complete, you must know how to install and use the program files that you downloaded. DigiComm produces and installs digital wireless communications products and technologies worldwide. Nancy Moore, the director of international sales and installations, has asked you, the computer support specialist, to equip staff members with several small programs, including an Internet file transfer program and a software compression/decompression program.

Internet

Understanding FTP

You use FTP to transfer files between computers that are connected to each other. FTP is widely used on the Internet to transfer files such as spreadsheets, pictures, movies, sounds, programs, and documents. Although you can easily transfer some files by attaching them to an e-mail message, many e-mail servers limit the size of attachments. FTP provides an alternative method for transferring larger files. For example, if you want a copy of a free program that you've seen on a friend's computer, you can use FTP to transfer the file from an Internet server to your computer. To download and install the utility programs that DigiComm staff members need, you need a program that can transfer files using FTP. You start by reviewing some of the terms you'll encounter as you work with FTP.

► FTP Client Program

An **FTP client program** is a program that resides on your computer and transfers files between your computer and another computer connected to it. Figure I-1 shows a popular FTP client program. The left pane lists the files and folders on the local computer (that is, your computer) and the right pane lists the files and folders on the remote computer.

► FTP Server Program

An **FTP server** stores the files that users running an FTP client program can transfer to and from their computers. An **FTP server program** runs on an FTP server. It allows file transfer to and from the server by FTP, and manages FTP access to the server's files. FTP is an operating-system neutral protocol. For example, you can use an FTP client program on a Windows 98 system to communicate with a large minicomputer that is running the FTP server on a UNIX operating system.

► Uploading Files

To **upload** a file means to send it from your computer to another computer. To upload files to an FTP server, you must use an FTP client program. For example, if you are working at home and need to submit a document to someone in your office, you could use an FTP client program to upload your document to your employer's FTP site.

► Downloading Files

To **download** a file means to receive the file on your computer from another computer. For example, if you are working at home and need a large file from work, you could use an FTP client program to download the appropriate file from your employer's FTP site.

► FTP Upload/Download Process

To use FTP to transfer files between your computer and another computer, you first connect to a remote computer and then log in by supplying a user name and a password. Figure I-2 illustrates the login screen for an FTP client program. You log in to an FTP server program in one of two ways:

- **Anonymous FTP**

You use **anonymous FTP** to log in to one of the many publicly accessible FTP servers, without having a personal account. The process is known as an anonymous login because "anonymous" is your user name. When you use anonymous FTP to connect to a publicly accessible FTP site, you are restricted to particular files and directories on the public server.

- **Full-privilege FTP**

The process of logging in to a computer on which you have an account (with a user name and password) and using the account to send and receive files is called **named FTP** or **full-privilege FTP**. After you log in to an FTP server with your user name and password, the FTP server program grants you access to the directories on the server that your account allows you to open.

FIGURE I-1: FTP client program

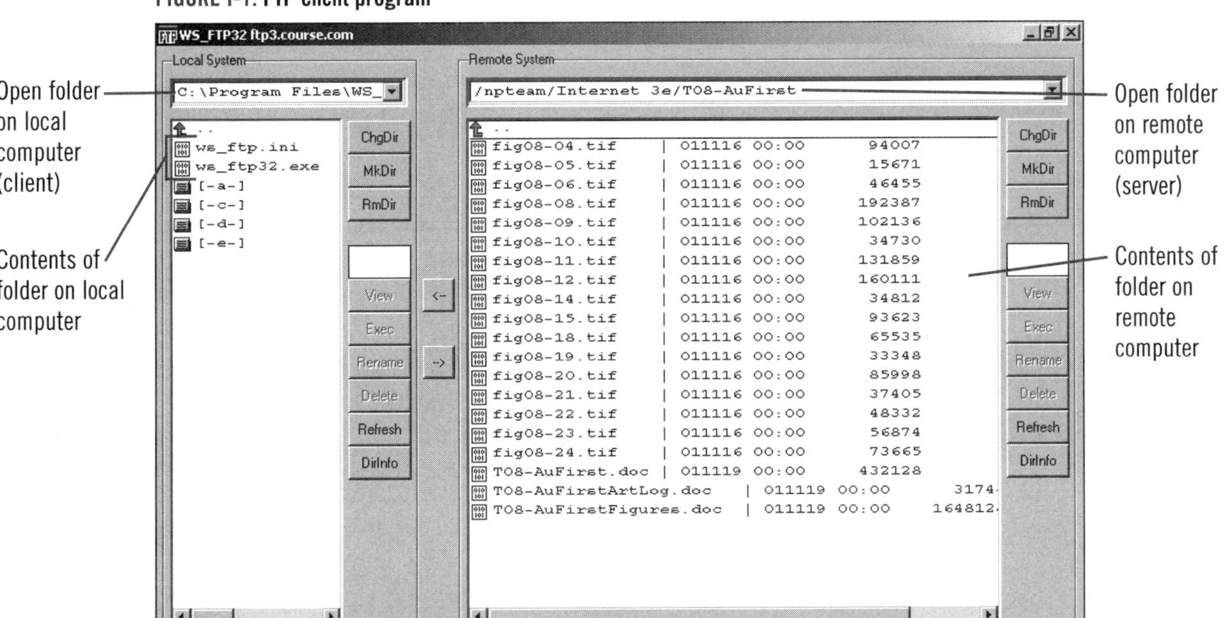

FIGURE I-2: Login screen for an FTP client program

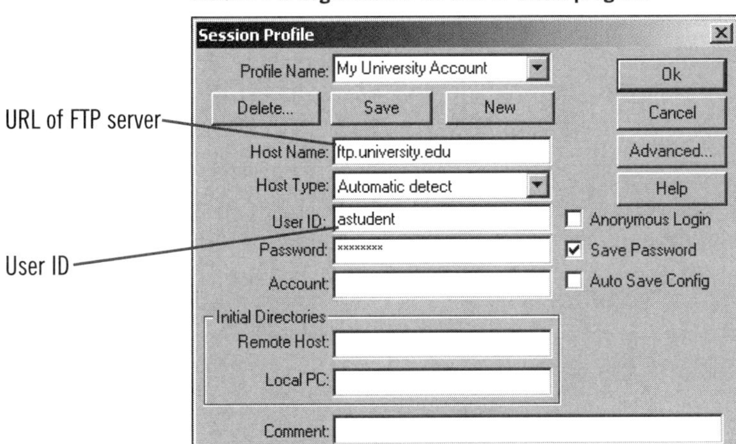

Checking files for viruses

Whenever you use FTP to download files, such as documents or programs from the Internet, you should check the files for viruses. Although you can configure anti-virus software to regularly scan the files on your hard disk to find infected files, the most popular anti-virus programs don't scan files while you're downloading them with FTP. However, you can set up anti-virus software to scan programs and documents before you open them. To ensure the safety of your computer when you download files with FTP, you can use a combination of these methods.

Internet

Locating Software Download Sites

Internet users can download many programs from the Internet at little or no cost. A large selection of programs is available online, from anti-virus software to interactive games. Download sites usually include downloadable programs that help you accomplish common tasks for working both on the Internet and offline. Because of the high cost of commercial software, using such free or low-cost software can save you significant money. To download software tools for the computers at DigiComm, you need an FTP client program. You conduct a search for information about FTP client programs so that you can determine which program you should download from the Internet.

1. Go to **www.course.com/illustrated/internet3**, click the **Unit I link**, then click the **Google link** under Lesson 2
2. Type **ftp client** in the text box, then click **Google Search**
3. Click the first few links on the results page to learn more about FTP client programs
   When you explore the selection of links returned by Google, you will find that some links are relevant and others are not. Table I-1 lists some of the best Web sites for downloading software programs. Links to these Web sites are listed in the Student Online Companion at *www.course.com/illustrated/internet3* on the Unit I page under Lesson 2.
4. Go to **www.course.com/illustrated/internet3**, click the **Unit I link**, then click the **Download.com link** under Lesson 2
   The Download.com Web site opens. You can select a category in which to search, such as Home & Desktop, Games, or Internet. Each category contains subcategories that allow you to narrow your search. You can also type a search expression.
5. Type **ftp client** in the Search text box
   Figure I-3 shows the completed Search text box.
6. Click **Go!**, then scroll down to review the search results
   A results page appears, similar to the one shown in Figure I-4. The results page includes links to Web sites with more information about FTP client programs and Web sites from which you can download FTP client programs. It also shows the date when each file was uploaded to Download.com's Web site, the number of times each file has been downloaded from the Web site, and the file size of the downloadable program.
7. Click your Web browser's **Back button**
   The Download.com home page appears.

CLUES TO USE

Freeware, shareware, and limited edition software

Freely downloadable software falls into three main categories: freeware, shareware, and limited edition software. **Freeware** is fully-functional software that is available to anyone at no cost and with no restrictions attached to its use. **Shareware** is usually available free of charge for a short evaluation period, after which users are requested to pay for its use. **Limited edition (LE) software** is a free, but restricted version of shareware that provides most of the functionality of the full commercial version. Users of LE software who like the software and want to use all of its functions can purchase the full version.

FIGURE I-3: Search expression for an FTP client program

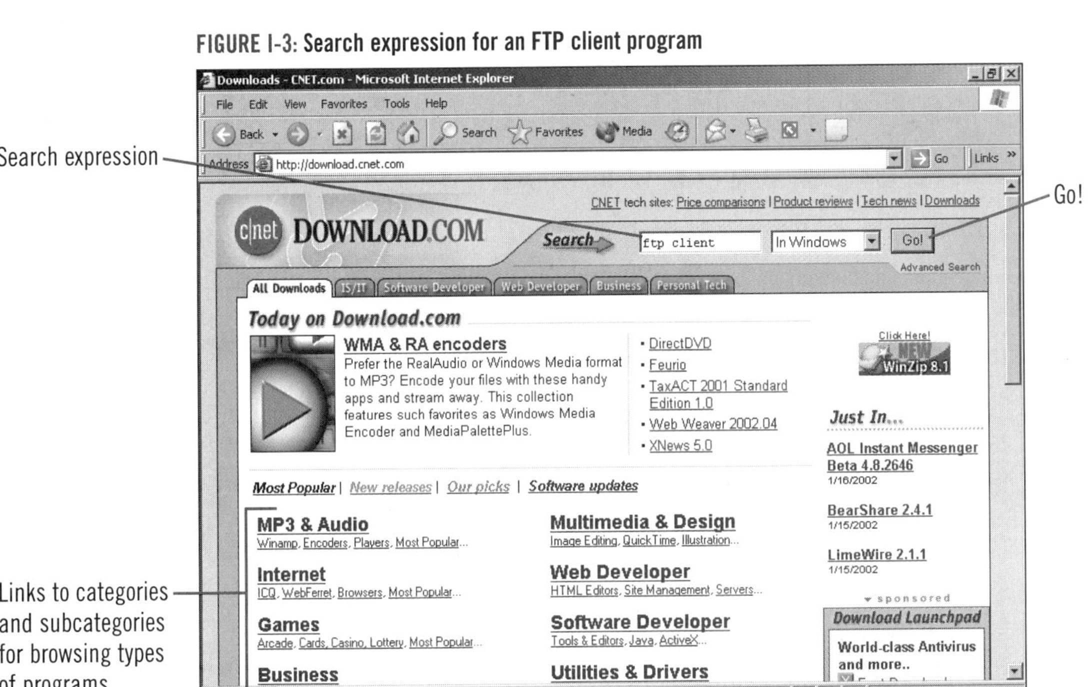

FIGURE I-4: Results page for an FTP client program

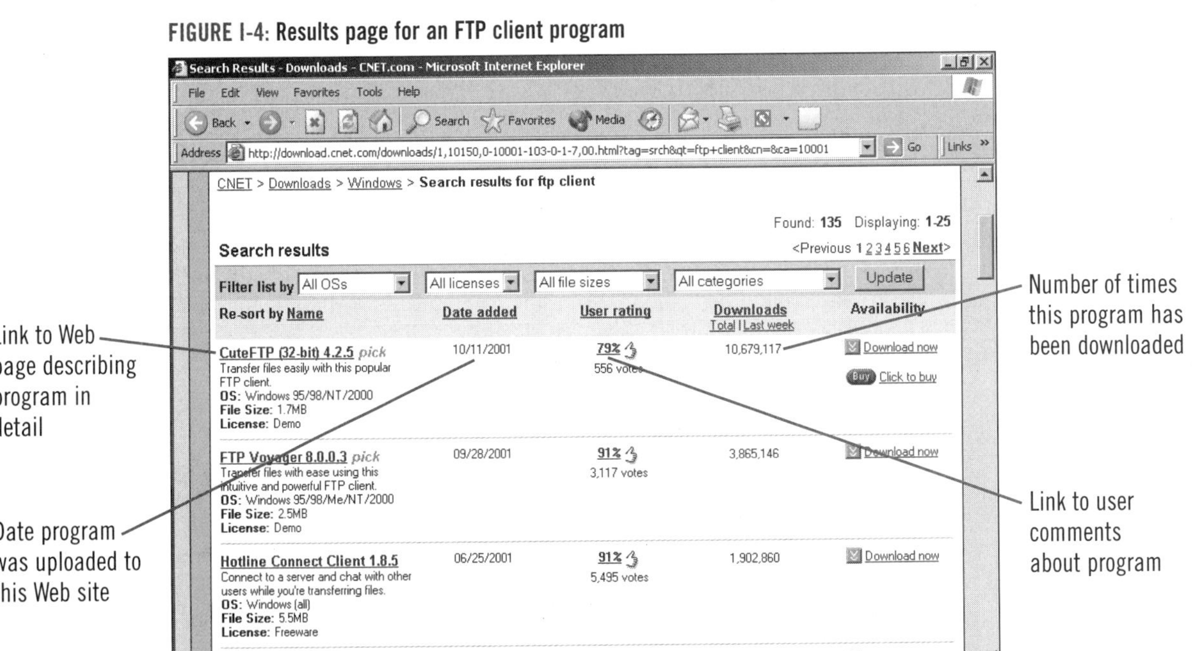

TABLE I-1: Web sites for obtaining software

web site	URL	description
Download.com	download.com	Contains freeware and shareware programs in many different categories
Tucows	tucows.com	Provides quick access to free, inexpensive, and full-cost software
Microsoft Download Center	microsoft.com	Provides enhancements and updates to Microsoft products and some free software
ZDnet Downloads	zdnet.com	Publishes ratings of various software programs based on tests and evaluations of users

Internet

Downloading an FTP Client Program

To begin using FTP, you need an FTP client program. You can use your Web browser to download an FTP client program from the Web. After you specify the program that you want to download, you will be prompted to save the program on your computer. When the download is complete, you can access the program file in Windows Explorer. The first utility you want to install on DigiComm staff computers is a user-friendly FTP client program. You download the WS_FTP Limited Edition FTP client program.

1. Go to **www.course.com/illustrated/internet3**, click the **Unit I link**, then click the **Ipswitch link** under Lesson 3
   The Ipswitch home page opens, as shown in Figure I-5.
2. Point to the **Downloads link** that appears on the bar at the top of the Web page, then click **Evaluation Software**
   The Ipswitch Evaluation Software Web page opens.
3. If necessary, scroll down the Web page, then click the **Try link** next to WS_FTP LE
4. Scroll down the Web page that opens, click the **English option button** under the Download the WS_FTP LE heading, then type your e-mail address in the Please enter your e-mail address text box
5. Deselect the **Please sign me up for the FTPplanet newsletter check box**
   Your screen should look similar to Figure I-6.
6. Click **Download Now!**
   A new Web page opens, along with a dialog box. If you are using Internet Explorer, the File Download dialog box opens; continue to Step 7. If you are using Netscape, the Enter name of file to save to... dialog box opens; skip to Step 8.
7. If you are using Internet Explorer, click **Save**
   The Save As dialog box opens.
8. Click the **Save in list arrow**, navigate to the drive and folder where your Project Files are stored, then click **Save**
   A dialog box displays the download progress.
9. If the dialog box remains open after the file is completely transferred, or if the Download complete dialog box opens, click **Close**
   The FTP client program file is saved on your computer.

Trouble?

If no dialog box opens after 15 seconds, click the click here link on the Web page that opens to start the download.

FIGURE I-5: Ipswitch home page

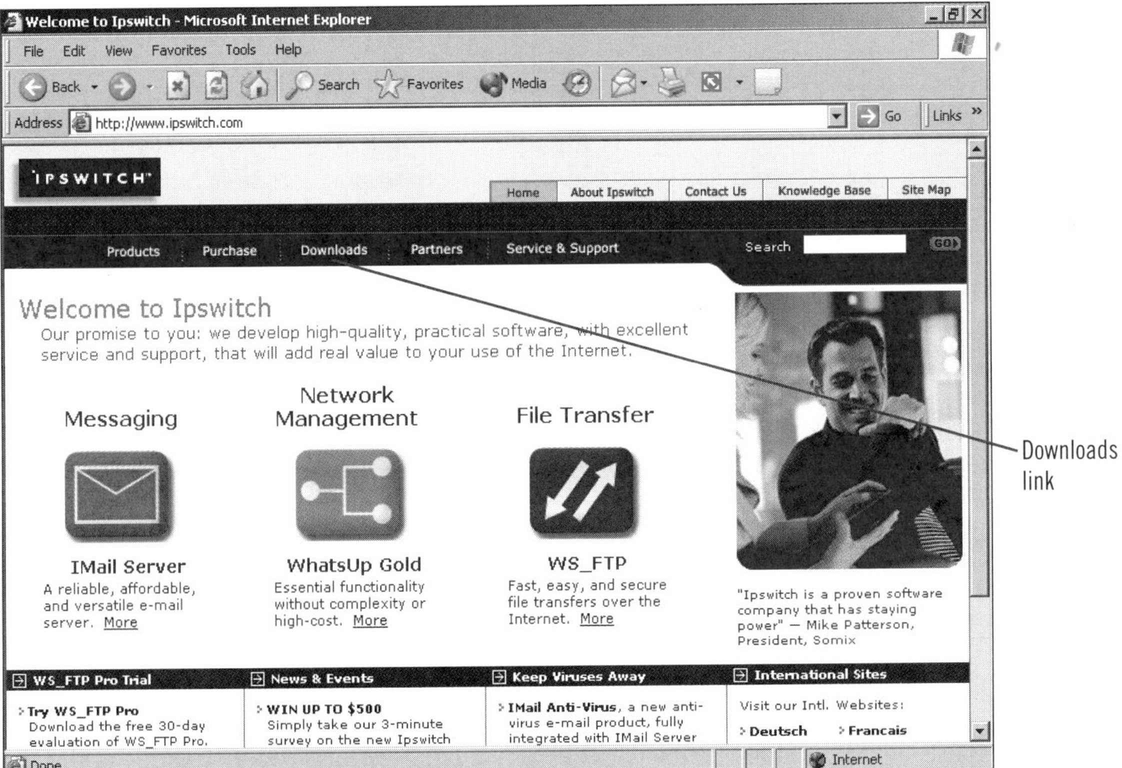

FIGURE I-6: Completed registration form

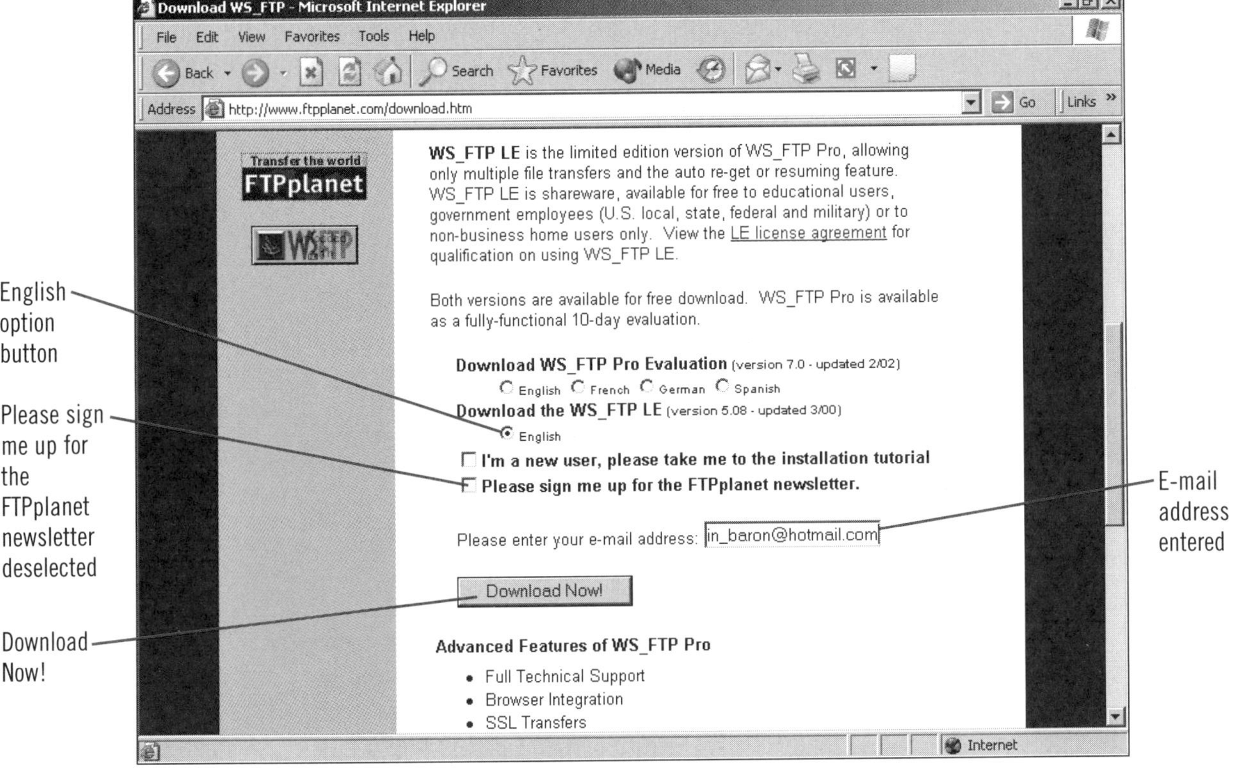

Internet

Installing an FTP Client Program

After you download a program from the Internet, you must install the program on your computer to use it. Usually, you can double-click a program file to install the program. The program file often facilitates installation by including an **installation wizard**, which is a series of dialog boxes that help you complete the installation process step-by-step. You checked with Savan Chen, manager of technical services at DigiComm, to verify that it's okay to install WS_FTP LE on the computers in your office. You install the program on your computer.

Warning

Ask your instructor if you may install the program.

Trouble?

If you don't see the file ws_ftple.exe listed, then double-click the file ws_ftple instead.

Trouble?

If a dialog box opens indicating that you have an "ini" file that will be erased, click No so the installing program does not destroy an important file.

1. Click the **Start button** on the taskbar, point to **Programs** or **All Programs**, point to **Accessories**, then click **Windows Explorer**
   The Windows Explorer window opens, as shown in Figure I-7.
2. In the left pane, navigate to the drive and folder where your Project Files are stored, then double-click **ws_ftple.exe** in the right pane
   The .exe file extension is an abbreviation for "executable," which means that the file is a program that you can run. A dialog box opens, showing two options.
3. If it's not already selected, click the **Install WS_FTP LE option button**, then click **Continue**
   A dialog box opens with option buttons corresponding to several types of users.
4. Click the **A student, faculty member... option button**, then click **Next**
   A dialog box opens with several check boxes, which indicate where and how you might use the program.
5. Select the **At school check box** in the Location section, select the **For academic work check box** in the Purpose section, then click **Next**
   The End User License Agreement appears, as shown in Figure I-8.
6. Read the End User License Agreement, then click **Accept**
   The WS_FTP LE Installation dialog box opens with a default destination directory.
7. Click **OK** to accept the default destination folder in which the program files will be stored, then click **OK** again to accept the preferred local destination folder for file transfers
   The default folder for both is C:\Program Files\WS_FTP. If you receive an error message indicating that the creation of a directory failed, enter a valid directory in the text box, then click OK; ask your instructor or system administrator if you are not sure which directories are valid on your computer.
8. Click **OK** to accept the suggested name "WS_FTP" for the Program Manager group name
   A WS_FTP window and a Congratulations! dialog box open.
9. Click **OK** in the Congratulations! dialog box, then close the WS_FTP window if necessary

FIGURE I-7: Windows Explorer window

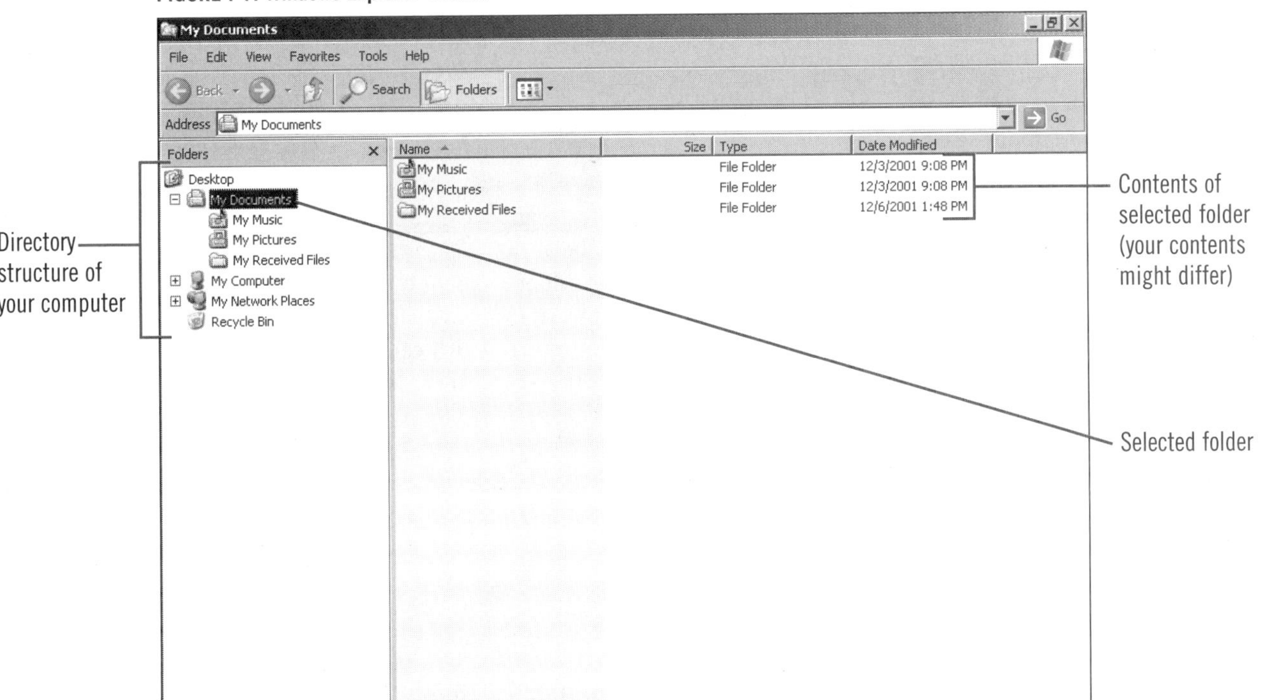

FIGURE I-8: End User License Agreement

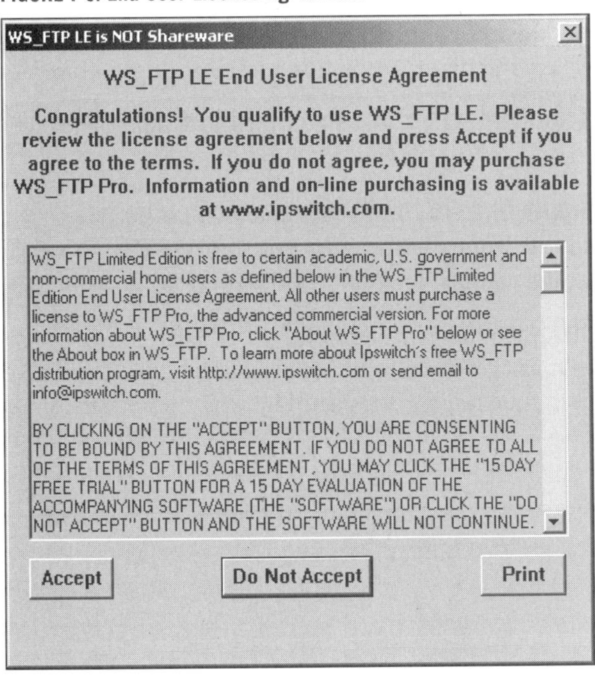

Internet

Internet

Setting Up an FTP Session

Before you can use an FTP client to download programs and files from another computer connected to the Internet, you need to create and save an FTP session profile. The **FTP session profile** is a collection of information about the FTP server that stores the program or files you want to download. The FTP session profile information enables you to connect to the FTP site that contains the files you want. If you want to connect to different FTP sites at different times, you need to create a different FTP session profile for each FTP site. The next file you want to download for DigiComm staff members to use is called WinZip. To download WinZip using WS_FTP, you first need to create an FTP session profile for the FTP server where the WinZip program is stored.

Trouble?

If you do not see WS_FTP on your Programs or All Programs menu, make sure that you downloaded and installed the WS_FTP LE program correctly. Ask your instructor or system administrator for help, if necessary.

1. Click the **Start button**, point to **Programs** or **All Programs**, point to **WS_FTP**, then click **WS_FTP95 LE**
   The WS_FTP LE program starts and the Session Properties dialog box opens. The Session Properties dialog box opens each time you launch WS_FTP95 LE.
2. Click the **General tab** if it's not already displayed, then click **New**
3. Type **WinZip** in the Profile Name text box, then press **[Tab]**
4. Type **ftp.winzip.com** in the Host Name/Address text box
   Many FTP sites on the Internet use the prefix "ftp" followed by the domain name. For example, the FTP site for Netscape is ftp.netscape.com. You can usually find an organization's FTP address on its Web site.
5. Select the **Anonymous check box**
   Selecting the Anonymous check box automatically places the text "anonymous" in the User ID text box and places a WS_FTP e-mail address in the Password text box.
6. Select the contents of the Password text box, then type your e-mail address
   Figure I-9 shows the completed General tab.
7. Click **Apply** to save the WinZip session properties
   Clicking the Apply button does not start the FTP process; it merely saves the FTP session profile information for the next time you want to access it to download a file.
8. Click **OK** to connect to the WinZip FTP site
   Various messages flash in the message area as the main WS_FTP LE window opens. In a few seconds, a tone might sound and the window appears, similar to Figure I-10.

Trouble?

If you receive an "access denied" message, the WinZip FTP site is busy. You can try again later, or just read the steps in the next lesson so you understand how to use an FTP client to download files.

FIGURE I-9: Session Properties dialog box

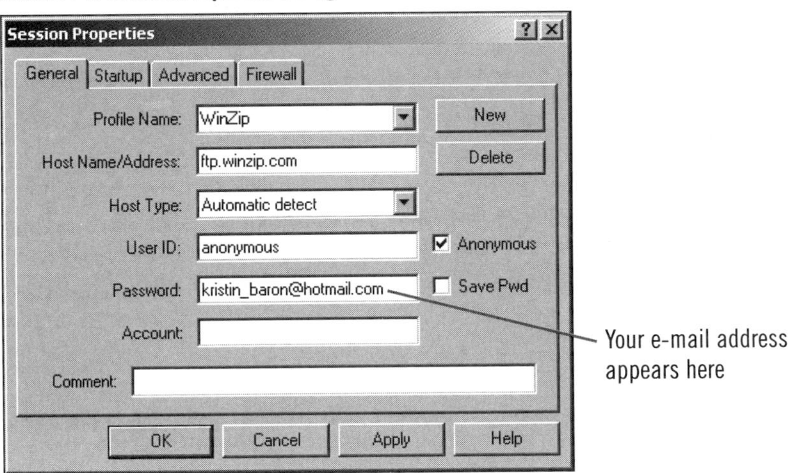

FIGURE I-10: WS_FTP client session with ftp.winzip.com server

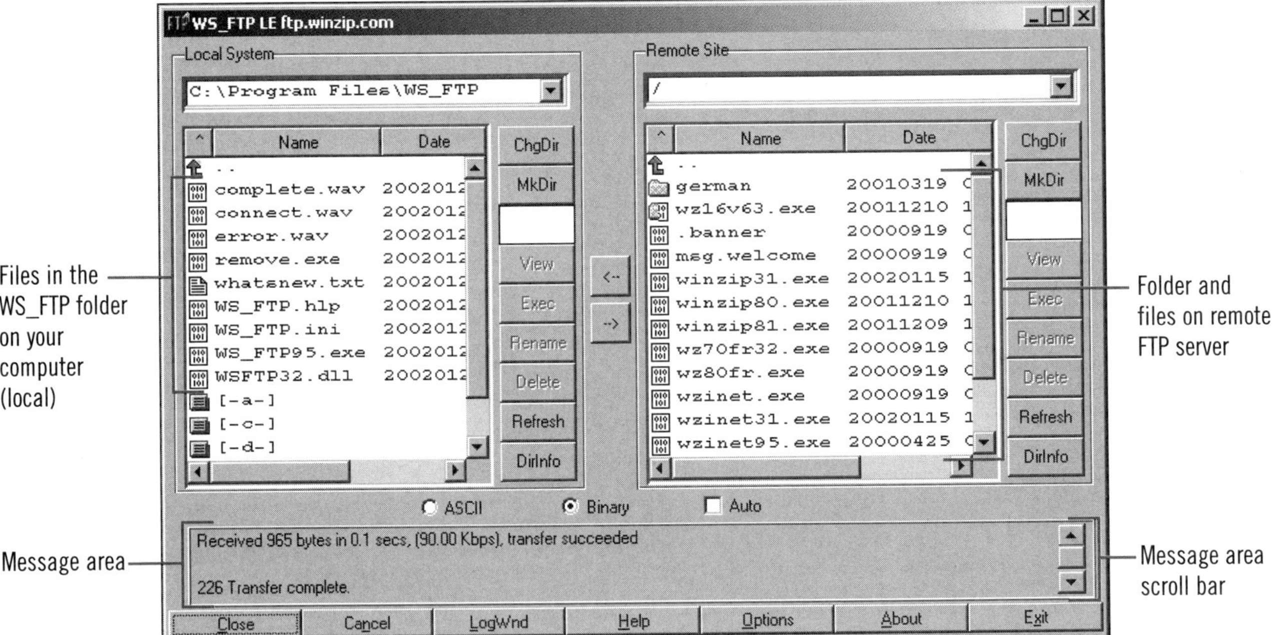

Internet

Internet

Using FTP to Download a Program

After you create a session profile and connect to an FTP site, you can download available files on the FTP server. You can use the WinZip FTP site you logged in to in the previous lesson to download a file compression program called WinZip. Now that you are connected to the WinZip FTP site, you use your FTP client to download the WinZip program.

Steps

1. In the left pane, double-click the **green arrow** at the top of the list until the directory text box at the top of the pane displays only a letter followed by :\
   Your screen should look similar to Figure I-11.
2. In the left pane, navigate to the drive and folder where your Project Files are stored
   The left pane displays your Project Files. It represents your computer, and the right pane represents the FTP server.
3. In the right pane, click **winzip81.exe**
   Figure I-12 shows the file winzip81.exe selected. If you don't see the filename winzip81.exe listed, go to *www.course.com/illustrated/internet3*, click the Unit I link, read the notes for Lesson 6, return to the WS_FTP LE program, then click the correct filename.
4. Click the **Download button**
   After you click the Download button, the FTP client program begins to download the selected file (winzip81.exe) from the FTP server shown in the right pane to the selected folder on your computer shown in the left pane. A Transfer Status dialog box opens with download progress information, as shown in Figure I-13. When the Transfer Status dialog box closes, the file transfer is complete and the winzip81.exe program is saved on your computer. The time required to transfer the program file varies according to your computer's connection type and speed.
5. After the file is transferred, click **Exit** at the bottom of the window
   You disconnect from the WinZip FTP site and the WS_FTP LE program closes.
6. Click the **Windows Explorer program button** on the taskbar, if necessary, navigate to the drive and folder where your Project Files are stored, then double-click the file **winzip81.exe** in the right pane
   The WinZip 8.1 Setup dialog box opens.
7. Click **Setup**, then click **OK** as many times as necessary until you see a window that says "Thank you for installing WinZip!"
   The WinZip Setup dialog box guides you through the WinZip installation.
8. Click **Next**, read the license agreement, click **Yes**, click **Next**, click the **Start with WinZip Classic option button**, click **Next** three times, then click **Finish**
   If the WinZip Tip of the Day dialog box opens, click Close. The WinZip program window opens.
9. Close WinZip, then if the WinZip dialog box opens asking you to register, click **No**

Trouble?

If your Project Files are stored in a different drive than the one shown at the top of the left pane, scroll down the file list in the left pane, double-click the drive where your Project Files are stored, then navigate to your Project Files folder.

Trouble?

If your computer doesn't allow you to install a program, ask your instructor or system administrator for instructions on how to proceed.

FIGURE I-11: Contents of local drive

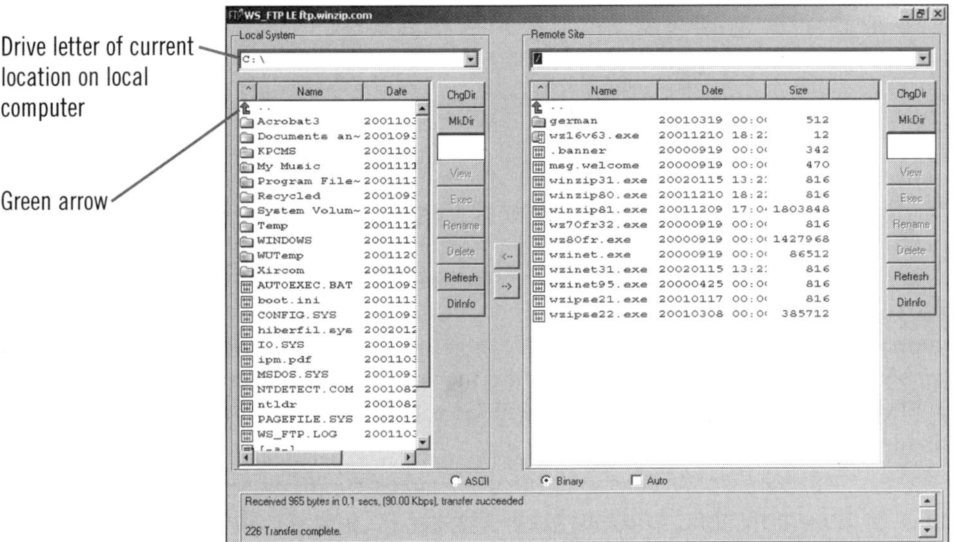

FIGURE I-12: WinZip program filename selected

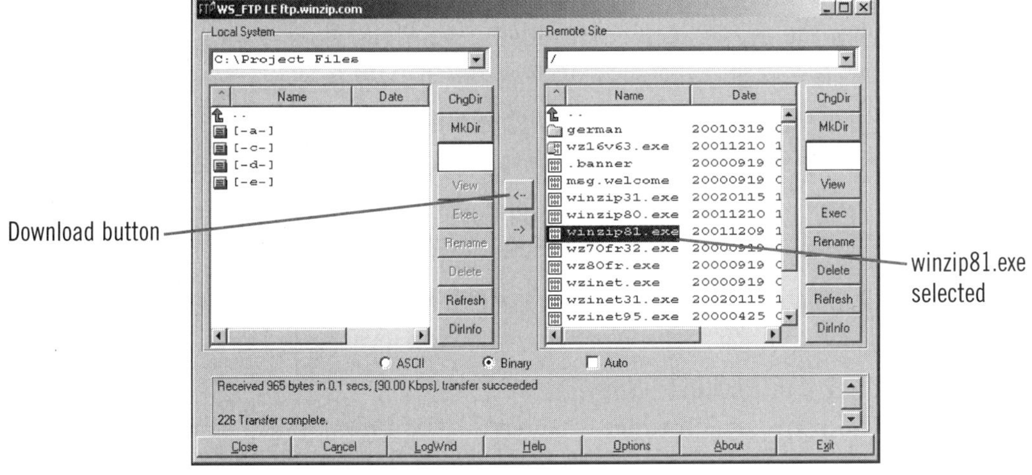

FIGURE I-13: Transfer Status dialog box

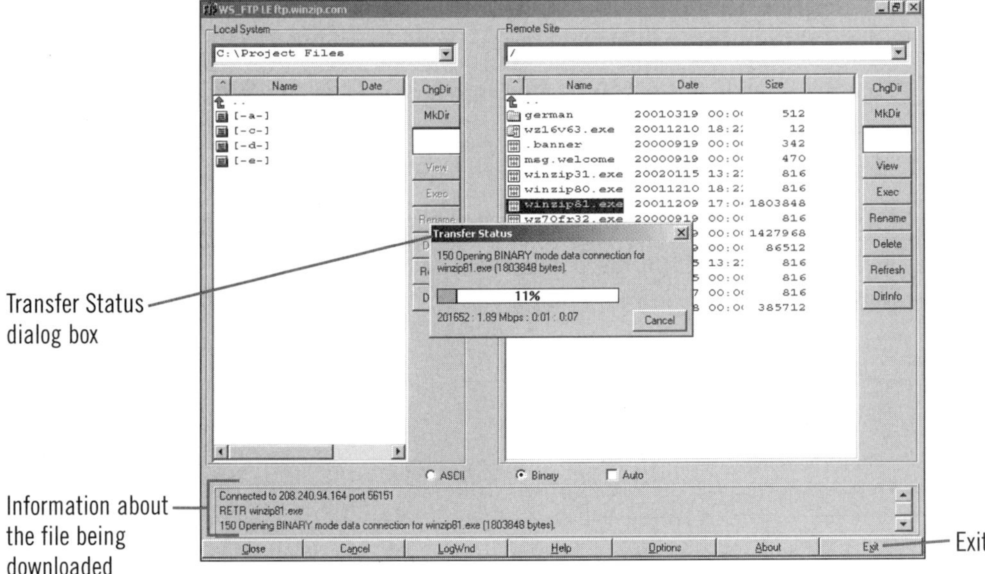

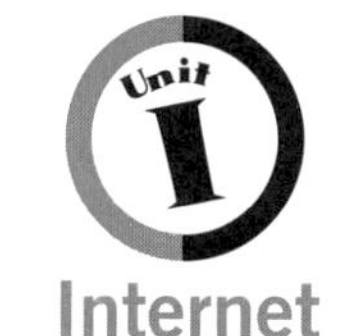

Internet

Downloading a .zip File

You use a **file compression program** to reduce a file to a fraction of its original size, creating a **compressed file.** The smaller file size of compressed files allows you to transfer files more quickly than full-size files via FTP or as an e-mail attachment. Compressed files can save you significant time downloading, especially over an Internet connection with a slow modem. The most common file extension for a compressed file is .zip, which is why some people refer to compressed files as **.zip files** or **zipped files.** Some of the staff members at DigiComm have been asking for a personal information manager (PIM) software program. After researching PIM software on the Web, you download the shareware program A+ Contact/Schedule Manager to evaluate it.

1. Go to **www.course.com/illustrated/internet3**, click the **Unit I link**, then click the **Download.com link** under Lesson 7
   The Download.com Web site opens.
2. If necessary, scroll down, click the **Business link**, then if necessary, scroll down to view the available subcategories
   Figure I-14 shows the subcategories listed on the Business Web page.
3. Click the **Personal Info Managers link**
   A list of PIM software programs appears.
4. Click the **Name link**, then scroll down to view the list of programs available
   The list of PIM software reappears, sorted by program name, as shown in Figure I-15.
5. Scroll down the Web page, then click the **A+ Contact/Schedule Manager 3.0 link**
   The A+ Contact/Schedule Manager 3.0 page opens.
6. Click the **Download Now link**
   If you are using Internet Explorer, the File Download dialog box opens. In Netscape, the Downloading csmt.zip dialog box opens.
7. If you are using Internet Explorer, click **Save**; If you are using Netscape, click the **Save this file to Disk option button**, then click **OK**
   A dialog box opens enabling you to specify the location where the file is saved.
8. Click the **Save in list arrow** to navigate to the drive and folder where your Project Files are stored, then click **Save**
   The file downloads to your computer.
9. If the dialog box remains open after the file is completely transferred, or if the Download complete dialog box opens, click **Close**
   The .zip file is saved on your computer.

Trouble?

The version number of the software is 3.0. If you do not see A+ Contact/Schedule Manager 3.0 in the list, locate A+ Contact/Schedule Manager with a number higher than 3.0.

FIGURE I-14: Business Web page on Download.com

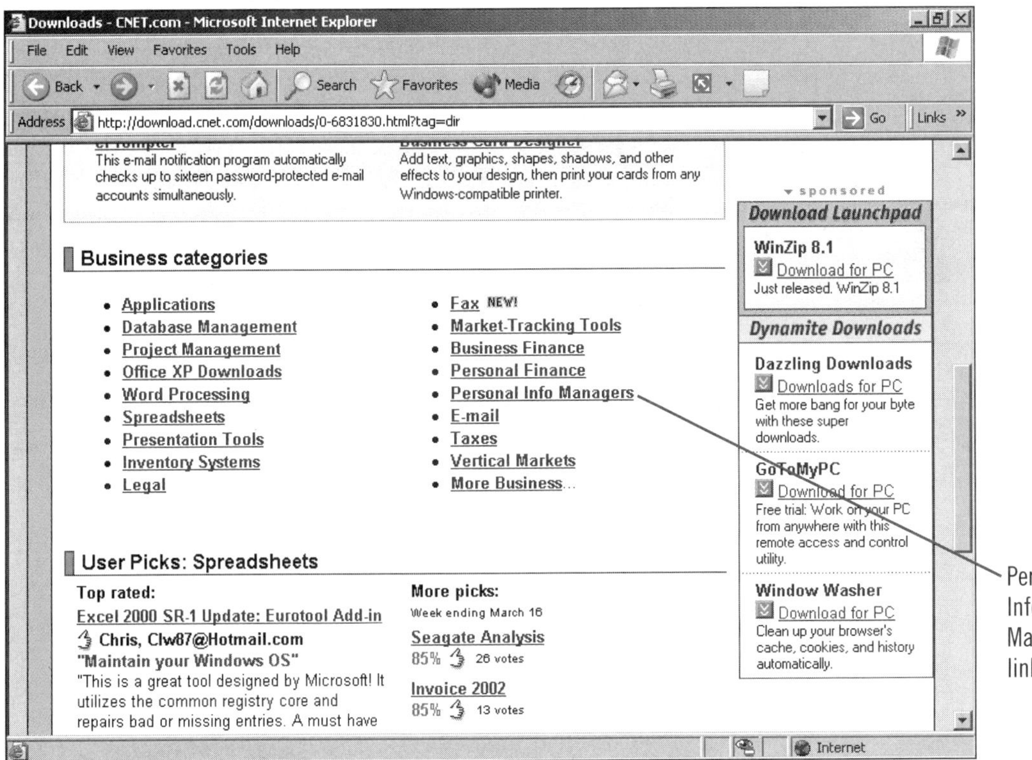

FIGURE I-15: Personal Information Managers page on Download.com

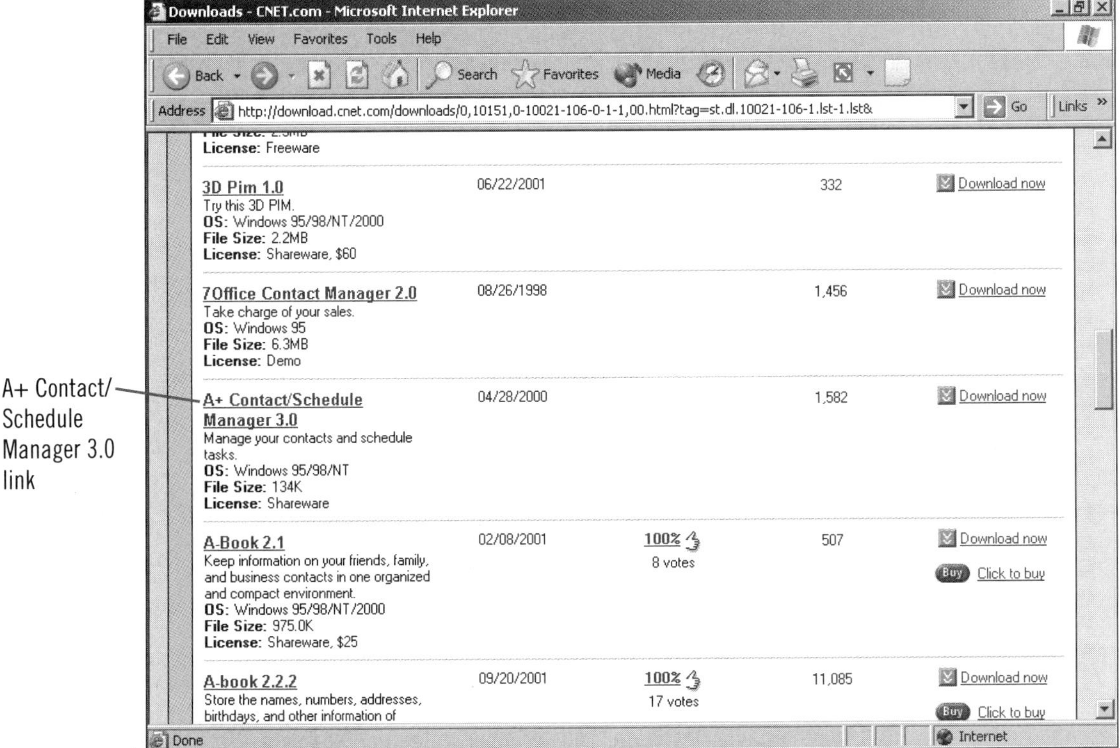

Internet

Opening a .zip File

After you download a compressed file, you must restore the file to its original size before you can open or run it. The process of restoring a compressed file to its original form is called **file decompression**, **file extraction**, or **file expansion**. To open a compressed file, you need a decompression program, such as WinZip. In the previous lesson, you downloaded a .zip file containing the PIM program. To evaluate the PIM program, you use WinZip to unzip the .zip file containing the PIM program and its documentation.

Steps

1. Open the Windows Explorer window, then double-click **csmt.zip**
   The WinZip dialog box opens as shown in Figure I-16.
2. Click **I Agree**
   The .zip file opens and all files in the csmt.zip file are listed in the WinZip window, as shown in Figure I-17. The files shown are all necessary to install and run the PIM software you downloaded.
3. Click the **Extract button** on the toolbar
   The Extract dialog box opens.
4. In the Folders/drives list, navigate to the drive and folder where your Project Files are stored
   Compare your screen to Figure I-18.
5. Click **Extract**
   The PIM files are extracted to your computer.
6. Close WinZip, then double-click **csm.txt**
   The csm.txt file opens in Notepad. The file contains information about the PIM program you downloaded, and a brief explanation of how to run it.
7. Close Notepad, then close all open windows

QuickTip

To extract a specific file in a zip file, click the file that you want to extract, then click Extract.

FIGURE I-16: WinZip dialog box

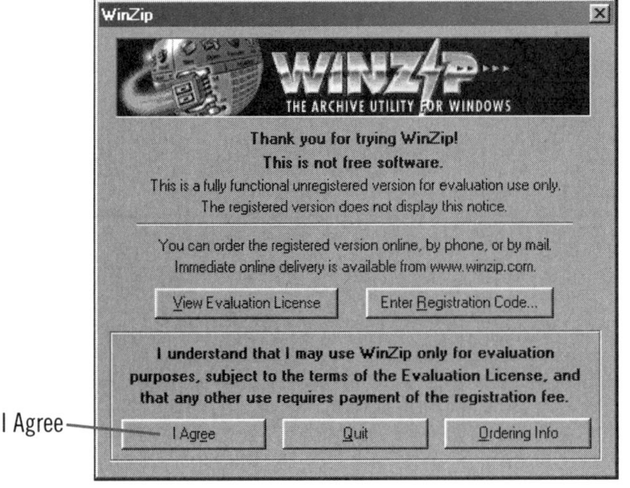

FIGURE I-17: Contents of csmt.zip

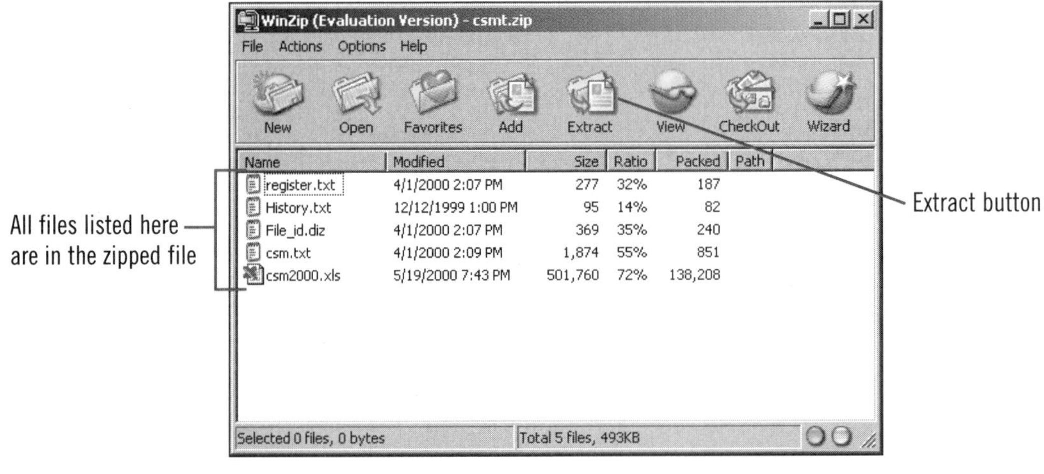

FIGURE I-18: Extract dialog box

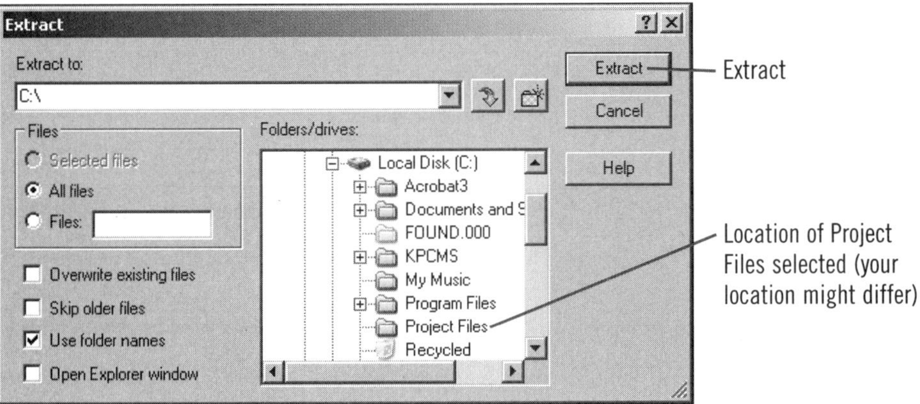

Internet

Practice

Concepts Review

Identify each element of the FTP client program window shown in Figure I-19.

FIGURE I-19

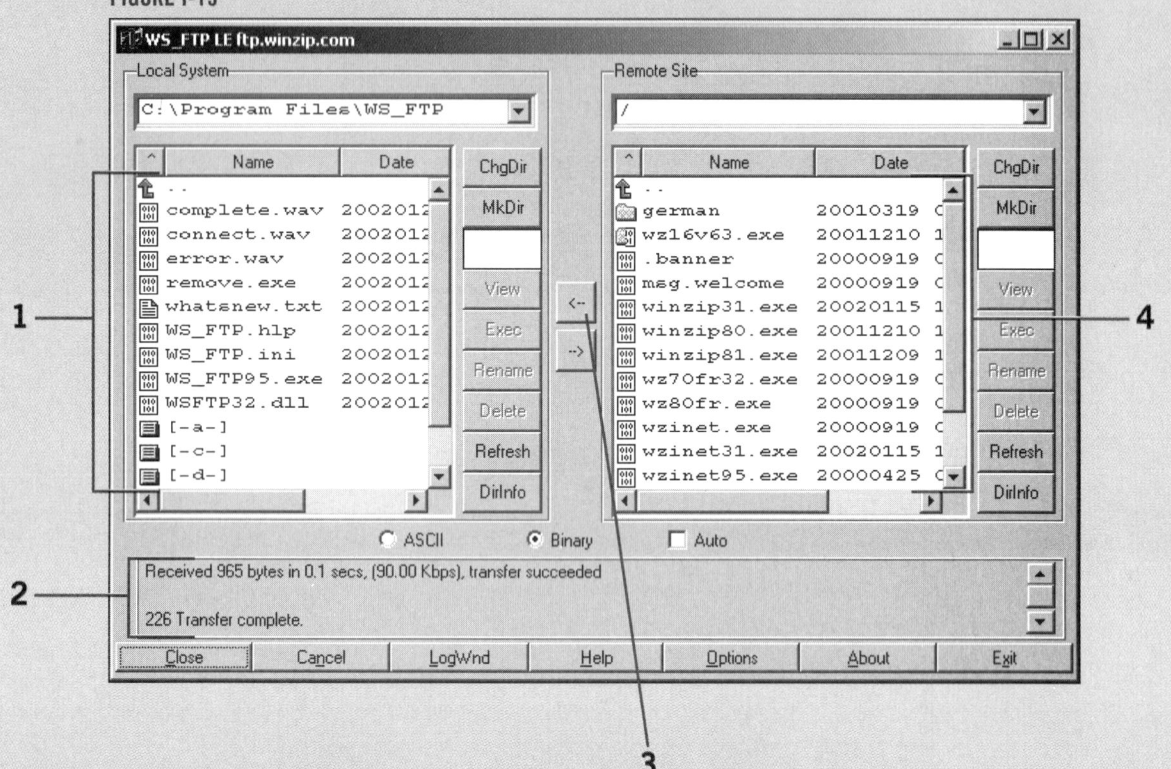

Match each term with the statement that describes it.

5. **Upload**
6. **Anonymous FTP**
7. **Shareware**
8. **FTP**
9. **Freeware**
10. **Download**
11. **.zip**

a. A method used to log in to public FTP sites
b. A type of software that you can download for free to use for a short evaluation period
c. To transfer files from a remote computer to your computer
d. A type of software that you can download for free with no restrictions on its use
e. A protocol used to transfer files between connected computers
f. A common extension for compressed files
g. To transfer files from your computer to a remote computer

Practice

Select the best answer from the list of choices.

12. To use full-privilege FTP, you must:
- **a.** Log in with the user name "anonymous."
- **b.** Have an account on the FTP server to which you're connecting.
- **c.** Use a specific FTP client program.
- **d.** Enter your e-mail address as your password.

13. Which user name do you enter to log in to a publicly accessible remote computer?
- **a.** Guest
- **b.** Anonymous
- **c.** Unknown
- **d.** FTP.COM

14. Limited edition software is:
- **a.** Fully-functional software that is available to anyone at no cost and with no restrictions attached to its use.
- **b.** The commercial version of a software program.
- **c.** A free, restricted version of shareware that provides most of the functionality of the full commercial version.
- **d.** Usually available at no cost for a short evaluation period, after which users are requested to pay for its use.

15. To use an FTP client program to download files and programs from a given server, you need to:
- **a.** View the server's contents in a Web browser.
- **b.** Start WinZip.
- **c.** Start Internet Explorer.
- **d.** Create an FTP session profile for the server.

16. FTP works:
- **a.** Only between computers connected via the Internet.
- **b.** Only between computers connected via a local network.
- **c.** Only between connected computers that are near one another.
- **d.** Between any connected computers.

Skills Review

1. Locate software download sites.
- **a.** Go to **www.course.com/illustrated/internet3**, click the **Unit I link**, then click the **Tucows link** under Skills Review 1.
- **b.** Search on the term **ftp**.
- **c.** Examine the search results, and read the reviews for at least three FTP client programs.

2. Download an FTP client program.
- **a.** Go to **www.course.com/illustrated/internet3**, click the **Unit I link**, then click the **CuteFTP link** under Skills Review 2.
- **b.** Click the **CuteFTP link**, then click the **Download Free Trial link**.
- **c.** Complete the online form with your e-mail address and information about your preferred language.
- **d.** Check with your instructor or system administrator for permission to download the CuteFTP program to your computer's hard drive.

- **e.** If you have permission, click **Download Now!**.
- **f.** Save the CuteFTP program where your Project Files are stored.
- **g.** If necessary, close any dialog boxes after the download completes.

3. Install an FTP client program.

- **a.** Check with your instructor or system administrator for permission to install CuteFTP.
- **b.** If you have permission, open Windows Explorer, then navigate to the drive and folder where your Project Files are stored.
- **c.** Double-click **cuteftp.exe**.
- **d.** Follow the installation directions.

4. Set up an FTP session.

- **a.** Open **CuteFTP**.
- **b.** Click the **Start trial button**, click **Yes** if an alert box appears, then close the Tip of the Day dialog box.
- **c.** Click **New** in the Site Manager dialog box, then complete the text boxes so that the dialog box appears as shown in Figure I-20.
- **d.** Click **Microsoft** in the list of General FTP sites.
- **e.** Connect to the Microsoft FTP site.
- **f.** Click **OK** when prompted.

FIGURE I-20

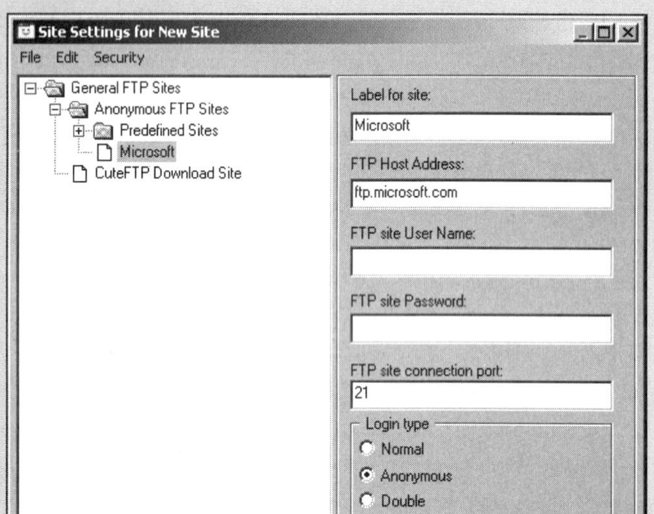

5. Use FTP to download a program.

- **a.** In the Microsoft FTP site, open the **deskapps folder**.
- **b.** Open the **games folder**.
- **c.** Open the **public folder**.
- **d.** Find a game file that appeals to you and that does not require much disk space. To find a game file, double-click the folder. For example, you could double-click the Baseball folder to find a selection of sound files that play recordings of baseball announcers. If the file sizes are not listed, click **View** on the menu bar, then click **Long listing**.
- **e.** In the left pane, navigate to the drive and folder where your Project Files are stored.
- **f.** Download the file you selected to your computer.
- **g.** When the program has downloaded, close CuteFTP.

6. Download a .zip file.

- **a.** Go to **www.course.com/illustrated/internet3**, click the **Unit I link**, then click the **artist.zip** link under Skills Review 6.
- **b.** Use the dialog box that opens to save the file to the drive and folder where your Project Files are stored.
- **c.** If necessary, close any open dialog boxes when the download is complete.

Practice

7. Open a .zip file.

  a. Open the **artist.zip file** from your Project Files folder.
  b. Extract the **birth.jpg file** to your Project Files folder.
  c. Close WinZip.
  d. Open the **birth.jpg file**.
  e. Close all open windows.

▶ Independent Challenge 1

A friend of yours owns an Apple Macintosh computer. The Macintosh runs its own operating system (MacOS) rather than Windows. Macs are also different from Windows computers in other ways. For example, the most prevalent type of compressed files for Macintosh users is the .sit file, rather than .zip. .sit is an abbreviation for the name of the program that creates these files, StuffIt. Your friend has downloaded a .sit file, but doesn't have a program to open it. She asks you to help her locate a program that can open a .sit file.

  a. Start your Web browser.
  b. Go to **www.course.com/illustrated/internet3**, click the **Unit I link**, then click the **Download.com link** under Independent Challenge 1.
  c. Search for "stuffit lite" (*Hint:* be sure to search in Downloads, rather than in Windows.)
  d. In the search results list, identify the most recent version of Alladin StuffIt Lite (the program name including the highest number), then click the link.
  e. Read the information about Alladin StuffIt Lite.
  f. Send an e-mail message to your instructor that includes the URL for the Web page on the Download.com site where you can download Alladin StuffIt Lite for Macintosh.
  g. Close your Web browser.

▶ Independent Challenge 2

You own Internet Adventures, a one-person consulting company that provides a variety of consulting services to small and medium-size companies. You charge an hourly rate to help companies find and download information on the Internet. You are working for a large CPA firm that wants you to create bookmarks and favorites for Web sites that are of interest to tax preparers. Some members of the tax-preparation team use Internet Explorer, whereas others use Netscape. When team members find interesting Web sites, they use their Web browser to create either a Netscape bookmark or an Internet Explorer favorite. The team members don't always have time to create a bookmark for the Web site in the other Web browser, so they end up losing some of the URLs. You remember reading a review about several shareware products that might be able to maintain a library of common bookmarks that Internet Explorer and Netscape can share.

  a. Start your Web browser.
  b. Go to **www.course.com/illustrated/internet3**, click the **Unit I link**, then click the **Tucows link** under Independent Challenge 2.

c. Click the **Windows link**.
d. If necessary, use the drop-down list to select your location, then click the link to a server that is the closest to your current location.
e. Click the **Internet tab** at the top of the screen.
f. Scroll down to the Web Browsers & Tools section, then click the **Bookmark Utilities link**.
g. On the Bookmark Utilities page, scroll down the list and click **Bookmark Converter 2.9**. If you cannot find that bookmark program in the list, then scroll down the list, and look for a bookmark program whose description indicates that it can convert bookmarks between Internet Explorer and Netscape.
h. Download the Bookmark Converter program, and save it where your Project Files are stored.
i. Install the program, if possible, then open it and examine its features.
j. Close all open programs.

▶ Independent Challenge 3

As the director of computing at Baseline High School, you and a staff of three people ensure that the school's computer lab of 45 PCs functions properly. Last week, a virus infected every computer in the lab, and you had to close the lab to prevent the virus from spreading to students' disks and other computers. Each lab computer has McAfee Virus Scan software installed, but the installed version does not recognize and cannot eradicate the new virus pattern. You need to download the latest virus data file from McAfee.

a. Start WS_FTP.
b. Create a new session profile using the profile name McAfee and the host address ftp.mcafee.com. Connect as an anonymous user, and use your e-mail address as your password.
c. Connect to McAfee's FTP site.
d. To see the antivirus data files on the remote computer, use the following pathname: /pub/antivirus/datfiles/4.x.
e. Change the local directory in the FTP client to display the location of your Project Files.
f. On the remote computer, select the filename that begins with "dat" and ends with the file extension .zip.
g. Get permission from your instructor first, if necessary, then download the file.
h. After the download completes, log out of the McAfee site and close WS_FTP.
i. WS_FTP creates a log file showing the date and time you downloaded the software, which is located in the same directory to which the file was downloaded. Locate the log file (named Ws_ftp.log) and open it with WordPad or Notepad.
j. Print the log file to show that you downloaded the anti-virus data file. Be sure to add your name and any other identifying information requested by your instructor to the document before you print it.
k. Close all open programs.

► Independent Challenge 4

HTTP, short for Hypertext Transfer Protocol, is a relative of FTP that's used for transferring Web page documents and other associated files from a Web server using an HTTP client (a Web browser). Your boss has asked you to create a short report on the similarities and differences between FTP and HTTP.

a. Start your Web browser.
b. Find information about what each protocol was originally designed for.
c. Find information about each protocol's most common uses today.
d. Find information about any overlapping uses between the two protocols.
e. Write at least two paragraphs summarizing your findings.
f. E-mail your findings to your instructor as an attachment.
g. Close your Web browser.

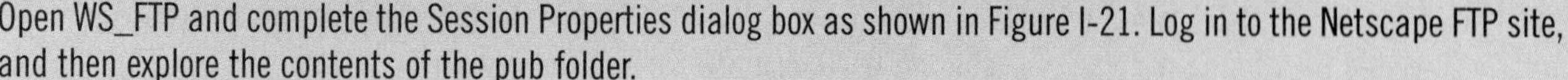

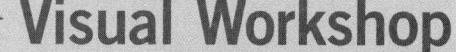

► Visual Workshop

Open WS_FTP and complete the Session Properties dialog box as shown in Figure I-21. Log in to the Netscape FTP site, and then explore the contents of the pub folder.

FIGURE I-21

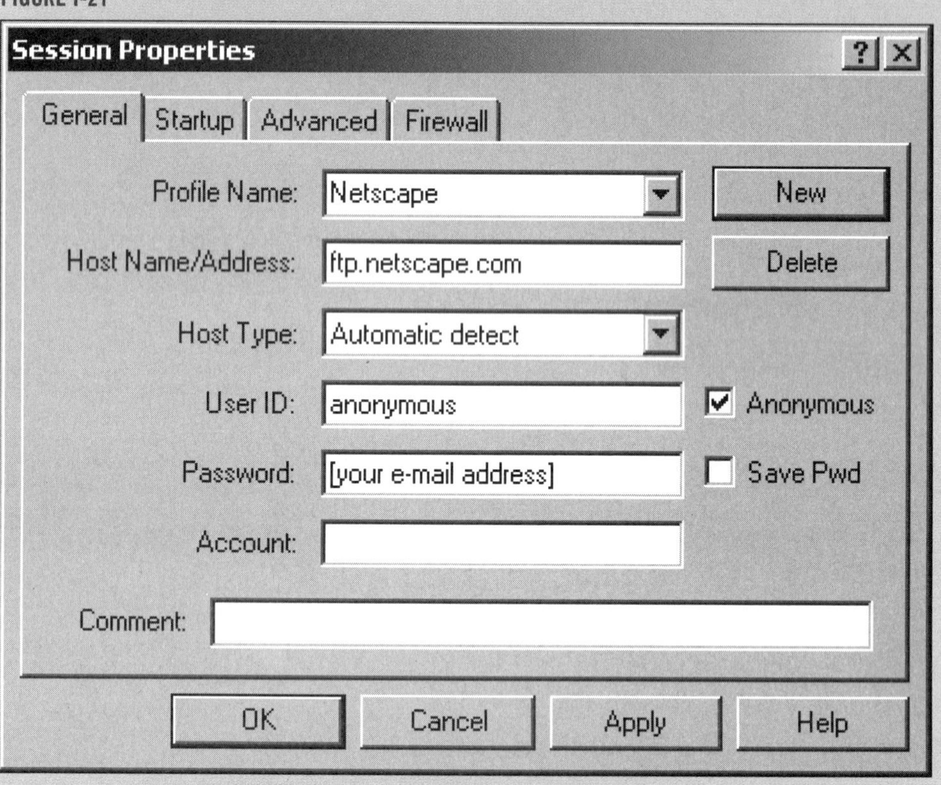

Internet

Increasing Web Browser Capabilities and Security

Objectives

- Understand browser extensions
- Locate browser extensions
- Install browser extensions with Netscape
- Install browser extensions with Internet Explorer
- Understand Internet security
- Minimize Web security risks
- Protect Web transactions
- Protect e-mail from viruses and interception

Many Web sites include files in file formats that Web browsers cannot display by default. You can enable a Web browser to interpret almost any file format on the Web by installing programs for the Web browser. These programs, known as **browser extensions**, are often small and can be downloaded for free. In this unit, you will install a browser extension. You will also learn about Internet security and privacy concerns, as well as your Web browser's capabilities for dealing with these concerns. Remes Video Productions (RVP) is a video production company. Mark Remes, the company's founder, has hired you to market the company on the Web by creating a Web site that includes samples of the company's video work. He also wants to be able to accept payments via the Web, and wants you to research concerns about the security of clients' personal information and other possible threats that are unique to conducting business over the Internet.

Internet

Understanding Browser Extensions

Many companies develop their own software to enhance the capabilities of Web browsers. These enhancements, called browser extensions, allow a Web browser to perform tasks that it was not originally designed to do. For example, some browser extensions can download and play audio clips or display movies. Some browser extensions are called **plug-ins** or **add-ons**, which are programs that a Web browser starts to display or play a specific file type. Plug-ins can start only from within a Web browser. Other browser extensions are called **helper applications** or **helper apps**, because they work with a Web browser to display or play a file. Helper apps can start independent of Web browsers. For example, a spreadsheet program can function as a helper application when a Web browser starts it to display a spreadsheet. You want to include video clips on the RVP Web site, and need to decide on a format that potential users can easily view with a Web browser. You begin the process by reviewing the types of browser extensions that are available for Netscape and Internet Explorer.

► Document and Productivity

Document and productivity browser extensions let you use a Web browser to read documents, such as documents saved in **PDF format**, a format that allows documents to maintain a consistent layout and format on different computers when viewed using Adobe Acrobat Reader. If your Web browser has Acrobat Reader installed, the Web browser can use the Acrobat plug-in to display and print files with .pdf extensions. If your computer has Microsoft Office installed, the Web browser can start Word, Excel, and other Office programs to display files with Office file extensions, such as .doc and .xls.

► Image Viewer

Image viewer browser extensions let the Web browser display graphics, such as interactive road maps or file formats other than the standard GIF and JPEG formats. For example, as shown in Figure J-1, the **iPIX** plug-in lets you view a specially-created digital image from all angles by panning an image left, right, up, or down to see it from the sky, ground, or to turn it in a circle. Real estate agents use iPIX to display a 360-degree view of the rooms in a house they have listed.

► Animation

Animation browser extensions, perhaps the largest category of browser extensions, enable you to view file formats that appeal to most of the senses. These browser extensions provide animation for images, games, and other animated content on the Web, allowing you to play interactive games, view animated interfaces, listen to streaming CD-quality audio music and speech, and view instructional presentations. One of the most popular animation extensions is **Shockwave**. Figure J-2 shows an example of a Shockwave-enhanced game. **Flash**, another popular animation plug-in, is installed automatically with Internet Explorer and Netscape.

► Sound Player

Sound player browser extensions let your Web browser play nonstandard audio file formats. Many sound player extensions, including Crescendo and Beatnik, play CD-quality streaming audio. RealPlayer and RealOne Player are widely distributed and play audio over a variety of slow and fast connections ranging from 56.6 K modems to faster cable modems. RealPlayer can also play streaming audio and video on the Web, though the music is less than CD quality. RealPlayer provides a feature called **buffered play**, in which music is downloaded and queued for play when the transfer/play rate exceeds your modem's speed.

► Video Player

Video player browser extensions deliver movies to Web browsers over the Internet. When you click a movie link, the movie downloads and begins playing in its own window. QuickTime, which plays video, sound, music, and 3-D, was one of the first movie players developed. Other successful movie players include RealPlayer, Microsoft Windows Media Player, and VivoActive Player. Some of these players download a complete movie before playing it, whereas others use streaming technology to play a movie before it has been completely downloaded.

FIGURE J-1: Web page containing iPIX image

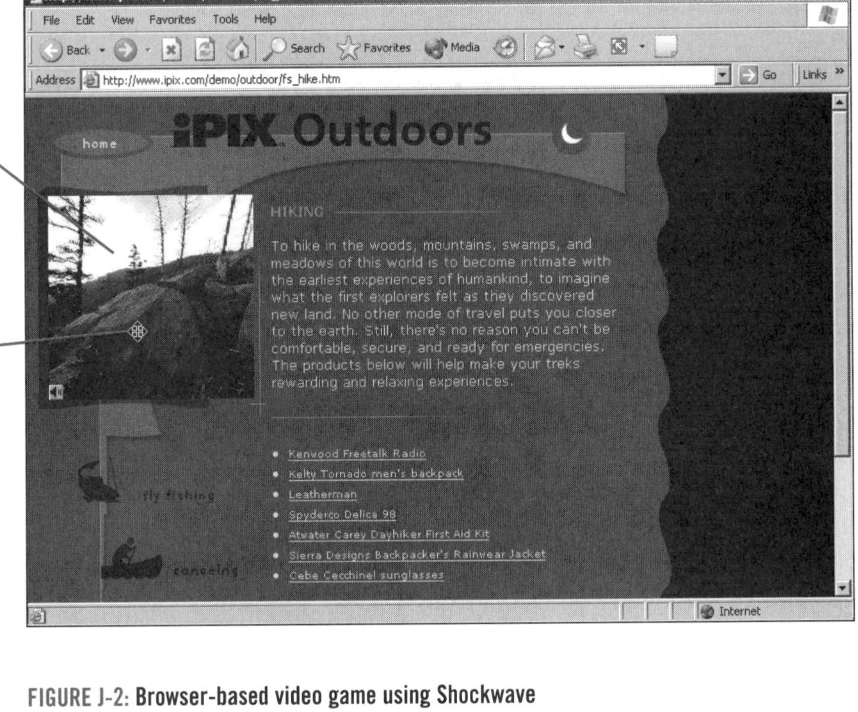
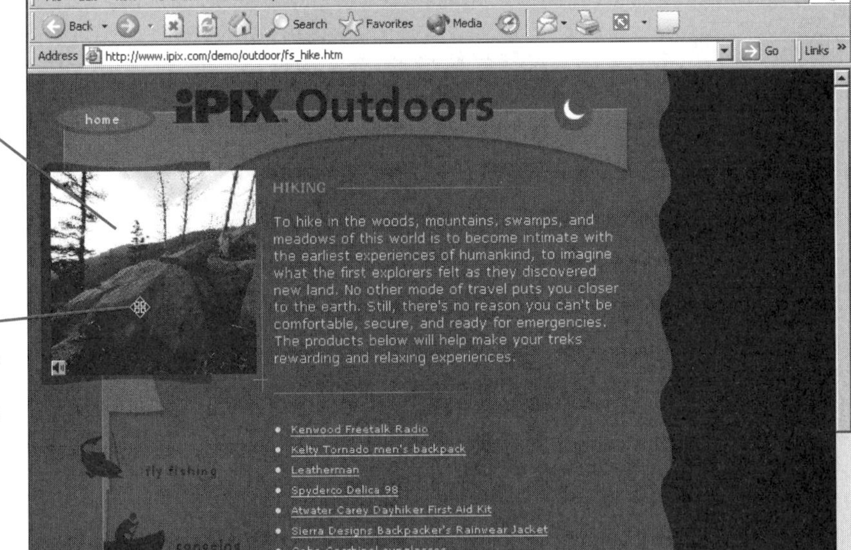

FIGURE J-2: Browser-based video game using Shockwave

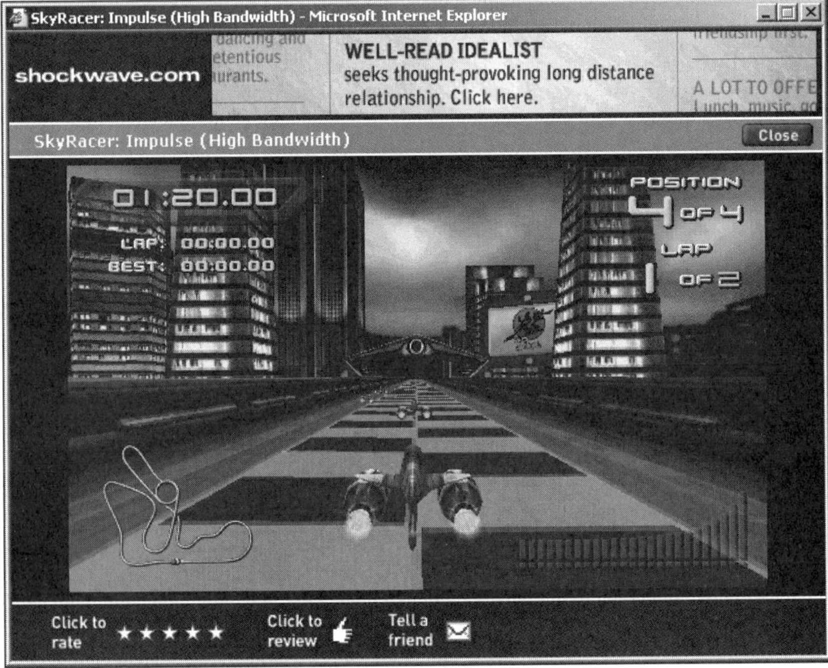

CLUES TO USE

How do you know when you need a plug-in?

When you are browsing the Web, you might encounter Web pages that indicate you need a specific plug-in to view or hear the Web page's content. If you do not have the required plug-in to play the content, nothing happens; you see only what your Web browser can activate, without hearing a sound, for example, or seeing a video. The Web page might also display an icon or empty frame, indicating that you are missing a plug-in. Many Web pages that require plug-ins display a dialog box that provides information about the missing plug-in and where to obtain it. You can often allow the Web browser to automatically install the plug-in right then and there, after which the full Web page content will be available through your Web browser.

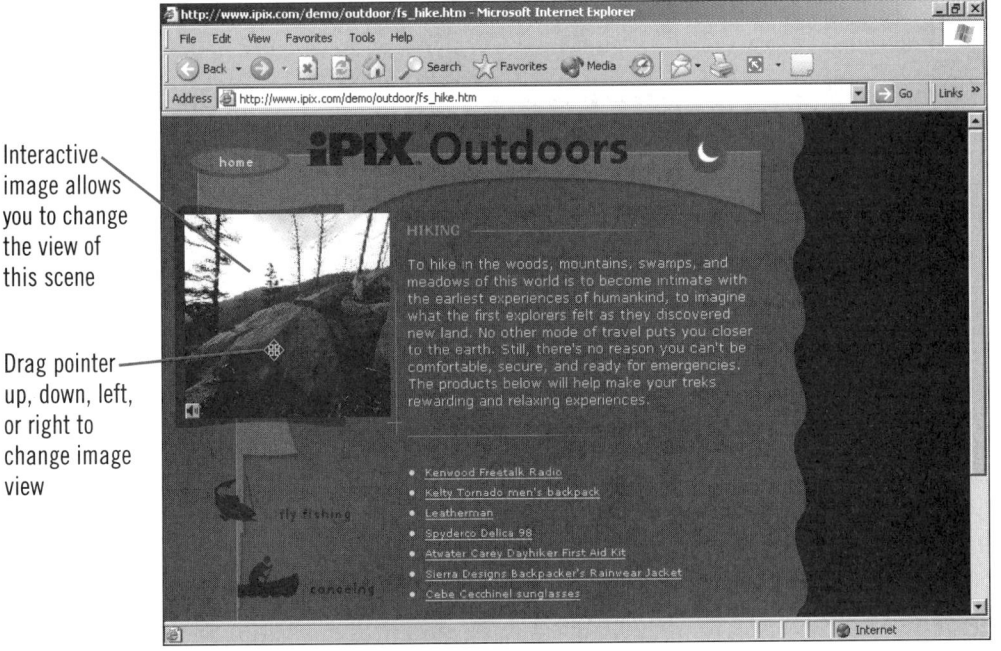

Internet

Locating Browser Extensions

You can find and download browser extensions from different Web sites. Some Web sites, such as Cnet.com, Tucows, and Yahoo!, include a list of links to browser extensions, which are grouped by category or function. Some of these Web sites indicate the number of times people have downloaded each browser extension, which acts as a popularity ranking. Some Web sites also provide user ratings. Before deciding on a video format for displaying samples of RVP's work on the Web site, you want to see which file formats are handled by the most popular and highest-rated browser extensions. You review the audio and video plug-ins listed on a couple of plug-in download sites.

1. Go to **www.course.com/illustrated/internet3**, click the **Unit J link**, then click the **Cnet.com link** under Lesson 2
2. Type **plug-ins** in the Search text box, then click **Go!**
3. On the Web page that opens, click the **Browser plug-ins link** in the Best Bets section
   The Plug-ins page opens and lists plug-ins in descending order by the date the software was added to the list.
4. Click the **Downloads link** below the Update button, then scroll down to view the most popular downloads
   Clicking a column heading sorts the list based on the contents of the column. The list is sorted in descending order based on the number of times each item has been downloaded, as shown in Figure J-3.

Trouble?

Your Web page might look different because the plug-ins and their statistics change over time.

5. Go to **www.course.com/illustrated/internet3**, click the **Unit J link**, then click the **Tucows link** under Lesson 2
6. Click the **Windows link** in the Desktop Software section, then if necessary, click the list arrow for your country to select the state or region in which you live or the one closest to you
7. If a list of mirrors appears, select a mirror closest to you
   The Welcome to Tucows Web page opens and displays featured downloads for the Windows operating system.
8. Click the **Internet tab** near the top of the Web page
   The Tucows Internet Software page opens and displays a list of categories for Internet software.
9. Scroll down the Web page as necessary, locate the Web Browsers & Tools category, click the **Web Browser Add-ons link**, then scroll down to view the plug-ins
   A Web page opens and lists browser plug-ins alphabetically by title, as shown in Figure J-4. For each plug-in, Tucows lists the title and version number, release date, type of license, rating, and file size.

FIGURE J-3: Most popular plug-ins available at Cnet.com

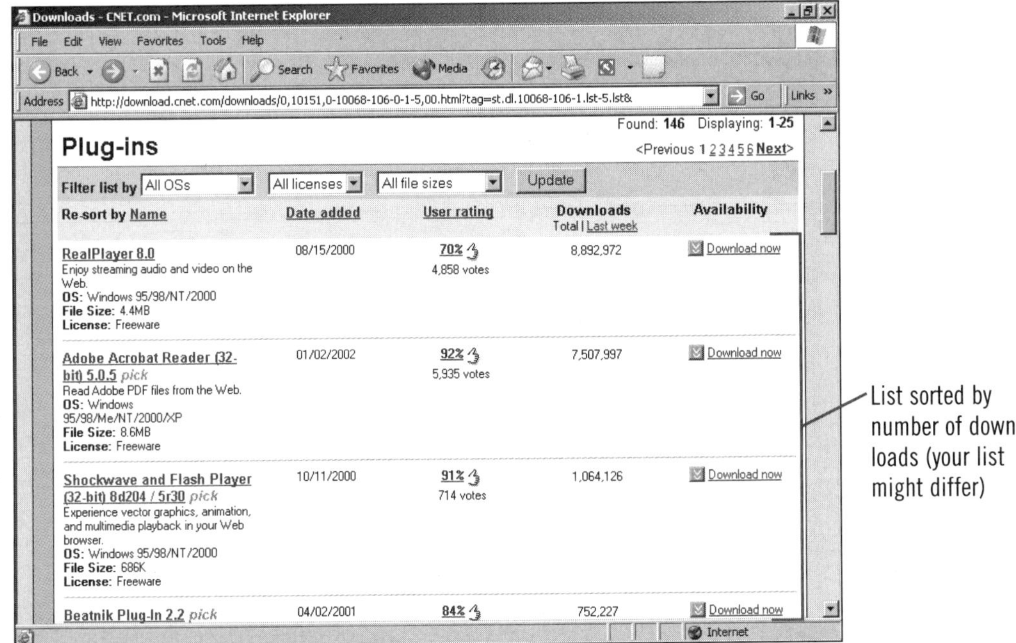

FIGURE J-4: Plug-ins available at Tucows.com

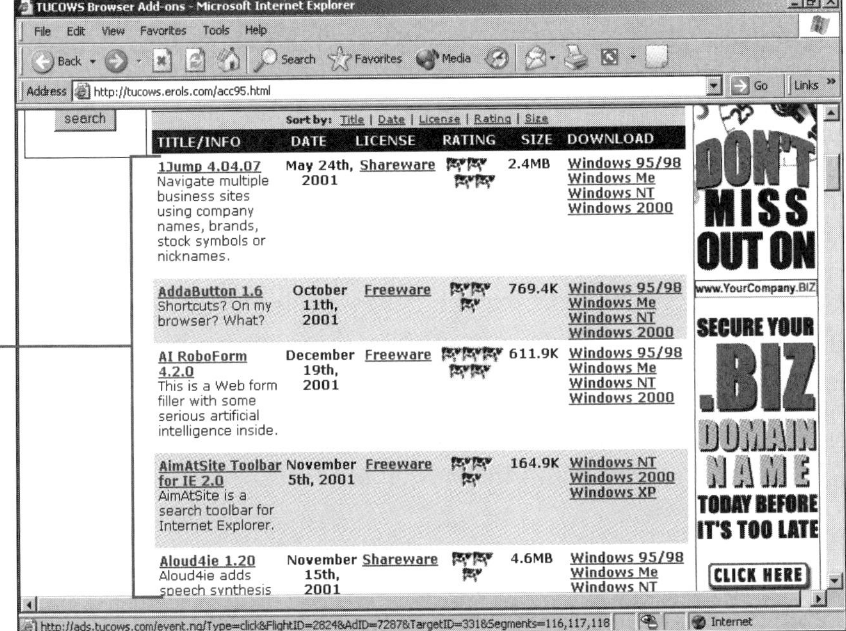

Clues to Use

Locating missing plug-ins

Sometimes your Web browser cannot perform the operation required by a file format, such as playing an audio file or displaying animation. When this happens, in some cases, a dialog box automatically opens, describing where to download the missing plug-in and how to install it. Some Web browsers automatically detect which plug-in a Web page requires and display a dialog box allowing you to download and install the plug-in. Most Web pages that require a plug-in to display or play their content typically contain a link to the Web site where you can download the required plug-in. When you click the link, the developer's Web site opens so you can download the plug-in. The plug-in then plays items, such as movies, animations, interactive games, slide shows, streaming audio, or background music, that are required to view the Web page correctly.

Installing Browser Extensions with Netscape

You download and install browser extensions just as you would other software for your computer. You first download the browser extension to your computer, then double-click it to run the installation wizard. Plug-ins are generally small programs that don't require a lot of system resources. Although many plug-ins are available, you should limit yourself to installing only plug-ins that you will use often. You investigate how easy it would be for potential Web site users to install a required plug-in by adding the Shockwave plug-in to your Web browser.

STOP ***Check with your instructor or technical support person before installing this plug-in. If you do not get approval to install it, read the instructions without performing the steps.***

1. Go to **www.course.com/illustrated/internet3**, click the **Unit J link**, then click the **Macromedia link** under Lesson 3
   The Macromedia download page opens.
2. Click **Download Now**
   The Enter name of file to save to dialog box opens.
3. Click the **Save in list arrow**, navigate to the drive and folder where your Project Files are stored, then click **Save**
   The Saving File dialog box opens, showing the download progress for the Shockwave installer file. The download is complete when the progress indicator shows 100%.
4. If necessary, close the Saving File dialog box, then close Netscape and any other applications that are running on your computer
5. Open Windows Explorer to display the contents of your Project Files folder, then double-click the **shockwaveinstaller.exe file**
   The Installing Shockwave Player dialog box opens, as shown in Figure J-5.
6. Click **Next**, verify that the version of Netscape you are using is selected, then click **Install**
   A dialog box displays the progress of the Shockwave installation.
7. Click **Continue**
   Netscape starts, and the player download center page opens.
8. If the Welcome to Shockwave dialog box opens, click **OK**, click the **13 or older option button**, click **Next**, enter your first and last names and e-mail address in the appropriate text boxes, deselect the **check box**, click **Next**, then click **Finish**
   The Installing Shockwave Player dialog box might display the download progress.
9. If necessary, click **Next**
   The animation, as shown in Figure J-6, demonstrates that Shockwave is installed correctly on your computer.

Trouble?

If you don't see shockwaveinstaller.exe, double-click shockwaveinstaller instead.

QuickTip

If the movie doesn't begin playing after a minute, click the Reload button, or close Netscape, and then restart Netscape to complete the installation.

FIGURE J-5: Installing Shockwave Player dialog box

FIGURE J-6: Shockwave installation test Web page

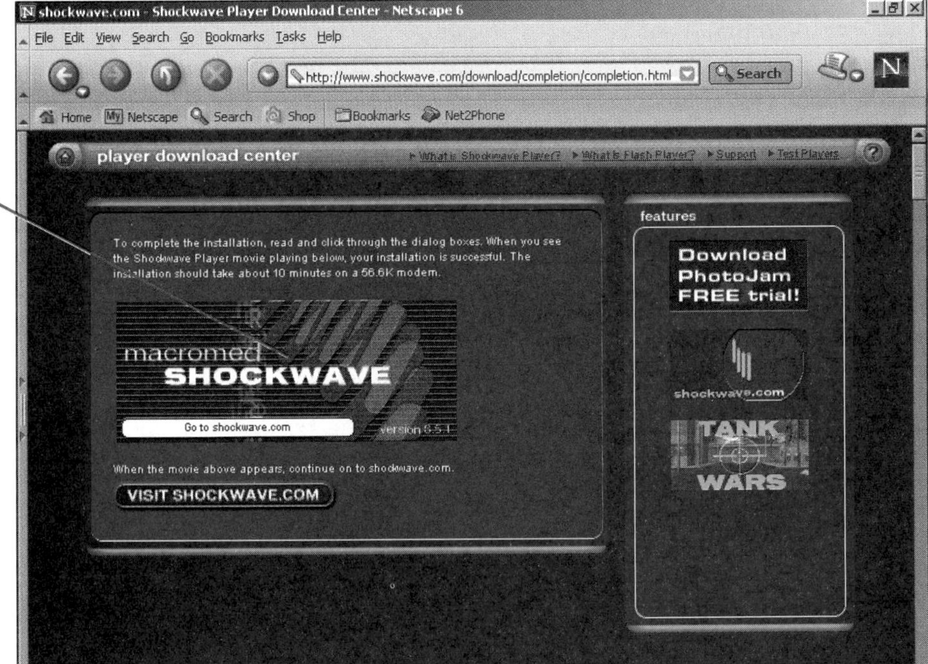

Internet

Installing Browser Extensions with Internet Explorer

You download and install browser extensions just as you would other software for your computer. Internet Explorer allows you to automatically download and install some browser extensions by simply clicking a link in a Web page. Plug-ins are generally small programs that don't require a lot of system resources. Although many plug-ins are available, you should limit yourself to installing only plug-ins that you will use often. You investigate how easy it would be for potential Web site users to install a required plug-in by adding the Shockwave plug-in to your Web browser.

Check with your instructor or technical support person before installing this plug-in. If you do not get approval to install it, read the instructions without performing the steps.

1. Go to **www.course.com/illustrated/internet3**, click the **Unit J link**, then click the **Macromedia link** under Lesson 4
   The Macromedia download page opens.
2. Click **Install Now**
   The Shockwave Player dialog box shows the progress of the download and installation, as shown in Figure J-7. When the installation is complete, the Welcome to Shockwave Player dialog box opens.
3. Close the Welcome to Shockwave Player dialog box
   The dialog box closes, and the Installation Complete dialog box opens.
4. Click **Next**
   The Welcome to Shockwave Web page loads, as shown in Figure J-8. The animation shows that Shockwave is installed correctly on your computer. If your computer has speakers, you might also hear accompanying music.
5. Close the Web browser window containing the Welcome to Shockwave Web page

Trouble?

If the Security Warning dialog box opens asking if you want to install software, click Yes. If the Open Browsers dialog box opens telling you that you must close your Web browser, close your Web browser, if necessary, then click OK.

FIGURE J-7: Shockwave Player dialog box

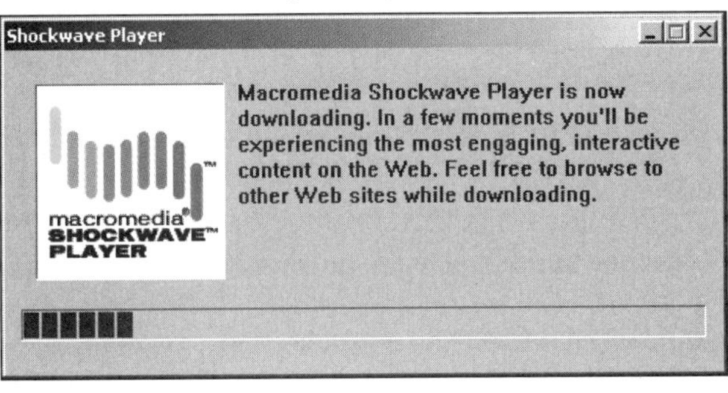

FIGURE J-8: Welcome To Shockwave Web page

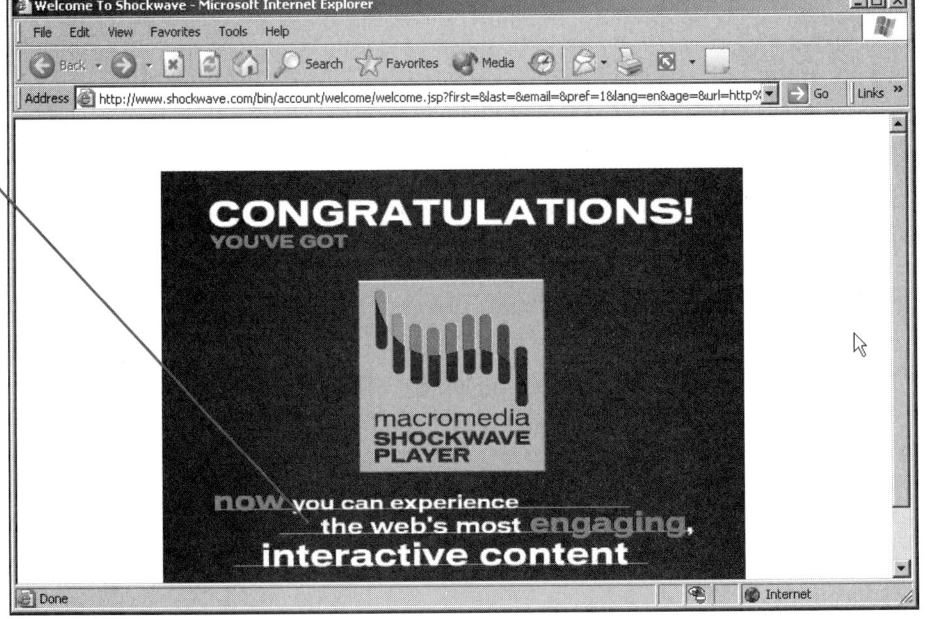

Animation shows that the Shockwave plug-in is installed successfully

Understanding Internet Security

Because any file can be uploaded or downloaded to the Internet, you always run the risk of downloading a harmful file. The potential presence of harmful files in many common Internet activities, along with risks, such as information theft or invasion of privacy, make it crucial to understand Internet security and to take steps to minimize your risks when you're online. As you continue to work on the new Web site for RVP, you research basic security concerns for Internet users to ensure that your Web site will be as accommodating as possible of its users' safety needs. In particular, you focus your research on the two most popular uses of the Internet: the Web and e-mail.

Web Security

Although many people use the Web every day without a second thought to security, the Web exposes users to a variety of security risks:

- **Computer safety**: The potential for the greatest damage comes from programs that Web pages can download to your computer and run. Such programs, known as **scripts**, **controls**, or **applets**, are generally benign and are used by Web page designers to enrich and personalize a user's interaction with a Web page. Many browser plug-ins, such as Shockwave, are controls or applets. Such programs can also be written with malicious intent, however, destabilizing programs and even risking data loss on a user's computer.
- **Data confidentiality**: Web sites commonly include forms where users can efficiently supply information to an organization. In addition to online shopping or donations, these forms are also used in other ways, for example, to sign up for an e-mail list. However, transmitting information across the Internet is not always secure; Figure J-9 shows an alert box in Internet Explorer that reminds users of this fact. If security features are not deliberately put into place by a Web site administrator, submitting information over the Web is about as secure as sending the same information on a postcard; people at both the sending and receiving ends can view the information without going through too much trouble.
- **Activity monitoring**: As you learned in Unit F, some Web sites store information on your computer in small text files known as cookies. Although some Web sites merely use cookies to preserve information about your preferences between visits, other Web sites might use cookies to collect information about your interests and then use this information to try to market products or services to you. Additionally, some Web sites attempt to glean information from all the cookies stored on your computer, meaning that any information stored in a cookie is at risk of being seen and used by anyone on the Web.

E-mail

Using e-mail can open users to computer safety risks. E-mail messages themselves are generally not harmful to a computer; attached files, however, can cause many different types of damage. A sender can attach an executable file known as a **virus** to an e-mail message. Viruses can cause various types of destruction to the recipient's computer. Other types of attachments are more worrisome and widespread, however. Harmful programs such as **worms**, which spread themselves using e-mail programs, can spread undetected around the world via the Internet in a matter of hours. Many Web sites, such as the one in Figure J-10, provide news and information about viruses, worms, and other e-mail threats.

FIGURE J-9: Security alert box in Internet Explorer

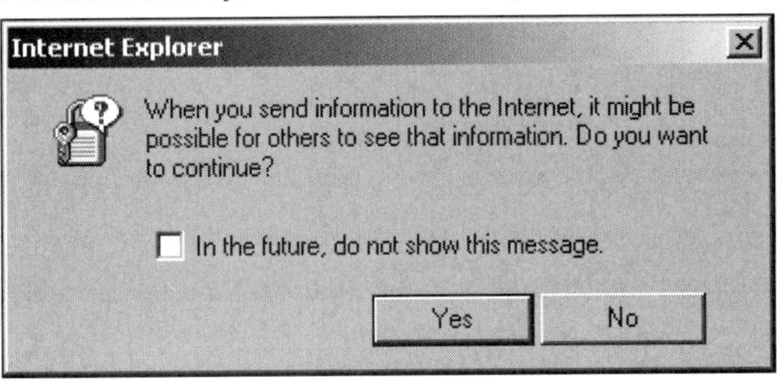

FIGURE J-10: Web page containing information about e-mail security threats

Internet

Internet

Minimizing Web Security Risks

The Web can expose users to many types of potential security risks. Fortunately, informed users can take simple **countermeasures**, which are procedures, programs, and hardware that detect and prevent computer security threats. Taking appropriate countermeasures makes Web use significantly less risky. You continue your research for RVP's Web site by learning about security risks that are most prevalent on the Web. You also look into popular countermeasures.

Web Page Programs

A program on a Web page, such as a script, control, or applet, can attack your computer. For example, a destructive **Java applet**, which is a program written in the Java programming language, can run and consume all your computer's resources. A **JavaScript program** can examine your computer's programs and e-mail a file from your computer to the Web server, which potentially compromises sensitive information, such as personal passwords. **ActiveX components** are Microsoft's technology for writing small applications that perform some action in Web pages. These components have full access to the files on your computer. For example, a hidden ActiveX component in a Web page can scan your hard drive for GIF and JPEG files and print them on any network printer, simply to drain resources and cause trouble. A renegade ActiveX program can reformat your hard drive. Web servers are also targets for such attacks. Recent programs have launched **denial of service attacks**, which slow down all Web traffic or make certain Web sites inaccessible. Although you cannot do much to protect Web servers from being attacked, you can protect your own computer. Popular Web browsers contain numerous options for limiting or blocking the types of Web page programs that run on your computer.

Sniffer Programs

The possibility of someone stealing your credit card number in a Web transaction is perhaps the most well-known security risk. This is possible because all Web traffic is divided up by the sender's server into uniform sized chunks of data known as **packets**; at any point along a packet's trip from source to destination, a user can identify and read packets for a certain network or user. A tool known as a **packet sniffer**, or **sniffer program**, allows a user to monitor and analyze network traffic. Used illegally, a packet sniffer can also capture data being transmitted on a network, including user names, passwords, and other personal information. In many cases, it makes no difference if others view the information you send and receive on the Internet. However, whenever you submit sensitive data, such as financial or other personal information, or view sensitive Web sites, you should ensure that the upload and download are protected by encryption. As explained in Unit D, **encryption** scrambles and encodes data transmissions to make it difficult for anyone intercepting the data to make sense of it. As shown in Figure J-11, popular Web browsers indicate that a Web page is encrypted by displaying a lock icon on the status bar. Additionally, the protocol in the Web page address generally begins with "https" rather than "http."

Cookies

Usually, cookies are used for harmless reasons, but they can pose a security threat. Cookies generally store information about your **click stream**, which is the sequence of links you click while visiting a Web site. Creating and saving cookies in this way is harmless. However, cookies can store user name, password, and credit card information, which allows illicit Web sites to store and use information about you without your knowledge. Web browsers offer many different options for dealing with cookies. All recent Web browsers allow you to prevent cookies from being saved on your computer. Although this choice totally eliminates problems with cookie misuse, it also blocks your access to some Web sites that rely on cookies for basic information about your preferences. For example, if you visit a Web site that requires a membership, without a cookie, you might have to sign in every time you open a new Web page on the Web site. Fortunately, recent Web browsers can also distinguish between different types of cookies, and might allow you to block more intrusive cookies while allowing harmless ones. Figure J-12 shows the cookie settings available in Internet Explorer.

FIGURE J-11: Web browser encryption indicators

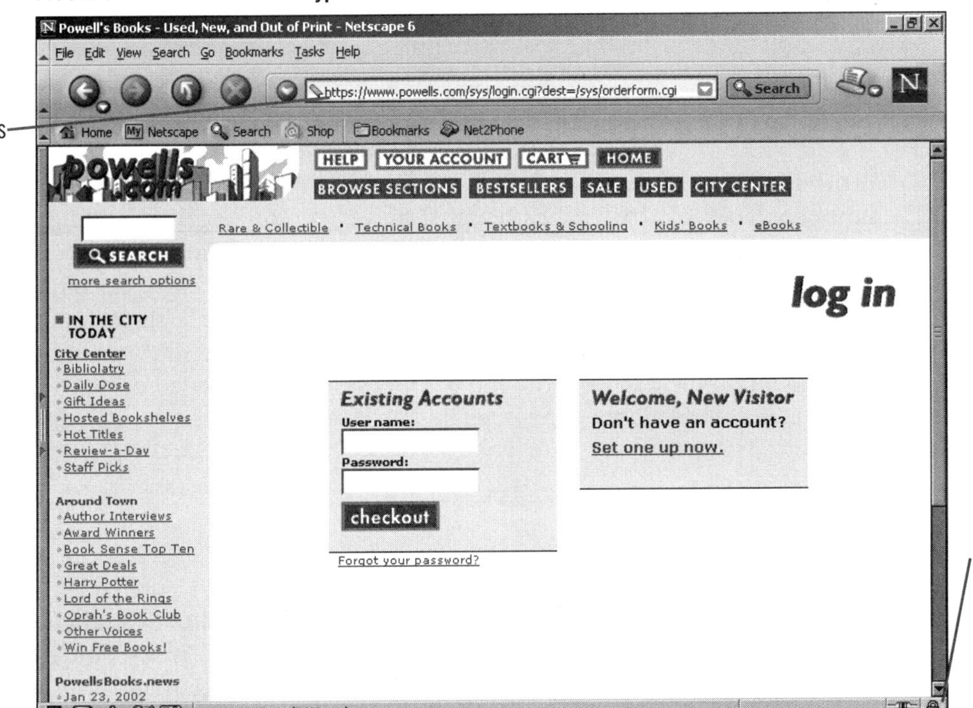

FIGURE J-12: Web browser cookie settings for Internet Explorer

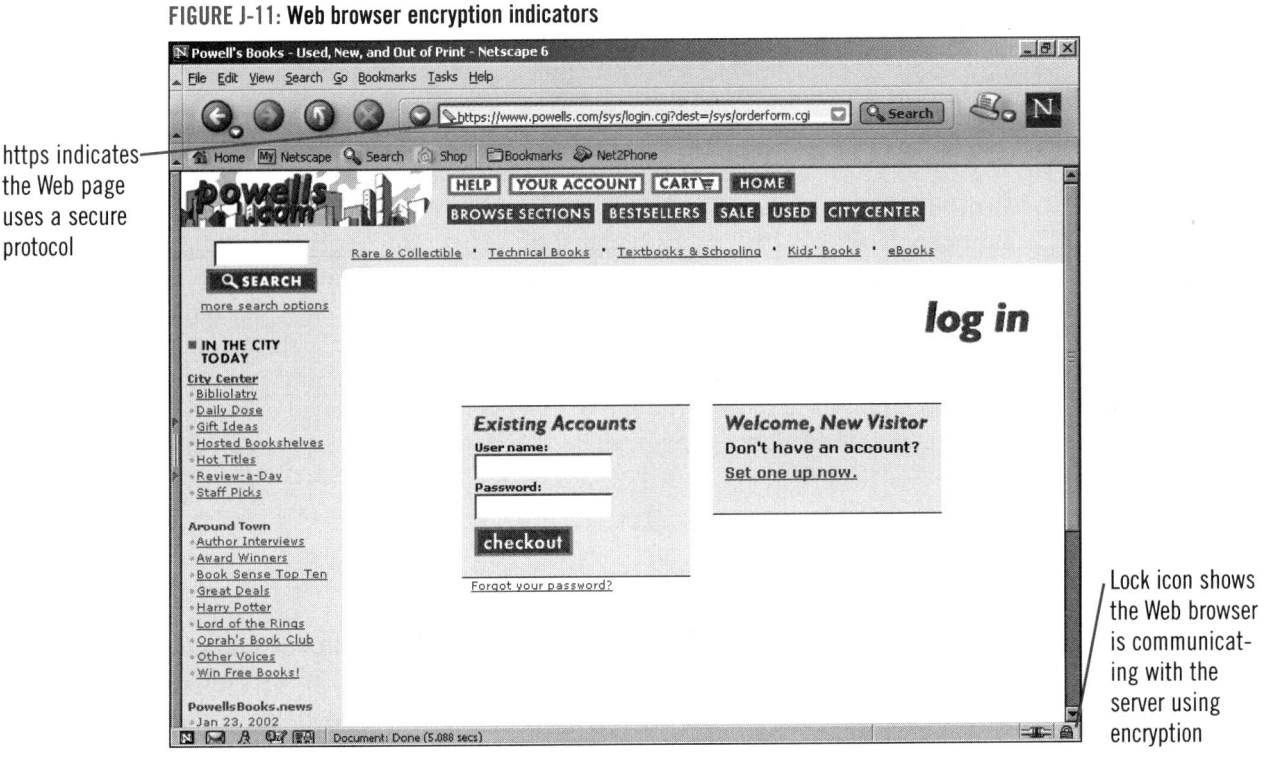

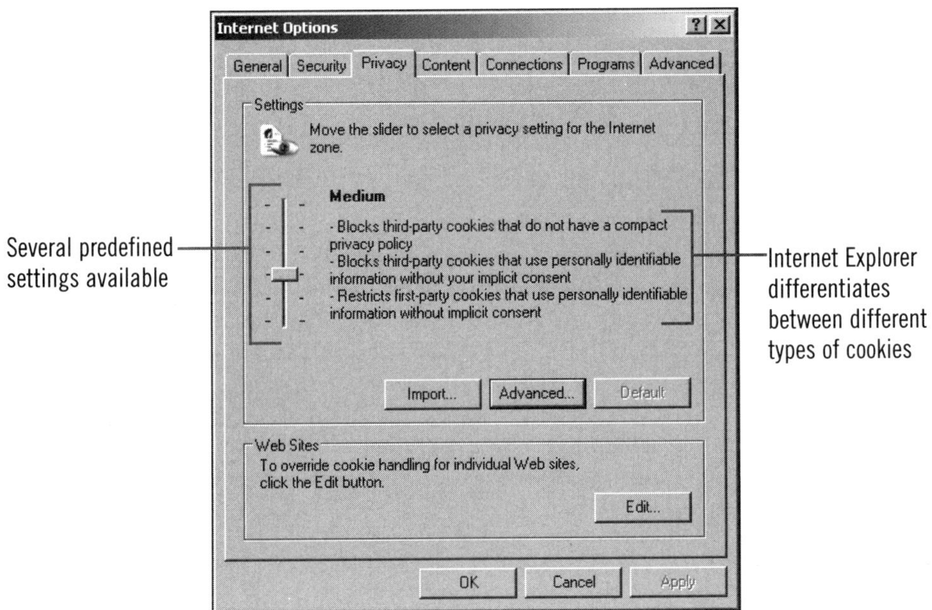

Internet

Internet

Protecting Web Transactions

As the number of Web users and the risks of security threats on the Web grow, the makers of the most popular Web browsers incorporate features that allow users to limit their risks as they use the Web. Although these features can largely protect users from many common threats, the tradeoff of increased security is sometimes a limitation on Web pages' customizability and interactivity. After you understand these tradeoffs, you can balance the amount of security you require with the importance of enhanced Web content. You want to be sure that important content on the RVP Web site will be compatible with users' security settings. You examine the settings available in the most popular Web browsers, Internet Explorer and Netscape.

In Internet Explorer:

1. Click **Help** on the menu bar, then click **About Internet Explorer**
   The About Internet Explorer dialog box opens, as shown in Figure J-13. This window shows your Web browser's version number and other details. The **cipher strength** listed in this dialog box is a measure of the encryption strength that the Web browser can use when exchanging information over a secure connection. Your Web browser might display a value between 40 and 128. A higher number indicates stronger encryption, and some online businesses consider only 128-bit encryption strong enough to ensure data security.
2. Click **OK**, click **Tools** on the menu bar, then click **Internet Options**
   The Internet Options dialog box opens.
3. Click the **Security tab**, then click **Custom Level**
   The Security Settings dialog box opens, as shown in Figure J-14.
4. Scroll down the Settings list box to view the available options
   The list box allows you to specify how to deal with many different types of Web page contents and programs, including ActiveX Controls, Java applets, scripts, and form content that is not encoded.
5. Click **Cancel**, then in the Internet Options dialog box, click **Cancel**
6. Close Internet Explorer

In Netscape:

1. Click **Help** on the menu bar, then click **About Netscape 6**
   The About Netscape 6 window opens, as shown in Figure J-15. This window shows your Web browser's version number and other details. The window also specifies the encryption strength that the Web browser can use when exchanging information over a secure connection. Your Web browser might display a value between 40 and 128. A higher number indicates stronger encryption, and some online businesses consider only 128-bit encryption strong enough to ensure data security.
2. Click the **Close button**, click **Edit** on the menu bar, then click **Preferences**
   The Preferences dialog box opens.
3. Click **Advanced** in the Category list
   The dialog box displays options for advanced preferences, as shown in Figure J-16. You can use this dialog box to enable or disable Java applets, Web page scripts written in the JavaScript language, and scripts included in e-mail messages.
4. Click **Cancel**
5. Close Netscape

FIGURE J-13: About Internet Explorer dialog box

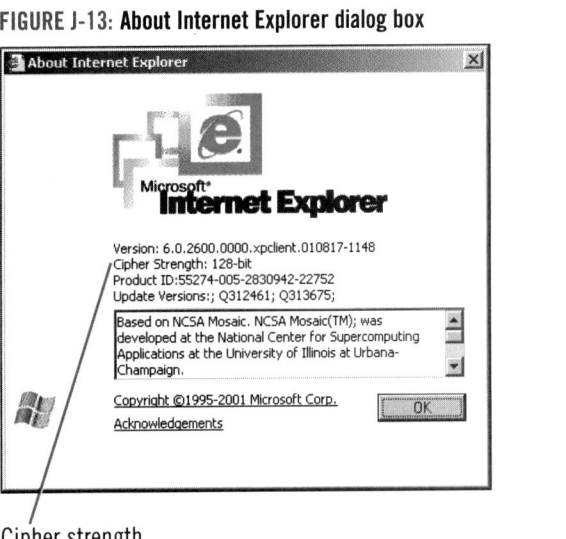

Cipher strength

FIGURE J-14: Security Settings dialog box

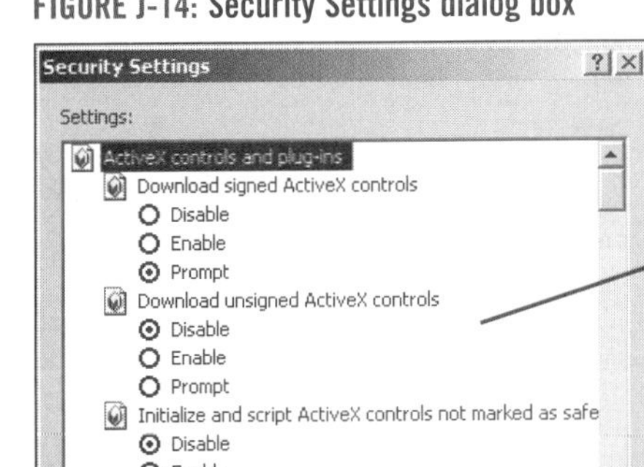

FIGURE J-15: About Netscape 6 window

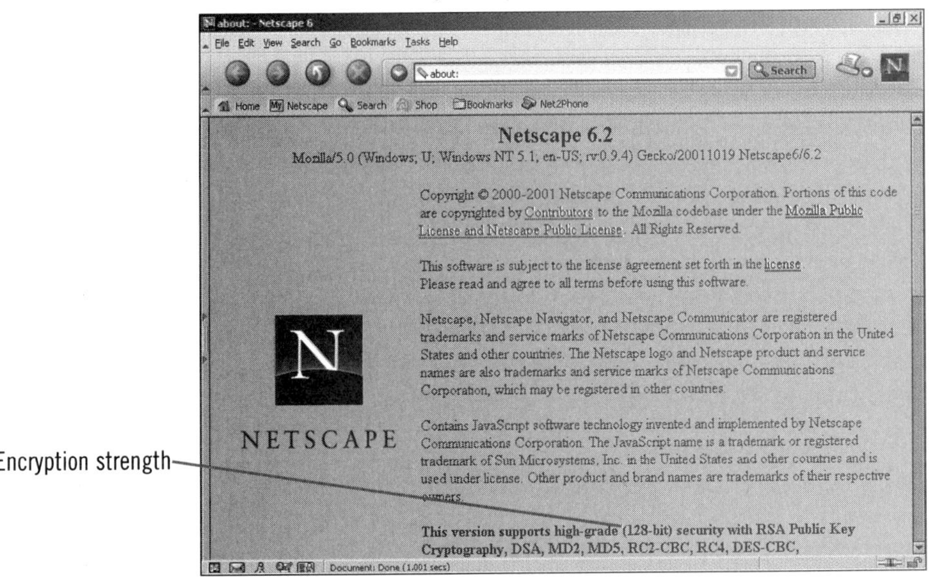

FIGURE J-16: Netscape advanced preferences

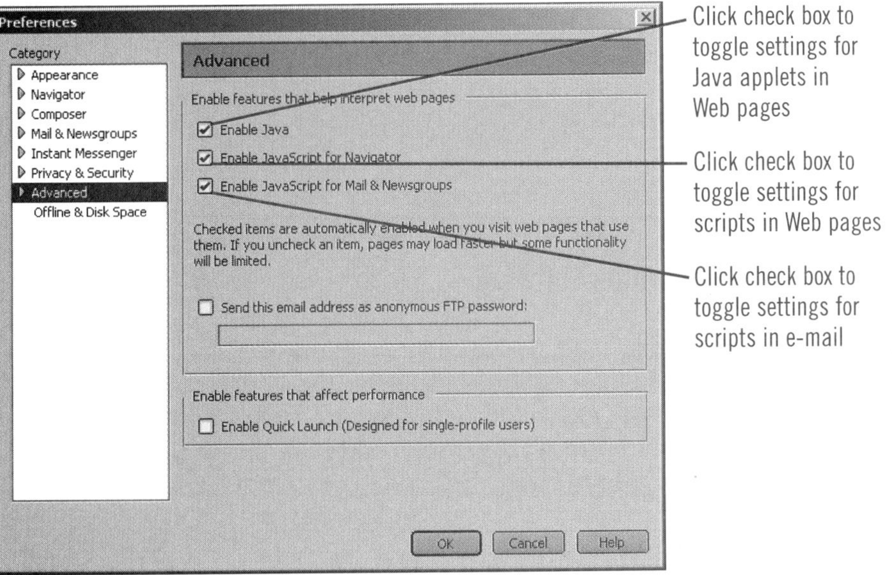

Internet

Unit J

Internet

Protecting E-Mail from Viruses and Interception

Although the Web is an important area to focus on for understanding Internet security, it's not the only area of concern. Protecting your computer when using e-mail must go hand in hand with Web protection to eliminate the most common Internet-based threats to your computer. Fortunately, you can greatly limit your exposure to destructive programs carried by e-mail by taking a few simple precautions, such as installing programs that protect your computer or verifying that your attachments are safe before you open them. As you conclude your preparatory research for the RVP Web site, you want to understand how e-mail risks might affect the company's online strategy. You review the steps customers might take in limiting their exposure to problems via e-mail.

QuickTip

Some Web-based e-mail systems, such as Hotmail, automatically check their users' e-mail messages for viruses.

Antivirus Software

As Units B and C explained, many types of programs have been specially designed to cause computer problems when downloaded as attachments with incoming e-mail messages. Worms and Trojan horses are destructive programs similar to viruses. Worms can not only perform undesired tasks when they run, such as deleting the contents of your hard drive, but they can also reproduce themselves by using the functions of e-mail programs like Netscape Mail and Microsoft Outlook Express to send out copies of themselves as attachments. Software is easily available, however, which can block damage from any viruses, worms, or Trojan horses that you might receive by e-mail. Such software, known as **anti-virus software**, also keeps such programs from using your e-mail program to reproduce. Figure J-17 shows the main options available for Norton AntiVirus, one popular brand of anti-virus software. Because anti-virus software is often available for free at colleges and universities, you should check with your instructor or system administrator to see if this software is available to protect your computer.

Handling E-Mail Attachments

In addition to using anti-virus software to protect your computer from harmful e-mail attachments, you can increase your e-mail security by modifying your e-mail practices. Most importantly, don't save or open attachments from anyone—even people you know well—without scrutinizing the e-mail message first. An attachment ending with .exe is a program file; opening it runs the program on your computer with unknown consequences. Always be sure you know what a program will do, and that you're certain of the sender's identity before opening it. Additionally, because worms replicate by sending nonsense messages to people listed in the victim's address book, make sure the accompanying e-mail message makes sense and is specific to you. If the message is short and general, even if it's from a friend, it might simply be a worm's trick to get you to open the attachment when you are not paying attention. If you get a lot of e-mail every day, using anti-virus software can be a worthwhile investment, because it can find and delete any viruses, worms, or Trojan horses attached to e-mail messages before they are even visible in your e-mail program.

Encryption Software

Like Web data, e-mail messages are sent across the Internet in packets. Therefore, a packet sniffer can be used illegally to intercept the contents of e-mail messages. If you use e-mail to send sensitive information, such as sensitive business information or financial data, it's good practice to use encryption software for e-mail. Like Web browser encryption, e-mail encryption scrambles a message's contents in a way that can only be decoded by the intended recipient. **Pretty Good Privacy (PGP)**, described on the download page shown in Figure J-18, is a popular program used to encrypt and decrypt e-mail. PGP can be downloaded for free from the Web for noncommercial use.

FIGURE J-17: Norton AntiVirus main options

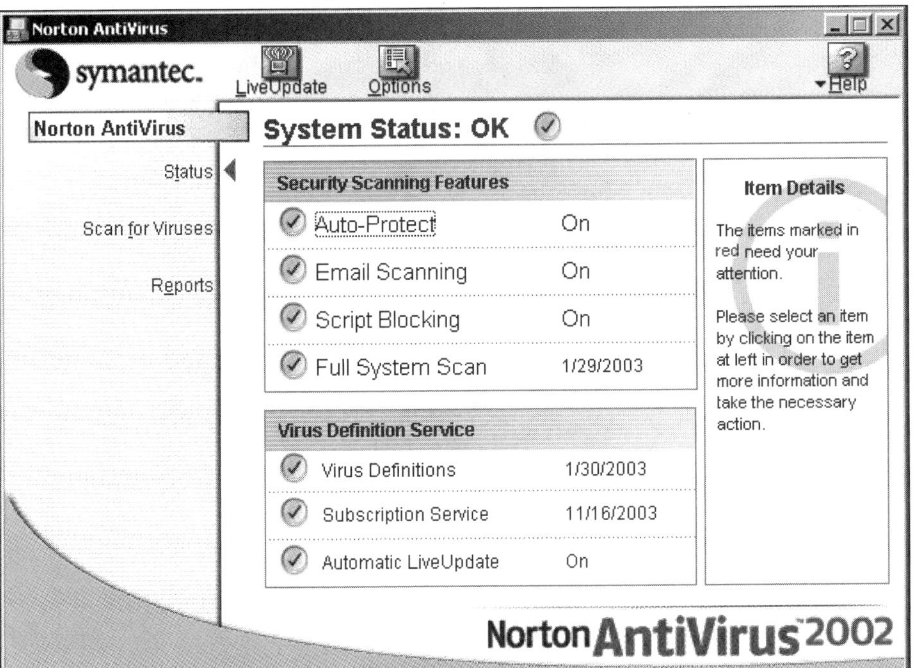

FIGURE J-18: PGP download page on Download.com

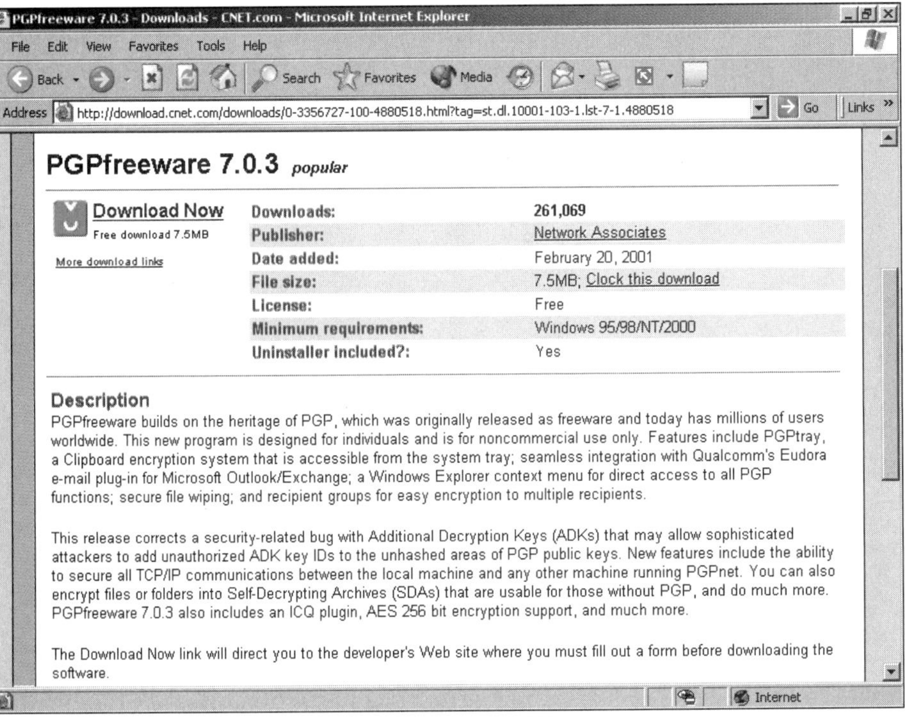

Internet

Practice

► Concepts Review

Identify the security threats associated with the countermeasures shown in Figures J-19 through J-21.

FIGURE J-19

1

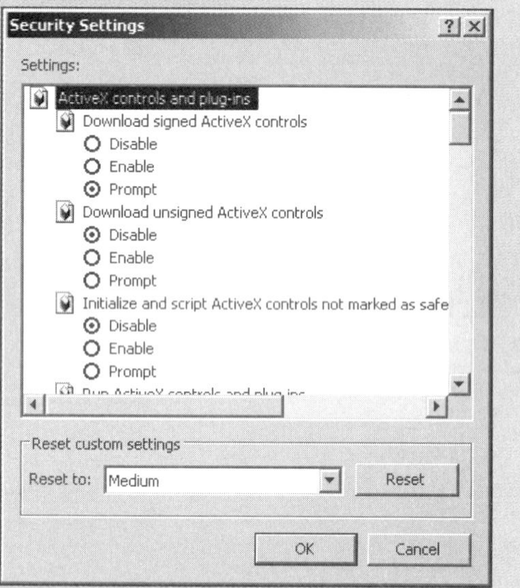

FIGURE J-20

2

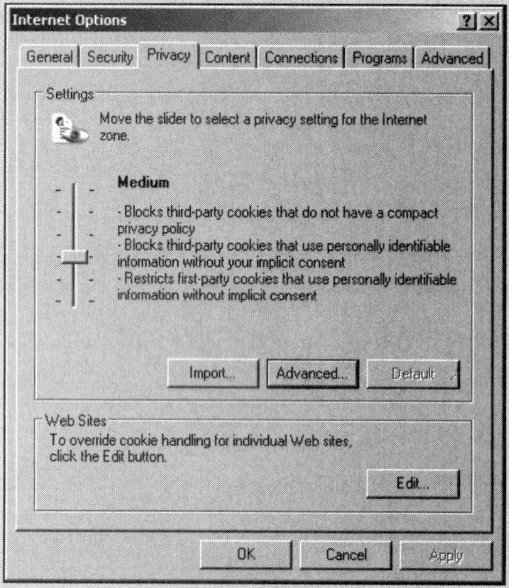

FIGURE J-21

3

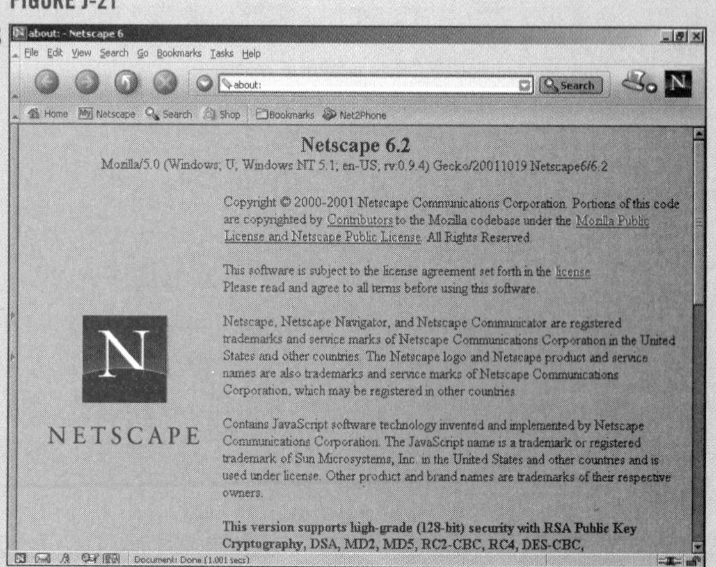

Practice

Match each term with the statement that describes it.

4. ActiveX component	**a.** A program that blocks damage from destructive programs you receive by e-mail
5. Cookie	**b.** A program you install to expand your Web browser's capabilities
6. Browser extension	**c.** A feature that makes it difficult for anyone intercepting data to make sense of it
7. Encryption	**d.** A type of program that runs in a Web page
8. Anti-virus software	**e.** A text file that Web sites can use to track your browsing habits

Select the best answer from the list of choices.

9. A browser extension is a(n):
- **a.** Program that you can only open from your Web browser.
- **b.** Executable file that causes harm to a computer.
- **c.** Small program that enables a Web browser to interpret a certain file format.
- **d.** Program that blocks damage to your computer from viruses, worms, or Trojan horses.

10. The best way to protect your computer against worms is to:
- **a.** Install anti-virus software.
- **b.** Prevent Web sites from storing cookies on your computer.
- **c.** Disable Web page programs in your Web browser.
- **d.** Use encryption software, such as PGP.

11. Cookies are an example of which security risk?
- **a.** Computer safety
- **b.** Data confidentiality
- **c.** Activity monitoring
- **d.** Viruses

12. A sniffer program is an example of which security risk?
- **a.** Computer safety
- **b.** Data confidentiality
- **c.** Activity monitoring
- **d.** Viruses

13. Which is an example of a browser plug-in?
- **a.** Anti-virus software
- **b.** Shockwave
- **c.** PGP
- **d.** Packet sniffer

Skills Review

1. **Locate browser extensions.**
   a. Go to **www.course.com/illustrated/internet3**, click the **Unit J link**, then click **Files32.com link** under Skills Review 1.
   b. Click the **Network & Internet link**, click the **Web Browser Tools link**, then click the **Web Browser Plug-ins link**.
   c. Scroll through the list to view the available downloads.
   d. Return to the Student Online Companion Web page for Unit J, then click the **Softpile.com link** under Skills Review 1.
   e. Click the **internet tab**, then click the **Browsers & Plug-Ins link**.
   f. Scroll through the list to view the available downloads.

2. **Install browser extensions with Netscape.**
   a. Go to **www.course.com/illustrated/internet3**, click the **Unit J link**, then click the **iPIX link** under Skills Review 2.
   b. Click the **iPIX Plug-In tab**, enter your name and e-mail address in the appropriate text boxes, verify that the check box is not selected, then click **send/download**.
   c. If an alert box opens informing you that the information will be sent over an unencrypted connection, click **Continue**.
   d. If the Software Installation dialog box opens, click **OK**.
   e. When an image appears at the bottom of the Web page displaying "You have successfully downloaded the iPIX Plug-in," click the **Demos tab**.
   f. Explore one of the links on the Web page that opens to view Web page images with the iPIX plug-in.

3. **Install browser extensions with Internet Explorer.**
   a. Go to **www.course.com/illustrated/internet3**, click the **Unit J link**, then click the **iPIX link** under Skills Review 3.
   b. Click the **iPIX Plug-In tab**, enter your name and e-mail address in the appropriate text boxes, verify that the check box is not selected, then click **send/download**.
   c. If the Security Warning dialog box opens, click **Yes**.
   d. When an image appears at the bottom of the Web page displaying "You have successfully downloaded the iPIX Plug-in," click the **Demos tab**.
   e. Explore one of the links on the Web page that opens to view Web page images with the iPIX plug-in.

▶ Independent Challenge 1

You work as a technology consultant, specializing in helping small businesses and independent contractors take full advantage of the Internet in their work. You generally install a couple useful browser extensions for your clients. You want to identify other useful extensions that your clients might find helpful in their work.

a. Start your Web browser.

b. Go to **www.course.com/illustrated/internet3**, click the **Unit J link**, then use the links under Independent Challenge 1 to locate and research a browser extension not already used in this unit.

c. Write a paragraph describing how the browser extension extends a Web browser's capabilities (what it does that a Web browser can't do alone).

d. Include the URL where you can download the browser extension on the Web. Also include the URL of a Web page that makes use of this browser extension. (*Hint:* such Web pages are often listed on the Web site of the company that makes the browser extension.)

e. Close your Web browser.

▶ Independent Challenge 2

You work as an intern for Portland Concrete Mixers while taking classes part-time. You recently spent a day in the office attending a training session on Internet security. Now that you understand more about Internet security and potential risks associated with using the Internet, you want to take steps to secure your Internet use at home as well. Start by finding out about your school's anti-virus resources.

a. Ask your instructor or system administrator if your school makes anti-virus software available to students and staff.

b. If your school does not make anti-virus software available, ask your instructor or system administrator about the school's plan for safe computing. Find out if other safeguards are in place to limit exposure to viruses for users of the school's computers. Summarize your research in a paragraph, then write another paragraph analyzing what you've found. State whether you think students and staff at your school are adequately protected against viruses, and why.

c. If your school does make anti-virus software available, download it to your computer and install it. Use information on your school's Web site along with the software's help section to understand and enable its main features. Also download the most recent virus definitions from the software company's Web site. Then write a paragraph describing the steps you took to download and install the software, and another paragraph summarizing the software's features.

Independent Challenge 3

You're interning in a lawyer's office for a summer. Because you understand some of the technical aspects of Internet security, your boss has asked you to evaluate PGP, a security program that she's considering using for sensitive communications.

a. Start your Web browser.

b. Go to **www.course.com/illustrated/internet3**, click the **Unit J link**, click the **Download.com link** under Independent Challenge 3, then search the Web site for PGP.

c. Open and read the Web page that gives an overview of PGP to understand how it works.

d. Return to the Student Online Companion Web page for Unit J, click the **PGP link** under Independent Challenge 3, then find more detailed information on the Web site explaining how PGP works.

e. Write at least three paragraphs summarizing your findings. Include a description of PGP's basic features, minimum computer system requirements, and the differences between the free version and the commercial version of PGP.

f. Close your Web browser.

Independent Challenge 4

In a class, you're discussing how to balance Web use with privacy concerns. You've been assigned to write a paper on whether all cookies are intrusive.

- **a.** Start your Web browser.
- **b.** Use the Web to research the different kinds of cookies.
- **c.** Write at least two paragraphs about a type of cookie that you might not want saved on your computer. Explain why you wouldn't want it saved on your computer, and include an example of how this type of cookie might be used by Web sites you interact with.
- **d.** Write at least two more paragraphs about a type of cookie that some Web users might find useful, including an explanation of why, and an example of how it might be used. Be sure to include the terms "third-party cookie" and "first-party cookie" in your descriptions, and explain what the terms mean.
- **e.** Close your Web browser.

▶ Visual Workshop

Go to **www.course.com/illustrated/internet3**, click the **Unit J link**, then click the **Download.com link** under Visual Workshop. Open a list of available browser plug-ins, then print the information page for a plug-in that interests you, like the one shown in Figure J-22.

FIGURE J-22

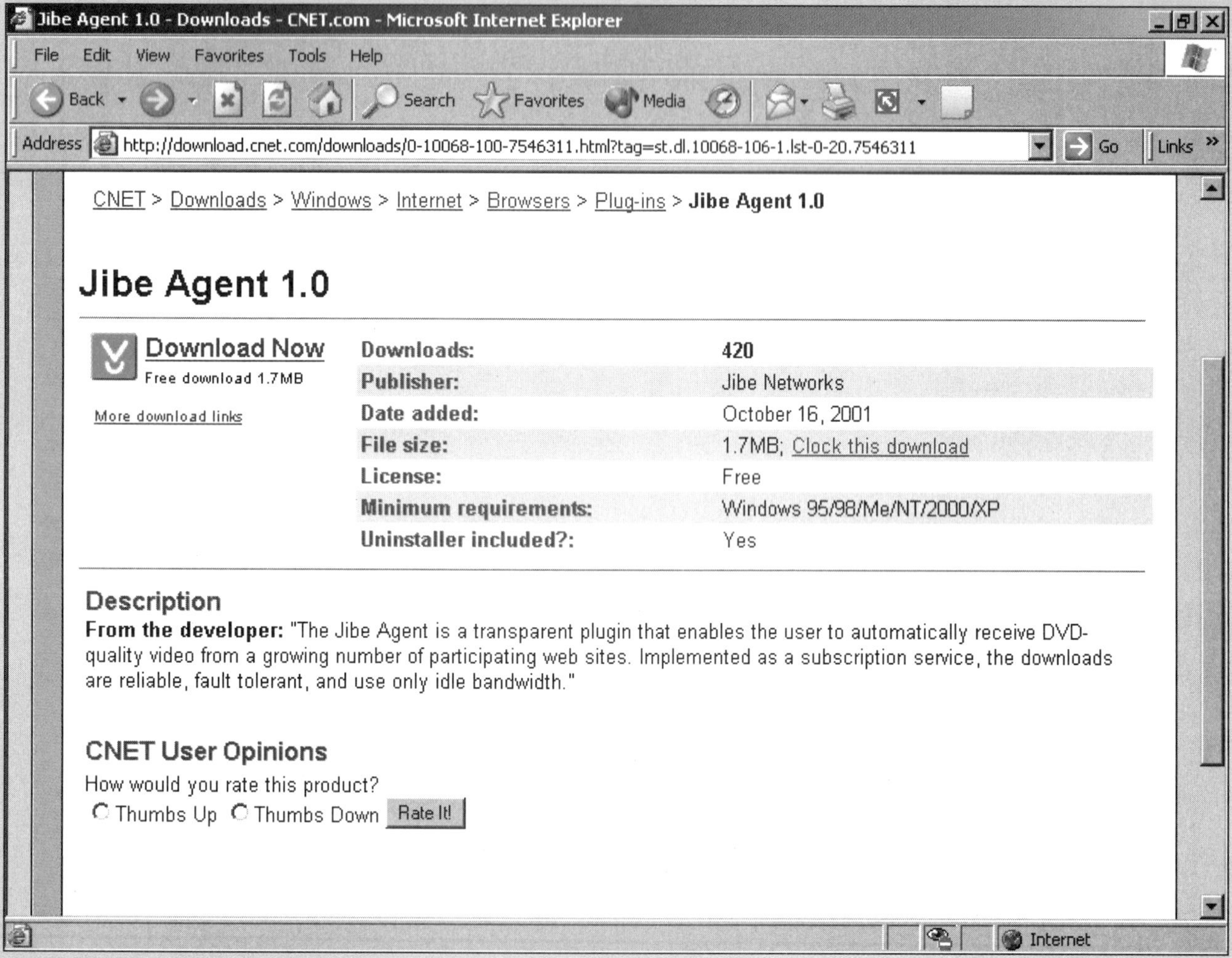

Jibe Agent 1.0 - Downloads - CNET.com - Microsoft Internet Explorer

File Edit View Favorites Tools Help

Back Search Favorites Media

Address http://download.cnet.com/downloads/0-10068-100-7546311.html?tag=st.dl.10068-106-1.lst-0-20.7546311 Go Links

CNET > Downloads > Windows > Internet > Browsers > Plug-ins > **Jibe Agent 1.0**

Jibe Agent 1.0

Download Now
Free download 1.7MB

More download links

Downloads:	**420**
Publisher:	Jibe Networks
Date added:	October 16, 2001
File size:	1.7MB; Clock this download
License:	Free
Minimum requirements:	Windows 95/98/Me/NT/2000/XP
Uninstaller included?:	Yes

Description

From the developer: "The Jibe Agent is a transparent plugin that enables the user to automatically receive DVD-quality video from a growing number of participating web sites. Implemented as a subscription service, the downloads are reliable, fault tolerant, and use only idle bandwidth."

CNET User Opinions

How would you rate this product?

Thumbs Up Thumbs Down Rate It!

Internet

Project Files List

Read the following information carefully!

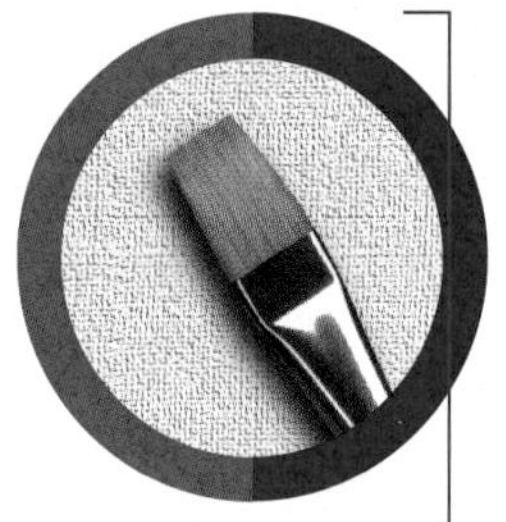

1. Find out from your instructor the location of the Project Files you need and the location where you will store your files.

- To complete many of the units in this book, you need to use Project Files. Your instructor will either provide you with a copy of the Project Files or ask you to make your own copy.
- If you need to make a copy of the Project Files, you will need to copy a set of files from a file server, standalone computer, or the Web to the drive and location where you will store your Project Files.
- Your instructor will tell you which computer, drive letter, and folders contain the files you need, and where you will store your files.
- You can also download the files by going to www.course.com. See the inside back cover of the book for instructions to download your files.

2. Copy and organize your Project Files.

Floppy disk users

- If you are using floppy disks to store your Project Files, this list shows which files you'll need to copy onto your disk(s).
- You will need one formatted, high-density disk for Unit B or Unit C. For each unit you are assigned, copy the files listed in the **Project File Supplied column** onto one disk.
- Make sure you label each disk clearly with the unit name (e.g., Internet Unit B).
- When working through the unit, save all your files to this disk.

Users storing files in other locations

- If you are using a zip drive, network folder, hard drive, or other storage device, use the Project Files List to organize your files.
- Create a subfolder for each unit in the location where you are storing your files, and name it according to the unit title (e.g., Internet Unit B).
- For each unit you are assigned, copy the files listed in the **Project File Supplied column** into that unit's folder.
- Store the files you modify or create in each unit in the unit folder.

3. Find and keep track of your Project Files and completed files.

- Use the **Project File Supplied column** to make sure you have the files you need before starting the unit or exercise indicated in the **Unit and Location column**.
- Use the **Student Saves File As column** to find out the filename you use when saving your changes to a Project File provided.
- Use the **Student Creates File column** to find out the filename you use when saving your new file for the exercise.

4. Important Notes for Units I and J.

Unit I requires that you download several files that won't fit on a floppy disk. If you are working in a lab situation, check with your instructor before completing Unit I to make sure that you are permitted to download, install, and extract files. If you do not have installation access, you should read through the lessons without performing the steps. Please see the Read This Before You Begin page for more information on software installation. The following lessons in Unit I require that you have an area on your hard drive (or a network drive) to download the files:

"Downloading an FTP Client Program"

"Using FTP to Download a Program"

In Unit I, the lesson "Downloading a .zip file" can be completed with a floppy disk. In Unit J, the lesson "Installing Browser Extensions with Netscape," can be completed with a floppy disk.

Unit and Location	Project File Supplied	Student Saves File As	Student Creates File
Internet Unit B			
Lessons	Physicals.wri	Unit B Physicals.wri	
Skills Review	Dinner Meeting.wri	Unit B Dinner Meeting.wri	
Visual Workshop	Recycle.wri		
Internet Unit C			
Lessons	Physicals.wri	Unit C Physicals.wri	
Skills Review	Dinner Meeting.wri	Unit C Dinner Meeting.wri	
Visual Workshop	Recycle.wri		

Internet

Glossary

Acceptable Use Policy The conditions under which individuals can use an organization's Internet connections; also known by the acronym **AUP**.

Active content Web page information that changes because of behind-the-scenes programs driving the Web page.

ActiveX components Microsoft's technology for writing small applications that perform some action in Web pages.

Address book A Netscape Mail feature that allows you to save e-mail addresses and other contact information.

Address book tab A navigation feature in Hotmail that contains options for managing your list of contacts.

Animated GIF file A multimedia file that combines several images into a single GIF file.

Anonymous FTP The process of logging on anonymously to an FTP server; the process is known as an anonymous login because a user types the user name "anonymous" instead of a personalized username.

Anti-virus software A software package that protects your computer from malicious programs.

Applet A type of program that Web pages can download to your computer and run.

Archive A Web page containing every message received and filed by a mailing list. An archive can be accessed by sending a command request for the messages from a particular time frame to the mailing list server.

ARPANET (Advanced Research Projects Agency Network) An experimental wide area network (WAN) that consisted of the four computers networked by DARPA researchers in 1969.

Attachment A file sent with an e-mail message.

AVI A file format commonly used for video on the Web.

Back button A button on a Web browser toolbar that allows you to go back to a previously viewed Web page.

Bandwidth A measure of the amount of data that can be transmitted simultaneously through a communications circuit.

Bits per second (bps) A measurement of bandwidth. A bandwidth of 28,800 bps means that 28,800 bits of data are transferred each second.

Bookmarks Shortcuts to Web sites you select.

Boolean algebra The branch of mathematics and logic invented by George Boole in the 19th Century. In Boole's algebra, all values are reduced to one of two values. In most practical applications of Boole's work, these two values are true and false.

Boolean operators Search terms that specify the logical relationship between the elements they join. Three of the basic Boolean operators—AND, OR, and NOT—are recognized by most search engines.

Bot See *Web robot.*

Browser extension A program that enables a Web browser to display a particular file format.

Buffered play An audio playback feature in which music is downloaded and queued for play when the transfer/play rate exceeds your modem's speed.

Cable Connections that use cable television lines to connect to the Internet. A cable connection can be as much as 170 times faster than an ordinary telephone line connection.

Cable modem A communication device that converts digital computer signals into radio-frequency analog signals that are similar to television transmission signals. The converted signals travel to and from the cable company on the same lines that carry the cable television service.

Category 1 cable A type of twisted-pair cable that transmits information more slowly than other cable types. Telephone companies have used twisted pair cable for years to wire residences and businesses.

Category 5 or 5e cable Types of twisted-pair cable that transmit information 10 to 100 times faster than coaxial cable. Category 5 cable and category 5e cable are used in computer networks.

Chat Instantaneous communication on the Internet or on the Web.

Cipher strength A measure of the level of encryption used by a Web browser.

Circuit switching A method used to transmit data in which all the data transmitted from a sender to a receiver travels along a single path.

Click stream The sequence of links you click while visiting a Web site.

Client Each computer connected to a server.

Client/server network A network consisting of one server that shares its resources with multiple clients. Client/server networks are commonly used to connect computers that are located close together (for example, in the same room or building) so that each computer can share such resources as a printer or a scanner.

Clip Art A collection of individual icons, shapes, and other graphics.

Coaxial cable Insulated copper wire encased in a metal shield that is enclosed with plastic insulation. A coaxial cable resists electrical interference much better than twisted pair cable and also carries signals about 20 times faster than Category 1 cable. Most cable television connections use coaxial cable.

Commands In a mailing list, messages that request the mailing list server to perform a specific action.

Communications circuits Pathways through which data can travel within or between networks.

Compose tab A navigation option in Hotmail that contains options for creating a new message.

Compose window A Netscape Mail window used to create messages.

Compressed file A reduced-size version of a file; created using a file compression program.

Configure To set up an e-mail program such as Netscape Mail or Outlook Express.

Contacts list A section of the Outlook Express window that displays the names of people and organizations whose contact information you have entered and saved.

Control A type of program that Web pages can download to your computer and run.

Cookie A small text file that a Web site stores on your computer.

Countermeasures Procedures, programs, and hardware that detect and prevent computer security threats.

Demodulation The process of converting an analog signal back into digital form.

Denial of service attack Malicious attack which targets Web servers with the goal of slowing down all Web traffic, or making certain Web sites inaccessible.

Digital Subscriber Line A high-speed Internet connection often provided by a phone company.

Domain name Identifiers made up of words and abbreviations that are assigned to IP addresses.

Download To receive a file from your computer to another computer.

Drafts folder A Hotmail folder that stores messages that you have written and saved but have not yet sent.

Drop To leave a mailing list.

DSL An abbreviation for Digital Subscriber Line.

DSL modem A specific type of modem required to connect to the Internet using DSL.

E-commerce See *Electronic commerce.*

Electronic commerce A business transaction between two parties conducted over various kinds of networks, rather than in person; also known as **e-commerce**.

E-mail Mail sent via a computer network, used to communicate electronically with people all over the world; short for electronic mail.

E-mail address A unique identifier that allows you to send e-mail to an individual or organization on the Internet.

Glossary

E-mail list A system that allows a group of people to communicate via e-mail about a subject of interest.

Emoticons Icons—such as :) and :-(— composed of standard typed characters, which chat and e-mail users find helpful to display humor and emotions in their messages; also known as **smileys**.

Encryption A method of scrambling and encoding data transmissions to reduce the risk that any person who intercepts the Web page as it travels across the Internet will be able to decode and read the Web page's contents.

Exploratory question An open-ended question that starts with general queries that lead to other, more specific questions.

FAQ See *Frequently Asked Questions.*

Favorites Shortcuts to Web sites you select.

Federal Networking Council (FNC) A council set up by the National Science and Technology Council's Committee on Computing, Information and Communications (CCIC) to meet the CCIC's research and education goals. The FNC also coordinates uses of its agencies' technologies by the commercial sector.

Fiber optic cable A connector that transmits information by pulsing beams of light through very thin strands of glass.

File compression program A program used to reduce a file to a fraction of its original size.

File decompression The process of restoring a compressed file to its original form.

File expansion See *File decompression.*

File extraction See *File decompression.*

File Transfer Protocol (FTP) A method used to transfer files between two connected computers.

Folder Bar A section of the Outlook Express window that displays the title of the folder that is currently open.

Folder list A section of the Outlook Express window that displays a list of commonly used folders.

Folders list A pane in the Netscape Mail window that displays six default folders, which you can use to receive, save, and store e-mail messages.

Forwarding Sending an e-mail message you receive to someone else.

Freeware Fully-functional software that is available to anyone for no cost and with no restrictions attached to its use.

Frequently Asked Questions A document containing the answers to common questions that users ask about a mailing list and its subject; usually referred to with the acronym FAQ.

FTP See *File Transfer Protocol.*

FTP client program A program that resides on your computer and transfers files between your computer and another computer connected to it.

FTP server A computer that stores files that users running FTP client programs can transfer to their own computers.

FTP server program A program that runs on an FTP server to allow file transfer to and from the server by FTP, and to manage FTP access to the server's files.

FTP session profile A collection of information about an FTP server that stores a program or files you want to download; FTP session profile information enables you to connect to the FTP site that contains the files you want.

Full-privilege FTP See *Named FTP.*

GIF A file format that compresses small or medium-sized images; acronym for Graphics Interchange Format.

Graphics Electronic files containing images or art.

Grouping operator See *precedence operator.*

Helper application A program that works with a Web browser to display or play a file; helper applications can function independent of a Web browser; also called **Helper apps.**

Hit A Web page that is indexed in a search engine's database and contains text that matches a specific search expression.

Home button A button on a Web browser toolbar that allows you to return to the home or start page for your Web browser.

Home page The main page around which all Web sites are organized, through which users enter the Web site and use links to open the pages they're looking for.

Home tab A navigation feature in Hotmail that shows links to news, shopping opportunities, and general links to other MSN sites.

Host name A name in an e-mail address of the computer that stores a recipient's e-mail. An at sign (@) separates the user name from the host name.

HTML anchor tag A tag that enables you to link multiple HTML documents together; the anchor tag enables users to easily open other Web pages that are relevant to the one they're viewing.

Hyperlinks Another term for links.

Hypertext links Another term for links.

Hypertext markup language (HTML) A computer language used to define the structure and behavior of a Web document.

ICQ An Internet chat client.

Inbox folder A Hotmail folder that stores your new messages.

Inbox tab A navigation feature in Hotmail that displays the list of messages you have received, aside from those that Hotmail suspects are unsolicited mail.

Inclusion operator See *precedence operator.*

Installation wizard A series of dialog boxes that help you complete an installation process step-by-step.

Internet A large collection of computers all over the world that are connected to one another in various ways.

Internet Engineering Task Force (IETF) A self-organized group that makes technical contributions to the engineering of the Internet and its technologies and is the main body that develops new Internet standards.

Internet Protocol (IP) Rules for routing individual data packets. Combined with Transmission Control Protocol in the acronym TCP/IP.

Internet Protocol address (IP address) A unique number that identifies a computer on the Internet.

Internet Relay Chat (IRC) A communications program used for chat.

Internet Service Provider (ISP) A business that sells Internet access to users and other ISPs.

Intranet A LAN or WAN that uses the TCP/IP protocol but does not connect to sites outside a firm.

IP version 6 (IPv6) A new Internet addressing scheme that will increase the number of IP addresses available on the Internet.

IRC See *Internet Relay Chat.*

Java applet A program written in the Java programming language.

JavaScript program A program written in the JavaScript programming language.

JPEG A file format that stores over 16 million colors and is useful for photographs; acronym for Joint Photographic Experts Group.

Junk Mail folder A Hotmail folder that stores e-mail messages from senders that you specify as bulk mailers, advertisers, or any Web site from which you don't want to receive mail.

Key term Each word in a search expression.

LE software See *Limited Edition software.*

Limited Edition software A free, restricted version of shareware that provides most of the functionality of the full commercial version.

Links Text, graphics, or other Web page elements that connect to additional data on the Web.

List moderator The person responsible for discarding any messages that are inappropriate for or irrelevant to the members of a moderated mailing list.

LISTSERV Software used to run mailing lists that users all over the world can join to discuss a variety of primarily issues and topics.

Local area network (LAN) A group of computers connected through NICs over a relatively short distance. Computers in a LAN are directly connected to each other.

Location operator A special search term that facilitates searches for terms appearing close to each other in the text of a Web page. The most common location operator offered in Web search engines is the NEAR operator.

Logical operators See *Boolean operators.*

Lurking The activity of silently observing the postings others make to a mailing list.

Mail client software A program that lets you send and receive e-mail, and store e-mail that you receive on your PC.

Mail server A server running special software for handling e-mail tasks.

Mail window The initial window that opens when you start Netscape Mail.

Mailing list A feature of an e-mail service or program that assigns a name to a set of e-mail addresses; also, a system that allows a group of people to communicate via e-mail about a subject of interest.

Menu Bar A Web browser component that contains common commands such as File, Edit, View, and Help.

Message body A section of an e-mail message that contains the actual content of the e-mail message.

Message header An element in an e-mail message window that contains all the information about the e-mail message.

Message header summary The display format of each e-mail message in the message list; it includes the subject of the message, the sender, and the date or time the message was sent.

Message list A pane in the Netscape Mail window that displays the contents of the folder selected in the Mail Folders pane; also, a section of the Outlook Express window that contains message header summaries.

Message window A Netscape Mail window that displays the same information as in the Message pane, but in its own window.

Messages In a mailing list, e-mail messages that express ideas or ask questions that each member of the list receives.

Meta-search engine A search tool that uses multiple search engines.

Modem A device that converts signals between a computer and the transmission line; short for modulator-demodulator.

Moderated mailing list A mailing list that is monitored by a person who reads and evaluates messages sent to the mailing list before sending the messages on to all the members in the mailing list.

Modulation The process of converting a digital signal to an analog signal.

MP3 A file format commonly used for audio on the Web.

MPEG A file format commonly used for video on the Web.

MUDs Adventure games that allow multiple users to assume character roles and play at the same time in order to interact with each other.

Multimedia A collective term for sound, animation, and video.

My Sidebar A Netscape Mail pane displaying customizable Web shortcuts that allow you to access the Web without switching to a Web browser window.

Named FTP The process of logging in to an FTP server on which you have an account (with a user name and password) and using the account to send and receive files; also called **Full-privilege FTP**.

Network Access Point (NAP) A physical location where networks connect to the Internet.

Network Created when two or more computers are connected to each other. A network allows computers to share resources such as printers or programs.

Network backbone The long-distance lines and supporting technology that transports large amounts of data between major network connection points.

Network Control Protocol (NCP) The first collection of rules for formatting, ordering, and error-checking data sent across a network.

Network Interface Card (NIC) A removable circuit board that connects a computer to a network of other computers.

Network operating system Software that runs on a server.

Newsgroup An electronic discussion group focused on a specific topic or range of topics; unlike a mailing list in which messages are sent to participants via e-mail, a newsgroup's posts are stored on Internet servers, sorted by topic.

Nicknames Shortened names for the e-mail addresses of people that you send e-mail to frequently.

Open architecture philosophy A set of guidelines that ensures that each network connected to ARPANET can continue using its own protocols and data transmission methods internally.

Packet A small chunk of data transmitted using the packet switching method.

Packet sniffer A program that allows a user to analyze and monitor network traffic.

Packet switching A method used to transmit data in which files and messages are broken down into small chunks of data called packets that are labeled electronically with codes for their origin and destination. The packets travel from computer to computer along the network until they reach their destination. The destination computer collects the packets and reassembles the original data from the pieces in each packet.

Plug-ins Programs that a Web browser starts to display or play a specific file.

PDF format A file format that allows documents to maintain a consistent layout and formatting on different computers when viewed using Adobe Acrobat Reader.

PGP See *Pretty Good Privacy.*

Post See *Posting.*

Posting A message sent to a mailing list; also, contributing to a mailing list by sending messages to the list.

POTS An acronym for plain old telephone service.

Precedence operator A symbol—usually parenthesis—that clarifies the grouping within a complex search expression.

Pretty Good Privacy A popular program used to encrypt and decrypt e-mail; also known by the acronym **PGP**.

Preview pane A section of the Outlook Express window that displays the contents of the message currently selected in the message list.

Printer-friendly link A Web page link that opens another Web page containing the same information as on the original page, but formatted like a printed page, rather than a Web browser window.

Printer-friendly pages Web pages that contain the information you want to print and are specially formatted to fit on a printed page.

Private chat Chat between two individuals.

Proximity operator See *Location operator.*

Public chat Chat in a group.

Query See *Search expression.*

QuickTime A file format commonly used for video on the Web.

Real-time Instantaneous.

RealAudio A file format commonly used for audio on the Web.

Refresh button See *Reload Button.*

Reload button A button on a Web browser toolbar that allows you to load again the Web page currently in the Web browser window.

Reminder An MSN calendar event that triggers an automatic e-mail message to you just before it happens.

Results pages Web pages that list links to Web pages containing the text that matches a specific search expression.

Router Each computer that an individual packet encounters on its trip through the network.

Routing algorithms Programs that routers use to determine the best path for packets.

Script A type of program that Web pages can download to your computer and run.

Scroll bar A Web browser component used to move up and down or side to side through the document window when viewing a Web page.

Search engine A special kind of Web site that finds other Web pages containing the word or phrase you specify.

Search expression The words or phrase you enter when you are conducting a search.

Search filter A search engine feature that eliminates Web pages from a search. The filter criteria can include such Web page attributes as language, date, domain, host, or page component (URL, link, image tag, or title tag).

Self-replicate The ability of a program (such as a virus, Trojan horse, or worm) to create, and in some cases distribute, copies of itself to infect computers.

Sent Messages folder A Hotmail folder that stores messages that you have sent.

Server A general term for any computer that accepts requests from other computers that are connected to it and shares some or all of its resources, such as printers, files, or programs, with those computers. A server can be a powerful PC or a larger computer such as a minicomputer or a mainframe computer.

Shareware Software that is usually available for free for only for a short evaluation period, after which users are requested to pay to use it.

Sign-in name See *User name.*

Signoff A common command used to leave a mailing list.

Smileys See *Emoticons.*

Sniffer program A program that allows a user to analyze and monitor network traffic.

Specific question A question that you can phrase easily and has only one answer.

Spider See *Web robot.*

Start page The first page that opens when a Web browser is launched, or the Web page that a particular Web browser loads the first time you use it.

Status bar A Web browser component that indicates the name of the Web page that is loading, the load status (partial or complete), and important messages such as "Document: Done."

Stop button A button on a Web browser toolbar that allows you to stop loading the contents of a Web page.

Streaming A technique for transferring sound and video files on the Web in which the Web server sends the first part of the file to the Web browser, then, while the Web browser begins playing the file, the server continues sending the remainder of the file.

Subscribe To join a mailing list.

T1 & T3 Connection A very high grade of service for connecting to the Internet that is often used by large companies and organizations that must link hundreds or thousands of individual users to the Internet.

Tags Programming elements used in HTML to format Web pages.

Task An MSN calendar entry that allows you to set up a long-term project, including start and end dates.

Telnet A tool that enables users to log on to a remote server.

Terms of Use A document specifying how a Web portal might use information that it collects about you.

Throughput The amount of data transmitted through a connector.

Title bar A Web browser component that shows the name of the open Web page and the Web browser's program name.

Top-level domain The last part of a domain name.

Transmission Control Protocol (TCP) Rules that computers on a network use to establish and break connections. Combined with Internet Protocol in the acronym TCP/IP.

Trash Can folder A Hotmail folder that stores messages that you have deleted.

Trojan Horses Variations of viruses, written with the intent of creating computer trouble.

Twisted-pair cable Consists of two or more insulated copper wires that are twisted around each other and enclosed in another layer of plastic insulation.

Uniform Resource Locator (URL) A four-part addressing scheme that tells the Web browser the transfer protocol to use when transporting the file, the domain name of the computer on which the file resides, the pathname of the folder or directory on the computer on which the file resides, and the name of the file.

Unmoderated mailing list A mailing list in which all members automatically receive all messages, regardless of content.

Unsubscribe To leave a mailing list; also, a common command to leave a mailing list.

Upload To send a file from your computer to another computer.

Usenet (User's News Network) A network that allows anyone who connects to it to read and post articles on a variety of subjects.

Usenet See *Newsgroup*.

User account User information stored on a server that sets up your e-mail address and account with an e-mail provider.

User name The identifying name in an e-mail address that is used to route an e-mail message to an individual whose e-mail is stored on a particular computer. An at sign (@) separates the user name from the host name.

Virus A piece of software that runs without your permission and does undesired tasks, such as deleting the contents of your hard disk.

Web-based e-mail service An e-mail service that allows you to send and receive e-mail using a Web browser.

Web bibliography A Web site that organizes information into categories and subcategories, just like a printed bibliography.

Web browser The software that you run on your computer to make it work as a Web client.

Web calendar A common feature on a Web portal which allows you to record details about upcoming events as you would in a planner book or calendar, and store them on the Web.

Web client A computer that makes requests of Web servers on the Internet.

Web directory A listing of links to Web pages that is organized into hierarchical categories.

Web document A Web page or other file, such as a sound or video file, available on the Web.

Web portal A Web site offering customized news along with features, such as a calendar and an address book.

Web robot A program that automatically searches the Web to find new Web sites and to update information about old Web sites that are already in the database. A Web robot also deletes information in the database when a Web site no longer exists. Also called a bot or a spider.

Web servers Computers that store the files that make up the Web; Web clients make requests of Web servers to display and interact with those files.

Web site A collection of linked Web pages that has a common theme or focus.

Wide area network (WAN) Several LANs connected together.

Wildcard character A character in a search expression that allows omission of one part of a search term or terms. Many search engines recognize the asterisk (*) as the wildcard character. For example, the search expression "export*" would return pages in many search engines that contain the terms exports, exporter, exporters, and exporting.

Wireless networks Networks that use technologies such as radio frequency (RF) and infrared (IR) to connect computers.

World Wide Web (WWW) A subset of the computers on the Internet that organize information in a user-friendly way.

Worms Variations of viruses that spread themselves via e-mail.

.zip file A compressed file; the most common filename extension for a compressed file is .zip.

Zipped file See *.zip file*.

Index

Index

Index

Index

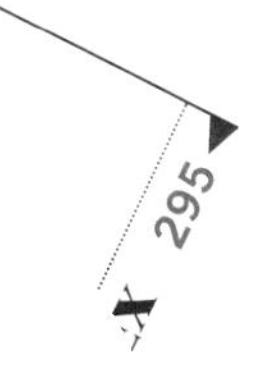